Books of Merit

Spirit of the Web

SPIRIT

Wade Rowland

OF THE WEB

The Age of Information
from Telegraph to Internet

Thomas Allen Publishers
Toronto

Library and Archives Canada Cataloguing in Publication

Rowland, Wade, 1944–

Spirit of the web : the age of information from telegraph to Internet / Wade Rowland.

Includes bibliographical references and index.

ISBN-13: 978-0-88762-227-4

ISBN-10: 0-88762-227-5

1. Telecommunication—History. I. Title.

TK5102.2.R69 2006   384.09   C2006-904030-3

Editor: Janice Zawerbny
Cover image: Alamy Images

Published by Thomas Allen Publishers,
a division of Thomas Allen & Son Limited,
145 Front Street East, Suite 209,
Toronto, Ontario M5A 1E3 Canada

www.thomas-allen.com

The publisher gratefully acknowledges the support of
the Ontario Arts Council for its publishing program.

We acknowledge the support of the Canada Council for the Arts, which
last year invested $20.3 million in writing and publishing throughout Canada.

We acknowledge the support of the Government of Ontario through the
Ontario Media Development Corporation's Ontario Book Initiative.

We acknowledge the financial support of the Government of Canada through the Book
Publishing Industry Development Program (bpidp) for our publishing activities.

10 09 08 07 06   1 2 3 4 5

Printed and bound in Canada

To Hilary and Simon, Web pioneers.

Foreword to the Third Edition

When I began writing this book in 1996 the World Wide Web was very new and pregnant with possibilities of historic import. As is always the case with breakthrough technologies, it was being greeted with a kind of ecstatic optimism. Just as atomic energy was to have led to an era of plenty built on electrical power so cheap it would not be worth metering, we were being told that the Web would bring transformative changes in social relations and economic processes, all of them beneficial. Today, the benefits are clearer than ever, as information media of all kinds converge on the Web, offering easier, faster access and enormously expanded choice. The depth and breadth of content is breathtaking, and is expanding by the hour. Commerce has been changed in ways unimaginable only a few years ago. It truly is a revolutionary development. But as in all revolutions, the gains are accompanied by loss, or its potential.

The darker side of potent new industrial technologies like plastics, pesticides, nuclear reactors and genetic engineering are often predictable from the outset, and the response is typically to search out technological solutions to these unwanted consequences. Experience has shown that our blithe faith in our ability to find such solutions in time to prevent irreparable damage, is as often as not misplaced. The "precautionary principle" that most people apply in their private lives and with their families—the idea that possible consequences need to be clearly understood and evaluated prior to taking risks—is not one that fits comfortably in a corporate capitalist economy. This is largely because both the industrial breakthroughs and the new industries that must be created to ameliorate the damage they cause are counted as progress and tallied in improved profits and national wealth statistics. Our current economic system is thus strongly biased in favour of risk-taking. And although the assumption that, where industrial technology is concerned, unwanted consequences will have a technological solution and there will always be a net benefit is no longer tenable, it is at least a rationally coherent arrangement.

But breakthroughs in communication technologies deal with the ephemeral and bring with them consequences that are much more difficult to predict and assess. Who can know or even guess the consequences of facilitating the exchange of ideas and information among people? Even less obvious are the results of improvements in human-machine communication brought about by advances in artificial intelligence. And if we did anticipate harmful outcomes, what possible solutions would we put in place? Technology is unlikely to rescue us from costs that are mainly social and political, psychological and spiritual.

If this edition of *Spirit of the Web* has a different tone than the first edition published a decade ago (and the second edition published in 1999), it is because some of the unwanted and unexpected consequences of the Internet revolution have begun to show themselves, both as potentials and as concrete irritations. While I remain optimistic about the possibilities for genuine social and economic progress resulting from this new and unprecedented meta-medium of communication, I, like many others, am now also much more aware of its potential for harm as a tool in the hands of the ever-present forces of exploitation and repression. In my case, the sources of this awareness have been, first, a knowledge of the hands-on experience of those around me who have been intimately involved in introducing e-commerce and second, a familiarity with the expanding academic literature being produced by my colleagues around the world in the relatively new discipline of communication and culture.

If there is one concern that is central to my revised assessment of the prospects presented by the new era in communication, it is that instrumental communication—communication aimed at getting things done, at producing results, at gaining satisfaction, at providing data, at increasing efficiency—is displacing communication that is designed to produce knowledge, to encourage questioning and speculation, to facilitate dialogue and debate, to enhance understanding. Both forms of communication are necessary, but in a world such as ours in which most communication is highly mediated by technology, and that technology is largely in corporate hands, the instrumental—which has profit potential— tends to squeeze out the truly communicative, which has little economic value even though it is the cornerstone of civilized life. The Web has enormous potential in both directions, potential that is just beginning to be exploited. But there are no natural laws at play that can guarantee a happy outcome; no invisible hand provided by the gods of communication or the implacable dynamics of physics or biology is guiding developments. What the Web becomes, for better or worse, is entirely in our hands. We need to recognize that fact and accept the responsibilities it entails.

I am indebted to my publisher, Patrick Crean, for his continued enthusiasm for this book, and to editor Janice Zawerbny for her astute editorial guidance. And, as always, to by wife Christine for her faithful support.

— Wade Rowland
Port Hope, 2006

Contents

Some Milestones in Communications Technology

1896   Marconi patents wireless telegraphy (radio)
1899   Fleming invents vacuum tube diode
1900   Marconi patents tuned circuit for radio reception
1901   Fessenden tests voice transmission by radio; Marconi bridges Atlantic by radio
1902   Trans-Pacific telegraph cable, Vancouver to Australia
1905   First practical photo-facsimile machine (Korn)
1906   First broadcast of voice and music on radio (Fessenden)
1907   De Forest patents vacuum tube triode
1918   Canadian Marconi experiments with scheduled radio broadcasts (Montreal)
1919   Radio Corporation of America (RCA) incorporated
1920   CFCF Montreal begins scheduled radio broadcasting
1921   Westinghouse establishes first U.S. commercial radio station, KDKA
1922   AT&T sells first radio commercials; BBC begins radio broadcasting in Britain
1924   First radio-facsimile transmission of photograph
1925   AT&T establishes first commercial radio network via telephone lines
1929   BBC begins experimental television broadcasts
1932   Fully electronic television demonstrated by NBC
1936   BBC begins scheduled television broadcasts; Turing invents digital computer
1939   NBC begins scheduled television broadcasts in New York
1942   First fully automatic digital computer (Harvard)
1943   Colossus, first electronic digital computer, England
1945   ENIAC, first electronic computer, United States
1946   First U.S. cable television systems
1948   Shannon publishes paper on Information Theory; transistor invented at Bell Labs

1949	Pilot Ace, first computer using Random Access Memory (Britain)
1950	Remington Rand UNIVAC, first commercial computer using RAM
1957	Sputnik 1, first artificial earth satellite (USSR)
1959	First integrated circuits (Fairchild Semiconductor)
1962	Distributed communications network proposed by RAND
1965	Early Bird, Syncom, geosynchronous communications satellites in orbit; first commercial digital telephone installations
1968–9	ARPANET launched using packet technology to link computers
1969	Bell Labs researchers develop collaborative, open source operating system called UNIX
1971	First computer chips, or microprocessors (Intel); e-mail invented (Tomlinson)
1972	Internet proposed at First International Conference on Computer Communication, Washington, D.C.; e-mail adapted to ARPANET, @ sign adopted
1974	TCP/IP protocols introduced, placed in public domain; CompuServe incorporated
1975	Intel 8080 microprocessor; Altar 8800, first personal computer (United States); Apple Computer incorporated
1976	First electronic telephone switching systems (United States); Microsoft incorporated
1977	Apple II personal computer introduced
1979	Usenet established
1980	IBM PC introduced, with Microsoft Disc Operating System (DOS)
1981	TCP/IP become uniform Internet protocols
1984	Macintosh computer introduced by Apple; Internet domain name system (DNS) introduced

1990	The World becomes first commercial Internet service provider (ISP)
1993	World Wide Web launched (Berners-Lee); Mosaic graphical interface Web browser (Andreessen)
1994	Netscape incorporated; first Internet shopping sites; first banner ads (for AT&T and Zema, a soft drink)
1995	Small-dish satellite television in United States; Yahoo! incorporated; Amazon.com launched; RealAudio audio streaming technology introduced; WWW becomes service with greatest traffic on Internet
1996	Browser wars—Netscape peaks at 87 percent market share; Microsoft Explorer launches at 4 percent
1997	TiVo launches, introducing the personal video recorder
1998	Google incorporated; Netscape sells to AOL, conceding browser war to Explorer
1999	Dot-com bubble bursts on NASDAQ; AOL purchases Time Warner
2002	BitTorrent introduced; Explorer market share peaks at 95 percent
2004	Open source Firefox browser launches; IBM sells its PC division to Chinese IT company Lenovo
2005	Number of WWW sites tops 70 million

Spirit of the Web

Prologue

Extensions of Man

THE PAGES THAT FOLLOW contain the story of a family of inventions: how they were conceived and then coaxed into existence and finally offered to an unsuspecting world. Linking together in unforeseen ways, they have created an entirely new and awesomely powerful medium of communication, the impact of which provides a running subtext and a collection of concluding thoughts and speculations to this story. The uses and effects, past, present and future, of these technologies are also on the menu, as are the stories of the lives, motivation and inspiration of some of the geniuses who bore them into the world. And because, as a group, these technologies have been instrumental in changing in the most profound ways our view of the world we live in, we will be looking into some of the philosophical ideas that have influenced their development, and which have in turn been shaped by those technologies.

The new medium of communication is in fact a *meta*medium— digital, interactive, multimedia—delivered by switched networks, the most visible current application of which is the Internet. It can be ranked among the handful of most important technical advances in history. Many predict that it will fuel the next great post-industrial economic transformation as it matures and realizes its full potential; it has already changed the way business is done in the world.

It will be—indeed, is now—the most sophisticated, engaging, all-embracing medium of communication ever seen on the planet. What does it communicate? Information—which is an assemblage of data (literally, "the given"). Information, through the application of intelligence and experience, produces knowledge. And knowledge is a modern economy's most valuable asset.[1]

Not everyone wishes to be on the welcoming committee for this new metamedium. The late educator and social critic Neil Postman is one of a number of commentators who have complained that modern communications technologies have conjured up an information deluge of scriptural proportions, one that has drowned or is drowning the last vestiges of coherent culture and intelligent discourse. He fears that what is most valuable in Western civilization will be swallowed up before we realize what is at risk, until, "years from now . . . it will be noticed that the massive collection and speed-of-light retrieval of data have been of great value to large-scale organizations but have solved very little of importance to most people and have created at least as many problems for them as they may have solved."[2] In a broader sense, he says, "the uncontrolled growth of [communications] technology destroys the vital sources of our humanity. It creates a culture without moral foundation. It undermines certain mental processes and social relations that make human life worth living."[3]

Postman proposes that all subjects be taught as history, so as to give context and meaning to information, as opposed to passing it on to students as a mere consumer product:

> To teach about the atom without Democritus, to teach about electricity without Faraday, to teach about political science without Aristotle or Machiavelli, to teach about music without Haydn, is to refuse our students access to The Great Conversation. It is to deny them access to their roots, about which no other social institution is at present concerned. For to know about your roots is not merely to know where your grandfather came from and what he had to endure. It is also to know where

your ideas come from and why you happen to believe them; to know where your moral and aesthetic sensibilities come from. It is to know where your world, not just your family, comes from.4

I would add that all subjects ought also to be taught within a framework of ethical thought. This is unavoidably the case in the liberal arts, the focus of Postman's concerns: how does one teach aesthetics or politics or English literature without discussing morality? But any adequate definition of culture needs to be broader than this, to include science, technology and their associated academic disciplines, as well as the social sciences. Economics, for example, has become the centre of gravity around which Western culture orbits, and to attempt to teach it without reference to moral philosophy is to ignore the nature of its relevance to society. Economics is a moral science, its roots deeply engaged with ethical thought, in particular with issues of fairness and equity in the distribution of scarce goods. Distributive justice is a subject that cannot be divorced from moral thought. The economic concepts of people as human resources, human capital and consumers are also fraught with (usually unexamined) moral implications.

Technology, too, has its moral dimension, as I'll be pointing out in more detail in subsequent chapters. Though the precise nature of the relationship is a subject of much debate, there is no question that technology, and science too, is to some extent socially constructed. In the case of science, this means that what we frequently regard as definitive, factual information about the nature of the world is actually an *interpretation* of the evidence presented by nature, which is seen by scientists, unavoidably, through the lens of contemporary academic prejudices and broader social needs and interests. The social construction of technologies means that they carry within their very structures the hopes and aspirations, fears and prejudices of the culture within which they were created, and more specifically of the institutions, and even the individuals, responsible for technological innovation. An increasingly important aspect of the social construction of technologies is the relatively new and novel role played by the modern business corporation, an entity that assumed its mature form as recently as the last third of the twentieth century. The corporation is, *by design*, incorrigibly self-serving and acquisitive, and that is reflected in the technologies it invents and disseminates.

It is in this spirit of acknowledging their historical and ethical contexts that this book explores the development of modern communications technologies. Its goal is to help readers understand where their sometimes bewildering world comes from. While it acknowledges the attitudes of Postman and other media critics, it is not a pessimistic work, mainly because it takes the historical narrative one step beyond where Postman left off, to the new era of networked computers and the Internet. If earlier critics have been harsh in their judgments of the impact of computers, it is perhaps because the true nature of these marvellous machines, their role as gateways to networks, had not yet fully emerged and was therefore not generally understood. Postman says, for instance: "Although I believe the computer to be a vastly overrated technology, I mention it here because, clearly, Americans have accorded it their customary mindless inattention; which means they will use it as they are told, without a whimper."[5]

Here, Postman is wrong on both counts. The biggest surprise in the tumultuous, astonishing history of the personal computer industry has in fact been the way people have *chosen* to use their machines—for record keeping and computation, certainly, but also and primarily as communications tools. Online publishing, email, newsgroups, Internet telephony and video conferencing, video and audio streaming, instant messaging, blogs (weblogs, or online diaries), the World Wide Web itself, were all unanticipated, user-driven applications of the personal computer. They came from the bottom up. It would be difficult to appreciate the value of an automobile or a subway train in the absence of a network of roads and railbeds; so we may forgive the Postmans of the world their short-sightedness, since it was difficult to appreciate the true potential of the computer as a communications tool prior to the very recent advent of national and global networks.

Furthermore, Americans, no less than Canadians or Britons or people elsewhere in the world, historically have been anything but submissive in the presence of technical advances in the area of communications. Computer engineers and marketers were not alone in being caught off guard by a public demand for applications they'd scarcely considered for their product: as we shall see, the same thing happened with the telephone and radio, and even, to some extent, with the telegraph.

It is likely that this ability to adapt, for purposes of personal communication, technologies that had been envisaged as industrial or institutional solutions goes back even further, to the printing press and even to the phonetic alphabet. People have always felt the compulsion to communicate with one another, as a means of discovering their world and creating their personal identity. A professor friend of mine likes to ask his undergraduate students: "If words carry meaning, where do they hide it?" The answer is that language must be accompanied by communication to have purpose; therefore the meanings of words do not exist in the words themselves, but are a product of the creative process of communication. Language, in other words, is a dynamic, social construct. It both reflects and creates the world we live in, by describing it and defining it.

We communicate with each other over both distance and time. Communication with those remote from us in time has been accomplished by recording techniques and devices ranging from the charcoal sticks and mineral paints of cave dwellers to the compact disc. Its success is determined both by the inherent durability of the storage medium and, perhaps less obviously, by the quality of the content being preserved. The quality of content helps to preserve it because it increases its perceived value, deterring casual destruction. Communication over distance, on the other hand, is concerned mainly with speed, and quality of the content is usually less important than its currency or timeliness. In general, the more immediate the message, the more valuable it is. Thus, the ideal distance-communication system operates in real time as does, for example, the telephone.

The quest for better distance communication, which is our main area of concern here, has been the quest for technologies which extend our principal "distance-capable" senses, vision and hearing, so that they may be employed at ever greater distance and with ever smaller time delays in communicating thought and information. It has led us from the megaphone to the drum, bugle and other musical instruments, to smoke signals and signal fires, to the optical telegraph and penny post, to the electrical telegraph, to telephony, to radio and television, and finally to today's digital multimedia delivered via switched networks, satellites and wireless cellular systems.

This raises an obvious question: What is all of this information used for? One analyst who has closely examined the issue, G.J. Mulgan, states that information in industrial societies is used principally for purposes of control. This may be the straightforward control of a machine that is regulated by feedback (for example, a thermostat), or it may be the complex cultural controls, from laws to customs, exercised by the various estates of society over a population in the pursuit of social order. "Information technology," he argues, is really a misnomer: the phrase should be "control technologies." The "information revolution" is really a shift toward more rapid, comprehensive and efficient methods of control of objects, processes and people.

Seen from this perspective, the burgeoning development of communications technologies, beginning with the telegraph and continuing through to the Internet, is a necessary response to the natural growth in size and complexity of industrial and post-industrial societies. The difficulties of control, and thus the need for information, grow disproportionately with the increasing complexity of any system: as the scale of a system doubles, the number of possible control points is squared. As well, improved communication both permits and encourages increased complexity, so that communication and complexity feed on one another to further accelerate demands for yet more information.

Information and the networks that distribute it have both positive and negative potentials, just as "control" has positive and negative connotations. They can mean the liberty that arises out of "peace, order and good government," as Canadians say, or they can be used for autocratic and repressive purposes. They can be used to enhance industrial productivity, making more efficient use of scarce resources and lowering prices to consumers, and they can, at the same time, be employed in regimenting workforces, sapping jobs of any vestige of the satisfactions that come with creative decision making. Information, at some level of analysis, may in principle be treated as a neutral commodity, but the technologies which make it useful by giving it a context are not: they have social and political implications that need careful examination. Mulgan writes:

> When governments introduced compulsory universal education, public libraries and later broadcasting, it was clear to many that beneath the rhetoric of benevolent liberal reform these were also deliberate attacks on the autonomous realm of working-class activity, with its own material base, its own networks of exchange and its own meanings. The self-education movements and subversive literary cultures of subordinate classes were effectively preempted and co-opted, as governments and ruling classes learned to use access, rather than the denial of access, as a tool of power.[6]

I will argue here that broadcast or unilateral communications technologies ("unilateral" because they move information in one direction only, from the top down), by their very essence, incorporate an authoritarian bias; that bilateral communications technologies ("bilateral" because information moves, or may be moved, in equal volumes in both directions), such as the telephone and the Internet, are intrinsically predisposed to the advancement of democracy. My reasoning, in a nutshell, is as follows: Broadcast communications technologies tend to promote hierarchical, pyramid-shaped organizational structures due to the fact that they originate information at one point (the apex of the pyramid) and disseminate the same information to all those on the receiving end (at the base of the pyramid). Bilateral technologies, on the other hand, of necessity organize laterally, through conversation, consensus and co-operation.

The technical advances that created the Information Age occurred during two distinct periods of great creativity. The first extends roughly from the middle of the nineteenth century through to the outbreak of World War I. It is an era in which the hitherto jealously distinct fields of science and what we would now call engineering, but was then called craft, came together in co-operation, with astounding results. Then a rift occurred. The nightmare carnage of the Great War wiped out a generation of the best and brightest idealists and intellectuals, and shattered the pre-war dream of human perfectibility through material progress and invention. In one of the truly pathetic ironies of history, one of the reasons for what seems an otherwise lunatic war was the technological optimism that was so pervasive in the pre-war period. It was believed on all sides that technology had brought the arts of war to such a pinnacle of sublime perfection that offensive military action would be devastating and irresistible, making a protracted conflict impossible. No one had paused to wonder what happens when an irresistible force meets an immovable object. The dreadful truth was that technical sophistication on both sides led to unbreakable deadlock and a sustained level of bloodletting unparalleled in human history.

The period between World War I and World War II is justifiably treated by most historians as a time of retrenchment, economic confusion, moral cynicism, and technical stagnation in many fields. It amounted to an uneasy bridge spanning the thirty years between two periods of global warfare, and was devoted to a regrouping of forces in preparation for a continuation of conflict. Following World War II, even after the worst of the physical devastation that had been inflicted on Europe and East Asia had been repaired, a sense of optimism was slow to rebuild. The forty-year Cold War with its truly terrifying nuclear arms race gave ample cause for despair over the uses to which advanced technologies were being put. The world had arrived at a state in which it had become possible, with the deliberate or accidental touch of a button, to exterminate virtually the whole of the human race and much of the natural ecosystem in which it had flourished, thanks to the supremely rational but deeply psychotic strategy of "mutually assured destruction." The Rationalist, technology-centred optimism of the late nineteenth century seemed laughable in retrospect. For a time immediately after World War II, technological development continued to build on the great advances of the late nineteenth century, which in turn had capitalized on the scientific discoveries of the previous two hundred years and more. But increasingly it was the science of the early twentieth century that began to drive technological innovation. Whereas earlier science had focused on the macrocosmic issues of the visible worlds of astronomy, physics and chemistry, this new science was involved with the previously unseeable and unsuspected world of atomic and subatomic, cellular and subcellular activity.

In the field of communications, the science of quanta or elementary particles has led to technologies of a radically different nature from those of the machine age. One aspect of their novelty can be seen in the convergence of late-twentieth-century digital computer technology with the analog electronic technologies of the late nineteenth and early twentieth centuries, including the telephone and radio. This convergence has led to the rapid ascendancy of digital over analog techniques and devices. (Analog technologies work by measuring; digital technologies work by counting. It is a distinction which may seem pedantic and obscure but which has nevertheless had profound effects on everyday life, as we'll see.) The impact of the digital revolution in communications (or, more broadly, information) technologies in turn is fomenting social change by placing unprecedented power in the hands of ordinary people around the world. It is at the same time enabling existing governmental and corporate power structures to resist this democratization in both the workplace and the political sphere. The ramifications have been startling and will be discussed at some length in the concluding chapters.

The trends sketched here point to the continuing relevance of questions raised by observers such as the historian of technology

Gene I. Rochlin, who wrote in 1974: "We seem no closer to the dream of a social structure in which industry is the servant of humanity rather than the forger of its chains. The chains may be more ephemeral now than they once were, but they still bind us to our machines."7

Is communications technology tightening those restraints or loosening them? The choice, in the end, is ours to make, and it is the central issue for the politics of the Age of Information.

PART ONE

THE ANALOG ERA

The Meaning of the Age of Information

F OR AS LONG as we have been building complex machines, humans have described themselves and their world in the context of those devices. The invention of the mechanical clock in medieval times gave rise to the notion of the clockwork universe, with its regular and predictable celestial events, and of God as a clockmaker. For René Descartes (1596–1650) and his Enlightenment-era contemporaries, humans were clockwork machines accessorized by an immaterial and inscrutable soul. Today, it is the computer that provides the imagery. Though the machine itself is still in its adolescence and the potential of the global computer networks is just beginning to be explored, we can see a further smudging of the boundary between human and machine in the fashionable notion of the brain as an elaborate biological computing device, and of intelligence as an emergent, perhaps generic quality of complexity in natural systems. And we have the Internet, a network of digital computers, proliferating, we are told, like an organic creature. Whether in the end substantial or illusory, this strange convergence between the animate and the inanimate, the organic and the inorganic, speaks to the power and endurance of the technological metaphor.[1]

If, as the technological optimists hope and the pessimists fear, the convergence between organic and inorganic intelligence proves to be more than mere metaphor, it is likely to mark humanity as profoundly as did Copernicus's momentous conclusion that the earth orbits the sun. When he published *On the Revolution of the Celestial Spheres* (1543) in the last year of his life, Copernicus changed the world. By observing that the movements in the heavens as they had been seen and understood from the dawn of history were an illusion created by the earth's motion around its star, he threw into question every other accepted truth about nature and the universe. If so obvious and fundamental a precept as the earth-centredness of the universe could be challenged and disproved, what other astounding revelations might be possible? Where else was the received wisdom of the ages in error? The medieval notion that all knowledge was contained within the Scriptures (as later complemented by the writings of the ancients of classical Greece) could no longer be sustained.

One might reasonably have expected the relegating of the earth to the status of just another celestial body—quite a step down from being the hub of the universe!—would have been a demoralizing experience for Western man. But the discovery came at a time when the return from Byzantium of many of the original texts of classical Greece had produced intense new interest in the ancients.[2] A resurgence of interest in the science and philosophy of classical Greece and Rome fuelled the growth of a new humanism, with which the Copernican revolution was in sympathy. Western civilization's values were set adrift with the loss of their moorings in the immutable, ordained truths of an unchanging universe, gradually to find a new anchorage in a renewed faith in values arising out of human wisdom. Experience, rather than zealous acceptance of received dogma, became the guide to understanding. And this had an inevitable impact on social values and the way in which they were expressed in politics. Petrarch, the chief humanist of the age, set the tone with his famous aphorism: "It is better to will the good than to know the truth." Explorers, making practical navigational use of the new cosmology and of new technologies of measurement, discovered and began exploring the western hemisphere. It was the time of Dante, Boccaccio, Rembrandt, the Medicis, da Vinci and Machiavelli.

The humanism based on rhetoric, the rediscovered philosophy of the Greek Sophists, flourished until about the mid-seventeenth century as a world view in which the truth was arrived at by observation and discussion of observed reality, in all its untidiness. "Man is the measure of all things" is the famous watchword of the movement. It meant, man is a centre of values; values are not external to him or in some way "given" or predetermined. The process of establishing truth was much like a courtroom trial in which material evidence is brought forward and examined according to accepted rules and conventions. As in law, once a decision has been arrived at, it becomes a precedent on which new "reality" can be built. The Truth was more invention than discovery, and therefore was not immutable. It could change if new evidence was presented. It is not difficult to see how humanism was a comfortable cradle for the modern, empirical science brought into the world through the successive ministrations of Copernicus, Kepler, Galileo, Descartes and, ultimately, Newton.

The fact that Newton was born in the year Galileo died (1642) is a coincidence of history made all the more striking by the inescapable metaphorical notion that Galileo died giving birth to Newton. The well-known (but often misunderstood) story of Galileo's conflict with the Roman Catholic Church, which insisted he recant his published conviction that the earth revolves around the sun, marks the climax of a long struggle by the Church to accommodate new physical knowledge of the universe without abandoning the metaphysical structures which defined its values.[3] With that incident, though by no means entirely because of it, came a historic parting of the ways between Religion and Science, between the spiritual and the material. Science flourished; the Church withered. Increasingly, Western societies looked to the victorious and robustly practical Science as a source of moral and ethical values, the sort of humanist values that had played such an important role at its birth.

Gradually, though, the accumulation of scientific knowledge led to a new determinism, more rational but, in retrospect, in some ways no less confining than the dogmatic religious faith it had replaced. In the new scientific world view, the universe was complete and perfect, a closed system whose mysteries could be discovered by rational analysis. Newton's physics epitomize this conception: Newton's universe was a well-oiled machine in which the whole was exactly equal to the sum of its parts and in which there were no surprises, no unexpected events once one understood completely the machine's workings. It was a linear world in which equations all plotted in straight lines or regular curves.[4] The values inherent in such a system could only be as fixed and invariable as the humanist's were mutable and subject to evolution, and over time, in its insistence on material, quantifiable answers to all phenomena, science would become as rigidly dogmatic as the medieval Church, until "[t]he world that people had thought themselves living in—a world rich with colour and sound, redolent with fragrance, filled with gladness, love and beauty, speaking everywhere of purposive harmony and creative ideals—was crowded into minute corners in the brains of scattered organic beings."[5]

And yet the one wilful blindness made no more sense than the other, since

> science deals with but a partial aspect of reality, and . . . there is no faintest reason for supposing that everything science ignores is less real than what it accepts . . . Why is it that science forms a closed system? Why is it that the elements of reality it ignores never come in to disturb it? The reason is that all the terms of physics are defined in terms of one another. The abstractions with which physics begins are all it ever has to do with . . .[6]

The role of a Creator and lawgiver in the universe devolved step by step from engaged participant, to detached observer, to Newton's Prime Mover, to a mere embodiment of the mathematical principles underlying material reality. God became a kind of constitutional monarch, a figurehead held over from a more naive era, held on to for nostalgic reasons.

The ascendance of the scientific rationalist world view was considerably accelerated by the first great broadcast-style communications technologies, the printing press and the mechanical clock, products of the sixteenth and fourteenth centuries respectively. Learning and literacy left the close confines of the monasteries and were made widely accessible, as were the techniques of organization. The two technologies combined to create what was, in its own way, an Age of Information.

The printing press, by fostering literacy, shaped our minds, our very thought processes. The mechanical clock, audible and visible in every prosperous town, day and night, taught people that the "river" of time was made up of quanta or bits; it taught them, some historians argue, to quantify. More concretely, by making it possible and practicable to organize time, the mechanical clock made it possible to organize production processes, with significant results, as Lewis Mumford has pointed out: "The gain in mechanical efficiency through coordination and through the closer articulation of the day's events cannot be overestimated . . . The modern industrial regime could do without coal and iron and steam easier than it could do without the clock."7

Although it was probably invented simply as a means of regulating monastic routines, the clock was, in late-twentieth-century terms, a potent piece of information technology that did its job by reducing uncertainty and increasing predictability. (Information may be defined, in fact, as "the elimination of uncertainty.") The information the clock created made it a powerful agent of control. It did no work on its own, but it came to govern those processes and machines that did, in much the same way that computers control processes today. It not only created information, however, it disseminated it, in broadcast fashion, to the four corners of the earth. At first, monastery bells ringing the seven daily calls to prayer became important to surrounding villagers, and soon clocks and watches everywhere were synchronized, giving life a universal and precise, though synthetic, regularity. Clock-created information, clock time, became virtually inescapable, and invaded cultures worldwide at every level.

But the clock did much more than that. By dissociating time from human activity, the mechanical clock created a new model of reality; more efficient, but in some ways impoverished. In bequeathing us the benefits of the ability to organize time, it also further distanced us from an essential part of our humanity, namely, the subjective, the emotional, the non-rational. It did this by promoting a method of thought whereby entities could be subdivided, the segment standing in for the whole as an abstraction of it. And this was a decidedly mixed blessing, as Mumford argued:

> Isolation and abstraction, while important to orderly research and refined symbolic representation, are likewise conditions under which real organisms die, or at least cease to function effectively . . . In short, the accuracy and simplicity of science, though they were responsible for its colossal practical achievements, were not an approach to objective reality but a departure from it. In their desire to achieve exact results the physical sciences scorned true objectivity: individually, one side of the personality was paralyzed; collectively, one side of experience was ignored. To substitute mechanical or two-way time for history, the dissected corpse for a living body, dismantled units called "individuals" for men-in-groups, or in general the mechanically measurable or reproducible for the inaccessible and the complicated and the organically whole, is to achieve a limited practical mastery at the expense of truth and of the larger efficiency that depends on truth.[8]

Society and its values had drifted from the faith of the medieval Roman Church to the renaissance of humanist thought to a new faith in the demonstrable truths of science, which more and more would be written in the supremely logical language of mathematics.

It was the determinist, rationalist position of the scientific materialists that was being advocated as recently as the early years of the twentieth century by Bertrand Russell and Alfred North Whitehead in their masterwork *Principia Mathematica*, a heroic attempt to integrate logic and mathematics in order to establish reason, once and for all, as the exclusive arbiter and verification of authentic knowledge. And then along came Albert Einstein with General Relativity, and mathematician Kurt Gödel with his proof that mathematics and logic, like all knowledge derived from formal systems, are inescapably incomplete and, in an important sense, "untrue," and quantum physicist Werner Heisenberg with proof that there are some realities under the sun that are forever indeterminate—simply cannot be known, ever. Added to that were the experimental demonstrations of the strange fact that in the quantum world the act of observation in some real sense creates what is observed, and of "entanglement," that phenomenon which connects everything in the universe with everything else, instantaneously. With these insights, the very foundations of the mechanistic, deterministic world view were fatally undermined. Pulverized, in fact. Rationalist civilization's verities could no longer be held to be definitive and invariable, since rational knowledge was now known to be indeterminate, incomplete and relativistic. The centre no longer held.

Once again we are left to fend for ourselves after being set adrift from a secure-seeming moral anchorage. We are currently in the midst of a revolution of outlook and perception no less disorienting and no less pregnant with possibilities than any experienced by our ancestors of the seventeenth and eighteenth centuries. It is being broadened and accelerated by the insights provided by our computer-mediated information networks.

The impulse to spread the net of science to take in more and more of life as it is experienced and observed led to quantum theory, and more recently to chaos theory. Reality in the Newtonian universe had been reduced to an affair of linear equations about static perfection largely because that is what was manageable with the technology (and the mathematics) of the day. Observations inconsistent with classical physics were set aside as irrelevant, or as a problem of information deficiency. It was assumed, in other words, that anomalous observations—if they were worth considering at all—would one day be brought into line with Newtonian law: "If we had more information, we'd be able to explain what was going on." Computers made that argument increasingly untenable because they removed many of the roadblocks to information acquisition and processing, allowing more and more of the real world to be brought into the closed system of physics and mathematics. We now understand that even very complex, seemingly chaotic systems obey rules—or rather, that we are able to describe such processes in mathematical terms that have the appearance of rules—but they are not the sort of linear rules set out by Newton. It takes a high-speed computer to discern their patterns. And thanks to quantum physics, we understand that the various entities that make up our universe are tightly interconnected, and that what happens to one affects all others, instantaneously. We are developing a conception of the world in which systems are best understood by examining their "bottom-up" behaviour rather than looking at them from the top down. This shift in perspective is a response to an understanding that natural systems were not created complete and fully mature, like Athena springing from Zeus's forehead, but rather evolved over time according to rules which we do not completely understand. Our concept of the world is much more biological, evolutionary, than Newton's.

Our brave new world exists on the edge of chaos, constantly in flux, forever changing, never quite exploding into complete anarchy but, because of its dynamism, alive in a way that Newton's was not. It is a world in which, increasingly, information and its communication seems to play a crucial role in maintaining dynamic stability in the midst of apparent chaos, much as human society depends on information and communication to organize itself at both the individual and collective levels.

The Information Age, we might then argue, is also the age of the return of the rhetorical-humanist world view, which is essentially a democratic outlook. Where determinist thought spawned utopian schemes of all descriptions, top-down societies all of them, rhetoric has been concerned with the give-and-take of real politics, real life and incremental, bottom-up progress. The Information Age brings with it a world view that maps our current understanding of physical reality and our highest aspirations for human progress and happiness much better than the machine-age paradigms it replaces.

But there is a worm in the apple. Determinism and its dogmatisms are alive and kicking, embedded in what might be called "the system," that is, the economic and political institutions which have been largely inherited from the era of high Rationalism in the seventeenth and eighteenth centuries. The market, the corporation, bureaucracies of all kinds, for all their modern sophistication, remain wilfully blind to those aspects of human life and aspiration that cannot be quantified. They deliberately avoid, on principle, the messy complexities of the moral, the aesthetic, the psychological—in fact, most of what constitutes the eternal Socratic notion of the good life. There remains entrenched in our culture the Rationalist belief that all scientific inquiry is productive, and that any and all technological innovation represents progress. To the extent that control or direction is needed, it is provided automatically (mechanistically) by the laissez-faire market economy.

How these conflicting views—the materialist-determinist and the humanist-rhetorical—are reconciled in the coming decades is a matter of historic consequence with few parallels. Technology may well hold the key. The new technologies of information and communication, products of the system and its chief sources of power, have been mastered with enthusiasm by the system's most effective opponents in the name of a more humane world. Whose interests these technologies best serve in the long run will decide the kind of world our children inherit.

2

The Need to Communicate

HUMAN COMMUNICATION began with touching, moved
on to gestures and vocalizations, and finally arrived at the
spoken word. Or so we can surmise: the process is one that
leaves no evolutionary footprints. How and why humans acquired
language remains a mystery. Two things seem clear at this stage of
our understanding. First, all healthy humans appear to be born
with a linguistic grammar hard-wired into their brains, and it is this
grammatical ability that allows them to learn to speak in whatever
language their particular culture may employ. Second, we learn who
we are through our communication with others, and it is communication with others of our own species that allows us to fully realize
our potential, to become all that we *can* be.

No one would call speech a technology, for the simple reason
that it is a function of the human body and mind, which, as far as
we know, are naturally occurring phenomena. They are nobody's
invention. Are *languages* technologies? Clearly, in their rules of
grammar and syntax, they are invented, purpose-built to facilitate
communication. But languages are not the kind of invention we
normally associate with technologies, in that they appear to have
emerged spontaneously out of linguistic abilities innate in all normal
human beings.[1] Spoken language is native to humans, and cannot

therefore be considered to be a *technical extension of human capabilities*, which is as good a definition of the word *technology* as any.

For our purposes, then, communications technology can be said to begin with writing, which is not innate, and which requires the adaptation and use of materials found in nature. The earliest-known writing has been discovered on Sumerian clay tablets dated to 3300 BC; hieroglyphic inscriptions began appearing in Egypt around 3100 BC. The Greek alphabet, to which we owe our own, was not invented until about 730 BC. And "invented" may be the appropriate verb here: judging from archaeological evidence, it appeared rather suddenly, and it was used from the beginning for what we would now call literary purposes, rather than for accounting, list keeping and other trade and bureaucratic functions. This has led some scholars to speculate that it was the fruit of a spontaneous act of creation by some brilliant but anonymous Greek thinker, who sought a means of making a permanent record of Homer's great epics, *The Iliad* and *The Odyssey*.[2]

As unlikely as that may seem, it is certainly true that the Greek alphabet made possible great refinement of the art of writing and composition because it was so flexible and adaptable, two virtues which derived from the fact that it was composed entirely of phonetic elements that, when assembled into a word, could be "sounded out" to extract their meaning. Other written languages of the period, like Egyptian hieroglyphics, were typically extensive and hugely complex, containing both phonetic content and symbols that represented complete words. Some symbols did multiple duty as ideas, names or words with more than one meaning. The Egyptian sign means "open," "hurry," "mistake" or "light" depending on the sign that follows (the determinative); it can also mean "becoming bald," and, as well, stands for the word *wn* (wen). The intended meaning could only be determined by the context, and if the reader had not previously memorized the symbol, it was next to impossible to decipher.

This meant that until the advent of early Greek writing, literacy was of necessity confined to small, highly trained elites. A ruler receiving a message recorded on clay would have to have it translated by his scribe, who would then compose the reply as well. At the receiving end, it would be decoded by another scribe and spoken aloud to the intended recipient. As a communications technology, this kind of writing had minimal impact on society at large because of its very limited penetration beyond the ranks of the professional.

By virtue of their literacy skills, the scribes of Egypt became quite influential in government since their records allowed them to predict the size of the harvest, estimate government revenue and allocate appropriations to government departments based on those estimates. In Babylon, the literate unfailingly mentioned this accomplishment on their seal-stones (which were not dissimilar in content to today's extended email signatures), in the same way that a present-day academic might list her degrees on her business card. Literacy was the key to high religious, commercial or government office.

It was a situation that would be repeated in the earliest days of personal computer communications, when the all but impenetrable MS-DOS reigned as the dominant operating system and only the highly skilled "computer nerd" was able to make the technology work. Or in the time of the telegraph, when messages were transmitted in Morse code, which could only be deciphered by trained telegraphers. Pre-Greek writing, like many of our present communications technologies, was *mediated* communication.

The Greek alphabet removed the need for mediation or interpretation—or, in the current jargon, it *disintermediated* reading and writing. In making widespread literacy possible, the alphabet also made it a socially desirable accomplishment, and the spread of literacy would have profound and surprising effects upon civilization. These did not go unnoticed at the time. Plato, and perhaps Socrates too, well understood that the medium is the message.

In his brilliant and persuasive *Preface to Plato*, Eric Havelock follows in the footsteps of Harold Innis and Marshall McLuhan with an engaging interpretation of Plato's *Republic* as an impassioned rejection of the oral culture that had previously dominated Greek life. Until writing was introduced, Greek culture was preserved and passed down through the generations by means of epic poetry, which, using mnemonic devices such as storytelling and rhythmic meter, conveyed social, legal, ethical, historical and religious information essential to the perpetuation of the civilization. McLuhan called it "the tribal encyclopedia . . . the specific operational wisdom for all contingencies of life . . . Ann Landers in verse." But oral culture, Plato asserted, stood in the way of intellectual growth, the growth of a true philosophy, because it trapped men's minds in a poetical or "musical" state in which understanding and learning are emotional and not rational, subjective and not objective, concrete and never abstract; are based on opinion rather than fact.

> [Plato] asks of men that . . . they should examine this experience and rearrange it, that they should think about what they say, instead of just saying it. And they should become the "subject" who stands apart from the "object" and reconsiders it and analyses it and evaluates it, instead of just "imitating" it . . . This amounts to accepting the premise that there is a "me," a "self," a "soul" or consciousness which is self-governing and which discovers the reason for action in itself rather than in imitation of the poetic experience. The doctrine of autonomous psyche is the counterpart of the rejection of oral culture.[3]

And it was the alphabet, Havelock asserts, that made this epochal change possible. He asks how the Greeks were able to shake themselves out of their poetic "somnambulance" and become a deeply analytical and speculative people, and answers his own question this way:

> The fundamental answer must lie in the changing technology of communication. Refreshment of memory through written signs enabled a reader to dispense with most of that emotional identification by which alone the acoustical record was sure of recall . . . No longer . . . was it a matter of "this corpse on the battlefield" but of "body" anywhere and everywhere. No longer

was it "this basket which happens to be empty but will be full in a moment": it is the cosmos which is empty or has emptiness always and everywhere.

Or, as Northrop Frye explains in his monumental *The Great Code*, with Plato

> the intellectual operations of the mind become distinguishable from the emotional operations; hence abstraction becomes possible, and the sense that there are valid and invalid ways of thinking, a sense which is to a degree independent of our feelings, develops into the conception of logic. What Homeric heroes resolve in their bosoms is an inseparable mixture of thought and feeling; what Socrates demonstrates, more especially in his death, is the superior penetration of thought when it is in command of feeling.[4]

By making possible the communication of thought through written words capable of unambiguous understanding by any reader, the alphabet cleared the way for the evolution of the detached intellectual state that makes philosophy or abstract analytical thought possible. Rational inquiry in turn led eventually to the scientific method, itself a branch of philosophy. And along the way the development of the person as individual, as opposed to compliant group-member, was made possible thanks to the new scope for independent thought. No less a role is claimed for the phonetic alphabet.[5]

Put another way, the alphabet allowed information to be removed from its human, emotional, tribal context for examination and evaluation, transmission and transformation. By making widely accessible the means of reliable transcription of thought and speech to durable, comprehensible and transportable text, it enabled people to display the contents of their mind for all to see and comment on—whether in the author's presence or not. It made of the mind (or at least its contents) an object distinct from the body, available for dissection and examination, while at the same time refining the abstract and theoretical from the raw stuff of the concrete and material. In doing this, literacy spawns individuality, as Marshall McLuhan argued:

> By their dependence on the spoken word for information, people were drawn together into a tribal mesh; and since the spoken word is more emotionally laden than the written—conveying by intonation such rich emotions as anger, joy, sorrow, fear—tribal man was more spontaneous and passionately volatile. Audile-tactile tribal man partook of the collective unconscious, lived in a magical integral world patterned by myth and ritual, its values divine and unchallenged, whereas literate or visual man creates an environment that is strongly fragmented, individualistic, explicit, logical, specialized and detached.

McLuhan is helpful in explaining why the phonetic literacy, in particular, led to changes more dramatic and long-lasting than previous forms of written communication, and is worth quoting at length on the subject:

> The phonetic alphabet was radically different from the older and richer hieroglyphic or ideogrammic cultures. The writings of Egyptian, Babylonian, Mayan and Chinese cultures were an extension of the senses in that they gave pictorial expression to reality, and they demanded many signs to cover the wide range of data in their societies—unlike phonetic writing, which uses semantically meaningless [i.e., devoid of real-world context] letters to correspond to semantically meaningless sounds and is able, with only a handful of letters, to encompass all meanings and all languages. This achievement demanded the separation of both sights and sounds from their semantic and dramatic meanings in order to render visible the actual sound of speech, thus placing a barrier between men and objects and creating a dualism between sight and sound. It divorced the visual function from the interplay with the other senses and thus led to the

rejection from consciousness of vital areas of our sensory experience and to the resultant atrophy of the unconscious.[6]

McLuhan had serious reservations as to whether the transition to literacy was an entirely positive development. The movement from oral to literate culture disrupted the previously balanced interplay of all the senses, "overdeveloping" the visual function and resulting in "a desert of classified data" largely devoid of context—context otherwise supplied by the aural and tactile senses. It distanced people from the world in which they live, and separated them from other people. One of the reasons he welcomed what he saw as a revival of orality in modern popular culture was that it promised to redress this long-standing "imbalance." In a famous *Playboy* magazine interview he was asked, "But aren't there corresponding gains in insight, understanding and cultural diversity to compensate detribalized man for the loss of his communal values?" He responded:

> Your question reflects all the institutionalized biases of literate man. Literacy, contrary to the popular view of the "civilizing" process you've just echoed, creates people who are much less complex and diverse than those who develop in the intricate web of oral-tribal societies . . . The internal world of the tribal man was a creative mix of complex emotions and feelings that literate men of the Western world have allowed to wither or have suppressed in the name of efficiency and practicality . . . There is much evidence to suggest that man may have paid too dear a price for his new environment of specialist technology and values. Schizophrenia and alienation may be the inevitable consequences . . .[7]

The notion of progress is one of the more vexing inventions of modern Western culture, and there is some suggestion that it too can be ascribed to literacy. Historians have noted that with widespread literacy came an increasing sense of anachronism, of the difference between the past and the present. The suggestion is that this is due to the fact that the record of the past was now available for careful scrutiny in the form of contemporary records, rather than being merely passed on through oral tradition. A sense of the difference between past and present was encouraged, and when that was combined with the optimism and self-assurance that was a cultural hallmark of the scientific revolution and the Enlightenment of the seventeenth and eighteenth centuries, we have *progress*—the peculiar ideology that defines the present as superior to the past, but not so desirable as the future, which will be better, indeed perfect. The past is dark and primitive while the future is bright and advanced; the present is a transition period that must be endured rather than enjoyed, a sacrificial hostage to the future.

The effects of phonetic literacy were greatly extended by the printing press, an invention of the fifteenth century ascribed to Johannes Gutenberg. It is generally recognized as the next great advance in communications technologies, one that is often alluded to by authors searching for adequate comparisons for today's computer network revolution. In making possible the mechanized duplication of manuscripts through the use of movable type, it did indeed transform the world, though not as quickly as is often suggested, and often in surprising and instructive ways. The printing press is credited with loosening the grip of orthodox Catholicism on Europe by making the Bible and other religious texts widely available. It also led to rapid advances in learning in almost every discipline, due to the widespread adoption of indexing, alphabetization, encyclopedic collections and other methods of organizing data. It arrested linguistic drift (fragmentation or "corruption" of languages) and paved the way for uniformity within European languages, thereby fostering the appearance of the nation-state. It was responsible for the ideas of copyright, plagiarism and patents. With it came the whole modern notion of authorship, virtually unknown in earlier eras of scribes and anonymous translators and interpreters.

But perhaps the most telling change wrought by the printing press is one that gets little attention in the libraries of tomes devoted to the subject. It is nicely summed up in a quotation that has been unearthed by Elizabeth Eisenstein in *The Printing Press as an Agent of Change*: "Why should old men be preferred to their juniors now that it is possible for the young by diligent study to acquire the same knowledge?" The question is asked by Jacob Filippo Foresti in his newly minted world history, published in Venice in 1483.[8] Communications technologies—whether the printing press or the World Wide Web—tend, in the modern vernacular, to level the playing field.

The printing press was a decisive step in the long process of abstracting and codifying information in discrete symbolic units, which made it reproducible with minimal erosion of content and easily transportable. But there were losses involved as well, as Frances A. Yates observed in the following passage from his *Art of Memory*:

> In Victor Hugo's *Notre-Dame de Paris*, a scholar, deep in meditation in his study . . . gazes at the first printed book which has come to disturb his collection of manuscripts. Then . . . he gazes at the vast cathedral, silhouetted against the starry sky . . . *"Ceci tuera cela,"* he says. The printed book will destroy the building. The parable which Hugo develops out of the comparison of the building, crowded with images, with the arrival in his library of a printed book might be applied to the effect on the invisible cathedrals of memory of the past of the spread of printing. The printed book will make such huge built-up memories, crowded with images, unnecessary. It will do away with habits of immemorial antiquity whereby a "thing" is immediately invested with an image and stored in the places of memory.

There was a certain snobbery in such reactions. In the sixteenth and seventeenth centuries, men and women of high social status resisted having their writings put into print, preferring to circulate them privately in manuscript form among those who it was felt were capable of understanding and appreciating them. When something found its way into print, it had escaped its author's control. There was also a sense that to print one's writing was to stoop to the level of a tradesperson, hawking thoughts and ideas like common commodities. Galileo thrived in a culture of privately circulated manuscripts, written mostly in Latin; he fell from grace when he published his views in book form in *Dialogues on the Great World Systems*. The love poetry of John Donne and Philip Sidney was circulated in manuscript for decades before finally being printed.

It was through newspapers that print cast its widest net. These began appearing in the early seventeenth century as adaptations of earlier manuscript newsletters delivered to small groups of subscribers and often dealing with diplomatic intelligence and other sensitive material. The first of these subscription newsletters to reach print in English, *The Corrant out of Italy, Germany, etc.*, was published in 1620 in Amsterdam, a liberal-minded city of refuge for victims of political and religious persecution from all over Europe. In the eighteenth century the role of sanctuary had shifted to London, and the press flourished: it has been estimated that in 1792, 15 million newspapers were sold in England. These were supplemented by a great number of weekly, biweekly and monthly magazines, or periodicals, such as the *Tatler* (1709) and the *Spectator* (1711). Most prided themselves on their independence, and coverage included everything from deep moral and aesthetic issues to politics, society and fashion. Correspondence from readers was encouraged and letters were often published.

By 1800 there were 178 weeklies and 24 daily newspapers in the United States, and it has been claimed that without newspapers and their ability to make criticism cumulative, the American Revolution would not have got off the ground. In Canada, under French colonial rule, the importation of printing presses had been forbidden, but after the British conquest and the end of the Seven Years War in

1763, a number of printers arrived from the American colonies to the south. The *Quebec Gazette* was established in 1764. The year 1783 saw the founding of the *Montreal Gazette*, and in what is now the province of Ontario, the *Upper Canada Gazette* was first published in 1793, in Niagara-on-the-Lake. Most of the early papers (including the very first in Canada, the *Halifax Gazette* of 1752) were offshoots of commercial printing concerns, and relied heavily on government business and the printing of official notices for their survival. Later start-ups, including William Lyon Mackenzie's *Colonial Advocate* in Upper Canada and Joseph Howe's *Novascotian* (both founded in 1824), challenged colonial rule and its institutions, as had prominent newspapers in the American colonies two generations earlier.

From the first, newspapers were criticized for trivializing the issues they covered, and for inaccuracy and misinformation. Then as now, there was justification for this criticism. But newspapers also helped create *public opinion*, a concept that came into currency in the last half of the eighteenth century and that has been explored and redefined as "public space" in our own time by philosopher Jurgen Habermas.[9] This concept has usefully placed the sphere of information, debate and exchange of ideas in the same context as physical public spaces such as town squares. The one is as deserving of protection from vested interests as the other, just as both are vulnerable to thoughtless misuse and malicious abuse by the public to whom they belong. For Habermas, the media are part of a wider system, which included, in the early days of newspapers, coffee houses, salons and clubs—places where ideas were discussed. The constituents and structure of that space—much different in our own time—have important effects on its social impact. To the extent that media are controlled by commercial interests solely for financial gain, and public space is transformed into the quasi-public space of the shopping mall and theme park, the public sphere may actually be diminished despite ease of transportation and a seeming abundance of media.

A medium of communication is more than merely a method of using symbols to encode, record and preserve thought. As the word is used today, it also includes the means of transmitting thought thus recorded. The phrase "the medium of television," for instance, takes in not just the aural, visual and textual matter that is presented to us, but also the technological infrastructure that packages this information in a way that allows it to be moved from place to place, that is, to be *delivered* to its audience. A book as a medium of communication includes not just the words it contains, but the paper and binding that make it portable and durable and allow the delivery of the message it contains. We might say, then, in a more abstract sense, the "medium" includes both the coding of the message and the delivery of the message. It is the "delivery" that makes the information accessible. As we pursue this examination of modern communications technologies, it will become evident that both aspects of media can have an impact on their users. Coding, as we've seen in the example of the alphabet, has received much more scholarly attention than delivery.

Until the era of the telegraph, which began in the mid-nineteenth century, communication and transportation were inextricably linked. There could be no reliable communication over distance without involving some means of transportation. Letters, for instance, had to be shipped from place to place on horseback or by stagecoach or by packet steamer. The early empires of Europe and Asia each developed a sophisticated postal courier system, which relied on a network of good roads for its efficiency. The ancient Persian postal system was much admired by the classical Greeks, who were unable to establish a similar network due to their fragmented political condition. But by far the most efficient of these early imperial systems was the Roman *cursus publicus*, a staged relay system of postal delivery whose speed was not to be duplicated in Europe until the eighteenth century. The importance of the Roman road network throughout Europe is normally thought of in terms of its usefulness in hurrying troops from place to place, but it served an equally important function in speeding mail on its way. It was thus a communications network in the modern sense, as well as a transportation network. The *cursus publicus* would outlast the Roman Empire, being adopted and maintained by the various barbarian rulers. It died a slow death only with the deterioration of the Roman road system that it ran on.

The modern national postal system had its genesis in the Europe of the seventeenth century, in the era of the emerging nation-state with its strong central government based on efficient command and control structures. So important was postal communication to government that what had been a collection of private services in most countries was everywhere taken over by the state and monopolized. Like the Romans, the European rulers thought the ability to communicate rapidly and reliably was a valuable strategic asset that ought to be in the exclusive hands of government. The regularity and security of these state postal systems was such, however, that there was immediate and ever-increasing pressure to open them up for non-official communication. Though this was resisted initially, governments everywhere were not long in recognizing the opportunity to make money by carrying unofficial correspondence, and this was common practice throughout Europe by the mid-seventeenth century. The issue of state security, which had been the main concern of those arguing against public carriage, and which is a recurring theme throughout the history of communications technology, was dealt with in legislation that permitted state postal inspectors to open suspicious mail. In Britain, a warrant was required; in other states this was seen as an unquestioned prerogative of the ruling regime. Interestingly, the continuing state monopolies on postal services were justified largely on the grounds that the public, through their government, had built and improved the network of roads on which the postal systems ran and were therefore entitled to share in the income earned through its use. In Britain, private postal concerns were permitted to continue doing business, but only over roads not used by the Royal Mail.

Before long, public use of British postal services exceeded the government's in volume, and per-unit costs fell steadily with increasing usage. By the 1820s, mail was averaging more than ten miles an hour around the clock in the British Isles, and a letter mailed in Manchester at 4 p.m. would reach London the next day at 10 a.m. With the advent of regular intercity rail service in the 1840s, delivery times would be even further reduced.[10] Jane Austen paid famous tribute to the British postal service in her novel *Emma*, through the character Jane Fairfax:

> The Post Office is a wonderful establishment! . . . The regularity and dispatch of it! If one thinks of all that it has to do, and all that it does so well, it is really astonishing! It is certainly well regulated. So seldom that any negligence or blunder appears! So seldom that a letter, among the thousands that are constantly passing about the kingdom, is even carried wrong and not one in a million, I suppose, actually lost! And when one considers the variety of hands, and bad hands too, that are to be deciphered, it increases the wonder.[11]

Mail was nowhere else nearly so rapid or efficient, but despite the fact that it was not uncommon for an international letter to take half a year to reach its destination, people corresponded in remarkable volume and frequency. "Even in France," notes historian Paul Johnson, "regarded as backward in this respect, the number of letters leaving Paris each day had risen to 36,000 by 1826 . . . In London, outgoing mail had long ago passed the 100,000 mark."[12] The very eagerness of the public everywhere to use even the slow and sometimes inefficient public post pointed to a great untapped demand for any innovation that would speed communication.

It was a British tax reformer and educator named Rowland Hill who first sorted out the true relationships in any communications network, from the Roman *cursus publicus* to the modern Internet. In an 1837 report entitled "Post Office Reform: Its Importance and Practicability," Hill demonstrated conclusively that transport costs were an insignificant portion of the overall cost of delivering a letter. In fact, he found that by failing to understand this, postal authorities were needlessly and very significantly increasing the cost of mail. This was because the complex distance-based system of postal tariffs then in place required armies of accountants and paper-pushers to administer. Hill proposed a single tariff for all letters delivered in Britain, regardless of distance, and he suggested it be a penny, which he had calculated was slightly higher than the actual average cost of delivery was likely to be under such a regime. (Parcels were charged by weight rather than distance.)[13] Ignored by officialdom, the penny-post idea nevertheless found many champions among the public, and politicians were persuaded to adopt it in 1840. It was, of course, a resounding success, greatly increasing both mail volumes and government revenues. The volume of mail handled in London by the post office reached 163 million pieces in 1863, and there were twelve daily deliveries. In 1901 the penny post was extended to the rest of the British Empire.

Cheap and rapid mail delivery of course facilitated all kinds of organization, and the historian Harold Innis has credited it, in part, for the popular revolts against the Corn Laws in Britain, in which organized political dissent from the industrial middle classes overcame the entrenched opposition of landowners to the repeal of import duties on grain.[14]

Politics aside, in finally agreeing to open their postal services to non-official mail, governments had implicitly accepted the principle that the administrator of the delivery network should stay clear of the business of content, except for official correspondence of its own. In other words, they had accepted the principle of the common carrier, which was later extended to the telephone and telegraph. Hill, in turn, had discovered that in a communications system the cost of establishing and maintaining the delivery network is trivial when compared with the revenue to be gained from the information traffic it will carry. This is particularly true, of course, when the network has been built to serve, or is able to serve, other purposes. The early mail services did not have to bear the entire expense of building and maintaining the road and rail systems they used, just as the Internet is greatly subsidized by the billions of dollars' worth of telephone infrastructure built up and paid for by earlier communication services. In this sense the Internet and the penny post can be thought of as value-added services, though in the case of the Internet the new service appears to be in the process of swallowing up all previous uses. But that is a story best told later on.

Prelude to the Telegraph

T HE HISTORY OF TECHNOLOGY offers no more important discoveries than those that enabled us to create and control fire and electricity. The former gave the human race the power it needed to thrive in a sometimes inhospitable natural environment; the latter gave us the ability to extend our senses far beyond our bodies and to communicate information and ideas with others of our species worldwide. We have lately discovered through quantum physics that these two sets of tools have much in common: they are in fact identical at the subatomic level where physical reality has its foundation and where information in the form of what we call energy is all there is.

Fire, of course, but electricity as well were abroad in the world and known to man from prehistoric times. Indeed, electricity in the form of lightning was the father to domesticated fire. Both fire and electricity would eventually provide motive power for people with work to do, survival to see to. As well, they both afforded means of projecting thought over distance. The signal fire has been used for rapid communication from time immemorial. According to legend as passed down to us by Aeschylus (525–456 BC) in his tragedy *Agamemnon*, news of the fall of Troy to the Mycenaean army was transmitted overnight to Mycenae, some 375 miles distant, by a string of island-hopping, mountaintop signal fires. A thousand years later the Greek historian Polybius (*c.*200–*c.*118 BC) reported on tests of a torch-telegraphy system that allowed transmission of complex messages. The twenty-four-letter alphabet was broken up into five parts, inscribed on five clay tablets. A signaller first raised, on his left, the number of torches corresponding to the tablet he wished the receiver to consult: one torch for tablet number one, two torches for tablet two and so on. Then, on his right side, the signaller raised the number of torches corresponding to the letter he wished the receiver to write down. As George Dyson has noted, "It would be another two thousand years before modern telegraphy instituted a digital coding of the alphabet as concise and unambiguous as this."[1] When the Spanish Armada threatened England in 1588, watchmen stationed all along the English coast gave the alarm, painting a picture later described by Thomas Babington Macaulay in *The Armada*:

> From Eddystone to Berwick bounds, from Lynn to Milford
>   Bay,
> That time of slumber was as bright and busy as the day;
> For swift to east and swift to west the ghastly war-flame spread,
> High on St. Michael's Mount it shone; it shone on Beachy
>   Head.
> Far on the deep the Spaniard saw, along each southern shire,
> Cape beyond cape, in endless range, those twinkling points
>   of fire.

Half a century later, John Wilkins (1614–72), Oliver Cromwell's brother-in-law, first secretary of the Royal Society and Bishop of Chester, revived Polybius's scheme for transmitting complex messages using a system of torches, and refined it with a method of encrypting the signal. The prolific inventor and experimenter Robert Hooke proposed "a method of discoursing at a Distance, not by Sound, but by Sight" in a speech to the Royal Society in 1684. By day, this method employed an alphabet of twenty-four symbols, large enough to be read at a distance through a telescope; by night, five lanterns were used.

It would be another century before a practical visual telegraph was developed in revolutionary France by the Chappe brothers. Claude Chappe began experimenting with machines for long-distance communication in 1790 with the idea that such a device might help protect the new republic, threatened as it was on all sides by hostile monarchist armies. He erected a test device in Paris the following year, hoping to demonstrate it to members of the Assembly, but it was torn down by a mob who took it to be a machine for communicating with enemies of the state. Undaunted, he set up at another site outside the city, only to have this apparatus too torn down by citizens who, this time, thought he must be signalling to royal prisoners in the Temple Tower. Finally, in 1793, the National Assembly's Committee of Public Safety agreed to finance an officially sanctioned trial, which was to be overseen by an eminent scientist and a leading mathematician. The test took place over the thirty-five miles between a Paris park and St-Martin-du-Tertre, with a midway post at Écouen. Each of the three installations consisted of a tall mast with two semaphore arms, which could be moved by means of ropes and pulleys through seven different positions, indicating numerals or letters of the alphabet. Messages were passed successfully in both directions and the device was hailed as miraculous. In its report to the committee, the evaluators concluded with the encomium: "What brilliant destiny do science and the arts not reserve for a republic which, by its immense population and the genius of its inhabitants, is called to become the nation to instruct Europe!" This set the pattern of euphoric enthusiasm with which each succeeding generation of communications technology would be received.

Chappe's telegraph was understood immediately to be of great strategic value. The scientist who had observed the test believed it was the best answer to those critics of the revolutionary regime who thought France was too big to be a republic. The Committee of Public Safety decided to erect lines from Paris to Montmartre to Lille. The first message the line carried, on August 15, 1794, brought word of the capture of Quesnoy from the Austrians. It took an hour for word to reach Paris; a mounted courier would have taken eleven. By 1844, France had over three thousand miles of telegraph line involving 533 signalling stations, and messages could be flashed from Paris to Calais in 4 minutes; to Brest in 6 minutes 50 seconds; to Bayonne in 14 minutes.

Since each arm of the telegraph could be deployed in seven distinct positions, and there were two arms, there were a total of 98 possible signal configurations ($7 \times 7 \times 2$). Six of these were reserved for special purposes, which left 92 for constructing the coded message. Chappe prepared a code book of 92 pages, the first page of which contained the letters of the alphabet and numbers. The following pages each contained 92 words or phrases. As with Polybius's ancient system, the signaller first indicated a page number and then a word or phrase on that page, and thus by stages a complex message could be built. Later, additional code books were added, expanding the number of possible signing options to over 25,000.

Chappe was disappointed that his creation was being exploited solely for military purposes and, as reported by historian Geoffrey Wilson in *The Old Telegraphs*, he proposed to Napoleon Bonaparte

> a pan-European commercial system stretching from Amsterdam to Cadiz and even taking in London, as he claimed to be able to correspond between Calais and Dover. He also proposed to relay stock exchange news daily. Yet another of his ideas was an official journal to be sent from Paris by post to all Departments and supplemented by a telegraphed summary of the news of the day . . . Unfortunately all these schemes were rejected as impracticable, but Bonaparte at least consented to the weekly transmission of the numbers of the winners of the national lottery.[2]

The lot of an important inventor is seldom an easy one. In our own era siege-length lawsuits challenging patents are the norm, and often they are enough to drive the principals to distraction. In

Chappe's day, challenges were more public and direct, and were carried out in the atmosphere of fervid politicking that surrounded the guillotine-happy revolutionary National Convention. While exhausting himself building telegraph lines, Chappe was forced to fight off challenges from several sources who claimed his inventions as their own. By 1804 he was becoming increasingly despondent; he suspected an attack of food poisoning to be a deliberate attempt to kill him. On January 23, 1805, he committed suicide by throwing himself down a well outside a telegraph station in Paris. The note he left behind said: "I give myself to death to avoid life's worries that weigh me down; I'll have no reproaches to make myself." He was just forty-two.

The success of Chappe's telegraph lines spurred the introduction of similar systems throughout much of Europe. Sweden was an early adopter, erecting lines as early as 1794. They remained in service in that country, often alongside or supplementary to the electrical telegraph, until 1891, longer than in any other European nation.

In every European country there was a nationalistic reluctance to adopt the proven French design without at least some indigenous "improvements." Bonaparte, on being shown a German technique that would improve the operations of his own telegraph, is said to have rejected it out of hand with the objection: "It's a German idea." When news of Chappe's telegraph arrived in Britain in 1794, it prompted this cheeky lyric, which appeared in a London musical production:

> If you'll only just promise you'll none of you laugh
> I'll be after explaining the French Telegraphe!
> A machine that's endowed with such wonderful pow'r
> It writes, reads and sends news 50 miles in an hour.
> Then there's watchwords, a spy-glass, an index on hand
> And many things more none of us understand,
> But which, like the nose on your face, will be clear
> When we have as usual improved on them here.

Adieu, penny posts! mails and coaches, adieu!
Your Occupation's gone, 'tis all over wid you.
In your place telegraphs on our houses we'll see
To tell time, conduct lightning, dry shirts and send news.

The "improved" system predicted in the song and in fact adopted by the British Admiralty was to be of little use as a clothesline: it was a radical departure from the Chappe model, consisting of six large wooden shutters mounted three over three in a massive frame. The shutters could be pivoted to a horizontal position with the pull of a rope, in which case they would be invisible at a distance. Combinations of visible and invisible shutters constituted a code for numbers and letters. To pass an average message between London and Portsmouth took about fifteen minutes; words were spelled out but often contracted by leaving out vowels. The brief preparatory message, or protocol, that preceded transmissions could be sent from Portsmouth to London and back, a distance of 130 miles, in three minutes!

During the British naval blockade of France that followed the Revolution, the first international telegraph network was established with a link between the systems in Denmark and Sweden, with a view to sharing intelligence on the movements of the British fleet. Following the Napoleonic Wars, Britain reverted to a telegraph system similar to the Chappe model, having discovered that its extended arms could be seen at a greater distance in adverse weather than shutters enclosed in their bulky frame. (Smog was a persistent problem in London: messages often had to be carried by courier to the city's outskirts for transmission.) Chappe's telegraph had the added advantage of being easily rotated to accommodate transmissions to stations at right angles to the main line, whereas the shutter telegraph was fixed in position.

Though in England, as in France, the visual telegraph was used almost exclusively for military purposes, the very fact that it facilitated rapid communication over great distances kindled the imaginations of contemporary writers who sensed the wider implications of such technologies. Alexandre Dumas, in *The Count of Monte Cristo*, described the machine in darkly ominous terms as "the insect with the black claws and the terrible name." The English journalist and editor Leigh Hunt wrote more optimistically in *The Town*: "Telegraphs now ply their dumb and far-seen discourses, like spirits in the guise of mechanism, and tell the news of the spread of liberty and knowledge all over the world."[3]

In the Americas, Canada has the distinction of having introduced the visual telegraph. In 1794, the same year the Chappe system was brought into service in France, Prince Edward, the future Queen Victoria's father and commander-in-chief of Nova Scotia, organized a system of flags, wickerwork balls and drums for signalling by day, and lanterns by night. Telegraph posts were built near Chebucto Head, at York Redoubt and on Citadel Hill in Halifax, and at the Naval Dockyard. When Edward moved his mistress, Madame St. Laurent, to more secluded quarters outside Halifax, on Bedford Basin, he had a telegraph installed there as well, on a hill behind the lodge. In 1799, newly promoted to commander-in-chief of all of British North America, he extended the telegraph to the Annapolis Valley, around the Bay of Fundy to Saint John, New Brunswick, and up the Saint John River valley to Fredericton. Another line, to give early warning of the arrival of shipping, was set up between L'Isle-Verte, below Rivière-du-Loup, and Quebec City, 120 miles farther up the St. Lawrence.

The first visual telegraph to operate in the United States was not a military but a commercial venture. Jonathan Grout Jr., a lawyer from Belchertown, Massachusetts, built a line modelled on descriptions of European systems he had seen in a magazine. It was designed to carry news of the arrival of shipping off Martha's Vineyard to Boston. Grout's line was superseded by the famous line run from Boston's Exchange Coffee House, a merchants' meeting place, all the way to Long Island Head and Boston Light. It made a profit from the outset, identifying and signalling the arrival of 799 vessels in 1825, a number that climbed to 2,104 eight years later. Because the cargoes known to be carried by these vessels would affect prices on landing,

advance news was of considerable commercial value. An early system
between New York and Philadelphia was used mainly to report stock
prices until, like others of its kind everywhere, it was made obsolete
in the mid-1840s by electric telegraphy.

By then, the visual telegraph had played out its crucial historical
role in establishing the value of rapid long-distance communication for both military and commercial ends, and had performed
the invaluable task of creating a market for the electric telegraph,
the device that heralded the twentieth-century era of light-speed
electronic communication by wire and through the air. Paul Johnson
succinctly sums up the reason why the visual telegraph was entirely
superseded and not merely complemented by the electric telegraph:
"It [the visual telegraph] was one of those good ideas not susceptible to fundamental improvement. In April, 1829, the system [in
France] was nearly 40 years old but when news of the election of
Pius VIII reached Toulon from Rome, at 4 a.m., it still took till
noon to get to Paris."[4] Frequently, new technologies coexist alongside older versions, as is the case, for example, with television and
its predecessors, radio and the cinema. Predictions of the demise of
the old in the face of the new proved to be inaccurate because the
technologies serve different purposes and fill different social needs.
But in the case of the telegraph, the electric version did exactly the
same thing as the visual model, and given its overwhelming technical superiority, it was bound to eradicate its predecessor.

Nevertheless, it would be a mistake to think of visual telegraphy
as a "primitive" means of communication. In its way, it was surprisingly sophisticated. All of the systems eventually developed complex
transmission protocols. These included elaborate dictionaries of
abbreviations that were an early form of compression; numerical
codes that contained entire stock or generic messages; initialization
sequences used on initiation of contact; error control protocols;
and codes for controlling the speed of transmission. The system was
quite secure, since there were no wires to be cut as in a modern telegraph or telephone system. In times of unrest or war, the telegraph
towers could be armed and defended.

But its speed could not be significantly improved. Nor could the volume of traffic it was capable of carrying be increased in any other way: it could pass only one message at a time. That meant that, in practice, it would be forever restricted to serving the exclusive needs of government and the military. There simply was not enough "bandwidth" to carry private or business messages, and without a commercial market, it was doomed to stagnation, ripe for replacement.

The transition to the early electric telegraph began in Britain in 1842 with the conversion of the old London–Portsmouth visual line to an electric system buried along the London and South West Railway right-of-way. The changeover was not universally applauded, for reasons that sound to a modern ear both quaint and very contemporary. Fears were expressed that the electrical line was prone to error and, worse, to sabotage: it would be no trouble for anyone intent on interrupting vital communications to simply cut the wire. But it was the loss of jobs and the attendant distress that was the focus of the *Times* of London's coverage of the switch. The newspaper noted that visual telegraph stations had long been operated by retired naval officers, who had no other prospect of employment, and listed a dozen such men by way of illustration: "Four of the above are [Battle of] Trafalgar men; one was a mate in Sir Richard Strachan's action in 1805; one was a lieutenant of the *Denmark* in the Walcheren expedition; one lost a leg at Navarino and all the others have distinguished themselves in their country's service."

In the event, operators were given three months' notice of termination and were granted permission to stay on rent-free in their stations. On the whole, it seems a more humane response to the fallout of technological change than we have come to expect in our own era of economic rationalization and corporate restructuring.

The "Invention" of the Electron

MODERN electronic communications technology begins with a brilliant British experimenter's coaxing to a climax several hundred years of slowly accumulating knowledge of electricity and magnetism. His name was Michael Faraday, and he posed himself a simple proposition: If electricity flowing in a wire can act on a magnet to deflect it (a phenomenon that had been described in 1820 by the Danish scientist Hans Christian Oersted), it ought to be possible to reverse that process, to *create* electricity using magnetism. It was the experimental discovery of the nature of electric current by Faraday (1791–1867) and the subsequent formalizing of the theory of electrical and magnetic fields by James Clerk Maxwell (1831–79), called by many the greatest scientist since Newton, that made possible light-speed communication beyond the line of sight.

The impact of their discoveries would be difficult to overstate. Biographer Bern Dibner said correctly of Faraday that, in discovering electrical induction, he did nothing less than "transform society into an ever-growing, integrated network."[1] Much of the remainder of this book is a narrative in support of that assertion.

Faraday is one of those figures whom editors of juvenile books and encyclopedias used to make much of, as a wholesome and altogether admirable role model for budding young scientists. *The Book of Knowledge*, a multi-volume children's encyclopedia first published in 1868, has several references to him, including a biography entitled "Michael Faraday, the Blacksmith's Son Who Helped to Change the World." Faraday, the article says,

> was born in 1791, the son of a poor London blacksmith. After very little schooling he was apprenticed to a bookbinder, and after working hard all day he would study science at night. One day a gentleman, on entering the shop, found the boy at work binding an encyclopedia, and studying hard at the article in it on electricity. The gentleman was surprised to see a boy so interested in a subject of such difficulty, and questioned him. He found that Faraday, working late at night, had already been making experiments of his own, though he was too poor to possess anything but an old bottle for his battery. The visitor was so pleased that he gave him four tickets for the lectures which Sir Humphry Davy was then delivering at the Royal Institution . . . [Faraday] made notes on what he heard, and then at the end of the lectures he went, in fear and trembling, to the great man and showed him his notes . . .[2]

Readers of a skeptical bent appropriate to the early twenty-first century may be surprised to learn that the story of Faraday's rise to prominence through hard work and native intelligence, his personal integrity and scrupulous honesty, not to mention his lifelong loyalty and devotion to his wife Sarah, are facts so well documented as to be unimpeachable. Not only that, he was by all accounts a superb platform speaker, and he initiated Christmas holiday lectures on science for the children of London that were nothing short of wonderful. His scientific writing is a model of clarity. Throughout his working life, he gave much of his modest earnings to charity. When he felt his intellectual powers waning late in life, he gracefully resigned his position as director of the Royal Institution, despite flattering pleas to stay on from those around him.

His early life was in fact harder than is suggested in the passage quoted above. His father was in poor health and unable to work regularly. Faraday, with his mother, older sister and younger brother, moved from lodging to lodging in west London. When his father died, his mother took in boarders. "My education," Faraday recalled in later life, "was of the most ordinary description, consisting of little more than the rudiments of reading, writing and arithmetic at a common day school. My hours out of school were passed at home and in the streets."

The benefactor with the lecture tickets is reliably identified as a Mr. Dance. In fact, though, Faraday on his own initiative (and with a shilling borrowed from his blacksmith brother) had earlier signed up for regular lectures on "natural philosophy" given by the City Philosophical Society in the evenings. During the two years of his attendance, he heard lectures on astronomy, geology, hydrostatics, chemistry and electricity, among other subjects. He took detailed notes and later wrote out each lecture in full and illustrated it with a natural draughtsman's skill and precision. He was eventually invited to address the society on the subject of the nature of electricity.

Faraday was twenty-one when he attended Humphry Davy's lectures at the Royal Institution, where Davy, a surgeon by trade, was employed as a professor in chemistry and geology. Continuing his City Philosophical Society practice, Faraday wrote out the lectures, and bound them in book form. His apprenticeship ended at about this time and he was engaged as a journeyman bookbinder with a Mr. De La Roche, who seems to have been a hard taskmaster. Faraday desperately wanted a job in science. As fate would have it, Davy was temporarily blinded by a laboratory explosion; Faraday, perhaps through the good offices of Mr. Dance, was taken on as Davy's secretary while the scientist recovered his sight. Later, Faraday sent Davy the bound and illustrated book of the Royal Institution lectures and asked for a job. Nothing was available at the time, but before long a young laboratory assistant at the Institution was fired for brawling. Davy sent for Faraday and offered him the position. He was formally hired by the board of governors in 1813 at a guinea a week, and given two rooms under the eaves to live in, with fuel and candles supplied. He was to remain with the Institution for the rest of his working life, making scores of significant contributions to chemistry, metallurgy and electrical theory and practice. None was half so important, however, as his discovery that passing a wire through a magnetic field will cause an electrical current to be generated in it. On that foundation, as elaborated and formalized by the great Cambridge physicist James Clerk Maxwell, has risen the modern edifices of both electrical engineering and electronics.

Nowadays we're pretty blasé about electricity, some of us even believing we have a reasonable understanding of how it works: electrons run through wires, setting up electromagnetic fields, lighting light bulbs and generating radio waves. The truth is, in the 150-odd years since Faraday's experiments, the mysteries of the electron have only got deeper and deeper, more and more inscrutable. The more science learns, the more magical it all seems. In exploring the world discovered experimentally by Faraday, science left behind the realm of sensory experience and entered a looking-glass universe of subatomic particles, where logic and common sense can no longer be counted on, where paradoxes abound, where insights into the true nature of the universe demand the abstract, intuitive understanding of the mystic in equal measure with the discipline of the scientist.

The universe as it was understood by Faraday was the three-dimensional world described by Newton, in which matter was composed of indestructible particles, space was an absolute and time was a river in which all change occurred, flowing immutably from the past, through the present, into the future. God, Newton believed, created the material particles, the forces between them and the laws governing their motion; then He set the whole construct running, and it is running still, a perfectly self-regulating machine.

But when Faraday induced an electric current in a copper wire by moving a magnet close to it, he did something Newtonian physics said was impossible: he converted mechanical energy required to move a magnet into electrical energy in a wire, even though there was no physical contact between the two objects. The whole notion of action-at-a-distance had long been consigned to the realm of the occult; two hundred years earlier the great Galileo had rejected his contemporary Johannes Kepler's (accurate) theory of gravitation and tidal motion for that very reason. The imaginations of Faraday and Maxwell were thus captured not so much by the result or action of the electromagnetic force they had observed as by *the force itself*, an area of inquiry that Newtonian physicists had all but ignored. It proved the key to a profusion of revolutionary scientific insights.

In translating Faraday's experimental discoveries into the precise language of mathematics, Maxwell found it necessary to describe the interaction between positive and negative electrical charges in a new way. It was not enough to state simply that unlike charges attract one another in some way analogous to the way masses attract one another in Newtonian gravitational theory. For the mathematics to work, he found he had to replace the idea of a force with a *force field*, a concept Faraday had arrived at intuitively from his laboratory observations. In Maxwell's model, an electrical charge creates a "condition" or "disturbance" around it that is felt as a force by another charge introduced to its area of influence. The area of disturbance is a "force field" and it exists whether or not another charge is brought into the picture.

It was a subtle but ultimately shattering change in our understanding of physical reality. In the Newtonian world, forces were firmly rooted in the physical entities they acted upon. In the new world of electrodynamics, forces had their own reality and could be studied independently of the objects they acted upon. Very soon it was understood that light is another form of electromagnetism, and that there was in fact an entire universe or spectrum of such disturbances, a continuum ranging from radio waves through visible light to ultraviolet, X-rays, cosmic rays and beyond. Maxwell's Rainbow, it has been called.

Maxwell's equations were to provide the necessary engineering data for the development of telegraphy, radio, television and computers, all very concrete examples of natural forces being harnessed to perform practical functions—to do work in the world. All electric communication stems from the notion that if electrons can be induced to flow in a wire or radiate through space, then it ought to be possible to communicate electronically by manipulating that electron flow in such a way as to carry intelligence—by dots and dashes, for example, generated by switching the electron flow on and off. The only trick was to develop suitable electron-generating devices at the transmitting end and appropriate electron-detecting devices at the receiving end. This proved simpler in the case of a wired connection than a wireless link, and wired telegraphy thus preceded wireless telegraphy or radio.

While Maxwell had made a great leap forward from Newton's conception of the universe, he still felt there needed to be a medium in which electromagnetic force fields exist, some substance in which these disturbances are created, and he proposed several under the rubric of "ether." Thus the comfortable familiarity of Newton's universe of action and reaction, cause and effect, logic and predictability, was salvaged and preserved for the next fifty years. The notion of orderly ranks of electrons marching through wires and streaming through the ether as electromagnetic waves at the touch of a telegraph key is an easy one to visualize, and it sufficed to carry us through the spate of invention that followed Faraday's discoveries. But it has little to do with what really goes on in electrodynamic processes. It is probably just as well that the early investigators were innocent of the insights that were to grow out of Faraday's and Maxwell's work: they would have thrown up their hands in despair at the idea of ever being able to harness so utterly bewildering a phenomenon as the electron.

Enter Dr. Einstein. In two papers published in 1905, Albert Einstein sought to resolve the discrepancies between Faraday's and Maxwell's electrodynamics and Newtonian mechanics. After all, both seemed to work in the real world, despite their apparent mutual contradictions; there must be a way to bring them together into a unified theory of broad application. The first of those papers, on "special relativity," remains among the most stunning intellectual achievements of the twentieth century. Quickly verified in detail through experimentation, it demonstrated that space is not three-dimensional, and that time does not exist outside space. There is a fourth dimension called "space-time" in which the two are inextricably bound together. Time is not a river; it is not inexorable; events that seem to take place simultaneously to one observer may be separated in time from the vantage point of another observer travelling at a different speed. Thus, all measurements involving time and space lose any absolute significance; they become *relative to the point of view of the observer*. Space and time are removed from their central position in the physical universe, to become merely two more elements of a description of physical phenomena.[3]

As Einstein was demolishing time and space as discrete theoretical phenomena, the new communications technologies arising out of electrodynamics were drastically altering the impact of time and space on day-to-day life and changing their meaning in popular perception. The telegraph, telephone and radio—even though their invention preceded Einstein's insights—were each spontaneously greeted in the popular media as having the miraculous ability to "annihilate time and space." On the day following Samuel Morse's first successful demonstration of the news-carrying capacity of his electric telegraph (he brought the results of the Democratic Party presidential nominating convention from Baltimore to Washington), the *New York Herald* observed: "Professor Morse's telegraph is not only an era in the transmission of intelligence, but it has originated in the mind . . . a new species of consciousness."[4] Time and distance were no longer what they once had been.

In the 1920s a polyglot group of scientists extended Einstein's insights in a sweep of great and sustained scientific creativity. They included Niels Bohr of Denmark, Werner Heisenberg of Germany, Louis de Broglie from France, Erwin Schrödinger and Wolfgang Pauli of Austria, and Paul Dirac of Britain, and together they mapped the unexplored territory of the subatomic particle, a field called quantum mechanics.

It may help to pause here for a moment to get some idea of the scale of the world of subatomic particles these scientists set out to explore. Travellers in southern Europe fortunate enough to find themselves among the ruins of the Minoan civilization on Crete, Santorini (Thera) and other islands often find it astonishing that, to the Romans, the Minoans were as remote in antiquity as the Romans are to us. John Gribben employs a similar kind of scale in groping for a way to convey the incredibly tiny phenomena of quanta in his book *Schrödinger's Kittens*: "In very round numbers, the quantum world operates on a scale as much smaller than a sugar cube as a sugar cube is compared with the entire observable Universe. To put it another way, people are about midway in size, on this logarithmic scale, between the quantum world and the whole Universe."[5]

Early in the history of the new discipline of quantum mechanics, it became necessary to deal with a paradox that has haunted it ever since. Einstein had demonstrated conclusively that light is composed of particles, which he called photons. Confirmed experimentally to exist, they are exceedingly strange entities: they always travel at the speed of light, have no mass, and because of their speed of travel, time has no meaning to them. Like other quantum particles, they are able to communicate with one another *instantaneously*, if need be, from one side of the universe to the other. Unfortunately, about a hundred years before Einstein, an English scientist named Thomas Young had proved that light is composed of waves. This too was tested and confirmed beyond dispute in many experiments. So light had been "proved" to be both a wave and a particle. Quantum physicists struggled with that for some time, but there was no way out. The answer had to be that light was indeed both particle and wave, and, by extension, other subatomic particles, including electrons, were also both waves and particles. In fact, it has recently been experimentally demonstrated that "objects" as large as atoms exist simultaneously in both states.

How can something be both a wave and a particle at the same time? The blithely outrageous answer agreed upon among the principal quantum mechanics investigators of the time was that subatomic entities have no concrete existence. They do not appear at specific times in specific places, but exhibit a "tendency" to exist.

This propensity is expressed in the mathematical form of a probability wave. According to Heisenberg, the probability wave "meant a tendency for something. It was a quantitative version of the old concept of 'potentia' in Aristotelian philosophy," which posited that all of reality exists in a kind of potential state that is brought into concrete form through interaction with human intelligence. Reality was an ongoing collaboration between what exists "out there" and the human subject, whose mind brings it into existence in the form in which we experience it. Heisenberg's indeterminacy principle "introduced something standing in the middle between the idea of an event and the actual event, a strange kind of physical reality just in the middle between possibility and reality."[6] In more concrete terms, the principle states that it is impossible to know both the velocity and the position of a subatomic particle at the same time. The more accurately one is known, the less certainty there will be about the other. In fact, the very idea of knowing exact position and velocity at the same time has no meaning at the quantum level. The indeterminacy or uncertainty of quantum physics is not the result of shortcomings of test instruments or of the indifference of physicists to concrete definitions. As Niels Bohr put it: "in quantum mechanics, we are not dealing with an arbitrary renunciation of more detailed analysis of atomic phenomena, but with a recognition that such an analysis is *in principle* excluded."[7] Our knowledge can extend only so far and no farther.

It gets stranger. A subatomic entity such as an electron can be said to exist only when its probability of being at a certain place at a certain time is 1; in other words, when it is certainly there. The only way to know whether it is certainly there, however, is for an intelligent observer to look and see it there. Until the observer observes, the probability of its existence is always less than 1: it may or may not exist. Until it is observed, it can have no concrete existence; it represents only a potential that may be described in terms of probability waves. It may or may not be there when the observer looks: if it is not there, it doesn't exist and the portion of the probability wave function indicating existence collapses; if it is there, it does exist, and it is the area of the probability wave function indicating non-existence that collapses. Without the observer, there can be no collapse of the wave function. Thus, the observer plays an integral role in quantum theory, in the very existence of particles. In a very real sense, the observer *creates* the particle through the act of observing it. Which makes him more than an observer, as pointed out by Princeton physicist John Wheeler:

> May the universe in some strange sense be "brought into being" by the participation of those who participate? . . . The vital act is the act of participation. "Participator" is the incontrovertible new concept given by quantum mechanics. It strikes down the term "observer" of classical theory, the man who stands safely behind the thick glass wall and watches what goes on without taking part. It can't be done, quantum mechanics says.[8]

All of this raises an even more interesting question. If quanta require the presence of an observer in order to exist, and if (as is the case) all observers are made up of quanta, what causes the observer to exist? That is, who observes the observer? For some, the only answer can be some sort of transcendent Being, akin to Newton's idea of God.

What is clear is that if quantum mechanics is correct—and for nearly a century it has passed every experimental test—then there is no substantive physical world, only a vast web of energy relationships. To try to extract discrete parts of the subatomic world for examination is futile, because there is no such thing as a "discrete part." As Einstein said: "We may therefore regard matter as being constituted by the regions of space in which the field is extremely intense . . . There is no place in this new kind of physics both for the field and matter, for the field is the only reality."[9]

Here is a more recent explication:

> The presence of matter (such as an electron) is merely a distur-

bance of the perfect site of the field at that place; something accidental, one could almost say, merely a "blemish". Accordingly, there are no simple laws describing the forces between elementary particles . . . Order and symmetry must be sought in the underlying field . . . The field exists always and everywhere; it can never be removed. It is the carrier of all material phenomena. It is the "void" out of which the proton creates the pi-mesons. Being and fading of particles are merely forms of motion of the field.[10]

Physicist David Bohm has written that, in the world of quantum physics, "parts are seen to be in immediate connection, in which their dynamical relationships depend, in an irreducible way, on the state of the whole system [and, indeed, on that of broader systems in which they are contained, extending ultimately and in principle to the entire universe]. Thus one is led to a new notion of unbroken wholeness which denies the classical idea of analyzability of the world into separately and independently existent parts . . ." Furthermore, Bohm states, "there is a similarity between thought and matter. All matter, including ourselves, is determined by 'information.'" In other words, he says, "'information' is what determines space and time."[11] Which helps to make the notion of an Information Age one of compelling interest at unexpected levels.

If the movement of electrons through wires and across space bearing human thought seems a magical idea, as it certainly did to the contemporaries of the early electrical experimenters, it is only because it is indeed *magic*. How it happens in specific detail is in a sense beyond comprehension.[12] It is unknowable in a rational, scientific way, because we are prevented in principle from having enough knowledge to make determinations that are not based on observation, due to the ambivalent wave/particle nature of these most basic of entities.

It is in this sense that the electron, the basis for all electronic communication, is an invention rather than a discovery.

The Electric Telegraph

A S THE FIRST of the practical applications to grow out of electrodynamic theory, the electric telegraph was slow to be accepted for the breakthrough technology that it was. Its value and potential were certainly not understood by the governments of Great Britain and the United States, each of which churlishly dismissed offers from its chief inventors to deed it to the state. Officialdom in both countries deemed the optical telegraphs then in use, along with the penny post, to be perfectly adequate for the job of handling necessary long-distance communication.

The idea that a new medium might lead to the creation of novel services and products, or might alter the traditional pattern of doing things in useful or interesting ways, was not considered. Wheatstone in Britain and Morse in the U.S. faced uphill battles to have their inventions adopted. Indeed, if there is a great puzzle in the early history of communications technologies, it is in the inexplicable inability of even the great inventors themselves to predict the public appetite for the services they were to provide. Samuel Morse and Alexander Graham Bell saw limited applications for their creations, mainly in business and government. Cyrus Field, the builder of the transatlantic telegraph cable, thought there "might" be enough traffic to warrant the expense; Guglielmo Marconi at first thought of radio as primarily a ship-to-shore service, a niche product. And they were the optimists.

The near-universal failure to see how these new communications technologies would play into humanity's innate gregariousness is a continuing mystery not confined to these early innovations. The greatest surprise among industry savants observing the early development of the personal computer was that people adapted it for use as a communications device. And very few so-called experts foresaw the explosive development of the Internet as a medium of mass personal communication in the 1990s. If there is anything these failures of imagination have in common, perhaps it is thinking that the technologies were too complicated for the public to be much interested in them. But in each case ordinary people in their wisdom saw the real worth of the devices in maintaining contact with other people, and forced the market to begin serving that need. Modern communications technologies, beginning with the telegraph, have this in common: their growth has been a phenomenon of what we nowadays call "demand pull," as opposed to "supply push." Throughout the modern history of communications, the public has been out in front of industry, regulators and government in recognizing the potential of new media.

The idea of the electrical telegraph is an old one. Although Samuel Morse apparently believed he was the first to conceive of the idea of transmitting intelligence over wires using electricity, he had many predecessors, and it was only his scant scientific training that prevented him from knowing as much. As early as 1753, an anonymous writer to the *Scots' Magazine* proposed a fully realized telegraph system that would use the movements of pith balls or the ringing of tiny bells activated by electrical currents to spell out messages. Each letter was to have its own wire. To prevent the "electric fire" from being dissipated in the atmosphere over long lengths of wire, the author proposed covering the wires with "a thin coating of jewellers' cement. This may be done for a trifle of additional expense; and as it is an *electric per se* [i.e., an insulator] will effectually secure any part of the fire from mixing with the atmosphere."

The suggestion reflects the contemporary understanding of electricity as having the mechanical properties of heat.

A more practical device using just one wire was built in 1816 by Sir Francis Ronalds and tested over more than forty miles of wire coiled on a frame in his London garden. An ingenious system of synchronized clockwork mechanisms at either end of the wire displayed each of the letters of the alphabet in turn, and when the correct letter appeared in the display window, the sending operator interrupted the circuit briefly to indicate to the receiving operator that he should copy that letter down. Ronalds sought an audience with the British Admiralty to demonstrate his device, but was informed by return mail that "telegraphs of any kind are now wholly unnecessary; and . . . no other than the one now in use [i.e., the visual telegraph] will be adopted."

Credit for the first working electromagnetic telegraph is generally given to Baron Pawel Schilling, who developed a system that used the deflections of a magnetized needle, and a code not unlike that attributed to Morse, to spell out words. Schilling built his telegraph in his hometown of St. Petersburg and demonstrated it to the czar in 1830 before travelling with it to the capitals of Europe. Czar Nicholas reacted with the instincts of a true autocrat: seeing in the telegraph an instrument of subversion, he forbade any mention of the device in the Russian press or scientific literature for the duration of his reign, with the result that Russia was among the last nations in Europe to adopt the new technology. Nicholas was in many ways a modern man, not the least in his understanding of information as both a means of control and, on the other side of the coin, a source of liberation.

Schilling's telegraph was seen in Heidelberg by William Cooke, a British dabbler in science with sharp entrepreneurial instincts. He at once saw commercial possibilities in the device and returned to England to develop it further. In search of sound technical advice, he formed a partnership with Professor Charles Wheatstone, the chair of the King's College (Cambridge) experimental philosophy department. In 1837 they jointly patented a needle telegraph that used five wires and five needles, which pointed to letters of the alphabet arranged on a grid; there was thus no need for the operator to know any code beyond the standard alphabet in order to receive a message. Problems with finding suitable insulating materials for the telegraph lines delayed commercial deployment of the device until 1846, when the two incorporated the Electric Telegraph Company and went into business. A major part of their market was the burgeoning railway industry. With improvements in rails and locomotives, speeds had increased to a point where a rapid means of communicating operational messages up and down track lines was needed to prevent collisions and other accidents, and the telegraph fit the bill.

It is an interesting and instructive fact that Wheatstone struggled for several years to find a solution to seemingly intractable problems with their telegraph—problems that had been solved a decade earlier by the Bavarian scientist Georg Simon Ohm. Ohm, for whom the unit of electrical resistance has been named, developed laws showing the relationship between electrical current, voltage and resistance in a circuit, and in those formulae was everything Wheatstone needed to know to iron out the bugs in his system. Clearly, communication among scientists and engineers was still at a primitive stage.[1] Schilling, a military man by profession and scientist only by avocation, published almost nothing in the scientific literature, and although Ohm did publish, his work remained unknown in England until Wheatstone unearthed it around 1840. It is evident that, had communication been better, development of the telegraph could have been accelerated by several years, perhaps as much as a decade.[2]

Samuel Morse was a portrait painter of genuine talent, a politician of pro-slavery, anti-Catholic and anti-immigrant prejudice, and a lifelong victim of poisonous pride who learned in mid-life of the electrical experiments of Oersted. His information came from fellow passengers on board the packet ship *Sully*, which carried him back to America in 1832 from studying and painting in Europe. In a gush of jingoistic hyperbole, an early American biographer of Morse titled his book *Samuel Morse: An American Leonardo*, but it is clear that Morse was far from that, having discovered none of the scientific principles associated with the telegraph, nor invented any electromechanical devices that were not already known in Europe. Indeed, his fellow countryman Joseph Henry, a man of milder disposition and scholarly modesty, had built a working telegraph at Albany in 1832, or perhaps even earlier. Henry published his work (and Morse saw it) but never sought a patent. There is even doubt that Morse invented the Morse code; that distinction is claimed for his associate Alfred Vail.

The code is an altogether ingenious conversion of the alphabet into binary, digital form based on dots, dashes and spaces. Vail is said to have worked out the details, perhaps at Morse's suggestion, by examining the numbers of various letters of the alphabet to be found in a printer's type drawer. The letters most frequently used, *e* and *t*, were assigned the simplest codings, one dot (·) and one dash (–), respectively. The letters *a* and *n* were assigned (·–) and (–·), and less frequently used letters such as *v* (···–) and *w* (·––) were given more complex combinations. Much effort was put into devising means of printing the code on paper tape, so that it could be translated into letters of the alphabet, until it was noticed that telegraphers were quickly able to do the decoding in their head simply by listening to the clicks of the telegraph receiver as its circuit opened and closed. It was this binary (two-element) code, and the rugged simplicity and cheapness of the system required for sending and receiving it (a telegraph key for transmitting and a simple electromagnetic sounder at the receiving end), that allowed Morse's system to eventually reign supreme over its competitors in the field. (It wasn't until the twentieth century that the theory of binary code was formalized, and it was recognized that any information that can be presented in symbolic form can be reduced to binary sequences of finite length. To encode the alphabet, as Morse and Vail discovered, it takes five sets of binary characters or *bits* [2^5=32], which explains why the early needle telegraph of Cooke and Wheatstone used five wires.)

Morse insisted until his death that he was the sole inventor of the electric telegraph, and his compatriots have been inclined to believe him, despite the evidence. Britain, however, refused him a patent and the U.S. Supreme Court, in its comment on one of the many lawsuits he energetically pursued in defence of his American patent, averred that Morse's claims were far too broad for even a generous interpreter to accept.

What is clear is that Morse was captivated to the point of obsession by the idea of developing an electric telegraph from the moment he conceived it on board the *Sully*. Living in penury on income from teaching art, Morse worked on his device fitfully until 1837, when he formed a partnership with the young engineer Alfred Vail, a wealthy New Jersey industrialist's son. In that year the U.S. House of Representatives asked the secretary of the Treasury to report to it on "the propriety of establishing a system of telegraphs for the United States." (The term *telegraph* in those days denoted, of course, the visual telegraph, as well as any other means of transmitting information over long distances.) Morse was among the many who replied to the circular distributed by the secretary asking for proposals. It was the beginning of a long and arduous process of convincing the government to finance testing of his device, which was patented in 1840, three years after Cooke and Wheatstone received a patent for their telegraph in England. Finally, in 1843, by dint of persistence and a new partnership with the well-connected congressman, lobbyist and speculator Francis O.J. Smith, Morse received approval from Congress to build an experimental line from Washington to Baltimore, some forty miles distant.

We tend to think in romantic terms of early technological triumphs, but what sold Congress on Morse's telegraph was mundane business logic. Though perennially improvident in his personal finances, Morse presented a soundly reasoned business case for the superiority of his electric telegraph over the visual telegraphs then in use. Taking the widely admired French network as his benchmark, he made some historically interesting comparisons:

> The French system of telegraphs is more extensive and perfect than that of any other nation. It consists, at present, of five great lines, extending from the capital to the extreme cities of

the kingdom . . . making a total of 1,474 miles of telegraphic intercourse. These telegraphs are maintained by the French government at an annual expense of over 1,000,000 of francs, or $202,000.

The whole extent, then, of the French lines of telegraph is 1,474 miles, with 519 stations . . . erected at a cost of at least $880 each—making a total of $456,720.

The electro magnetic telegraph, at the rate [of] . . . $461 per mile (and which, it should be remembered will construct not *one* line only, but *six*) could be constructed the same distance for $619,514—not one-third more than the cost of the French telegraphs. Even supposing each line to be only as efficient as the French telegraph, still there would be six times the facilities, for not one-third more cost. But when it is considered that the French telegraph, like the English, is unavailable [due to inclement weather and darkness] the greater part of the time, the advantages in favor of the magnetic telegraph become more obvious.[3]

Morse estimated potential earnings from operations of the Washington–Baltimore line at $600,000 a year, and drove home his case with an argument that has a distinctly modern ring:

An important difference between the two systems is, that the foreign telegraphs are all a burden upon the treasury of their respective countries; while the magnetic telegraph proposes, and is alone capable of sustaining itself and producing a revenue.[4]

In his report to the U.S. Treasury secretary on completion of the Washington–Baltimore line, Morse was of course enthusiastic about its potential, though the instances he gives of its usefulness seem, from this distance, to quaintly understate the case:

An instance or two will best illustrate [the great utility] of the telegraph: A family in Washington was thrown into great distress by a rumor that one of its members had met with a violent death in Baltimore the evening before. Several hours must have elapsed ere their state of suspense could be relieved by the ordinary means of conveyance. A note was dispatched to the telegraph rooms at the Capitol, requesting to have inquiry made at Baltimore. The messenger had occasion to wait but *ten minutes* when . . . the answer returned that the rumor was without foundation. Thus was a worthy family relieved immediately from a state of distressing suspense.

An inquiry from a person in Baltimore holding the check of a gentleman in Washington, upon the Bank of Washington, was sent by telegraph, to ascertain if the gentleman in question had funds in that bank. A messenger was instantly dispatched from the Capitol, who returned in a few minutes with an affirmative answer, which was returned to Baltimore instantly; thus establishing a confidence in the money arrangement, which might have affected unfavorably (for many hours at least) the business transactions of a man in good credit.[5]

The question of state versus private ownership of this new and in some ways radically superior means of communication was debated on both sides of the Atlantic, the differing outcomes establishing important precedents. In most of Europe, the telegraph was incorporated into state postal monopolies from the outset. In Britain, Wheatstone and Cooke's firm operated in competition with another large company for nearly twenty years before both, along with the telegraph businesses of the railway companies, were purchased by the Royal Mail under the Telegraph Act 1868. (Several of the previous owners, flush with cash, invested in companies involved in overseas communication, with the result that Britain quickly came to dominate international telegraphy. The strategic significance of this in terms of trade and international relations did not go unnoticed in Europe and the United States.) But state involvement had been foreseen from the outset. The act that incorporated the Electric Telegraph Company (1846) empowered the home secretary to temporarily take control of the company's telegraph operations in times of civil unrest. He did just that in April 1848, when the Chartist movement for social and economic reform, with branches across Britain, threatened open revolt in that year of European rebellions.

There was strong sentiment favouring state ownership in the United States as well. The postmaster-general, who had operated the Washington–Baltimore line in 1845, asked "how far the government will allow individuals to divide with it the business of transmitting intelligence—an important duty confided to it by the Constitution, necessarily and properly exclusive. Or will it purchase the telegraph, and conduct its operations for the benefit of the public?" He left no doubt where his sympathies lay: "An instrument so powerful for good and evil," he said, could not "be safely left in the hands of private individuals uncontrolled by law."[6] Morse himself was amenable to selling his invention to Washington, but the fact that the line had operated at a loss of more than $2,800 on revenues of just $3,284 in the first six months of 1845 seems to have neutralized whatever resistance there was in Congress to private ownership, and the line was returned to Morse and his backers. Thus was the pattern set for future developments in electronic communication.

Just seven years after Morse sent the first signal down the Washington–Baltimore line, there were more than fifty telegraph companies in the United States. The system was a confusion of competing companies using different technologies and protocols over redundant lines, and patent disputes were rife. In that year, 1851, the New York and Mississippi Valley Printing Telegraph Company was incorporated with initial capital of $360,000 and a number of cross-directorships with prominent railways. In 1856, after gobbling up several competing systems and linking "western" (Midwestern) lines to the east, it changed its name to the Western Union Telegraph Company, known to all as simply Western Union. Between 1870 and 1890 the number of its offices grew from 3,972 to 19,382. In New York in 1890, it employed 444 telegraph operators, among them the young Thomas Edison, and nationwide it was handling 80 percent of all telegraph traffic.[7] Western Union would eventually absorb 562 of its competitors, claiming all the while that telegraphy was a "natural monopoly" made necessary by the need for network integration and common standards, as well as costly research and development. Its monopoly status was officially sanctioned in 1943 by a special act of Congress. The model of a state-sanctioned, regulated private monopoly was one that would be used in the U.S. again in the cases of the telephone and radio.

The looming American Civil War (1861–65) provided the impetus needed to drive the telegraph out across the Great Plains and the deserts of the American heartland to the new settlements on the west coast. President Abraham Lincoln judged the communications link essential in keeping California loyal to the Union. The lines were force-marched inland from both coasts and eventually met in Salt Lake City in October 1861. The challenges of crossing so much open, unsettled territory were formidable. Not the least of these was the fact that in much of the Nebraska and Colorado territories, the Cheyenne and Arapaho Indians were at war with the American government. Whenever the opportunity arose, the Indians tore down telegraph lines and attacked the isolated telegraph stations. But repairs were effected with surprising speed and energy. In one episode, repair crews protected by army howitzers rebuilt eight miles of telegraph line, replacing poles that had been burned or chopped down, and restrung another twenty-two miles of damaged wire in forty hours of continuous pick-and-shovel labour. In more normal circumstances, new line could typically be thrown up at a rate of between three and eight miles a day, depending on the terrain, with twenty-five poles per mile, each set in a five-foot-deep hole dug with special long-handled spades.

When the line was finished and signals flashed from Atlantic to Pacific for the first time, the *New York Times* intoned:

It is with almost an electric thrill that one reads the words of greeting yesterday flashed instantaneously over the wires from California. The magnificent idea of joining the Atlantic with the Pacific by the magnetic wire is today a realized fact. New York,

Queen of the Atlantic, and San Francisco, Queen of the Pacific, are now united by the noblest symbol of our modern civilization.

National purpose played a large role in this mammoth construction feat, though perhaps not so great a role as the promise of equally mammoth profits. The eastern portion of the line from Omaha to Salt Lake City had been financed by a million-dollar stock sale; its actual cost was $147,000. The western line from Salt Lake to California is estimated to have cost just $500,000. Telegraph companies initially charged a dollar a word on the new transcontinental line, and even at that breathtaking rate there was plenty of demand for the service.[8] Once it became possible to communicate instantly from one coast to the other, it became necessary for business to do so.[9] Companies that did not take advantage of the new communications link could be quickly outmanoeuvred by competitors who did. Commodities speculators, in particular, had to keep informed by the quickest means available if they were to stay in business, and that meant using the telegraph to check prices of gold, silver and other commodities. In the same way, government communication had to be carried out at the maximum speed available even in peacetime, if only because political courtesy demanded it.

Nor was owning a telegraph line the only way to get rich in telegraphy; owning a glass factory would do just as well. Some lines used as many as two thousand insulators per mile to mount many converging wires. Manufacturers turned out millions of insulators on high-speed glass moulding machines introduced in 1865.

In Canada and Australia, where centres of population were even more widely dispersed than in the U.S., the telegraph was welcomed with equal enthusiasm, and from the beginning carried more traffic per mile—frequently double the quantity—than in Britain or Europe. The Melbourne *Argus* bubbled with exuberance over "this most perfect of modern inventions," and wondered "what will be left for the next generation upon which to expend the restless enterprise of the human mind," now that the acme of technological perfection had been achieved. From its beginnings with the Toronto, Hamilton and Niagara Electro-Magnetic Telegraph Company (1846) and the Montreal Telegraph Company (1847), the Canadian industry had stretched from the Atlantic as far west as Manitoba by 1880. In 1881 Western Union bought out major Canadian operators and briefly took control of the industry. The Canadian Pacific Railway entered the telegraph business in 1883 in competition with Western Union, to be joined early in the next century by the government-owned Canadian National Railway's telegraph arm. The two railways operated telegraphy in Canada as an oligopoly until they formally merged their telecommunications services in 1967.

The era of the early telegraph was one of mammoth and daring engineering undertakings. As media historian Daniel Czitrom has observed, writers of the period frequently considered the telegraph alongside other marvels of the age, the steamship and the railway. And yet, "the inscrutable nature of the telegraph's driving force made it seem somehow more extraordinary."[10]

Mysterious electricity, an early historian of the telegraph wrote, "seems to connect the spiritual and the material." Another reflected: "The mighty power of electricity, sleeping latent in all forms of matter, in the earth, the air, the water, permeating every part and particle of the universe, carrying creation in its arms, is yet invisible and too subtle to be analyzed . . . Its mighty triumphs are but half revealed, and the vast extent of its extraordinary powers but half understood."[11] The words chosen by a young woman of Samuel Morse's acquaintance[12] to be the first transmitted by the Washington–Baltimore prototype line were, "What hath God wrought!"[13] Historian and telegraph promoter T.P. Shaffner, in concluding a review of all previous forms of communication, said of the telegraph: "But what is all this to subjugating the lightnings, the mythological voice of Jehovah, the fearful omnipotence of the clouds, causing them in fine agony of chained submission to do the offices of a common messenger—to whisper to the four corners of the earth the lordly behests of lordly man!"[14]

The special significance accorded the telegraph, and other electrical means of communication, is wrapped up in the way "communication" was defined, according to Czitrom:

> Praisers of "universal communication" [made possible by the telegraph] no doubt had in mind the most archaic sense of the word: a noun of action meaning to make common to many (or the object thus made common). The notion of common participation suggested communion, and the two words shared the same Latin root, *communis*. . . . Those who celebrated the promise of universal communication stressed religious imagery and the sense of miracle in describing the telegraph. They subtly united the technological advance in communication with the ancient meaning of that word as common participation or communion. They presumed the triumph of certain [Christian] messages . . .[15]

The telegraph, wrote one enthusiast,

> gives the preponderance of power to the nations representing the highest elements in humanity . . . It is the civilized and Christian nations who, though weak comparatively in numbers, are by these means of communication made more than a match for the hordes of barbarism . . . [The telegraph] binds together by a vital cord all the nations of the earth. It is impossible that old prejudices and hostilities should longer exist, while such an instrument has been created for an exchange of thought between all the nations of the earth.[16]

For commentators like this one, the telegraph, as an instrument of the ineffable, quasi-spiritual stuff called electricity, was more than just an invention: it was a moral force in the world. This was a view shared in varying shades and degrees by many on both sides of the Atlantic. In Britain, it was seen as a providential tool that would assist in extending the beneficent (and highly profitable) influence of the Empire to the far corners of the world; in America, it became an agent of the manifest destiny of the American people to achieve wealth, greatness and world moral leadership. The Canadian historian of technology David F. Noble has argued convincingly that the technological enthusiasm of the West has historically been an essentially religious drive, a search for an earthly surrogate for Salvation, a return ticket to Eden and its perfection.[17] Nowhere is the evidence for his claim more compelling than in the ecstatic welcome given to new technologies of communication.

The telegraph did in fact point the way to a remarkable future that could only be dimly suspected by even the most astute nineteenth-century observers, though it would serve up a plentiful dose of Aldous Huxley's techno-nightmare *Brave New World* along with intimations of the Biblical Eden. As George Dyson has pointed out in *Darwin Among the Machines*, electric telegraphy, a digital medium, provided an evolutionary pathway for the digital computer. Early in commercial telegraphy's development, paper-tape machines were introduced that allowed an operator to encode messages "off-line," storing them on punched tape for automatic transmission when circuits were available—an early version of the next century's store-and-forward computer networks. The electro-mechanical relays inserted periodically along extended telegraph lines to amplify waning signals would later serve as logic gates in experimental computers, and the data input mechanisms for those computers were frequently adapted from high-speed teletype equipment, using punched tape as the storage medium.

A Worldwide Web

FOR THE BUSINESS INTERESTS behind the great telegraph enterprises that were to develop in Europe and North America, it was not so much the moral value of improved communication as the example of mountainous profits on the U.S. transcontinental line that provided the primary incentive for undertaking the seemingly impossible task of linking the two continents by wire. The story of the laying of the first transatlantic marine cables is remarkable in its own right and a magnificent tribute to nineteenth-century engineering prowess. But there was also a little-remembered, outrageously ambitious scheme to tie Europe to North America through the back door, via British Columbia, Alaska and Siberia. It was undertaken by Western Union in 1865, with the co-operation of the governments of the United States, Canada and Russia.

With the transatlantic cable project suffering one failure after another (as we'll see in a moment) and being dismissed in the conventional wisdom as a pipe dream, while the trans-America line was a roaring success, Western Union fell under the spell of a promoter named Perry D. Collins, who convinced the directors that an overland route to Europe via Russian Alaska and Siberia was the way to go. What he proposed seems in retrospect sheer lunacy, given the weather conditions, distances and terrain involved, but the confidence of the age in its engineering capabilities appears to have been boundless. And the need for rapid communication with Europe was clear: when President Abraham Lincoln died from an assassin's bullet on the morning of April 15, 1865, word was received in San Francisco within the hour; Europe found out on April 26, eleven days later, when the steamer *Nova Scotian* docked in England.

The *New York Times* expressed the blithe opinion of many who had grown skeptical of the prospects of ever making a successful transatlantic link: "If there is ever to be electric communication with Europe, it will be by imitating the splendid example the United States has thus given in our transcontinental line. The bubble of the Atlantic submarine line has long ago burst, and it is now seen to be cheaper and more practicable to extend a wire over five-sixths of the globe on land, than one-sixth at the bottom of the sea."

Work was begun on the line within days of the end of the Civil War in the summer of 1865, with construction of sections linking San Francisco to New Westminster, British Columbia, and from there up the Fraser River to Quesnel in the B.C. Interior. Other crews were put to work on line stretching across the largely unexplored mountain ranges of Russian Alaska to the Bering Strait. A third work party sailed to Siberia to explore a route and construct line from the Bering Strait (which was to be spanned by a short underwater link) eighteen hundred miles southwest to Okhotsk at the mouth of the Amur River. A seven-thousand-mile Russian-built line from Okhotsk to St. Petersburg would provide the final connection to Europe and its growing web of telegraph communication.

The Russian party included a twenty-year-old telegrapher named George Kennan, who kept a diary thanks to which we have a detailed record of the events of the next two years. Kennan and the other Americans spent the summer of 1865 and the following winter mapping a route south. By early 1866, they had been out of touch with the rest of the world for nearly a year. It wasn't until August of that year that two supply ships arrived in a village on the Sea of Okhotsk, bearing sixty American construction workers and cargoes of building supplies and construction tools from San Francisco, two months away by sea. A third supply vessel arrived in September. Over the following winter, six hundred Siberian labourers were hired and three hundred horses were purchased to cut and haul twenty thousand telegraph poles, in temperatures that often dropped to –60° Fahrenheit. In the spring of 1867, work on the line began in earnest, with confident predictions that it would be completed right to St. Petersburg by late 1869.

It was on the evening of May 31, 1867, that an American whaling ship appeared over the horizon and dropped anchor in the Siberian port settlement where the American expedition was headquartered. The following morning a party of Americans rowed out to the *Sea Breeze* to be greeted by the astonished captain.

"Have you been shipwrecked?" he asked them. What other explanation could there be for Americans to be stranded in such a remote corner of the globe?

Kennan explained that they were building a telegraph line, at which point the captain volunteered the devastating news that the transatlantic cable had been completed more than a year earlier and was functioning well. San Francisco newspapers, he said, were routinely publishing European news that was only a day old. Kennan and the other dispirited men were to learn from newspapers on board the whaler that construction had been halted on their own line through British Columbia seven months earlier. It wasn't until July that a second vessel arrived at the little port, with official news from Western Union that the entire project had been abandoned. The Americans were told to sell off their tools and building materials as best they could and return home. It is said that glass insulators sold as tea mugs can still be found in Siberian farmhouses.

The line from the U.S. border to Quesnel was purchased by Canada in 1870. Abandoned poles and spools of wire left along the broad right-of-way cleared to the north of Quesnel were salvaged by local Indians, who used the copper for nails and fishing spears, and for binding logs together in footbridges and other construction projects. A famous native-built suspension bridge made almost entirely of telegraph wire spanned the river at Hagwilgaet for decades. Thirty years after the line was abandoned, the great Klondike gold rush saw the right-of-way north of Quesnel used as a highway to the gold-fields. The Canadian government at last completed the telegraph link from Quesnel to Whitehorse to assist in the policing and administration of the Yukon Territory during the gold rush.

Western Union and its shareholders had spent $3 million on the aborted project, a sum that gains significance when compared with the $7 million paid the following year by the United States to purchase all of Alaska from Russia. A traveller to the Skeena and Bulkley rivers in northern British Columbia in 1872 penned a haunting epitaph to the project:

> Crossing the wide Nacharcole River and continuing south for a few miles, we reached a broadly cut trail which bore curious traces of past civilization. Old telegraph poles stood at intervals along the forest-cleared opening, and rusted wires hung in loose festoons down from their tops, or lay tangled in the growing brushwood for the cleared space. A telegraph in the wilderness! What did it mean? When civilization once grasps the wild, lone spaces of the earth it seldom releases its hold; yet here civilization had once advanced her footsteps, and apparently shrunk back again, frightened at her boldness . . .[1]

The Atlantic submarine cable that dashed Western Union's plans for a back-door link to Europe was a high-water mark of nineteenth-century technological achievement. It bore all the hallmarks of Newtonian physics expressed in machines: it pushed the limits of engineering of all kinds to an extent that gives pause even to the modern observer. Everything about it was monumental, larger than life. Given the materials and technology then available, the laying of a wire cable right across the Atlantic Ocean seems every bit as impressive a feat as sending a man to the moon.

It took five attempts, beginning in 1857 and ending with success, finally, in 1866. One man, the American wholesale-paper tycoon Cyrus W. Field, provided the bottomless supply of energy and optimism required to carry the project to completion through years of heartbreaking failures and long delays caused by the Civil War. (He made more than fifty Atlantic crossings in the process, suffering from seasickness each time.) In 1856, having successfully laid cable across the Cabot Strait to connect Newfoundland with mainland Canada, he formed the Atlantic Telegraph Company with the British engineer Charles Bright and brothers John and Jacob Brett, who had laid the first cable across the English Channel in 1851.

The first foray was launched, with great fanfare and speech making, from Valentia on the southwest coast of Ireland. The British and American governments had each supplied a warship rigged for cable laying. The frigate USS *Niagara* was to lay the first half of the cable from Ireland, accompanied by its escort USS *Susquehanna*; HMS *Agamemnon* was to meet *Niagara* at mid-Atlantic, splice the cable and carry on to Trinity Bay in Newfoundland, escorted by HMS *Leopard*. The job went smoothly at first, until, four hundred miles into the Atlantic, a swell caught the stern of *Niagara*, lifting it high into the air. Before the men on board could react, the cable parted and dropped out of sight beneath the waves. The ships were forced to return to Britain, and Field had to raise new capital for a second attempt.

The squadron set out again with fresh supplies in June 1858. This time the plan was for *Niagara* and *Agamemnon* to meet and join the cable at mid-ocean, *Agamemnon* then heading for Ireland and *Niagara* steaming slowly for Newfoundland. Several cable breaks in the first few days forced the vessels to return to Valentia to resupply before setting out once again for mid-ocean and a fresh start. The ships had steamed to within a few hundred miles of their mid-Atlantic rendezvous when they encountered one of the worst Atlantic storms ever recorded. The heavily laden *Agamemnon* was nearly capsized, and saved only by superb seamanship. *Niagara* survived as well, although her cable had been thoroughly scrambled below decks, resembling a mass of cooked spaghetti.

Six days after the storm, the two ships met and the cable was spliced. They steamed off in opposite directions. Within an hour, the cable had broken as it was being paid off *Niagara*'s deck. A fresh splice was made, and the exercise began again. A day later the cable broke once again, but this time under water. A third splice was made, and now the operation went smoothly while 146 miles of cable was laid. Then the cable parted at *Agamemnon*'s stern and dropped into the ocean. There was no longer enough cable for another attempt, and the squadron returned to Britain, thoroughly disheartened.

There were those on shore who counselled abandoning the project as impossible, but Field and other optimists prevailed, and on July 17 another attempt was mounted with the same ships. There were no celebrations this time when the vessels departed for mid-ocean, only faint hope and foreboding. Tension on board was palpable as they spliced the cable and crept east and west toward their respective destinations. On August 4, *Niagara* entered Trinity Bay, Newfoundland, while lookouts on *Agamemnon* raised the Irish coast. The ocean had finally been bridged, and the link worked, though there were disturbing problems with weak signals and long gaps when nothing could be heard.

The success triggered rapturous celebrations on both sides of the ocean. In Britain, Charles Bright was put on the Queen's honours list and received a knighthood at the tender age of twenty-six. Field was hailed as a hero. In his hometown of New York, festivities included a church service, two parades, a banquet and speeches. The streets were alive until well after midnight. So enthusiastic was the fireworks display that night that it set the city hall alight and burned it down. And in the state capital, Albany, "crowds of persons flocked to the newspaper offices and Telegraph offices for confirmation of the news, which most at first doubted, but when the conviction of the truth of the report forced itself on the public mind, the scene in the street was as though each person had received some intelligence of strong personal interest . . . The people are wild with excitement."[2] In reflecting on the spontaneous exhilaration that greeted the news, the *New York Times* referred to the telegraph as a "divine boon," and added: "From some such source must the deep joy that seizes all minds at the thought of this unapproachable triumph spring. It is the thought that it has metaphysical roots and relations that makes it sublime."3

But Field could not enjoy the celebrations, because he and a few others shared the awful secret that all was not well with the cable. It continued to work only intermittently, and messages took hours to transmit when they should have taken minutes. Later investigations indicated that the rubber-like gutta percha insulation had broken down on portions of cable that had been stored in sunlight at the manufacturing plant in England. Further damage was done by experimenting with high voltages to boost the signal strength. The link lasted only two months; a total of seven hundred messages were transmitted before it died forever.

It was a terrible blow for Field, who became, as dethroned heroes often do, an object of scorn and ridicule, excoriated in the press that had so recently lionized him. Remarkably, he persevered, arguing that the brief success of the 1858 cable had proved beyond doubt that the idea was feasible. So enormous was the potential for profit, and so great was the importance assigned to the project by the governments of the United States and Britain, that Field was eventually able to raise enough capital and government guarantees for yet another attempt. By then, cable-making methods had improved, as had telegraphic instruments and cable-laying technology.

Ultimate victory was assured by putting into service as a cable-layer the British vessel *Great Eastern*, at the time of her launch in 1858 (the year of Field's first, partial success) the biggest ship afloat, five times larger than her nearest competition at nearly 700 feet long with a displacement of 27,000 tons. Her twin 60-foot side paddlewheels weighed 90 tons each, and gave her superb manoeuvrability. Her single cast-iron screw propeller was 24 feet high and weighed 36 tons. Her coal-fired engines developed 11,000 horsepower. Only a vessel of this size could manage the great weight of the more than 2,000 miles of armoured and insulated copper cable that needed to be paid out on the voyage from Ireland to Newfoundland: though only a little bigger around than a thumb, it weighed in at about 7,000 tons.

But, once again, success was not to come without bitter setbacks. On the first attempt, in 1865, there were four signal failures on the cable in the first four days out from Ireland. Each time, the wire had to be rolled back on board the ship, inspected for damage and repaired. Sabotage was suspected, since the failures had been caused by tiny needles of wire shorting the cable to its outer casing of wire armour, and all had occurred when the same crew was on duty. Eventually, however, it was determined that the fault had been in the brittle composition of the outer shielding, which had a tendency to splinter. Redoubling their caution and signalling constantly through the line back and forth to Ireland, the crews continued paying out cable until *Great Eastern* was within 660 miles of Newfoundland. There, another fault was detected, and while the line was being hauled on board for repair, it snapped and dropped back to the sea floor 3 miles below.

Plundering the huge ship's stores for enough rope, the captain rigged a grapple and steamed back and forth across the cable's track. Twice the crew snagged it and raised it from the ocean floor, but both times the grapple line parted under the strain. Finally there was not enough line left to try again. *Great Eastern* sailed back home.

A new company was organized by Field and his backers, and financing was arranged. New cable was manufactured over the winter at the rate of 20 miles a day. On July 12, 1866, *Great Eastern* sailed from Valentia with more than 2,300 miles of cable stored in her ample holds. On July 27, at 5 p.m., the ship's crew dragged the cable ashore through the surf at Heart's Content, Newfoundland. It was soon operating perfectly. Two weeks later, with Field aboard, the ship returned to the site of the previous year's break and, dragging with new, stouter grappling gear, raised the broken cable. The crew cleaned it up, attached telegraph equipment and tried signalling Ireland. It worked! Field strode manfully to his cabin, closed the door and collapsed in tears. There were now two functioning transatlantic cables.

Despite the awesome logistics of these early transatlantic undertakings, by 1892 there were ten such telegraph links spanning the ocean, where the indefatigable Field and the backers of the original success had wondered whether there would be enough demand to pay for one. The economics tell the story of the rapid expansion: A message on the first cables cost about five dollars a word. Working at speeds of up to seventeen words per minute, the potential revenue from each cable was calculated at upwards of $2 million a year. The total investment for all five original cables, three unsuccessful and abandoned, one broken but repaired and one completely successful, plus ancillary lines across Newfoundland to Nova Scotia and on to New York, was about $12 million over twelve years, much of that guaranteed by long-term contracts with the governments of the United States and Great Britain. By 1867, Field had paid off all his company's creditors with an added 7 percent interest. Cable stock that had sold for 30 guineas per £1,000 (about 30 cents on the dollar) was paying £160 in annual dividends.[4] The bottomless, pent-up demand for rapid communication made it a sound business proposition despite the enormous costs and risks.

The globe was effectively girdled when in 1905 the Pacific was spanned by two cables linking Vancouver with Australia, jointly developed by the British, Canadian, Australian and New Zealand governments. A section between Vancouver and the Fanning Island coral group in the Pacific was the longest in the world, at 3,500 miles. In 1930, with the world sliding calamitously into economic depression, there was a worldwide web of about 350,000 miles of telegraph line. About 265,000 miles of that was long-distance trunks, including transoceanic links. British private and government interests were by far the largest owners of long-distance cables, with the United States a distant second. Britain's Eastern Telegraph Company had long-established cable links with India, Australasia, the Far East, Africa and South America, making it the largest cable operation in the world. The system amounted to 136,000 miles of cable, and it was carrying about 70 million words a year.

As long as the telegraph held its monopoly on long-distance communication, ample profit was a foregone conclusion for any cable-laying endeavour. The industry, as one might expect in these circumstances, became technically conservative and administratively hidebound. It took radio's competition to prod cable telegraphy into making renewed technical advances in the 1920s and 1930s. The baffling and debilitating problem of capacitance, or storage capacity, on the line was at long last overcome. Undersea cables behave electrically like capacitors, with the insulated central conductor as one plate and the outer armour of wire as the other. A feature of capacitors is that they store electricity until fully charged and then allow current to flow as a discharge. The effect was that code had to be sent very slowly in the early cables in order to be received distinctly at the other end. If it was sent too quickly, characters would be lost in the charging period; words would pile up and the backlog would never reach the other end in intelligible form. Early transatlantic cables were limited to speeds of about 15 to 17 words per minute.

This was a problem that could be safely ignored so long as the cables held on to their monopoly on transoceanic communication, but when radio arrived, telegraph engineers got busy. It was discovered that if the cable were "loaded" (i.e., if the inductance to ground were increased) by wrapping the centre conductor with a ribbon of a nickel-iron alloy called Permalloy, the capacitance problem could all but be eliminated. The loading or increased inductance had the effect of lowering the cable's capacitance. Speeds on these new loaded cables reached 400 words per minute, with dramatic consequences for the cable operator's bottom line. This and other technical advances made it possible, at last, to transmit telephone signals. As well, techniques for laying undersea cables were developed to the point where, in 1928, a high-capacity cable was laid and in operation between Newfoundland and the Azores, a distance of 1,341 miles, in just eight days.

The last of the scores of transatlantic telegraph cables that were laid in the hundred years following Field's first successes was abandoned in 1966, with telegraph traffic switching over to newer, more efficient telephone cables and to satellite transponders. Fibre optic cables of undreamed-of capacity now span both the Atlantic and

Pacific oceans, carrying everything from live television pictures to e-mail.

As the global cable web grew, so did the reality of a global market, now that shipping movements, prices, supply and demand could be learned instantly for stocks and bonds and currencies and for staple commodities such as minerals and foodstuffs. The effect on the grain market was typical: the telegraph, combined with a parallel improvement in ground and marine transport technologies, involved North America directly in what had been a European-dominated world market for grain. In 1874, the cost of shipping a bushel of grain across the Atlantic was 20 cents; in 1904, it was 2 cents. Grain exchanges in Canada, Britain, the United States and Australia were in constant communication, and the buying and selling of grain became transoceanic, at world prices. Turn-of-the-century proponents of globalization lauded the development as lowering prices and making crop specialization feasible; others worried about the loss of diversity in agriculture in individual nations, as "inefficient" sectors were threatened by foreign competition. Ironically, the era of free trade that had begun early in the nineteenth century, and which British prime minister Benjamin Disraeli and other European leaders assumed in 1860 was a permanent fixture in world markets, died as rapidly as the expiry of trade treaties would allow in the 1880s, and high tariff walls were a feature of international trade right up to World War II. The telegraph was a major factor behind the change: it instantly created powerful lobbies in commodities sectors and in industry for protection from "too much" foreign competition, pressure that politicians in Europe and North America were unable to resist.

While the telegraph enabled business to operate more efficiently, its impact in transforming the public's patterns of information consumption was perhaps even more important. For one thing, the telegraph changed the definition of "news." Until the telegraph, newspapers, apart from strictly local coverage, had consisted mainly of analysis and interpretation of events that were often days, even weeks or months, old. With the telegraph, newspapers got into the national and international spot-news business, and freshness supplanted relevance as the most important defining characteristic of the product. In other words, the telegraph made relevance in news less relevant. Thoreau put his finger on it when he commented in *Walden*: "We are in great haste to construct a magnetic telegraph from Maine to Texas; but Maine and Texas, it may be, have nothing important to communicate . . . We are eager to tunnel under the Atlantic and bring the old world some weeks nearer to the new; but perchance the first news that will leak through into the broad flapping American ear will be that Princess Adelaide has the whooping cough." Once it became possible to bring newspaper readers word of events from around the world on the very day they occurred, it became *necessary* to do so. News moved away from being analysis and interpretation of events of interest and importance to readers—useful or functional information—toward a simple recitation of happenings.

What kind of happenings met the definition of "news"? To some degree, the fact that events occurred at all made them news, or news*worthy*; the more dramatic or unexpected the occurrence, and the farther from home, the more weight its exoticism carried in the balance with its possible relevance to readers. The fact that "Princess Adelaide has the whooping cough" became news of the highest order, as was made clear in the first news bulletin ever carried by transatlantic cable. Transmitted from England and addressed to the Associated Press on August 27, 1858, the complete, unedited text read:

EMPEROR OF FRANCE RETURNED TO PARIS SATURDAY. KING
OF PRUSSIA TOO ILL TO VISIT QUEEN VICTORIA. HER MAJESTY
RETURNS TO ENGLAND 31ST AUGUST. SETTLEMENT OF
CHINESE QUESTION: CHINESE EMPIRE OPENS TO TRADE;
CHRISTIAN RELIGION ALLOWED. MUTINY BEING QUELLED,
ALL INDIA BECOMING TRANQUIL.[5]

The great news wire services were formed to satisfy the newly created demand for news of the world and put its supply into the hands of professionals. Before the Associated Press in the U.S. and Reuter in Britain, Agence France Presse in France and the forerunners to the Canadian Press in Canada, most telegraph news had been provided by telegraph operators in the employ of the telegraph companies. In Canada, that meant that Canadian Pacific Telegraphs controlled the flow of news across the continent, and the company was not averse to turning off the spigot to newspapers that dared to criticize CP in their pages. In the U.S., the Associated Press newspapers fought a long and expensive battle with the Morse interests and Western Union to gain unrestricted, uncensored access to the wires for news. It ended in a settlement so cozy that the AP and Western Union, which had grown to become America's biggest corporation, were the objects of mounting criticism as a two-headed monopoly controlling what should have been a public utility. The collusion between the two was the focus of intense disappointment, especially among those who had been most enthusiastic in greeting the telegraph's arrival—disappointment that the bright promise of the telegraph as a divinely given instrument of moral force and a common carrier of intelligence should have fallen into the hands of crass commercial monopoly.

The news agencies, like some of the more responsible newspapers, tended to subscribe to more or less thoughtful standards for the definition of news, including in their characterization the notion of information needed by citizens to organize their lives and make responsible choices in a democratic society. However, they were all dependent for their survival on the satisfaction of the maximum number of subscribers, and idealism was inevitably forced to find a modus vivendi with coarse commercial imperatives.

Media critic Neil Postman says of the telegraph that it "gave a form of legitimacy to the idea of context-free information; that is, to the idea that the value of information need not be tied to any function it might serve in social and political decision-making and action, but may attach merely to its novelty, interest, and curiosity."[6] The news organization became the buyer and seller of the generic commodity called "news."

When broadcast news was still young enough to be idealistic, CBS News writing guidelines forbade calling the newscast a "show," in order to preserve, to the extent possible, the distinction between news and entertainment. ("Program" or "broadcast" were the preferred nouns.) In the 1990s, after network television had fallen into the hands of multinational entertainment conglomerates and business school–trained management specialists, this quaint tradition was relegated to history and the coffee-shop conversation of the few aging news people who had somehow survived the multiple rounds of layoffs. Today, it is not unusual in newsrooms to hear the word "content" used in preference to any of the more descriptive terms for news and information programming. Plane crash, budget speech, obituary, flood: it's all "content," nicely demonstrating Postman's reminder that news has become a commodity, a "thing" to be bought and sold.

Postman argues correctly that the value of any information (as distinct from entertainment) depends on its usefulness to the recipient, which can be further defined as the possibilities for action it presents. News of happenings or circumstances that will never impinge on the recipient's life, and which allows no action by the recipient in response to it, is of very little, if any, use to anyone.[7] With the coming of the telegraph, the proportion of the information flooding into people's lives that had any relevance to them— that presented any possibility for action, and could thereby be said to be "useful" to them—dwindled dramatically. Furthermore, says Postman:

> Prior to the age of telegraphy, the information–action ratio was sufficiently close so that most people had a sense of being able to control some of the contingencies in their lives. What people knew had action-value. In the information world created by telegraphy, this sense of potency was lost, precisely because the

whole world became the context for news. Everything became everyone's business. For the first time we were sent information which answered no question we had asked, and which, in any case, did not permit the right of reply.

Thus, the telegraph's contribution was "to dignify irrelevance and amplify impotence."[8]

It is not a new idea. The London *Spectator* put the argument even more eloquently and succinctly nearly a century earlier:

[With] the recording of every event, and especially every crime, everywhere without perceptible interval of time the world is for purposes of intelligence reduced to a village . . . All men are compelled to think of all things, at the same time, on imperfect information, and with too little interval for reflection . . . The constant diffusion of statements in snippets, the constant excitements of feeling unjustified by fact, the constant formation of hasty or erroneous opinions, must, in the end, one would think, deteriorate the intelligence of all to whom the telegraph appeals.[9]

The nineteenth-century American critic W.J. Stillman accused the telegraph of having

transformed journalism from what it once was, the periodical expression of the thought of the time, the opportune record of the questions and answers of contemporary life, into an agency for collecting, condensing, and assimilating the trivialities of the entire human existence. In this chase for the day's accidents we still keep the lead, as in consequent neglect and oversight of what is permanent and therefore vital in its importance to the intellectual character.[10]

The early, uncritical enthusiasm for the telegraph had begun to seriously erode by the end of the century. "In place of the enormous faith invested in the telegraph by the earliest observers," notes Daniel

Czitrom, "late nineteenth-century thinkers increasingly identified the telegraph and the modern newspaper as both symptom and cause of the frantic pace of industrial life." Eventually, "the disturbing challenge of the periodical press to classical notions of culture began to elicit troubling doubts about the ultimate cultural import of modern communication."[11]

Perhaps, though, too much blame has been placed on the telegraph for the trivializing of news and the debasement of content in the periodical press. Prior to the introduction of the telegraph, newspapers everywhere had been involved in a radical restructuring of their approach to doing business known as the "penny press revolution." It began with the *New York Sun*, a newspaper launched in 1833 by a twenty-three-year-old printer with minimal capital and a consequent pressing need for cash flow.[12] To achieve the latter, Benjamin Day adopted the high-risk strategy of selling his newspapers for a penny a copy, well below the cost of printing. His competitors charged 5 or 6 cents. To bridge the gap between sales revenue and printing costs, Day intended to sell as much advertising as he could, a plan that required him to boost his circulation rapidly to levels that would make potential advertisers take notice. This he accomplished by instituting street sales through vendors called paperboys.

Day's business plan worked: within two years the *Sun* was selling 15,000 papers a day in a city of 218,000. The previous circulation leader, a mercantile paper called the *Courier and Enquirer*, had been selling 4,500 copies. (In London, the highly respected *Times* was selling 10,000 copies a day in a city of two million.) The *Sun* was soon followed by another bootstrap operation, James Gordon Bennett's *New York Herald*. The revolution had begun. Both papers focused their attention on the sensational and the scandalous. The *Sun* became famous for a blatant hoax in which it claimed in a number of stories that a famous astronomer working in South Africa had "made the most extraordinary discoveries . . . winged creatures much like men and women on the moon, as well as magnificent structures, such as the great Temple of the Moon, built of polished sapphire." Bennett sought sales with graphic reporting on the axe murder of a beautiful prostitute in a New York brothel. The public was shocked and affronted, but circulation soared. Sales numbers were crucial to both papers not simply because of the revenue produced, but because they were the key to attracting advertisers.

As more newspapers joined the fray in New York and other major centres (New York boasted a dozen newspapers in 1840), the real impact of the revolution began to emerge through the noise and dust of the great circulation battles. In shifting the focus of their attention from subscribers to advertisers as their principal source of revenue, newspapers were effectively making advertisers their most important clients. It only makes sense that if a majority of income is derived from advertising, advertisers will be front of mind in the business planning and development processes, as well as in mapping daily news coverage. In the earlier subscriber model, the reader had been king, and supplying his needs was the focus of the newspaper's energies. In the new model, readers were means to an end, and satisfying advertisers was the focus. In the old system, readers had purchased news, editorial comment and entertainment; in the new model, advertisers purchased readers. The content of the newspapers, seen as bait to attract readers to be sold to advertisers, now had to appeal to as wide an audience as possible, which meant, in effect, seeking out the lowest common denominator in taste, attention span and intellectual ability among readers.

This led, on one hand, to pandering to a common penchant for violence, sex and sensation, and on the other to the more respectable trend toward "objectivity" in news coverage. Whereas earlier, subscriber-financed newspapers had worn their politics and social concerns on their sleeves, the new breed of paper would eventually claim to report on events in a fair, balanced and unbiased way. Objectivity had its ethical rationale, but for publishers it was mainly a commercial strategy aimed at attracting readers from across the political spectrum and, by doing so, boosting the circulation numbers that were the object of advertisers' undivided attention. The introduction of objectivity in reporting is best seen as part of a broader trend toward the homogenization of news, an attempt to always please as many readers as possible, while avoiding content that might conceivably offend any significant number of subscribers.

The role of the telegraph in all of this was to make available to a new breed of newspaper editor a growing and ultimately almost unlimited pool of stories with which to "bait" readers and thereby satisfy advertisers, stories from all over the world featuring the bizarre, the horrific, the titillating, the tragic and the frightening. In doing this, the new technology certainly helped to shrink the world, if only in the public's perception. The twentieth century, it was predicted, would be the beneficiary of the new possibilities for global community building, and there is no doubt that the telegraph provided many tangible benefits, not the least of which was the rapid dissemination of truly significant news and information. However, given that century's unparalleled record for bloodletting, whether the telegraph and succeeding global media were, on balance, truly beneficial is at least open to debate.

Late in the twentieth century, the laying of cables beneath vast stretches of ocean and across continents once again inspired extravagant hope and ebullient predictions. These modern cables are fibre optic lines of such vast capacity that they are making satellites obsolete for data transmission. Whereas copper submarine cables can carry only a few dozen telephone circuits, or about 2,500 kilobits of data per second (kbps), the new cables can carry 120,000 circuits, or about eight gigabits per second (gbps)—about 3,200 times more data. FLAG (Fibre-optic Link Around the Globe), completed in 1997, stretches 17,400 miles from England to Japan, via Gibraltar and the Mediterranean Sea, Egypt, the Red Sea, India, Malaysia, China and Korea. FLAG Telecom Holdings and GTS Telecom have constructed a fibre optic system across the Atlantic called FLAG Atlantic-1. FLAG Pacific-1, a cable system from the west coast of the United States and Canada to Japan, was finished in 2002. With those three systems combined, along with backhaul additions in certain countries along the route, FLAG's network alone had a 40,000-mile reach.

It was clear by this time, however, that despite burgeoning growth in Internet and other users, fibre optic cable capacity had been overbuilt worldwide, to the extent that demand in many countries lagged 80 percent or even more behind available bandwidth. This created pressure to extend household broadband service worldwide, doubtless a healthy development. It now seems clear that bandwidth for the transmission of data of all kinds can be extended virtually indefinitely, when it is needed. The wiring of the world continues apace, and the hope that it will lead to better lives for the planet's inhabitants has not died.

The Invention of
the Modern Inventor

THE PERIOD of European and North American history from about 1860 to the outbreak of World War I in 1914 is one of exceptional interest to students of social history and technology, who have variously dubbed it the Age of Materialism, the Age of Invention and the Second Industrial Revolution. It is essentially a period in which the scientific discoveries of the previous two hundred years were exploited to produce practical devices for everyday use. These included an array of electric and electronic communications devices as well as the electric incandescent light and the internal combustion engine, a lightweight, portable power plant that made the automobile possible. As well, enormous advances were made in chemistry and pharmaceuticals; steel-frame construction demonstrated in the Eiffel Tower made possible the first skyscrapers; iron bridges spanned impossible distances; and railways transformed commerce and created nations.

It was an era of breathtaking developments in geopolitics as well. The great European imperial expansions were in full swing. Between 1870 and 1900, Great Britain alone acquired about five million square miles of territory in the eastern and southern hemispheres. It was not the land the imperialists were after so much as the markets represented by the people who inhabited the land, as noted by J.D. Bernal in his *Science in History*:

> Already towards the end of the [eighteen] sixties the first, simple, optimistic phase of early capitalism was beginning to draw to an end . . . The enormous productive forces liberated by the Industrial Revolution were by then beginning to present their owners with the problem of an ever larger disposable surplus. This could not, under capitalism, be returned to the workers who made it. When invested at home it led to even greater production and to a more hectic search all over the world for markets that were soon filled. The result was colonial expansion, minor wars, and preparation for the larger wars which were to come in the next century.[1]

The telegraph, like the telephone and many other technical achievements of the era, is a "modern" invention in that it owes its genesis to scientific research. Prior to Michael Faraday's work, virtually all technology had been the result of empirical discoveries by practical men searching for solutions to practical problems. Motives for innovation were thus as varied as the human condition, and not exclusively or even primarily economic in nature. It is argued, for instance, that the primary motivation for the widespread adoption of wind and water mills in the Middle Ages was the Christian view that menial labour requiring brute force to the exclusion of the intellect was inhumane, and inconsistent with the doctrine of the intrinsic value of all human beings. In other cases, innovation was suppressed despite economic logic. The Muslim world, for example, refused to adopt the printing press for several centuries after its introduction in Christian Europe. The reasons for this are obscure, but are presumed to have been rooted in a (justified) fear that widespread availability of books would undermine existing power structures.

From the pre-Christian era through to the mid-nineteenth century, technology and science had been distinct traditions. The intelligentsia of classical Greece shared a well-known prejudice against manual labour in its most literal interpretation: they relegated to lower social strata the farmer and miner, but also the artist and artisan, and even the musician, all of whose work, being manual, was stigmatized by the taint of slavery. Indeed, it is a prejudice that has proved remarkably resilient, despite Jewish rabbinical and Christian teachings to the contrary, and the monastic idea of *laborare est orare*, work is worship. Historian Sir Desmond Lee has remarked: "That the upper and controlling classes in Greece and Rome thought poorly of manual labour in the sense that they regarded it as a lower class occupation is undoubted. The texts speak clearly enough . . . But I would ask in reply at what time in the world's history has the attitude of the upper and controlling classes been different? When have they commended manual labour as a way of life, except for other people or in sentimental pastoral?"[2]

However, beginning in the nineteenth century with Faraday and men like him, a new relationship between theory and practice was forged: technology provided problems for science and science provided experimental knowledge that allowed technology to progress. A new community of practitioners evolved, people who had scientific and mathematical knowledge and who also had an intimate knowledge of technology. They came to be called engineers, not a new coinage but the revival of a term used sporadically since it had first appeared in twelfth-century Catalonia, in connection with specialists in siege engines and fortifications.

The age-old class structure that had relegated technology to the trades, while stereotyping practitioners as trained but not educated, broke down. By the mid-twentieth century, Arthur Koestler was able to write of the person who did not understand and appreciate technology as being every bit as much a "barbarian" as one who had no interest in or appreciation of art. For technology, he observed, is after all a human product, growing not only out of humanity's need to improve its material lot but also out of its love of play and adventure.[3] Morse and Vail, Marconi, Edison, Bell and Fleming are all exemplars of Koestler's insight into the soul of the gifted engineer.

Nevertheless, experience in the twentieth century, particularly in its second half, has made it possible to question the extent to which modern technology does in fact represent humanity's highest aspirations and most sublime qualities, as opposed to our baser economic drives. In fact a convincing argument can be made that the conditions under which much late-twentieth-century technical innovation has taken place have effectively eliminated all facets of motivation except the economic from the invention equation. Since this is an issue that will be raised explicitly and implicitly a number of times in succeeding chapters, it is worth a brief exploration here.

With the possible exception of Fleming, the inventor-entrepreneurs mentioned above also exemplify, particularly in their later careers, an important social and political phenomenon described eloquently in David F. Noble's *America by Design*: "From the outset the engineer was in the service of capital and, not surprisingly, its laws to him were as natural as the laws of science . . . The technical world of the engineer was little more than the scientific extension of capitalist enterprise; it was through his efforts that science was transformed into capital."[4] Noble goes on to quote A.A. Potter, the founding dean of the faculty of engineering at Purdue University, as summarizing the relationship this way: "Whatever the numerator is in an engineering equation, the denominator is always a dollar mark."[5]

The rise of the modern engineer was fostered by and concurrent with the rise of the great industrial corporations which, by exploiting the fecundity of the wedding of science to craft, would come to dominate economic and, thus, social existence in the industrial nations of the world. Prior to this, practical arts had been the helpmate of science. Following the marriage, the reverse was true: science came to be more and more in the service of the practical arts, or engineering. This was a crucially important turning point in the history of technology, bringing into intimate contact, as it did, two quite different sets of motives and ideals.

Initially, the distinction in values was subtle. On the one hand, science wished to reach an understanding of the universe for its own sake; on the other, engineering sought to apply that understanding for the happiness and well-being of humanity. Who could be blamed for seeing it as a marriage made in heaven? However, as the nineteenth century wore into the twentieth and the power of the technology-based corporation grew, a disturbing gulf arose between the objectives of the partners. Science's goals remained essentially the same (though engineering increasingly encroached on its territory); but engineering's goals merged with those of the corporation, which were, by definition, to maximize return on investment. It can be argued, and often is, that this science–engineering–corporate nexus is the most effective system yet devised for providing widespread material well-being. Nevertheless, it has the effect of making social goals subservient to corporate goals. Throughout most of history prior to World War I, this would have been regarded as an intolerable affront to civilized values; today, it is widely acquiesced in by a society conditioned to accept it as the natural and inevitable order of things.

The rise of the industrial corporation, with its phalanxes of professional engineers, also brought with it the evolution of the great industrial laboratories, to which so many of the twentieth century's technological advances owe their existence. The GE lab opened in 1901 with a staff of eight; in 1902, there were 102; and by 1932, when Irving Langmuir brought it its first Nobel Prize,[6] it employed more than 600 researchers. In 1907, several Bell research establishments were amalgamated with Western Electric. In 1911, the famous Bell Labs were established, with a mandate to undertake fundamental scientific research. By 1925, more than 3,600 people were employed there, and it was the largest and best-equipped research facility in the United States, including those of the best universities. It won the first in a long series of Nobel Prizes in 1937. Similar research centres were established in the oil, automotive, steel and chemical industries. In 1920, there were 526 American companies boasting in-house research facilities; by 1983, there were more than 11,000.

The indispensable David Noble describes the difference between the new industrial and the traditional university laboratory this way:

Whereas the university researcher was relatively free to chart
his own paths and define his own problems (however meager his
resources), the industrial researcher was more commonly a sol-
dier under management command, participating with others in
a collective attack on scientific truth. [The role of the scientist
within a large industrial lab] came more and more to resemble
that of the workmen on the production line and science became
essentially a management problem.7

In addition, corporations increasingly played a leading role in
financing and in other ways moulding and shaping the engineering
faculties at major universities, especially in the United States. From
the industrial corporation's point of view, engineering schools
were providers of what we have lately come to refer to as "human
resources," and corporations were at pains to see that students were
trained according to corporate requirements. The very nature of university education was shifted in the direction of corporate priorities.

The corporatization of technical innovation did not eliminate
the freelance inventor. A study of seventy key inventions of the first
half of the twentieth century shows that about half of them came
from independent inventors.8 These include Bakelite plastic, the
automatic transmission, the ballpoint pen, Cellophane, the cyclo-
tron, insulin, the gyrocompass, the jet engine, colour photographic
film, xerography, the zipper and the safety razor. But the momentum in favour of the corporate lab had nevertheless been firmly
established.

Paradoxically, perhaps, technology throughout this era of materialism and the rise of corporate capitalism was seen increasingly as
holding the key to realization of the humanist aspirations of Victorian civilization. Modern technology, it was argued, had ended
slavery (by making industrial processes using wage labour cheaper
than maintaining slaves); and technology had elevated the status of
women and children, rescuing them from the "dark Satanic mills"
of early industrialism (by making their jobs redundant). Technology had provided the means to banish hunger, made social welfare

a reality, linked the peoples of the world (some of them, at least) in instantaneous communication. Might it not be expected to eliminate such remaining evils as warfare and prejudice and inequality as well?

The prospects seemed encouraging. But there was a problem growing like a cancer at the core of the concept. In the United States, Britain and most other industrial countries, the patent system had long been the key to encouraging innovation. It was designed to guarantee that the inventor of a new product or process would be the first to benefit financially from its production, and it was available only to individuals: corporations need not apply. It also allowed the inventor to release details of his creation to the public without fear of having it stolen, thus, in theory, further accelerating the process of innovation. It had grown out of the granting of royal "letters patent" or monopolies on trade and industrial processes, initially with no foundation in law other than the authority of the monarch. As early as the seventeenth century in England, however, it had been regularized in statutes passed by Parliament granting seventeen years of exclusivity to inventors who met the legislation's criteria. Abraham Lincoln described the patent process, in words later engraved over the entrance to the U.S. Patent Office in Washington, as adding "the fuel of interest to the fire of genius." The purpose was to serve the public interest by encouraging inventors to make their work public by describing it in a patent application, while at the same time protecting their ability to profit from it.

But as corporations got involved (they were officially recognized as "persons" in an 1886 U.S. Supreme Court decision),[9] they naturally acted to make the system work on their behalf. This inevitably meant that it worked increasingly against the interests of the lone inventor, who was the corporation's main competition in the field. Corporate managers were to develop a number of tactics, including the "pooling" of their patents (gained through purchase from inventors or by virtue of the fact that the patent holders were corporate employees) with those of troublesome competitors. In these cartel-like arrangements, companies that had been mutually hobbled by constant patent litigation agreed to divide up the industrial land-scape under complex and often secret contracts which eliminated strife between them and barred the door against new entrants. Corporations also sought out and purchased any and all patents related to their field of interest, and then ferociously defended their intellectual property rights in the courts. Here is how the first president of Bell Telephone candidly described the tactic:

> It appears to me that the policy of bringing suit for infringement on apparatus patents is an excellent one because it keeps the concerns which attempt opposition in a nervous and excited condition since they never know where the next attack may be made, and since it keeps them all the time changing their machines and causes them ultimately, in order that they may not be sued, to adopt inefficient forms of apparatus.[10]

L.H. Baekeland, one of the founders of the plastics industry and the inventor of Bakelite, was equally blunt, if more judgmental, in his observation of the patents scene in 1909:

> Before the courts, the poor inventor is entirely at the mercy of a legalized system of piracy . . . This game is so successfully played that I know of rich corporations here in the U.S. whose main method of procedure is to frighten, bulldoze, and ruin financially the unfortunate inventor who happens to have a patent which he is not willing to concede to them on their own terms, which is to say, for next to nothing . . . Thus has it come about that an otherwise liberal patent law intended for the protection of the poor inventor has become a drastic method for building up powerful privileges in the interest of big capitalistic combinations.[11]

Many corporations established "industrial research" departments, whose task was to follow closely patent applications and news of industrial developments, so that patents could be purchased or, if that were not possible, in-house inventors could quickly secure related patents with which the original inventor could be harassed in court. The Bell Telephone Company began its life in 1875 with two patents; in 1935 it held 9,225, acquired through purchase, mergers and in-house research.

As independent inventors found it more and more difficult to patent and commercially exploit their innovations, more and more of them chose to accept the proffered job opportunities with corporate R&D departments. There, they would have security and the satisfaction of working out their ideas with the best equipment and facilities and with help from corporate colleagues. But policy within AT&T, General Electric, Western Electric and most other research-based corporations forced them to sign over to the employer patent rights to their inventions, without compensation beyond their salary.

Such patent reform as was from time to time adopted by the U.S. Congress tended to serve corporate interests rather than those of the lone inventor. According to Noble,

> The successful reform efforts between 1900 and 1929 . . . brought the American patent system more closely into line with the needs of corporate industry. They set the basis for a "formalism" in the handling of patents which progressively eliminated the individual inventor who, unlike the large corporations with their well-staffed legal departments, was not equipped to cope with its intricacies and complexities.[12]

Once corporations became deeply involved in the process, invention was no longer strictly something that grew out of human needs; new consumer needs were instead created by inventions, to promote corporate growth. Edison, for example, did not invent the incandescent bulb and then merely speculate on how it might be used. He built on a range of earlier scientific discoveries and technical advances to fabricate a practical bulb: that meant a high-voltage, low-current bulb, one which would meet the commercial requirements of a system of widespread electrical distribution as he envisaged it.

The bulb had to be cheap, it had to last for many hours before burning out, and it had to operate in such a way as to minimize the cost of the electrical generation and distribution system behind it. Edison did not invent the electric light so much as *electric lighting*. And he did it not so much to fill an obvious existing need as to create a product that would, through its very existence, *create* a need.

The focus and direction of invention had been redefined and, one might say, rationalized. It was an enormously successful technique, and it led to the creation of entire new industries. These

> arose in and helped to perpetuate a social climate where the possession of material goods was becoming a sign of status, where desires were replacing needs as a reason for the acquisition of products. The search for market expansion in the automobile industry was to lead Henry Ford first to adopt mass production (previously used in stockyards and at Sears Roebuck), then mass advertising, and then credit buying to broaden mass consumption. The auto industry is the archetype of the twentieth-century consumer industries: it was among the first to create a necessity out of a luxury and subsequently to alter the very fabric of society to perpetuate its own market.[13]

Once progress in technological invention became independent of the inspired individual and came to reside in the group processes of the corporate industrial laboratory, incremental change became more or less continuous, and finally even predictable. The current state of the art in any technology pointed clearly to the direction of expected development, and increasingly, timelines could be assigned in advance for future "breakthroughs" made by teams of engineers and scientists working in corporate R&D labs. For this reason, it has been said that the real significance of the Age of Invention lies in the invention of the modern process of invention.

It seemed an unassailable power structure, liable to persist like the pyramids. But we'll see how social rather than corporate ideals did come to be served by the flurry of recent invention surrounding computer-mediated communications technologies, particularly software—this in spite of, rather than because of, the role played by corporations and their R&D labs and patent research offices. And we'll see how narrow corporate interests were effectively subverted by massive government financing of early Internet development, as well as by the anarchic behaviour of the early software hackers who, as a matter of principle, made their most revolutionary products available to the world free of charge. Partly because of the power of new communications and information technologies, and partly because of a socially conscious ethic that characterized early entrepreneurship in computer software innovation, the corporate-engineering grip on the direction of technological development has been seriously challenged in recent years. But the corporation is fighting back, using all of the immense financial, legal, political and technological resources at its disposal. The outcome of this historic struggle is still in doubt.

The Telephone

EVERYBODY KNOWS who invented the telephone, but there is a sense in which the invention of the telephone *system* might be attributed to someone far less famous than Alexander Graham Bell. His name is Theodore Vail, and he was neither scientist nor engineer, but a professional manager, the first general manager of the Bell Telephone Company. Bell himself fit the traditional mould of the bohemian inventor for whom wealth was not the main goal and who was content to leave further development of his breakthrough device to others. It was an archetype he helped make obsolete through the success of his company and the leading role it would play in the corporatization of innovation. As we'll see, Vail provided the second half of the modern invention equation, the commercial half, by understanding that the telephone was of commercial value only insofar as it was part of a network.

History, though, has granted to Bell the undisputed title of inventor of the telephone itself—if only by a whisker. As if in a photo finish at an Olympic event, Bell's agent had hardly had time to gather his papers and leave the U.S. Patent Office on February 14, 1876, when a law clerk for Elisha Gray puffed up the stone steps, clutching the inventor's sketches and specifications for an almost identical device. Gray, retired co-owner and chief engineer of Western Electric,

the principal hardware supplier to Western Union, was philosophical. He wrote to his patent attorney, "The talking telegraph is a
beautiful thing in a scientific point of view . . . But if you look at
it in a business light it is of no importance. We can do more . . .
with a wire now than with that method . . . This is the verdict of
practical telegraph men."[1] Having missed out on "the most valuable patent ever issued" by an excruciating two hours, Gray had the
consolation of having taken out fifty others during his long career,
while Bell faced the ordeal of defending his own through some sixty
lawsuits between 1879 and 1897. Most significant among these would
be the epic patent fight with Western Union.

The two experimenters had the insight that led to the telephone
at virtually the same time. Each was trying to solve the commercially
important question of how to squeeze more than one signal down a
telegraph wire, Bell as a freelance inventor and Gray as an acknowledged authority in the practical applications of electricity. Both were
testing transmission techniques that allowed vibrations of different
frequencies to be sent down the line simultaneously and separated at
the receiving end by devices tuned to respond to those frequencies.
It occurred to each of them that it ought to be possible to transmit
enough different frequencies to replicate the human voice. What
was needed was a device that would increase or decrease the amount
of electricity sent down the transmitting wire in exact correspondence with the variations in volume and tone of the voice. Bell won
the development race, but only just, and probably because of his
background in speech pathology and as a trainer of the deaf. Gray,
an established inventor and electrical experimenter of long standing,
approached the problem as one of finding a way to get electricity to
carry sounds imitating speech; he saw the telephone as an extension
of telegraphy. Bell, from his background in teaching the deaf to
speak, saw the problem as getting an electrical apparatus to imitate
human physiology. He had in fact done his most productive work
on the telephone receiver only after a medical friend had given him
a complete human ear from a cadaver, and he was able to observe
how delicate and sensitive was its mechanism. He once said, "Had

I known more about electricity, and less about sound, I would never have invented the telephone." Whereas Gray saw the telephone in terms of its potential for improving commercial and industrial productivity, Bell saw it as an extension of man.

It took Bell a year after his patent was issued to get his invention to work. His first success was achieved using a copy of Elisha Gray's device, which employed the variable resistance of an acid solution to convert sound vibrations into electrical impulses.[2] His famous words to collaborator Thomas Watson on March 10, 1876— "Watson, come here. I want you."—were uttered because he had spilled some of the acid on his clothes and worktable. It would be several more months before he could get his own invention, which used a vibrating metal diaphragm and an electromagnet, to work. But it proved to be a far superior instrument. The microphone, or sender, and receiver, or earpiece, were identical; in fact, early telephones used the same piece of equipment for both talking and listening, and subscribers were alerted not to "talk with the ear and listen with the mouth." What made it possible was Bell's discovery of how little electrical energy was required for the system to transmit speech. The device used a thin metal disc placed close to an electromagnet. The vibrations of the plate when struck by sound waves were enough to induce a tiny electric current in the wire coils of the magnet, which was then transmitted along wires to the receiving device. The receiver's electromagnet, reacting to the fluctuating current flowing through it, acted on the metal disc, causing it to duplicate the vibrations of the sending disc. The telephone thus "spoke."

Bell demonstrated his invention at the Philadelphia Centennial Exposition just two months after his first laboratory successes. There, the prestigious judging committee would likely have overlooked his modest booth among the scores of scientific displays (including the first electric light bulb, the first grain-binder and Elisha Gray's multi-wavelength telegraph) had not Dom Pedro de Alcatrana, the second emperor of Brazil, appeared on the scene with his wife and entourage in tow. Dom Pedro recognized Bell, with whom he shared an interest in teaching the deaf, and paused to greet him. He was persuaded to listen to a demonstration, and was volubly astonished. "My God, it speaks!" he exclaimed. The judging committee members, caught up in the eddy of public and press interest created by the emperor, had little choice but to politely follow suit and try Bell's invention. Among the members were such luminaries as Joseph Henry, the foremost American physicist, and William Thomson, later to be Lord Kelvin, perhaps the world's leading authority on electricity and inventor of a galvanometer that had been instrumental in the success of the transatlantic telegraph cable. Said Thomson: "It does speak! It is the most wonderful thing I have seen in America!" And Henry said: "This comes nearer to overthrowing the doctrine of the conservation of energy than anything I ever saw!" Reporters furiously scribbled notes. (Colleagues elsewhere that day were receiving the first telegraphic reports of Custer's last stand.)

For the remaining weeks of the exhibition, the telephone was its star attraction. As had been the case with the telegraph, people found it impossible to believe the device could work until they had actually tried it. So remote was it from their everyday experience, they simply could not take it in. Some who saw it work thought there must be a hole through the wire along which sound waves passed.

Buoyed by the Philadelphia success, Bell and his associate/collaborator Thomas Watson formed the Bell Telephone Association in partnership with two financial backers, Gardner Hubbard and Thomas Sanders. The group had great difficulty raising capital, and in 1877, in desperation, they tried to sell the rights to the invention to the Western Union telegraph company for $100,000. Just a decade after the great Alaska–Siberia telegraph debacle, Western Union president William Orton made the stupendous blunder of turning the offer down. Other potential investors shared Orton's apparently low opinion of the commercial promise of Bell's invention: the fledgling company was starved for capital and in dire straits.[3] Sanders, a shoe manufacturer and the only member of the Bell directorate with any money to speak of, pushed his credit to the limit to keep the venture afloat, more out of gratitude for Bell's having taught his deaf son how to speak than out of any business sense. Hubbard, the group's untiring promotion maestro, was also attached to the project as much by sentiment as anything else: his daughter, also deaf, was Bell's fiancée and future wife. Fewer than eight hundred telephones had been sold, mostly in pairs to businesses with special communications needs.

To make matters worse, Western Union chose this moment to change its mind about the telephone's commercial potential. The company had been supplying business customers with sophisticated printing telegraphs and automated sending devices that could transmit sixty words a minute; they were seen as the ultimate in business communications technology. But a Western Union subsidiary reported to head office that, despite these improvements, several of its customers had recently switched to Bell's telephone. That galvanized the telegraph giant into action. It formed a telephone company of its own, seeded it with $300,000 in capital, and appointed Thomas Edison, Elisha Gray and a third inventor, Professor Amos Dolbear, to its engineering staff. It announced that it had "the only original telephone," invented by its three engineers, and that it was ready to supply "superior telephones with all the latest improvements." It was a thinly veiled threat that it was prepared to mount a protracted and expensive court challenge to Bell's patent if need be, a tactic typical of the freewheeling, brawling practices of the robber-baron era in American business (and, sadly, not untypical today). Western Union was at the time controlled by one of the legends of the breed, William H. Vanderbilt, who summed up the prevailing ethic with the famous quip: "The public be damned. I am working for my stockholders." Vastly experienced in the takeover or elimination of competing businesses, Western Union expected a quick success against the puny Bell Association.

Edison had in fact invented a single-purpose transmitter that was markedly superior to the dual-purpose transmitter-receiver used in the tiny Bell system. It was essentially the same device as is used in today's telephones: a microphone containing a cylindrical "button" of carbon particles that, when compressed by sound waves, provide a reduced resistance to an electric current flowing through them. The electric current varies, in other words, with the sound waves produced by the speaker's voice. This variable current is then applied to the electromagnet within the metal-disc receiver at the other end of the conversation, causing the disc to vibrate in sympathy with the speaker's voice.

Edison's carbon microphone thus required something Bell's telephone did not: electric current from a battery. The strength or amplitude of the electrical current flowing through the wires to the receiver was not dependent on the loudness of the voice using the transmitter, as it was in Bell's telephone, but on the battery current flowing through the microphone button; the sound waves produced by the voice simply modulated this current.[4] In compensation for this added complexity, Edison's microphone provided the enormous advantage of acting as an amplifier of sound waves, which meant that voices could be transmitted more clearly over greater distances. Western Electric's first test of the device took place over 160 miles of existing telegraph line, and was a complete success.

The Edison microphone was an enormous competitive asset for Western Union. Bell's customers soon began demanding a transmitter as effective as Edison's. The situation facing the beleaguered company was now so bleak as to seem hopeless.

Then, the unexpected happened. The Western Union strategy boomeranged. The very fact that the great telegraph conglomerate was jumping into the telephone business legitimized the industry overnight, and gave retrospective credence to all the promotion work done by Bell and Hubbard over the past year, as they demonstrated the invention in auditoriums and church basements all over the eastern United States.[5] Very soon, the delighted Sanders found himself leasing telephones at the rate of a thousand a month. Half a dozen wealthy businessmen put up $50,000 in capital. And, in a moment of inspiration, the company hired Theodore Vail as its general manager.

Vail would become one of the legends of American business management, both for his masterful piloting of Bell Telephone and for his management philosophy. He was exactly the right man for the job. His family had operated the historic Speedwell Iron Works in Morristown, New Jersey, for generations. And—small world!—Alfred Vail, the indispensable associate of Samuel Morse, was his cousin. Young Theodore had grown up amid telegraph lore on the Vail estate where Morse had lived in genteel poverty for several years. Most importantly, Theodore Vail had been a department head in the U.S. Postal Service, where he was responsible for implementing notable efficiencies. Telephone historian Herbert Casson noted that "by virtue of his position [in the Postal Service] he was the one man in the United States who had a comprehensive view of all railways and telegraphs. He was much more apt, consequently, than other men to develop the idea of a national telephone system."[6] Which is exactly what he did. What made Vail a uniquely valuable leader was his understanding of the importance of networks. As a consequence, he focused on making the company a nationwide institution, with standardized equipment and practices, and rates designed to encourage system expansion; the value of the telephone, he knew, resided in the network rather than the appliance. It may seem a commonplace observation today, but it was a rare insight at the time, when communications networks were in their infancy.

With a conventional economic product—for example, gasoline—if the customer base expands by 10 percent, then sales can be expected to increase by 10 percent; the relationship is linear. But in a network, if the customer base expands by 10 percent, the value of the network *to each and every subscriber* increases at the same time, and network traffic can be expected to increase accordingly. Revenues expand at a rate much greater than in a linear relationship.

It was with the network in mind that Vail continued the early Bell policy of leasing rather than selling telephone equipment. For the network to function, technical standards needed to be uniform across the system; incompatible equipment would lead to inefficiencies and breakdowns. Bell had a choice: it could publish its technical criteria for network equipment and allow competing companies to sell appliances that would meet those standards, or it could restrict use of the network to Bell equipment and preserve the standard in that way. The first option would have been, in modern terms, an *open* network architecture; the second one, the one chosen, was a *closed* architecture. These two approaches to maintaining uniform standards across a network are much in evidence in the modern world of computer communication. Each has its advocates, although proponents of open systems can point to indisputable evidence of increased innovation and more rapid technical development due to the benefits of competition. The explosive early development of the Internet was assisted by the fact that it is a system with open technical specifications.

Prior to Vail's network insights becoming widely accepted, the manifest destiny of the telephone as a home appliance was not immediately clear, even to many of its backers. At first it was believed its main market was limited to business and commerce, it being too expensive for the average householder. This was particularly true in most of Europe, where Sweden was the sole exception that proved the rule. Britain, France, Germany, Russia, Austria-Hungary all lagged far behind the United States and Canada in adopting the telephone.

For a time, telephone promoters experimented with various broadcast applications for the device. As late as 1890 a vice-president of AT&T described "a scheme which we now have on foot, which looks to providing music on tap at certain times every day, especially at meal times. The scheme is to have a fine band perform the choicest music, gather up the sound waves, and distribute them to any number of subscribers."7 In London, Paris and Budapest, telephone technology was actually used for wired broadcasting from the 1890s until displaced by radio broadcasting. In Budapest, Theodore Puskas's six-thousand-subscriber "telephonic newspaper" network broadcast to paying subscribers fourteen hours a day with a mixture of stock market reports, news, music and drama, which sounds remarkably familiar to a modern ear. It remained in business until it was merged into the new Hungarian radio broadcasting organization in 1925 and became merely a "cable" delivery system for radio broadcasts. Historian Carolyn Marvin notes: "Photographs and illustrated advertising posters show that subscribers listened to the [telephone broadcasting service] through two small round earpieces hanging from a diamond-shaped board mounted on the wall. The audience for which the service was intended apparently possessed wealth, education and leisure. Its cultural relaxations were those of the opera and the theater. Its attachment to sport was aristocratic."[8] A copycat service set up in Newark, New Jersey, in 1911 appears to have been a victim of its own success: demand for subscriptions far outstretched the company's financial abilities to supply equipment, and it soon went bankrupt.

A number of telephone companies on both sides of the Atlantic offered either news or scheduled musical entertainment as an incentive to new subscribers, and there were many experiments in broadcasting concerts, particularly operas, over the wires. Church services were another frequent subject of experimental broadcasts. In Woodstock, Ontario, in 1890, an enterprising pub owner anticipated Court TV of one hundred years later by placing telephone microphones in a local courtroom for a notorious murder trial of the day. There were twenty receivers in the tavern, which patrons could rent for 25 cents an hour; four more were available in a private room for ladies.

The failure of wired broadcasting to put down roots may be attributed at least in part to technical reasons. An early problem with the system was the steady weakening of the audio signal as more and more subscribers signed on. By the time suitable amplifiers were developed, radio was a competing reality that afforded the key advantages of reception beyond wire lines and true portability. Nevertheless, it would be an oversight not to list lack of vision among telephone company executives as one of the reasons as well. They seemed wholly preoccupied with enlisting subscribers and fighting their court battles.

Late in 1878, Western Union went to court claiming Bell had infringed Elisha Gray's patent rights to the telephone, and the Bell Telephone Company, newly reorganized and recapitalized, and with Vail at the helm, met the telegraph giant head-on with the country's best patent attorneys. The case carried on for a year before ending with stunning suddenness when Western Union withdrew its suit and sought a negotiated settlement. It had become clear it could not win in court. Under the settlement, Western Union agreed to admit that Alexander Graham Bell was the sole inventor and that his patents were valid, and to retire from the telephone business. Bell, for its part, agreed to buy the Western Union telephone system, pay Western Union a royalty on revenue from telephone rentals for fifteen years, and keep out of the telegraph business. Elisha Gray's Western Electric was given a monopoly contract to supply the Bell system with hardware. It was, all things considered, a brilliant victory for Bell.

An engineer who worked at Edison's Menlo Park research establishment during the period, Francis Jehl, summed up the consequences succinctly in his memoirs: "The Bell instrument is a delicate hearer, while the Edison transmitter possesses a good lung and speaks loudly, so that each does its share of the work, and, together, they have formed an ideal combination and have made the telephone a universal success."[9] With the settlement, Bell shares soared to $1,000. The American Bell Telephone company was organized, capitalized at $6 million dollars. By 1882 the company had doubled it size, and gross earnings reached a million dollars. Bell, Watson and Sanders cashed in their chips to become wealthy men, leaving further commercial development to others. Bell went on to explorations in aircraft and hydrofoils and a dozen other areas at his Cape Breton, Nova Scotia, retreat; Watson founded a successful shipbuilding venture; Sanders lost most of his money in a Colorado gold mine venture; Hubbard became a founder of the National Geographic Society.

Three years after the settlement, in 1882, American Bell purchased Western Union's research and manufacturing arm, Western Electric. In 1907, Bell's new corporate parent, American Telephone and Telegraph Company (AT&T), coolly wrote a cheque for $30 million to purchase control of Western Union itself. AT&T would go on to become the world's largest corporation.[10] By 1900 it had twice as many miles of line as Western Union (five times as many by 1905), and it had installed well over a million telephones in the United States and Canada. Another million had been installed by independent phone companies. So numerous were telephones that the proliferation of overhead wires in cities was becoming a serious blight, and major engineering efforts were devoted to finding the right kind of cable for underground burial. There suddenly appeared dense forests of 80- to 90-foot poles, each carrying thirty or more cross arms and three hundred wires. For decades, many a North American city looked as if it had grown a grotesque system of nervous ganglia on the outside of its skin.

It was in November 1892 that the first automated telephone switchboard went into operation, in La Porte, Indiana, serving about seventy-five subscribers. The facts of its origins are somewhat comical. It was started by an irate Kansas City undertaker, Almon B. Stowger, who was convinced the local telephone operator was turning his business away to a competitor. His automated switching device made her redundant. Stowger's system involved a rotary switch-arm operated by electrical relays that were controlled from the subscriber's phone. The system used four buttons on the phone to "dial" hundreds, tens and ones; the fourth button was to release the connection once the call had been completed. The buttons were replaced by the familiar finger wheel in 1896.[11]

The success of the Stowger switcher was an event of great significance, for the switchboard provided the means by which the telephone could be fully exploited. It meant that the telephone network would become an *addressable system*, that every telephone could be linked to any other telephone, that users could choose where they wanted to be when they made a call. And with automation, there was no practical limit to the size of the network. It was the automated switchboard that made possible the realization of Vail's network vision, and it granted users an entirely new freedom to move from place to place while still remaining in social contact. The telephone switchboard was the linchpin to a communication system that made the world a noticeably more secure and predictable place.

As the telephone showed promise of becoming an international medium, cultural commentators expressed their concerns. Perhaps the most trenchant of these, and certainly the most interesting, were based on the medium's ephemeral nature, and the risk that might pose to truthfulness in communication. Even before the adjective "phony" had been coined, novelist H.G. Wells observed that with electric media, "The businessman may sit at home . . . and tell such lies as he dare not write."

With technology steadily improving, attention turned to long-distance telephony as a new growth area, though it took some imaginative marketing to get the public used to the idea: most people thought of the telegraph when it came to intercity communication. This was partly because it was, and would remain for decades to come, much cheaper than long-distance telephony, and also because telegrams were hand-delivered to the recipient. A telephone call obviously required that both the caller and the recipient have telephones (or access to a Bell facility at the appointed time), and prior to the post–World War II recovery boom, only a small fraction of homes had phones. In New York, a special long-distance salon was set up at Bell headquarters; customers were picked up in cabs and escorted over oriental carpets to silk-draped booths, where their calls were placed. Transcontinental calls would have to await the development of the vacuum-tube amplifier as a by-product of radio; transoceanic telephony by wire rather than radio would become possible only at mid-twentieth century with further improvements in electronics.

Transmission over even moderate distances involved two problems beyond the straightforward amplification hurdle: distortion and interference on the one hand and, on the other, the need to multiplex signals, putting more of them down the same wire so as to get maximum commercial value from very expensive long-distance cables. Telegraphy shared these difficulties, though on a less complex level due to the relative simplicity of the signals being transmitted.

Answers did not come easily. The early grounded-circuit telephones were plagued with baffling noises. Casson provides a colourful description:

> This was, perhaps, the most weird and mystifying of all telephone problems . . . Such a jangle of meaningless noises had never been heard by human ears. There were spluttering and bubbling, jerking and rasping, whistling and screaming. There was the rustling of leaves, the croaking of frogs, the hissing of steam, the flapping of birds' wings. There were clicks from telegraph wires, scraps of talk from other telephones, and curious little squeals that were unlike any known sound. The lines running east and west were noisier than the lines running north and south. The night was noisier than the day, and at the ghostly hour of midnight, for what strange reason no one knows, the babel was at its height. Watson, who had a fanciful mind, suggested that perhaps these sounds were signals from the inhabitants of Mars or some other sociable planet[12] . . . "We were ashamed to present our bills," said A.A. Adee, one of the first agents, "for no matter how plainly a man talked into his telephone, his language was apt to sound like Choctaw at the other end of the line."[13]

The answer to the worst of the early noise problem turned out to be getting rid of the ground return system and instead using a two-wire connection. This (very expensive) conversion was begun in 1883. To help defray some of the cost of doubling up on circuits, a method of "ghosting" a third conversation on two lines was developed.[14]

The real solutions, however, would have to wait until the middle of the twentieth century and the introduction of electronic amplification and pulse code modulation. Pulse code modulation reduced analog (continuously variable) signals to digital, binary code, the simplest possible and therefore least error-prone signal configuration—

off–on, or 0–1. This was done with elegant simplicity by sampling the analog electrical signal produced by the telephone's microphone at regular intervals (many times a second), assigning a binary code to the pitch and amplitude of the wave at each point, and transmitting that code as a stream of ones and zeros. At the receiving end the binary information was decoded and translated back into an analog waveform duplicating the original electrical impulses produced by the microphone. In this form the electrical signal could be converted back into sound by the vibrations of the telephone receiver's diaphragm. It was a relatively simple matter of software programming to identify and eliminate electrical interference from a binary message, and replication of the signal by the many amplifier/repeater stations along the route of telegraph lines no longer involved the introduction of error or distortion as it had with the more complex analog waveform. Binary information could be replicated ad infinitum with little or no error.

Pulse code modulation meant that several telephone conversations could be carried simultaneously on a single line. This was accomplished by interleaving *packets* of binary information in the interstices between wave samplings and in pauses in conversation. The first digital telephone transmission was recorded by Bell Labs in 1956, and the first commercial installations were made by Illinois Bell in Chicago in 1962. The system was called T1 and could carry twenty-four voice signals, or 1.5 megabits of information, over a standard pair of wires.

Now operating in digital mode, telegraph and telephone communication were ready for wholesale adoption of the ultimate digital machine, the electronic computer. Introduced initially for improved automatic error (distortion) correction, buffering and switching, the digital computer would swiftly become the mainstay and workhorse of both systems. Increasingly, the telephone and telegraph systems that shared so much history and so many of the same technologies were being melded together as the telecommunications industry.

The first entirely electronic telephone switching systems were installed in the United States in 1976. Special-purpose computers, they could handle half a million calls an hour as well as special services including toll-free 1-800 numbers and call forwarding. By 1980, more than half of all calls in North America were being switched electronically. A decade later the AT&T system could boast of handling 61 billion calls a year on its 2.75 billion circuit miles of facilities, a system that was now entirely digital from end to end.

A Convivial Technology

O F ALL THE SIGNIFICANT new technologies of the late nineteenth and twentieth centuries—the telegraph, the automobile, the jet aircraft, nuclear energy, television (the list could go on)—the telephone shares with electric lighting the unusual distinction of near-universal public approval. Large numbers of people devote vast amounts of time and energy to criticizing almost every other highly visible technology as perverse and dangerous in one way or another. There are remarkably few jeremiads of the telephone.[1] Why is this?

There is a clue to this mystery in the fact that as an interactive, point-to-point communication device, the telephone had two powerful advantages over that other destroyer of time and space, the telegraph. First, the telephone enabled users to reach one another directly. To send a telegram, by contrast, one had to rely on a series of intermediaries from telephone operators and order clerks to telegraph operators and messengers. The second, and more profound, difference was that the telephone put the electrical encoding device—in this case, the microphone—in the hands of the user. You did not have to know Morse code to use the phone. You did not need an operator's licence, or special training, or special equipment, or official permission to use it. Ordinary speech did the trick.

Philosopher and social critic Ivan Illich includes the telephone in his list of modern technologies that foster self-realization by enhancing "the ability of people to pursue their own goals in their unique way." Illich calls these "convivial" tools:

> Tools foster conviviality to the extent to which they can be easily used, by anybody, as often or as seldom as desired, for the accomplishment of a purpose chosen by the user. The use of such tools by one person does not restrain another from using them equally. They do not require previous certification [licensing] of the user. Their existence does not impose any obligation to use them. They allow the user to express his meaning in action.[2]

Most hand tools and simple mechanical devices meet this definition, whereas nuclear power plants and modern, computerized automobiles do not. Convivial tools (and institutions) foster self-reliance and self-realization; "manipulative" tools foster dependency, passivity and alienation. But even simple tools can be made non-convivial, or manipulative in Illich's terms, if they are restricted "through some institutional arrangements. They can be restricted by becoming the monopoly of one profession, as happens with dentist drills through the requirement of a license and with libraries or laboratories by placing them within schools."[3]

The conviviality of a tool really has nothing to do with its level of technological complexity. As we'll discover, radio fits the definition of a convivial tool that was made manipulative by institutional arrangements. The telephone, however, with its complex hi-tech network, has fit Illich's definition of a "convivial," or people-friendly, technology from its introduction, and continues to do so. "Anybody can dial the person of his choice if he can afford a coin," notes Illich. "The telephone lets anybody say what he wants to the person of his choice; he can conduct business, express love, or pick a quarrel. It is impossible for bureaucrats to define what people say to each other on the phone, even though they can interfere with—or protect— the privacy of their exchange."[4]

If one were to rate communications technologies according to their conviviality, the telephone would rank near the top of the list, right after the alphabet and the printing press, which Illich has called "almost ideally convivial. Almost anybody can learn to use [printing presses], and for his own purpose. They use cheap materials. People can take them or leave them as they wish. They are not easily controlled by third parties . . . The alphabet and the printing press have in principle deprofessionalized the recorded word."[5]

In the same way, the telephone "deprofessionalized" rapid long-distance communication. The telegraph (and radiotelegraph) required trained and licensed intermediaries—telegraphers—to interpret messages; telegraphers were the modern-day equivalent of the ancient Egyptian scribes. Effective two-way radio communication has long been restricted to those who can obtain the requisite government licences. Only the telephone, among these technologies, is truly people-friendly. Not only is it cheap and simple to use, but it gives the user exactly what he or she wants of it, rather than what some third party wants the user to get. By this definition, the Internet would also qualify as convivial.

Put another way, the telephone permits unmediated conversation. Given the social importance of conversation, or the sharing of person-to-person communication, to the species from pre-hominid days onward, it is not difficult to see why such a useful extension of this fundamental means of social intercourse would be warmly welcomed.

At yet another level, people appreciate the telephone almost unreservedly because it is a tool that works for *them*, when so many other technologies require them to work for the machine. It is not necessary to alter ordinary behaviour in any way in order to make use of the telephone; one simply uses it when it's needed. Applications such as voice mail and telemarketing, which tend to reverse this equation, are disliked and reviled, with justification.

It is helpful to look at these issues through the lens provided by the philosopher Jurgen Habermas. Habermas had the misfortune to grow up in wartime Germany in a family that clung to Nazi sympathies to the bitter end. He was a member of the Nazi youth movement, as were most German children, and at fifteen he was sent to serve on the western front, where Hitler's armies were being decimated in the dying days of the war. He has spoken of the shattering realization he experienced in following the post-war Nuremberg trials of Nazi war criminals, which exposed the lies and perversions of beliefs that had been forced upon him as a child. As an exceptionally bright, though shy, university student (he was born with a cleft palate that has caused a slight facial disfigurement and a minor speech impediment) Habermas was driven to try to understand how his country could have been duped by Nazi propaganda and institutions. Deeply engaged as a public intellectual in debates surrounding the evolution of democracy and its institutions in Europe and around the world, his writings have been credited with inspiring several of the successful anti-Communist revolutions in Eastern Europe in the late 1980s. He placed great emphasis on the need for authentic communication in society, and on the concomitant need for the creation and preservation of public spaces in which such communication can freely take place.

Habermas distinguishes between the instrumental and the truly communicative when he considers what is generically known as communication. Instrumental communication is aimed at getting things done, at satisfying wants. To be effective it needs to be simple and straightforward, clear of ambiguity. As such, it is amenable to machine duplication, and much of the world's economic and bureaucratic business is in fact carried on automatically, in the background, as it were, by computers and other devices. Habermas calls this institutional arena of highly automated communication "the system." Genuine communicative action, by contrast, is aimed at mutual understanding, and it employs language and experience of the real world of people, with all its emotion, ambiguity, playfulness, concern for values, and general, unavoidable fuzziness. The arena in which this kind of communication takes place he calls the "life world," with its public spaces dedicated to encouraging just such fruitful, if "inefficient," human interaction.

Habermas recognizes that societies need both varieties of communication. But he warns that unless we choose our institutions and technologies carefully, we can find ourselves living in a world (or in his case, returning to a world) in which the system overwhelms the life world, in which we spend our time conforming to rules rather than engaging in dialogue, carrying out tasks rather than partaking of experiences we can share with fellow humans. Our lives will increasingly be lived according to patterns that have no human meaning or significance.

If we can think of Habermas's "systems" as mediated communication, or, in Illich's terminology, "manipulative" or "non-convivial" technologies, we can see how life in such a world becomes more and more complex in the sense of more dependent on rules and regulations and less dependent on the consensus and understanding arrived at through true communication.[6] In a world dominated by non-convivial technologies, our choices will be increasingly restricted to those dictated by technology. Meaning and understanding will be marginalized in favour of required procedures and processes, and reasonable behaviour will be defined in terms of conformity to these requirements.[7]

For Habermas, then, as for Illich, our choices of tools of communication are important, in that some promote and encourage the values of the life world, while others favour the system's idea of productivity—getting things done efficiently, regardless of other, more human, considerations.

It should be acknowledged here that, when it was first introduced, the telephone did have its share of critics, especially in Britain, where it was feared that it would promote the breakdown of barriers between the classes. The problem was precisely the telephone's unmediated character. After all, if anybody could have a telephone, the lady or gentleman of the manor would have no idea who might be on the other end of the line when he or she answered the incessant ring, much less what the caller might say. The risk of being exposed to unseemly language and other forms of rudeness—or simply of having to speak to someone to whom one had not been properly introduced—was high. Of course, the solution was to not have a telephone, or to keep it safely tucked away in the servants' quarters (where a servant could mediate between caller and recipient). Market penetration of the telephone in Britain was significantly slower than in North America in part for this reason, and in part because of the disparity in average affluence. In America, the class argument was heard, but it was discreetly framed in terms of unnecessary invasions of the privacy and tranquility of the home, which proved a considerably weaker deterrent to adoption of the device.

All of this serves to highlight the fact that the telephone was to become (and remains) a powerful democratizing influence. It accomplished this, albeit unconsciously, by the stratagem of having all telephone users *subscribe* to the system. It was this fact of common subscription to a shared system that was the equalizing factor. The system treated everyone the same: nobody's voice, nobody's ring, was louder than anybody else's on the telephone network. The appliances themselves, thanks to the system's demands for technical uniformity, were pretty much alike whether they were to be found in a palace or a tenement. (Western Electric marketed coloured telephones for the first time in 1954.) British communications theorist Colin Cherry observed that

> we are so accustomed to such ideas today that we may forget that such liberties of approach by one person to another, irrespective of rank, did not exist in such egalitarian forms in the nineteenth century. Letters of introduction might have been needed, for example. The telephone service, at one stroke, introduced this totally new concept—that persons of all ranks could be members of the same subscriber organization, with common rights, rights of "membership."[8]

In the early 1970s, the telephone industry attracted its share of criticism from the anti-establishment counterculture in North

America. But it was the establishment and not the technology that came under fire. The technology, in fact, was a source of deep fascination for an emerging subculture of technological whiz kids known as "phone hackers" or "phone phreaks." Homemade "blue boxes" that could manipulate the long-distance phone network by imitating its coded audio signals were distributed widely throughout North America. They allowed the user to make long-distance calls without paying for them. Phone phreaks took pleasure in manipulating the system for its own sake, in bouncing a call through the network, off satellites, across oceanic cables and perhaps back to the phone in the next room. It was the computer switching and the network system that intrigued them; few were in it for the money, although it is estimated by AT&T that $20 million in free calls were made using blue boxes in each year of the 1970s, until the company upgraded its security measures, ending the fad. Many phone phreaks found themselves deeply involved in the computer industry as it, and they, matured during the seventies and eighties. Two well-known blue box manufacturers, remembered for the high quality of the products they sold around the San Francisco Bay area, were Steve Jobs and Steve Wozniak, who went on to establish Apple Computer.

In its business and institutional (as opposed to domestic) uses, the telephone extended and amplified the impact of the telegraph in creating global markets. But Marshall McLuhan has argued that it also had an important impact on organizational structures, tending to "flatten" them. The telephone introduced "a seamless web of interlaced patterns of management and decision-making," McLuhan claimed. "It is not feasible to exercise delegated authority by telephone. The pyramidal structure of job-division and description and delegated powers cannot withstand the speed of the phone to bypass all hierarchical arrangements, and to involve people in depth."9

One challenges McLuhan at one's peril, but there is good evidence that the impact of the telephone on bureaucracies was in many cases just the opposite: while it permitted geographic decentralization, it encouraged organizational pyramid-building. Urban

police forces, for instance, rebuilt their operations around the telephone call box. Police officers, who had previously patrolled streets
more or less autonomously to prevent crime and occasionally to
apprehend suspects, were by 1917–18 more likely to be assigned
to squad cars stationed at call boxes, where they would wait for an
order from the police dispatcher to respond to a crime in progress or
already committed. The telephone centralized authority and control
at the precinct office rather than on the street, and moved police
away from crime prevention to a more purely reactive stance. Steven
Lubar writes, in *Infoculture*:

> Many businesses used [the telephone] to centralize operations,
> a process already started by the telegraph and by other trends
> in American management. Salesmen were required to report in
> every day and get instructions. The telephone, *Telephony* maga-
> zine opined in 1906, "has curtailed the functions and respon-
> sibilities of a district manager as the cable has those of an
> ambassador." The phone made it easier to separate manufac-
> turing plants from the offices where company sales and man-
> agement staff worked, helping to create downtown office
> districts.[10]

Telephone historian Herbert Casson claims that, in the early
days in which he was an observer, the phone also had a salutary
effect on manners. Speaking of the telephone operator, invariably a
woman, Casson says:

> To give the young lady her due, we must acknowledge that she
> has done more than any other person to introduce courtesy
> into the business world. She has done most to abolish the old-
> time roughness and vulgarity . . . She has shown how to take
> the friction out of conversation, and taught us refinements of
> politeness which were rare even among the Beau Brummels
> of pre-telephonic days . . . This propaganda of politeness has
> gone so far that today the man who is profane or abusive at the

telephone, is cut off from the use of it. He is cast out as unfit for a telephone-using community.[11]

If there is anything we don't like about the telephone, it is its insistent nature. McLuhan points us to what must be one of the most bizarre demonstrations on record of this aspect of the phone, as described in the pages of the *New York Times*:

> On September 6, 1949, a psychotic veteran, Howard R. Unruh, in a mad rampage killed thirteen people, and then returned home. Emergency crews, bringing up machine guns, shotguns and tear gas bombs, opened fire. At this point an editor of the *Camden Evening Courier* looked up Unruh's name in the telephone directory and called him. Unruh stopped firing and answered, "Hello."
> "This Howard?"
> "Yes . . ."
> "Why are you killing people?"
> "I don't know. I can't answer that yet. I'll have to talk to you later. I'm too busy now."[12]

The abuse of the private and personal quality of the telephone (the quality that makes its ringing so irresistible) by telemarketers, pollsters and others is a serious issue and one that is increasingly being addressed by governments. Washington instituted a national "do not call" registry in 2003, and within months it contained the phone numbers of tens of millions of Americans. Marketers who call registered numbers are subject to substantial fines. A year later, Canada announced it would follow suit.

It is perhaps paradoxical that the intimacy of the telephone should be a characteristic of what is a public space. But society has defined the telephone system as a public utility and the network as public space from the earliest stages of the technology's development. Governments have either taken over responsibility for telephones outright, as in Britain and much of Europe, or they have granted closely regulated private monopolies, as in Canada and the U.S., on the understanding that the space created by the network is public and the monopoly is there to serve the public interest. The 1902 government of Sir Wilfrid Laurier in Canada, for example, passed legislation that required Bell Canada to provide service to any person within its monopoly territory "with all reasonable dispatch," and forbade changes in rates without government approval.

As we've already noted, the telephone industry was slow to realize that the device's most valuable application would be in personal communication, and even slower to see that they were creating a new form of agora, or public space, with their networks of wire. To the extent that they did realize it, they resisted the trend. Telephone companies everywhere initially did all they could to discourage "frivolous" chatter over their lines, insisting that the resources must be used for legitimate business purposes, much like the telegraph. Women, in particular, were discouraged from using the phone, it being assumed that their conversations would be of small substance! But ordinary users prevailed in their superior though "non-expert" understanding of the telephone's real utility, and by the 1920s phone companies had seen the handwriting on the wall and were beginning to encourage social uses of the appliance. And women at home with children continued to use it, as they had from the beginning, for the very useful purpose of keeping in touch with family and friends in the community.

Surprisingly few studies have been done of how people use the telephone in their daily, domestic lives. Those that exist indicate that it has become an integral part of the social structure, whose value is difficult to measure in monetary terms. When the Australian telecommunications authority considered bowing to pressure from local telephone companies that wanted to switch to a fee-for-time charge from the existing flat rate for local calls, sociologist Ann Moyal was prompted to gather some research data on how Australian women use the phone, in the belief that "important social data should be added to the equation." Moyal found that the cross-section of women studied made from two to six calls a week for "instrumental" purposes such as setting up appointments for themselves and their families, volunteer activities or in pursuit of information. These calls normally lasted from one to three minutes. On the other hand, the women made between fourteen and forty-two personal or "intrinsic" telephone calls a week, many of them long distance. (Habermas would regard these as representing true "communicative action.") Respondents confirmed "that the prime importance of the telephone in their daily life related to 'sustaining family relationships' and to their contact with children, parents and to a less regular extent, with siblings, grandchildren and other members of the family." One particular family relationship stood out above the others in terms of telephone time consumed: "A singular proportion of these calls and time is devoted to communication between mothers and daughters, who establish telephone contact daily or regularly throughout the week, and maintain an intimate and caring telephone relationship across their lives." Communication was particularly intense when the daughter was in a child-bearing or child-caring mode.

The value of this kind of communication for social stability and quality of life would be difficult to overestimate, and yet it is precisely the kind of telephone use that has been derided over the years, even when it has not been actively discouraged by the telephone companies. Moyal calls it "a pervasive feminine culture of the telephone in which kinkeeping, nurturing, community support, and the caring culture of women forms a key dynamic of our society."[13] Legislators and regulators who try to restrict this kind of communication do so at their peril, Moyal suggests.

The virtual space created by a telephone network, the space in which conversations take place and through which data flows on its way to its destination, has been variously called the "telecosm" and the "telesphere." The law in democratic societies treats it as sacrosanct, in the same way in which the law treats real public space as affording inviolable communal rights to all citizens. The law also recognizes that there are limits to those rights, and responsibilities that come with them. Defacing public property is an offence; citizens are expected to put their litter in trash bins. No one has the right to tell me how to deport myself in a public space—unless what I'm doing prevents others from enjoying their rights to the space. The same or analogous rights and responsibilities exist in the virtual public space of the telephone network. Some of the affronts to the conviviality of the telephone system, such as voice mail and automated call answering and recorded advertising messages, are merely the equivalent of boorish behaviour in real space. But others, such as unsolicited marketing calls and harassing calls from collection agencies, have been made illegal in many jurisdictions because they present a threat to the continued healthy functioning of the network. Just as persistent solicitation or threatening behaviour causes people to avoid some urban public spaces, abuses of the telephone network result in more and more levels of interference between users in the form of call screening devices of various kinds. Just as real public space infested with annoying and threatening people can fester and die and be lost to the public, so are virtual spaces at risk and in need of policing.

Nowadays we think instantly of blue-uniformed, gun-toting officers when we think of policing, but professional police forces are a recent innovation. Before the bobby appeared on London streets in the days of Wellington and Napoleon, policing public spaces was handled largely by the citizenry that owned them and used them. A little "self-policing" in the public space of the telephone network, in the form of letters to offenders and other lobbying activities, can go a long way toward keeping it a safe and healthy environment. It would also be an appropriate response in an era in which we are discovering that institutional responses to public problems are not always the best idea: the well-meaning ministrations of government and regulators can be more dangerous than the condition they aim to cure. We are all citizens of the telesphere, and we need to take our individual responsibilities seriously.

The development of radio is the next chapter in the sequential story of communications technologies, but we must jump ahead briefly here to acknowledge the very significant merger of the telephone with radio to produce the phenomenon of the mobile phone, better known in North America as the cell phone, after the cellular nature of the radio network that receives and hands off calls from one transceiver (cell) to another. The mobile phone combined the personal nature of telephone communication with the ability of radio to break loose from the land line network, allowing the user to roam at will, to be reached literally anywhere on the globe. Although the first mobile phone licences were granted in the U.S. in 1983, it wasn't until 1989 that the million-subscriber mark was reached, thanks to the miniaturization of the appliance itself. By the mid-1990s the cell phone had become a social phenomenon throughout the developed world: Finland, Italy, Britain, Canada and Japan all exceeded the U.S. in subscriptions per capita. In 1995, there were about 91 million cellular subscribers worldwide. By 2000, the number had risen to 946 million, a tenfold increase. By the dawn of the twenty-first century, mobile telephony had developed significant markets for mobile text messaging and photography, and had begun exploring video applications.

In the Third World, mobile telephony leapfrogged traditional land line technology to make the mobile phone globally ubiquitous. Outside the OECD, between 1995 and 2000, telephone subscriber growth was about 130 percent for land lines and over 2,300 percent for cellular phones—there were 14 million mobile subscribers at the beginning of this period and 342 million by the end. Twenty-seven countries had annual growth rates of over 100 percent in the period, which means they achieved a better than sixtyfold cumulative growth in mobile telephone penetration. In that five-year period, Senegal went from roughly 100 subscribers to 390,000; Egypt from 7,000 to nearly 3 million; Romania from 9,000 to almost 4 million. An additional forty-four countries with no measurable wireless penetration in 1995 had measurable numbers by 2001.[14]

In terms of its social impact, mobile telephony has been a mixed blessing. In countries with weak communication infrastructures, the mobile has enabled a leap ahead into the world of "connected intelligence"[15] without the massive expense of installing conventional wired networks nationwide. This has, overnight, brought the undoubted advantages of telephony to billions of people worldwide. But the benefits of "keeping in touch" offered by the phone can become a burden if one is never able to be *dis*connected. There is almost always a control element to communication, and when communication resources and opportunities improve, so do opportunities for control by what Habermas calls the system. Corporations have found that more productivity can be squeezed from managers and other workers if they are constantly reachable, which has meant that the concept of being "off duty" has vanished for many. This takes its toll both socially and psychologically. The notions of privacy and solitude begin to seem quaintly inefficient to some, sadly nostalgic to others.

The next step in the integrating of the telephone into the worldwide communication and information cloud that is the Internet is well under way, with industry forecasts suggesting that most mobile phones will have wireless Internet access before the end of this decade. The telephone is morphing into a personal communication device capable of everything the desktop or laptop computer with high-speed Internet access can do. It can communicate aurally, textually and visually, in real time, and it can do so asychronously, depositing messages to be read by the recipient later. As the cost of these do-everything devices continues to fall, distribution will become virtually ubiquitous, surpassing even the phenomenal market penetration of the standard cellular phone.

The mobile telephone industry markets its products as personal freedom devices, focusing on the individual. The new do-everything phone "becomes literally your personal communications centre . . ."[16] In the context of Habermas's thought, this is "system-speak." The notion of "personal" communication is almost an oxymoron, like one hand clapping, since real communication is a process involving at least two persons, the most important of whom is the listener. What is crucial in communication is the reception of information, that is, *understanding*. And so the truly significant thing about the evolving field of personal communication by mobile telephony is not so much the "freedom" offered to the individual user as the expansion of the public space we've been calling the telesphere: it is a social rather than a personal phenomenon that is growing up around us.

The Invention of Radio

W ITH THE INVENTION OF RADIO, we arrive at the appearance of a communications technology that has two unique, defining characteristics, both subjects of fascination, one innately occurring and the other imposed artificially for complex political and economic reasons. The first of these characteristics is its ability to communicate information at great distances without wires or other material connections between sender and receiver. The second is its adoption as a medium of mass communication, wherein messages originating at a central transmission point are broadcast to many "dumb" or passive receivers, which may be located anywhere within the transmitter's range.

The quality of "wirelessness" is one of great scientific and technological significance. The adoption of a unilateral or one-way model for radio as a public appliance, on the other hand, raises issues of historic social and political significance that spill into our own era, and speak directly to our relationship to the new computer-mediated communications technologies. Understanding radio and its history is the key to a comprehension of the major social and technical issues surrounding both television and the Internet. The next several chapters will therefore be devoted to this engrossing and illuminating saga.

And we will begin with Guglielmo Marconi, though that is not, strictly speaking, the beginning of the story. The world celebrates Marconi as the "father of radio" not because he invented it, but because he recognized its potential as a communications technology. The phenomenon of radio waves and their creation by electricity, as he freely acknowledged, had been discovered by others. They were a cosmopolitan group. In constructing experiments to test mathematical predictions published by James Clerk Maxwell in 1873, Heinrich Hertz found that waves of electrical energy did indeed emanate from an electrical spark, as Maxwell's equations had predicted, and that this energy spread in concentric circles through space, travelling at the speed of light. He published his findings in 1888, but he died before he was able to pursue the practical possibilities held out by this phenomenon.

Few people, in fact, seem to have grasped the real import of Hertz's discovery. There was one amazingly prescient exception: British scientist Sir William Crookes, writing in a contemporary magazine, saw "a new and astonishing world" emerging from Hertz's work. "Rays of light will not pierce through a wall, nor, as we know only too well, through a London fog. But the electrical vibrations of a yard or more in wave length . . . will easily pierce such mediums, which to them will be transparent . . . Here, then, is revealed the bewildering possibility of telegraph without wires."[1]

By the time Marconi began his experiments in wireless telegraphy in 1894, the key discoveries and inventions out of which the technology would be built had all been made. It remained for the young inventor to put them together in a practical package, and he could hardly believe his good fortune at having been given that opportunity. "I could scarcely conceive," he said years afterward, "that it was possible that their [radio waves'] application to useful purposes could have escaped the notice of eminent scientists." But invention requires more than technical knowledge and imagination; it demands, as well, an ability to correctly anticipate how the invention might best be used, or, in Marconi's words, its "application to useful purposes."[2] Marconi's great insight, his masterpiece of creative thinking, was in seeing radio's potential value as an instrument with which it would be possible to communicate messages *to distant recipients whose position was unknown.* No other means of communication permitted this seemingly impossible feat.

Marconi himself perfectly defined the secret of his success as a pioneer in a speech he gave late in his life to the Royal Institution of Great Britain: "Long experience has . . . taught me not always to believe in the limitations indicated by purely theoretical considerations or even by calculations. They are, as we well know, often based on insufficient knowledge of all the relevant factors. I believe, in spite of adverse forecasts, in trying out new lines of research however unpromising they may seem at first sight."[3]

He had early seen the most exciting possibilities for his apparatus in providing ship-to-shore communication, a need that could not be served by either telegraph or telephone, and with that in mind he chose to develop his ideas in the world's greatest maritime nation, Great Britain. With the backing of his mother's Anglo-Irish family (the Jamesons of Irish whiskey fame), Marconi patented his wireless telegraph in England. The year was 1896, and he was just twenty-two.

Within three years of securing his patent, he was operating a handful of small coastal radio stations and had equipped several ships with radio gear. It was by most standards a thriving business, though overextended in the manner of many a start-up firm: by 1898 his Wireless Telegraph and Signal Company was capitalized at $500,000. But competition was snapping at his heels, in Germany from the principals of what would eventually become the Telefunken company, and in the persons of Reginald Fessenden and Lee De Forest, both of whom were making significant advances in radio technologies in the United States. Marconi's marketing instincts and his determination to maintain leadership in the fast-developing field led him to announce his intention to link North America to Europe by radio, a feat deemed by conventional wisdom to be not just impossible, but absurdly so.

Since radio waves were known to travel in straight lines, and since the curvature of the earth makes it impossible to draw a line of sight between two points on the surface more than about one hundred miles apart, one hundred miles was, in the unanimous scientific opinion of the day, the limiting distance for practical radio communication. Between North America and England there was a mountain of ocean more than 160 miles high! Marconi, however, suspected that radio waves would travel along the earth's surface, following the curvature according to well-understood laws of diffraction of light. Indeed, he had conducted experiments in which he had received signals at twice the distance line-of-sight calculations told him were possible. He went to his board of directors with a bold proposition: he wanted funding released to build two stations, one on each side of the Atlantic Ocean.

Neither Marconi nor his scientific detractors were correct in terms of what we now know about long-range radio propagation. Radio waves do indeed travel in straight lines, as the scientists said, but they also bounce off the underside of the ionized (electrically charged) layer high in the atmosphere known as the ionosphere, and are thus reflected back to earth far beyond the horizon. In some conditions they will be reflected back up to the ionosphere by the earth's surface, leading to transmissions of several "hops" covering globe-girdling distances.

Marconi's initial choice of location for his North American station was Cape Cod, Massachusetts. There, he had a replica of his new Poldhu, Cornwall, station built, near the village of South Wellfleet. Before the tests could take place, however, the Poldhu antenna array blew down in a storm. A smaller substitute antenna was quickly lashed together. Then the antenna at Cape Cod was demolished in a September gale. A temporary array was set up, a fan of wires strung between two 150-foot masts. A November nor'easter brought that down before it could be put into service.

Haunted by visions of being beaten to the punch by competitors in America or perhaps Germany or elsewhere, the inventor hastily packed a few wicker trunks with wire, some kites and balloons, and a selection of receiving devices and set out for Newfoundland, geographically the closest spot in North America to his Cornwall station and therefore, presumably, the easiest transatlantic hop for radio waves. There, he was warmly welcomed by Governor Sir Charles Cavendish Boyle and Prime Minister Sir Robert Bond, who gave him use of an abandoned military hospital on Signal Hill, a windswept promontory six hundred feet above St. John's Harbour, looking straight out to sea in the direction of England. He could scarcely have found a more appropriate location for his experiment. Signal Hill had been used in communications since the sixteenth century, when a signal cannon was put in place. During the Napoleonic Wars, signal flags had been flown there, warning ships at sea about navigation hazards and weather. When Marconi arrived, work had just been completed on Cabot Tower, a monument commemorating the four hundredth anniversary of explorer John Cabot's landing on the beaches below.

By December 9, Marconi and his two assistants had finished assembling their equipment in a ground floor room of the barracks, and Marconi cabled Poldhu to begin transmitting the letter *s* continuously between the hours of 11 a.m. and 3 p.m. from December 11.

Gale-force winds played havoc with kite-borne antennas lofted by Marconi's men, but then, just after noon on December 12, 1901, Marconi heard, very faintly but nevertheless distinctly, the *tap, tap, tap* of the letter *s* being repeated over and over. It could only be the station at Poldhu, two thousand miles away. His assistant, George Kemp, clapped on the headphones and confirmed what he had heard. Faint signals were also heard on the following day. Marconi cabled word of the success to London and then informed the press on December 14. The news caused a sensation that rippled around the globe. On December 15, the *New York Times* began its story with: "Guglielmo Marconi announced tonight the most wonderful scientific development in modern times."

But the news caused consternation in the London offices of the Anglo-American Telegraph Company, which owned the enormously expensive England-to-Newfoundland undersea cable over which Marconi had sent his telegrams to Poldhu. Marconi's success confirmed their worst nightmares: the upstart new radio technology would begin competing with them for overseas traffic, with the huge operating advantage of not having to lay cable. The company immediately wired Marconi, ordering him to cease and desist, or face a lawsuit for damages on grounds that Anglo-American had monopoly rights to telegraphy in Newfoundland. The damage was real: Anglo-American's stock on the London exchange had plummeted steadily in the days following Marconi's announcement. At stake was a business that, by 1900, involved twelve transatlantic cables carrying about 25 million words a year at 25 cents a word.

Marconi, it is reported, greeted the threat with a dismissive laugh, but the governor and council of Newfoundland were suitably affronted on his behalf. On December 20, the council passed a resolution stating: "The Council are much gratified at Signor Marconi's success, marking as it does, the dawn of a new era in transoceanic telegraphy, and deplore the action of the Anglo-American Company." A celebratory banquet was held in St. John's and the council visited the wireless station en masse in a show of solidarity.

It was a telling episode, and it served to underline a watershed between nineteenth- and twentieth-century technology, between the monumental and imposing, and the small and ephemeral.[4] No one has described this difference so well as Marconi's daughter Degna in her delightful biography *My Father, Marconi*:

> In the eyes of the world what Marconi had done with two balloons and six kites was magic, an occult modern mystery. The Field achievement [of the first transatlantic undersea cable] was by comparison pedestrian and cumbersome. He himself had written when he was taken aboard the *Great Eastern* to see the ship's crew through their heavy labours, towards the end of the cable-laying voyage, that there had been on board "ten bullocks, one milk cow, 144 sheep, 20 pigs, 29 geese, 14 turkeys, 500 fowls as live stock and dead stock in larger numbers, including 28 bullocks and eighteen thousand eggs." Nor was this all. When they dragged the ocean floor to bring up the "slimy

monster," they had to use twenty miles of rope twisted with wires of steel in order to bear the strain imposed by thirty tons of cable. It took two hours even to lower it to the bottom. As against this, Marconi had instantaneously caught his intangible train of waves with a kite that could be packed in a wicker hamper and weighed a few ounces.[5]

In some scientific quarters, the news caused plain disbelief. Why was no independent witness present, just Marconi himself and a co-worker? How was it possible for radio waves to be heard so far beyond the horizon? Thomas Edison, asked for comment by a New York newspaper, said: "I do not believe that Marconi has succeeded as of yet. If it were true that he had accomplished his object I believe he would announce it himself over his own signature." Marconi, in turn, asked to comment on Edison's skepticism, told a reporter the signals were absolutely genuine, and that Governor Boyle, at Marconi's request, had cabled the fact to King Edward.

As recently as the 1980s (the last time anybody checked) there were still scientists and engineers who believed it was impossible for Marconi's Poldhu station, transmitting in daylight on a frequency assumed to be about 820 kilohertz (near the bottom of today's AM radio band), to have reached Signal Hill, and it does seem a technically problematic proposition in light of what is known today about absorption of such long-wave signals by the atmosphere during daylight hours. It is possible that Marconi was hearing one of the many harmonics of the main Poldhu signal, reaching him on much shorter wavelengths not so much affected by daylight and the ionizing effects of sunlight on the atmosphere.

In any case, the controversy became moot three months later when Marconi sailed from Southampton to New York aboard the liner *Philadelphia*, which he had equipped with the latest in receiving equipment and an elaborate masthead antenna. On that trip, signals from Poldhu were heard loud and clear during daylight hours up to a distance of 700 miles, and more than 2,000 miles at night. This time, there were plenty of witnesses.

When it came to finding a commercially and geographically salubrious site in North America for a permanent terminus for commercial transatlantic service, Marconi made a surprising choice. Geography indicated Newfoundland as the best location (assuming Anglo-American's objections could be overcome), but Marconi was now confident that his signals could reach much farther, into more commercially promising regions of the continent; while commerce suggested Cape Cod, his original selection, nearer to the big American markets. But Cape Breton Island in Nova Scotia won the contest, thanks to some aggressive entrepreneurial thinking on the part of the Nova Scotian and Canadian governments.

Word had spread quickly of Marconi's decision to leave Newfoundland, and there had been many offers of assistance. Alexander Graham Bell cabled him from his lab in Cape Breton to offer a place to work. Cape Breton member of Parliament Alec Johnston knew that the inventor would disembark from his steamer at North Sydney on the island, where he would catch the train for New York. He met Marconi on the dock and immediately suggested that Cape Breton would make an ideal North American terminus for his continuing experiments. There were no telegraph monopolies in Canada, he explained, and the island's eastern coastal cliffs afforded a clear shot to Poldhu. Within hours, the Nova Scotian premier, G.H. Murray, was in North Sydney, twisting Marconi's arm as well. The train for New York left without him. Cornelius Shields, the manager of the Dominion Coal Company, which owned the local railway and much of the land in the area, was dragooned into service, and Marconi was bundled aboard a special railway car, to be shown likely transmitter sites between Sydney and Louisbourg.

Between the villages of Bridgeport and Glace Bay, the rail line crossed a flat headland high above the ocean, and here the train was stopped. While the engine idled, chuffing smoke and seeping steam, Marconi and his companions strode through the grass and scrub to the cliff's edge, the ocean stretching before them into a blue haze. When Shields saw Marconi's enthusiasm, he offered on the spot to give him the land free of charge.

That evening, over dinner in the Sydney Hotel, enthusiasm waxed further. The Nova Scotians told Marconi they believed the federal government in Ottawa would be willing to finance construction of his station, and if it was not, money could be raised locally. The next day, Marconi was whisked by rail to Ottawa, where he received an immediate appointment with Prime Minister Sir Wilfrid Laurier. By the following night, contracts had been drawn and the Government of Canada had pledged $75,000 to cover the complete construction costs of establishing a wireless station at Table Head, Nova Scotia. Marconi now continued his interrupted journey to New York, no doubt suitably impressed with the diligence of Canadian officialdom, and pleased to have substantial portions of his company's research and development costs underwritten.

By 1902, Table Head was in routine communication with Poldhu, the first regular transatlantic radio link.[6] Two years later, the station and its four tall wooden antenna masts were torn down and relocated farther inland, on land now known as Marconi Towers. It was paired with a new station at Clifden, Ireland, and they became the twin termini of the world's first commercial radiotelegraphic service.[7] To send a message cost 17 cents a word, the price of a decent breakfast in many a restaurant. However, this sum compared well with the undersea cable prices of the Anglo-American Telegraph Company, which were 24 cents a word.

Marconi's considerable gifts as a businessman were not in managing corporate bureaucracy; he left that to growing ranks of company subordinates. But he was astute at choosing employees for key positions, and was capable of engendering fierce loyalty thanks to an absence of what the British call "side," coupled with his willingness to get down in the trenches and operate the equipment or help out with repairs at the isolated radio stations he'd built. In his early life of meteoric success (including a Nobel Prize in physics in 1909) he overcame an innate shyness to enjoy the attention he attracted, especially from women. He was a regular in the pages of *Vanity Fair*, an early twentieth-century celebrity likely to be mobbed wherever he went in the world. His first wife divorced him after tolerating many a romantic dalliance. Both she and Marconi would remarry, he choosing a woman twenty years his junior. Soon after, he converted to Catholicism, and soon after that he installed a permanent radio link between the Vatican and the Pope's summer retreat at Castel Gondolfo, using the "impossibly" short wavelength of fifty centimetres. He would continue experimenting with short wavelengths, which he felt were being unjustifiably neglected by the engineering community he had helped to establish.

In 1923, apparently after much soul-searching, Marconi concluded it was his patriotic duty to join Italy's Fascist Party. Mussolini was understandably delighted to have the support of such a celebrated international figure, and throughout the subsequent years until Marconi's death he made frequent use of the inventor as a roving diplomat and apologist for Fascist foreign policy.

Marconi died on July 21, 1937. The following day, almost all of the world's radio stations, including broadcast stations, observed two minutes of silence. It was the first and last time since radio's invention that the planet's airwaves had been so silent.

Radio Goes International

ARCONI and his London backers had always had a global vision for the company, and they pursued it with remarkable diligence. By 1899, an American arm of the company had been established and an ambitious, worldwide shore-station construction program was under way. By 1903, the Marconi companies dominated wireless telegraphy to a degree that was beginning to cause international concern. Fiercely protective of its many patents and its commercial leadership, the company refused to sell its equipment; it was available only for lease (along with a Marconi-trained operator), an arrangement that allowed the user a certain number of words per month, beyond which surcharges kicked in.

Its shore stations, scattered by now around the world, refused to carry messages originating from non-Marconi equipment other than distress signals. A word was coined for all of this: *Marconiism.* It meant that Marconi was not selling equipment so much as "communications," an effective and far-sighted business strategy. From a modern perspective, it amounted to a means of controlling the technical standards by which communication took place. Closing the system architecture is an approach to market control that has been used throughout modern communications history, notably by Bell Telephone. Marconi and his backers realized that, as had been the case with the telephone, the real money was in the network rather than the hardware.

Given Marconi's suffocating dominance in strategically located shore stations and its market command in shipboard equipment, it was exceedingly difficult for other manufacturers to break into the industry. This raised wider geopolitical issues: Britain already controlled a majority of the world's growing web of transoceanic telegraph cables; other nations, particularly Germany at this time, were loath to allow her to monopolize international communications by dominating wireless telegraphy as well. Problems were cropping up on a more mundane level as well. The airwaves were becoming more and more chaotic in the complete absence of law, national or international, to regulate the use of transmitting equipment. The temptation to play with the equipment when it was not being used for official messages was too great for most operators to resist. In his *History of Radio*, Gleason Archer records:

> Operators, whether on Naval or merchant ships, attained importance out of all proportion to their actual daily duties. They were in a class by themselves. Soon they began to run wild . . . Human nature in its most arrogant form soon bedevilled the new medium of communication. Gossip between friends could and did crowd out messages of life and death on the high seas . . . The only way in which urgent messages could be gotten on the air when two gossiping cronies held the ether was to lay a book or other weight upon the transmitting key and thus blanket them with such a roar of interference that they were obliged to desist. This process, however, was time-consuming and provocative of feuds . . .[1]

Accordingly, the International Radiotelegraphic Conference was organized in Berlin in 1903, and attended by the Great Powers and a host of smaller nations. Standards for certification of wireless operators were drawn up. It was agreed by the nations that CQD would be the international distress signal, and that signals preceded by it would be given immediate priority over all other traffic. The more difficult issue of opening up the architecture of the worldwide radiotelegraphic network to allow free exchange of messages among different carriers was debated hotly, with Britain and Italy obdurately supporting the Marconi position against Germany and other backers of open exchanges. The conference ended on a rancorous note when the deadlock could not be resolved, with the result that Marconi maintained its stranglehold on commercial radiotelegraphy. But at the second conference, in 1906, with Germany, France, Russia, the United States, Spain, Hungary and Austria aligned behind the idea, the open exchange of messages was adopted. Coastal stations would now have to accept messages from ships at sea and transmit traffic to them without distinction as to the manufacturer of their equipment.[2]

The question of public access to the airwaves was debated throughout this period with some vigour. The issue was framed in the context of the rights of "amateur" radio and its growing ranks of hobbyists. Earlier in the century, there had been no clear distinction between amateurs and professional, i.e., commercial, operations. Equipment being used by amateurs was often superior to that of commercial operators; as do-it-yourself hobbyists, they could adopt all the latest advances in tuners and other technology without having to worry much about patent rights. "How-to" plans were provided in the growing literature of magazines and books on radio. The first of the periodicals, *Modern Electrics*, sold 9,000 copies in its second year of operation (1909); by the end of 1910, circulation had leaped to 30,000. But by about 1908, commercial radiotelegraphy had become a substantial industry with bright profit prospects for the future, and friction grew inevitable.

With little in the way of domestic or international regulations in place, amateurs inevitably interfered with commercial stations. Clinton DeSoto describes the situation in his history of amateur radio in America, *Two Hundred Meters Down*:

If a commercial station wanted to do any work, it was usually necessary to make a polite request for the local amateurs to stand by for a while. If the request was not polite, or if an amateur–commercial feud happened to exist, the amateurs did not stand by and the commercial did not work. Times without number a commercial would call an amateur station and tell him to shut up. Equally as often the reply would be, "Who the hell are you?" or "I've as much right to the air as you have." Selfish? Undoubtedly. And yet, the amateur did have equal right to the air with the commercial, from any legal or moral standpoint. He was seldom interrupting important traffic—contrary to accusations that have been made, there is no authoritative record that amateurs ever seriously interfered with any "sos" or distress communication: on the contrary, there are instances when the constantly watchful amateurs heard distress calls which were not picked up by the regular receiving points. And he was even then doing a useful work developing new and better radio equipment through his patronage of the manufacturers of parts and apparatus.

Nevertheless, the fact that there was money to be made in commercial services would help to spell the end of the freedom of the so-called "amateur"—actually, the *citizen*—to roam the radio spectrum at will. (This topic is explored in greater depth in chapter 13, "Commodifying the Airwaves.") Ironically, in the doomed fight against regulation that ensued, it was the Marconi company that proved to be the amateur's greatest ally: the company saw in the burgeoning numbers of amateurs both a pool of trained prospective employees and a market for their radio components. Marconi argued that the interference problem was not so much the fault of amateur operators as a matter of inferior (i.e., non-Marconi) equipment being used by the commercial operators who were doing most of the complaining. It was a self-serving argument that nonetheless was substantially correct.

Throughout the history of radio's technical development, there has been tension between two approaches to achieving elbow room on the airwaves. If radio can be thought of as a new continent and Marconi as its Columbus, then the early attempts to reach lower and lower into the long wavelengths—where Marconi and others believed signal reliability would be greatest—can be likened to extending the frontier of settlement. Later, radio experimenters would find fertile new territory in ever-shorter wavelengths, higher up the spectrum in the direction of visible light. At the same time, refinements in both receiving and transmitting circuitry and components made it possible to squeeze more and more signals into adjacent frequencies at any point on the spectrum, without causing interference; "population density" could be increased throughout the territory.

Of course, there was no way of knowing of these technical developments in advance, and the public access controversy was carried on for many years on the faulty premise that usable radio spectrum was severely limited by the perceived need to use only long waves. As well, the lack of selectivity in receivers and the extremely greedy bandwidth characteristics of the early spark transmitters were taken as givens.[3]

While the territorial dispute simmered, radio had already demonstrated its potential in a spectacular way with the 1899 collision between the coal ship *R.F. Matthews* and the *East Goodwin* lightship off the coast of Britain, the first recorded instance of the use of radio saving lives. The dense fog made distress flares invisible, but the *East Goodwin* happened to be taking part in a demonstration of Marconi radio systems and the ship was able to signal for help. As a result, no lives were lost.

Whatever residual doubt may have lingered about the commercial future for wireless telegraphy evaporated a decade later, in 1909, in one of those events that shape the future of a medium by capturing the public's attention and making the medium's potential plain. In January of that year, the White Star passenger liner ss *Republic* had been groping her way through dense winter fog off Nantucket Sound when suddenly a grey mass loomed ahead. With a grinding crash, the ss *Florida* drove her prow into the steel of the *Republic*'s hull, tearing a mortal gash.

Holed and sinking, the *Republic* was able to call for help thanks to an on-board spark-gap radio rig and a doughty operator named Jack Binns. Newspaper accounts breathlessly told the story of how Binns coaxed his transmitter into operation and began sending the signal CQD over and over. The cry for help was heard by a powerful Marconi-equipped United States Coast Guard station at Siasconset and was retransmitted to ships in the area. These included another White Star vessel, the *Baltic*, some two hundred miles away. The *Baltic* raced to the scene of the collision, using bearings provided by Binns. Before the *Republic* sank, all of her surviving passengers and crew were transferred to the *Baltic* and *Florida*. Only five lives were lost among the 460 passengers and crew aboard the *Republic*, and the world applauded. Marconi stock prices surged.

A colourful account in a contemporary children's encyclopedia concludes: "It is a thrilling thing to think of, these ships drifting in the fog, talking to each other over sixty miles of space, carrying along an invisible ocean new life for a thousand beating hearts." Radio operators like Binns were the heroes of juvenile fiction, the darlings of newspaper reporters, the astronauts of their day; to be one, it was necessary to have the right stuff. Binns himself had a small subsequent career in vaudeville, demonstrating his signalling talents, and was contracted by a publisher to provide forewords for the Radio Boys book series. "The escapades of the boys in this book are extremely thrilling," he wrote, "but not particularly more so than is actually possible in everyday life."

Three years later, as the mighty *Titanic* lay dying under a starry sky in frigid April waters off Newfoundland, the ss *California*, close enough to effect a rescue, steamed on despite the sinking liner's increasingly frantic distress calls. *California*'s wireless operator was off duty, asleep in his bunk. One thousand, five hundred and thirteen lives were lost. That clinched it for radio: international regulations soon prescribed twenty-four-hour manning of shipboard stations and a station for every vessel carrying more than fifty passengers. Marconi stock shot up from £55 to £225 on the London exchange even before the *Titanic* survivors had arrived in New York harbour, and American business went on a speculative binge of investment in the new technology that would not be repeated until the days of Apple and Intel, Yahoo! and Google.

How Radio Works

T
HE RADIO REVOLUTION started with a remarkably pro-
saic piece of technology put together by Heinrich Hertz in
1886. Hertz, in seeking a laboratory confirmation of electrical theory as laid out in the mathematical equations of James Clerk
Maxwell, devised a rudimentary transmitter of electrical waves. Two
one-metre-long metal rods with small metal spheres on one end
and flat metal plates on the other were mounted on a horizontal
plane so that the metal balls could be brought close to one another.[1]
A source of electric current (a Leyden jar battery) was connected to
the rods, negative side to one, positive to the other. When that was
done, a spark jumped the gap between the metal balls. According to
Maxwell's theory, that ought to cause electromagnetic oscillations
to be set up in the rods, and these in turn would produce radio
waves in space. To receive those hypothetical waves, Hertz used a
receiver that was simplicity itself. It was a length of wire with small
metal balls on each end, bent into a loop so that the balls were close
together. The theory predicted that when the transmitter was spark-
ing and thus radiating, a spark ought to be observed jumping the
receiver "gap"—and it was. The electrical waves travelling through
space from the transmitter's spark set up a current in the receiving

loop. It was rather like the action of tuning forks on one another, only it happened in inscrutable, mysterious silence, and at the speed of light. In electrical terms, it was as if a wire (the receiving coil) had been moved through an electromagnetic field (the radio waves moving past it): a current was induced to flow in the wire. Hertz found that those invisible waves could be detected at considerable distance—all the way to the other side of his laboratory! And he demonstrated that radio waves exhibit all the characteristics of light, including speed, refraction, reflection and polarization.

Historians, like Marconi himself, have sometimes marvelled at the fact that Hertz did not seem to see the potential for his experimental device as an instrument of wireless communication. But Hertz was a scientist and not an engineer: he was out to fry even bigger fish. His confirmation of Maxwell's equations proved the existence of electromagnetic fields, and thereby undermined the foundations of the seemingly impregnable three hundred-year-old edifice of Newtonian physics. Electromagnetic field theory would lead to a hundred inventions, of which radio may not even be the most important. It also led a Swiss patent clerk named Albert Einstein to write a paper on "special relativity," announcing the dawn of the atomic age.

Science's success has been based on its ability to isolate areas of nature and study them intensively, ignoring for the purposes of simplification the linkages of the delineated study area with the rest of the natural world. In this context, electromagnetic theory described in terms of billiard-ball electrons, solar system atomic structure and waves through "ether" worked well enough to allow practical engineers such as Marconi and his successors to build instruments and appliances that performed useful functions. But the descriptions were very far from the reality as understood by science even as early as the first transatlantic radio message. From the perspective of today's physics, what happened when Hertz induced a spark to jump the gap in his receiving loop is, on the one hand, immensely more complicated than anyone could have suspected and, on the other, more intimately connected to our lives.

Einstein and the quantum physicists who followed him demolished the notion of electrons and other subatomic particles as bits of matter existing in the void of space, or in some insubstantial, indefinable substance called "ether." Both matter and empty space, we have come to understand, are illusions and ether is merely a convenient fiction. What, then, was going on in Hertz's radio apparatus? It certainly had nothing to do with orbits and billiard balls. Physicist Hermann Weyl wrote:

> According to [quantum physics' update of Faraday's field theory] a material particle such as an electron is merely a small domain of the electrical field within which the field strength assumes enormously high values, indicating that a comparatively huge field energy is concentrated in a very small space. Such an energy knot, which by no means is clearly delineated against the remaining field, propagates . . . like a water wave across the surface of a lake; there is no such thing as one and the same substance of which the electron consists at all times.[2]

According to quantum field theory, the propagation of radio waves through space is the distillation of patterns of energy out of the electromagnetic fields that are the fabric of space/time. There is a real sense in which Hertz's transmitter and receiver were connected despite the space between them—in which *every* transmitter and receiver everywhere are always connected—by the cosmic web of potentialities waiting to be realized. What happened in Hertz's receiving loop was that a potential created by the application of electricity to the transmitting rods was realized, the information for that realization having been carried across the intervening distance by wavelike disturbances in the fabric of space/time. Radio communication is not the sending out of something from a transmitter to be detected by a receiver, but the actualizing of an energy or information link that always exists as a potential. When we shine a flashlight in the dark, we do not think of the process as "transmitting photons," we think of it as revealing what is there to be seen. In the same way, radio reveals, and in doing so taps directly into the fabric of existence in the universe to facilitate communication. Small wonder we find it so fascinating.

Marconi's early experimental work in radiotelegraphy was simply an elaboration of Hertz's basic experiment, inspired by an inventor's instinct for what would work in the real world outside the laboratory. He first attached a long vertical wire (an antenna) to one side of the gap in Hertz's transmitter, and attached the other side to the earth. No doubt it was the knowledge that the telegraph used an earth return for its circuits that inspired the thought. By doing the same with the receiving loop, he was gradually able to increase the distance over which he could successfully transmit from 300 yards to two miles, then across the English Channel and then, finally, across the Atlantic.

One of the early engineering problems facing Marconi was the fact that spark-gap signals were extremely broad-banded: each transmitter used a spectacularly wide chunk of the radio spectrum, and the result was that no two stations could operate in close proximity to one another without causing intolerable interference. In short, radio signals were not tuned to specific frequencies. Sir Oliver Lodge, whose early experiments with Hertzian waves had in part inspired the young Marconi, developed a method for tuning both transmitters and receivers to a resonant frequency, outside which radio waves were greatly attenuated. Radio transmitters thus equipped used much less power and ate up much less spectrum. Marconi improved on the idea, developing the modern "tuned circuit" and patenting it in 1900.

As these early advances were made in the techniques of radio wave transmission, parallel improvements came to receiving. Early in his experiments, Marconi switched to a more sensitive radio wave detection device called a "coherer," which exploited the elementary fact that an electrical current passing through a wire creates a magnetic field. He sealed nickel and silver filings in a cigarette-sized glass tube with a silver plug at each end, and placed the tube in the gap in the receiving loop (which had by now evolved into a coil, or series of loops). When the presence of radio waves induced a current in the receiver wire, the current would find its way into and through the filings in the glass tube, setting them up in an orderly alignment, causing them to "cohere" or clump together, forming a good conductor of electricity.[3] A tiny hammer-like tapper was used to unclump or "decohere" the particles so that they could detect the next incoming waves, supplied by a closing of the Morse key at the transmitter. Radio waves, in effect, caused the glass tube and its filings to act as an on-off switch. An electric current from an auxiliary supply, when attached to the coherer, would be switched on and off according to the presence or absence of radio waves in the receiving circuit, and this auxiliary current could be used to ring a bell or activate some other electrical sounding or printing device. If the tiny decoherer hammer was activated in this way as well, the presence of a continuous radio signal would be indicated by a rapid on-off switching of the coherer and a consequent buzzing noise from the sounder.

A similar chain of events takes place today when the homeowner activates an automatic garage-door opener with a small radio transmitter in her car: the transmitted radio waves activate a small, sensitive relay (the coherer), which in turn switches on household electrical current to a motor, which winches up the heavy garage door. A mechanical arrangement switches off the motor when the door reaches the top of its range of travel.

The coherer worked, but only just. Elegant though it was in its highly polished mahogany stand and finely machined brass fittings, it was an electromechanical solution to an electronic problem. An electronic solution would have to wait for the vacuum tube.

An interim answer of great importance was provided by the discovery in 1903 of the crystal detector by the American physicist Greenleaf Whittier Pickard. Pickard noticed that certain mineral crystals were good conductors of electric current in one direction but poor conductors in the opposite direction—in other words, "semiconductors." Why this should be, he did not know, but he immediately saw that these crystals might be used as detectors in radio circuits. They had the obvious advantage of not needing a mechanical "decohering" mechanism, but they also had the ability to change the high-frequency alternating current of radio waves into a pulsating direct current. In effect, the crystal detector behaves like the flap valve in a hand pump on a water well: the valve lifts open in one direction only and thus allows water to move up the pipe when the pump handle is worked, creating a suction (and lifting the valve flap), but closes itself against water trying to escape back down the pipe into the well when suction is released, that is, when the handle is moved up in preparation for the next downward stroke. The up-and-down motion of the pump handle is analogous to an alternating current; the unidirectional flow of the water is like a pulsating direct current; and the flap valve plays the role of a semiconductor, converting incoming, alternating current to an output of pulsating direct current.

The conversion of radio waves to direct current was a crucially important step in developing improved receivers, since direct current was many thousands of times easier to detect with electrical metering devices than alternating current, which typically changed its polarity or direction of flow many times a second and thus appeared to most early instruments as no current at all. Furthermore, a pulsating direct current would actuate electromagnets such as those in telephone earpieces and headphones and loudspeakers, whereas alternating current would not, due to the same problem of rapidly switching polarity. Thus the direct current generated within the receiving device by radio waves—or "detected," in the lingo of the medium—would be audible in earphones or a loudspeaker as a sustained note as long as the current was present, rather than a simple "click" marking the onset of an alternating current. (This made it possible to transmit dots and dashes, and, eventually, the human voice and music.)

A wide range of mineral crystals were found to operate this way, including galena, iron pyrites, carborundum and silicon. For many years the crystal detector, though delicate and finicky to adjust, was a mainstay of the market in inexpensive radio receivers, and it deserves recognition for its important role in popularizing the medium. It was, in fact, the precursor to and inspiration for that ubiquitous present-day semiconducting device, the transistor.

Shortly after the crystal detector came the vacuum tube revolution, which would at last let radio explore its full potential. It would also make long-distance telephony possible, and give birth to electronic data processing and ultimately the digital computer. It is a classic tale of how the scientifically informed tinkerings of engineers can lead to useful new devices.

Thomas Edison was in the early stages of development of electric light bulbs when he noticed the mysterious phenomenon later to be known as the "Edison effect." Parts of the inside of the glass bulbs were somehow becoming coated with a thin black film, even though all the air had been evacuated from the bulbs to prevent the carbon filaments from burning out. What could be causing this peculiar phenomenon? Edison suspected it was caused by "molecular" bombardment of the glass from the filament, and he probed the bulb with a wire attached to a galvanometer. Sure enough, the galvanometer needle was deflected, betraying the presence of an electrical current flowing through the vacuum from the filament to the probe wire. This was the summer of 1880. A little more tinkering and he might well have noticed that the current would flow only in one direction within the tube (just as it did in a semiconductor crystal), and thus have discovered a practical system of wireless telegraphy using vacuum tube detectors more than a generation ahead of time.

But Edison was focused on making his electric light bulbs commercially viable. The extra element he inserted into the tube didn't solve his blackening problem, so he turned to other matters of more immediate practical concern. He revisited the puzzling phenomenon in 1882 and again early in 1883, and learned that the current passing through the tube varied in amplitude with the voltage applied to the filament. On the basis of that information he patented what was essentially a laboratory toy, a device for measuring voltage using an incandescent lamp with a second element inserted. It was the first patent in electronics. He demonstrated it for the world to see at the 1884 Philadelphia Electrical Exhibition. Still no one understood the true implications of what he had observed. The puzzle of the minuscule electric current flowing within an evacuated light bulb was left to an English investigator to solve.

John Ambrose Fleming was a young engineering teacher at Cambridge, a former student of the great James Clerk Maxwell, when he was asked by the newly organized British Edison Electric Light Company in 1882 to become a scientific consultant—in effect, a consulting engineer. He began almost immediately to examine the Edison effect. Meanwhile, the German scientists Julius Elster and Hans Geitel conducted a number of experiments on electrical conduction in an evacuated bulb, and reported that current flowed in one direction only. Again, no practical application of this phenomenon was suggested. Fleming, always, it seems, overloaded with a combination of teaching, textbook writing and consulting work, eventually picked up the threads of the mystery again in 1889. He had a number of bulbs built by glass-blowers, using a variety of electrode arrangements. His experiments confirmed the one-way flow of electricity in a vacuum containing a heated electrode and a second element. He had come within a hair's breadth of inventing the electronic vacuum tube, but he was once again sidetracked by other matters for several years.

In 1895, Fleming had another batch of assorted lamps built, conducted another set of experiments and published another long paper. This time he noted that a vacuum tube—or "valve," as he called it—could, because of the one-way conduction phenomenon, be used to "rectify" an alternating current, or, in other words, convert it to direct current. This was because electrons would flow from the filament to the second element or "plate" within the tube only when the two elements had opposite electrical charges, i.e., when the filament was negative and the plate was positive. When both the plate and filament were negative, no current would flow (electrons would not be attracted to the plate). Thus, only half of the positive-negative waveform of alternating current would pass through the tube, and that half was direct current, that is, current of a single, rather than alternating, polarity or charge. (It would be two more years until physicist J.J. Thomson proved the existence of the electron; Fleming attributed the current flows he'd monitored to "negatively charged molecules.")

Fleming's findings received little public notice, overshadowed as they were by the astonishing discovery of X-rays and Marconi's exciting demonstrations of wireless telegraphy. The scientist's strange inability to grasp the practical applications of his discoveries has been a source of intense, vicarious frustration for historians of his life and work. George Shiers, writing in *Scientific American*, is typical:

> With Edison's sharp intuition, or the deep perception of [Sir Benjamin] Thompson, or perhaps more freedom from pressing duties, Fleming could have leaped into the twentieth century simply by combining the elements of his lamps. He could have suggested the possibilities of using his glow lamp as a rectifier for small currents (such as radio waves) . . . Even more important, he could have placed a zigzag wire (which he had put into one of his models) between the other electrodes (just to find out what would happen, as Edison would probably have done) and thereby have anticipated Lee De Forest in inventing the three-element vacuum tube.[4]

Shiers seems to sigh before continuing: "None of these leaps, however, would have been characteristic of a man as methodical and cautious as Fleming." For the third time in his sixteen-year investigation, Fleming put the bulbs away in favour of other matters.

By 1899 wireless telegraphy was well on the road to full-scale commercialization, and Fleming was contracted as a consultant to the Marconi Wireless Telegraph Company, and put to work designing the power supply for the experimental wireless station at Poldhu, Cornwall. It was during this work that he had, at long last, "a sudden and very happy thought" that his test lamps were "the very implement required to rectify high-frequency oscillations"—in plain language, to detect radio waves. Finally, he was close to making his historic invention. He quickly wired together a simple spark-gap transmitter and a receiving circuit, using a two-element tube almost identical to the one Edison had constructed ten years earlier. The experiment worked immediately: Fleming had discovered a new means of detecting radio waves. He called it, without much apparent thought to marketing, the "thermionic valve."

The radio waves collected by an antenna were led to the "plate," a metal cylinder surrounding the filament inside the "valve." Whenever the radio waves were present and in the positive half of their alternating cycle, a current would flow (electrons would be attracted) from the heated filament (which was negatively charged) to the plate. When radio waves were in the negative phase of their alternating cycle, no current would flow. And of course, no current would flow when no radio waves were present. The presence of direct current could easily be monitored with a meter such as a galvanometer, or it could be heard in a telephone headset. Fleming's valve was both sensitive and durable, and it gradually replaced earlier detector types in Marconi equipment beginning in 1907.

The American inventor Lee De Forest took the Fleming valve a giant step further by experimenting with a third element within the tube, which he called a "grid." The resulting device has been called one of the most important inventions in history. And for poor Fleming, it was a source of frustration and unhappiness for the remainder of his life. He could not accept that De Forest, a brash, egomaniacal and none too scrupulous young American, had done anything more than make a minor modification to his thermionic valve. Given the record of Fleming's meticulous experiments over so many years, there is some justification for this position. Nevertheless, De Forest patented the three-element tube (in 1907) and Fleming did not.

De Forest had been working on the problem of an improved method of detecting radio waves for several years, even experimenting with the rectifying properties of gas flames. In 1905, after he heard of Fleming's work, it occurred to him that if a grid—a wire bent in a zigzag shape—were to be placed between the filament and the plate in a Fleming valve, it ought to be possible to alter the strength of the electron flow in the tube by applying different charges to the grid, which would act as a kind of electric gateway between filament and plate. De Forest's revolutionary insight was that the grid would make it possible to greatly amplify a weak, variable current, such as a radio signal. It was no problem to get a very strong electron flow streaming from the filament to the plate by using a battery in a circuit connecting the two. A weak current (radio waves, for example) applied to the grid could now be used to regulate that flow, by changing the grid's polarity (widening and narrowing the gate) as the weak current fluctuated through its positive and negative cycles. The strong primary current would in this way be made to duplicate the characteristics of the weak grid current, only at much greater strength or amplitude. The incoming radio signal would be both detected *and amplified.* De Forest hurriedly drew up plans for the device and took them to a glass-maker.

In his autobiography, he recalled:

> I hurried to my laboratory carrying in my pocket the world's only supply of three-electrode vacuum tubes. They were just two in number, and I was eager to test them to determine whether my latest invention, a tiny bent wire in the form of a grid inserted between the carbon filament and the platinum plate . . . could bring in wireless signals over substantially greater distances than other receiving devices then in use . . . To my excited delight I found that it did; the faint impulses which my short antenna brought to that new grid electrode sounded many times louder in the headphones than any wireless signal ever heard before. I was happy indeed.[5]

This simple device, which had taken so long to arrive at and which De Forest called the "audion," was the foundation of all modern electronics, including the electronic computer, until it was superseded by the transistor.

De Forest, who did not count modesty among his slim reper-toire of social virtues, was apt to call himself "the father of radio" at the drop of a hat. Many others have awarded that title to Marconi. But if it's radio as we currently understand the word—what we hear when we switch on a radio in the kitchen or car—Reginald Fes-senden probably has as much right to the title as anyone.

While Marconi and De Forest were still preoccupied with solving the problems of wireless telegraphy, Fessenden was experimenting with voice transmissions by radio. By inserting a carbon microphone in a radio transmitter's output, he was able to "modulate" the radio waves, or superimpose on their shape the subtle variations in sound of a human voice. At the receiver, these variations would be captured in the detection circuit and passed along to the earphone, where they would be reproduced. By December 1900, using equipment of his own invention, he had been able to transmit his voice, super-imposed on the crash and thunder of a spark-gap signal, over a dis-tance of about a mile. The first words spoken (shouted, actually) on radio were: "Hello one, two, three, four. Is it snowing where you are, Mr. Thiessen? If it is, telegraph back and let me know."[6] With this success, Fessenden went to work on the transmitting side of the equation, to get rid of the characteristic din of spark transmission while preserving the voice, and by 1906 was ready to demonstrate a practical "radiotelephone."

Fessenden was born in Quebec, moved to Niagara Falls and Fergus, Ontario, as a youth, and was educated at Trinity College School in Port Hope, Ontario, and Bishops' College in Lennoxville, Quebec. Between 1887 and 1890 he worked in the laboratories of both Edison and Westinghouse, doing original research into the properties of electricity. In 1892 he established the electrical engi-neering department at Purdue University and a year later accepted an invitation to join the faculty of Pittsburgh University's engineer-ing department. In 1899 he attempted to return to Canada, but his application for an advertised faculty position at Montreal's McGill University was turned down because he lacked a university diploma. Fessenden would eventually be credited with more than five hundred inventions in the fields of radio, sound and optics. Early in his career he had the good fortune to find the backing of two Pittsburgh bankers, who supported him during his period of greatest productivity in radio, eventually sinking more than $2 million into his experiments. In 1902, the three of them formed the National Electric Signaling Company with Fessenden's patents as the nugget of value. Fessenden was to give his unfortunate partners many a sleepless night as he burned through huge sums of capital in obsessive pursuit of his goal of refining radiotelegraphy and perfecting the transmission of voice by radio.

An early assistant, Roy Weagant, recalled:

> He could be very nice at times, but only at times. His voice boomed like a bull . . . He had no regard for cost; he once sent for a 100-horsepower boiler and had it shipped by express. The more anything cost the better he liked it. He was sometimes unsound technically, but he more than made up for it by his brilliant imagination. He was the greatest inventive genius of all time in the realm of wireless.[7]

Another assistant, Charles J. Pannill, worked with Fessenden from 1902 to 1910. He wrote:

> He had a great character, a splendid physique, but what a temper! Many of us were fired on more than one occasion, and usually on some slight provocation. When he had cooled off, he was sorry and hired us back, always at higher pay . . . Fessenden could think best when flat on his back smoking Pittsburgh stogies; that's when he got his real ideas.

In 1905, Fessenden's company built a state-of-the art experimental station at Brant Rock on the Massachusetts coast. It was equipped with Fessenden's latest invention, a steam-driven, high-speed alternator-type transmitter that would prove to be the climax of spark technology, soon to be superseded by the high-power vacuum tube. His station already held the distinction of being the first to establish reliable two-way communication by radiotelegraphy between North America and Europe. In November 1906, a test transmission of an assistant's voice was heard in Scotland. On Christmas Eve, 1906, with no fanfare, Fessenden made the first real radio broadcast. An early historian of the medium reports:

> Early on that evening, wireless operators on ships within a radius of several hundred miles sprang to attention when they heard the call "CQ,CQ" in Morse code. Was it a ship in distress? They listened eagerly, and to their amazement, heard a human voice coming from their instruments—someone speaking! Then a woman's voice rose in song. It was uncanny! Many of them called to officers to come and listen; soon the wireless rooms were crowded. Next someone was heard reading a poem. Then there was a violin solo; then a man made a speech, and they could catch most of the words. Finally, everyone who had heard the program was asked to write to R.A. Fessenden at Brant Rock, Massachusetts—and many of the operators did. Thus was the first radio broadcast in history put on.[8]

Fessenden went on to perform a series of tests that greatly improved both the range and the quality of his radio broadcasts. Wireless technology had been lifted to a new level, an advance comparable to the leap from the telegraph to the telephone. However, the fact scarcely seemed to register on the public consciousness, and it was not until 1920, fourteen years after the first broadcast, that radio really caught fire as a consumer product. As late as 1914, the president of the Wireless Society of London predicted a future for radio in which receiving stations would be set up in special auditoriums resembling cinemas, and audiences would listen "*viva voce* [to] all the prominent speakers of the day, although they might be speaking hundreds of miles away."[9] The notion of a radio in every home still seemed too far-fetched to consider.

Until voice transmission became widespread, radio was to remain in the realm of the laboratory curiosity for most people. For those who understood how it worked, it held endless fascination, and amateur radio operators abounded. But the fact that communicating was done in Morse code and the equipment, even when it was not homemade, required a degree of expertise to operate meant that for another decade and a half radio was well buried in the consciousness of the majority of people. We might say in today's idiom that the interface between sender and receiver was just too complicated.

Nevertheless, radio magazines abounded, and there were articles in all the popular science periodicals with instructions on how to construct and operate transmitters and receivers and build antennas. The author of a popular American how-to series of books was soon earning royalties in six figures. Parts manufacturers were reaping a bonanza and, in the process, patent rights were often scandalously abused. Lawsuits proliferated.

Carneal has an evocative description of the era that will find resonance in the experience of many a late-twentieth-century parent of computer kids:

> At just about this time [1910] the word "radio," heretofore a mysterious "force" that only the scientist understood, sprang into being. It was ushered in by a motley group of people, mostly boys and young men, working all alone on crude homemade apparatus in the isolation of their own homes. These young people, scattered over the country, were engaged in the strange pastime of "fishing" things out of the invisible space around them, at first dots and dashes and later words and music that come from nowhere . . . Parents, at first indulgent of the strange and not inexpensive devices their youngsters brought into the home, began to gape in wonder as they donned their headsets and actually listened to music coming to them out of the air. They did not understand in the least how it happened.

It seemed mysterious beyond words. Their amusement died out as they found themselves listening to an explanation of the vast intricacies of "radio."[10]

Fessenden himself, at home in the laboratory and radio "shack" in the company of engineers and experimenters, was ill adapted for the world of business and legal affairs. His partnership with the Pittsburgh bankers fell apart early in 1911, when the bankers ousted him from the company and took control. At issue was profitability, and Fessenden's interest in advancing the science of radio at the expense of commercial considerations. It was a classic case of what current management texts call "founder's syndrome," which is defined as an excessive interest in the quality of the product and customer satisfaction at the expense of maximum return on investment. This was the dawn of the era of the modern, professionally managed and publicly held business corporation, and as the twentieth century progressed, many another inventor and company founder would find himself similarly disenfranchised by professional business managers and finance specialists, who were trained to wring maximum profit from the inventor's creations on behalf of anonymous shareholders.

Commodifying the Airways

THE TRANSFORMATION of mainstream radio from a freely accessible, two-way technology to a one-way, heavily regulated broadcast medium took place in two main stages. First, governments everywhere took radio out of the hands of ordinary citizens. Then, in the United States, they turned it over on an all but exclusive basis to commercial, profit-making enterprises; while in Britain and most other European nations, it was put in the hands of a government agency. By the end of the transformation, radio had become a "manipulative" rather than a "convivial" technology in Illich's terms; part of "the system" from the perspective of Habermas. The transition merits detailed examination, since it is a story replete with cautionary tales and lessons of history that are directly applicable to today's media environment. The saga hinges on the trauma of World War I.

When "the war to end all wars" began, amateur radio operators in Europe and North America were required to dismantle their stations for the duration, ostensibly to eliminate the possibility of accidental or deliberate disruption of military radio traffic. All radio communication, including private commercial radiotelegraphy carried on by Marconi and a handful of other companies, was placed under the control of the military. To expedite the production of the great quantities of wireless equipment required by the armed forces, all patent disputes were frozen and manufacturers were permitted to use any and all technical innovations, whatever their source.

During the war, wireless was of limited use in ground engagements due mainly to the weight, bulk and unreliability of field sets and the fact that the enemy could listen in on transmissions. Its potential for military applications was nonetheless made clear before the fighting had ended. Radio's most significant contribution was in providing immediate feedback from artillery spotters flying over enemy lines in aircraft equipped with relatively compact, low-power transmitters. They could see where a shell had landed and radio back instructions for correcting the aim. At sea, where weight and bulk were unimportant, and where constant movement over great distances was a prime factor in warfare, wireless revolutionized naval strategy and tactics by permitting worldwide coordination of battle fleets. Ships no longer had to maintain visual contact with one another to coordinate operations, and they were able to benefit almost immediately from intelligence gleaned by their command establishments onshore.

When the war ended, governments everywhere showed a reluctance to relinquish to their citizenry control over radio. It had become a technology of strategic significance for the Great Powers; leadership in the field of radio communications was an important military asset and would likely become even more important as the science evolved. The transoceanic telegraph cables, which until now had formed the backbone of the world's communication system, had shown themselves vulnerable to warfare. When fighting began in 1914, Britain herself had cut or otherwise disabled most of the global undersea telegraph network to keep it from falling into enemy hands. Overland cables were likewise vulnerable, particularly in Europe, where a line of any length inevitably crossed several frontiers. In a world that had quickly grown to depend on rapid international communication, radio was now seen as a crucial backstop to the telegraph system.

From the point of view of the British and American post-war administrations, putting the medium back in the hands of what was perceived to be an undisciplined rabble of amateur operators simply would not do. Moreover, the tangle of conflicting patent claims and lawsuits would have to be sorted out, and quickly, so that technical development could proceed. And finally, it was now seen as imperative, for reasons of national security, that foreign nationals be prevented from owning any significant portion of a nation's radio industry.

The U.S. and Britain found diametrically different solutions to these post-war problems. In the U.K., the government of the day placed radio in the hands of the Royal Mail, which had long regulated the telegraph and telephone businesses. Private commercial broadcasting was outlawed, and British Marconi resumed its accustomed arm lock on the international radiotelegraph business.

A similar plan for public control of radio was proposed in the United States, and had the backing of the navy and significant support in Congress. Congressional hearings were held in December 1918. Navy Secretary Josephus Daniels testified: "We strongly believe that having demonstrated during the war the excellent service and the necessity of unified ownership, we should not lose the advantage of it in peace." He argued that the navy "is so well prepared to undertake this work and to carry it on that we would lose very much by dissipating it and opening the use of radio communications again to rival companies."

Leading the opposition to the bill in committee testimony were the head of the American Radio Relay League, representing American radio amateurs, and the president of American Marconi, which was essentially a branch plant of British Marconi and the country's principal commercial radiotelegraph operator prior to the war. Informed opinion on Capitol Hill at first predicted adoption of the bill, but opposition was vocal and well organized. Before the end of the month, the committee had voted unanimously to shelve the measure; the idea of state monopoly in a thriving industry was too much for American legislators to stomach.

This, of course, left the strategic military issue unresolved. Sooner or later, President Woodrow Wilson would have to return commercial assets to their owners (presumably as soon as the armistice being negotiated in Paris had been signed), and foremost among the owners was American Marconi. Wilson's position was described by one of his wartime advisers in a 1937 interview:

> [The] President had reached the conclusion, as a result of his experience [at the armistice talks] in Paris, that there were three dominating factors in international relations—international transportation, international communication, and petroleum— and that the influence which a country exercised in international affairs would be largely dependent upon their position of dominance in these three activities; that the British obviously had the lead and the experience in international transportation—it would be difficult if not impossible to equal her position in that field; in international communication she had acquired the practical domination of the cable systems of the world; but that there was an apparent opportunity for the United States to challenge her in international communications through the use of radio; of course as to petroleum we already held a position of dominance. The result of American dominance in radio would have been a fairly equal stand-off between the U.S. and Great Britain—the U.S. having the edge in petroleum, Britain in shipping, with communications divided—cables to Britain and wireless to the U.S.[1]

The issue became all the more urgent when General Electric reported that British Marconi had placed an order for several of the advanced high-power transmitters GE had built on the model of Fessenden's Brant Rock station. It was an enormous order, worth more than $5 million. The alternators, massive pieces of machinery that resembled the electrical generators found at a small hydroelectric station, were the state-of-the-art in radiotelegraphy. The more powerful models could be heard around the world, and they were far superior to the equipment being used by Marconi.[2]

Alarmed at the potential strategic consequences of the deal, the U.S. Navy, in the person of Admiral William Bullard, director of naval communications, stepped in behind the scenes at the behest of President Wilson to abort the sale in the name of national security. In response to General Electric's plaintive cry that it would have to cease production of the alternators and lay off workers without a sale to *someone*, and that, in any case, nothing short of a state monopoly could succeed in usurping Marconi's dominance, Admiral Bullard proposed setting up a government-sponsored, private American corporation with the resources necessary to compete internationally.[3]

The proposal was to establish a government-sanctioned cartel— never, of course, identified as such in public—under the name of the Radio Corporation of America, or RCA for short, which would be owned by General Electric and other participating companies (including Fessenden's lamented National Electric Signaling Company).[4] The cartel would be the customer GE needed to keep its war-bloated manufacturing arm afloat. GE managers jumped at the suggestion.[5]

As a prelude to establishing RCA, General Electric, with the active encouragement of the U.S. government, negotiated the purchase of all the assets of American Marconi. "Negotiation" may be a trifle euphemistic for what occurred in the panelled boardrooms of British Marconi when GE honchos arrived for talks: it was made clear to the British company that the government of the United States would under no circumstances allow Marconi to continue to dominate wireless telegraphy in America, and that the offer being made by General Electric was the best they could expect. It was well known that there were powerful interests within the American government pushing for outright state control of radio, in which case Marconi's American interests would have been nationalized in any case. Faced with what was essentially an ultimatum, the company in 1919 agreed to divest itself of its American assets.

The strategic political question nagging the Americans had thus been addressed. But it did not stop there. A year later, British Marconi, France and Germany's Telefunken all found themselves on the receiving end of intense diplomatic pressure from the U.S. and its new radio conglomerate over plans to develop a powerful wireless station in Argentina. Telefunken had already begun construction on a station there; the British wanted to beat them to the punch if at all possible, as did the French. France and Britain were outraged, then, when the Americans presented an ultimatum demanding that any station in Argentina or anywhere else in the western hemisphere be operated by a board of directors on which the United States would be given veto power. Over several weeks of negotiations in Paris in 1921, the Americans prevailed. This was an explicit embodiment of the Monroe Doctrine, under which the United States had since the 1820s claimed all of Central and South America as its exclusive economic and political sphere of influence, the theatre of its "manifest destiny."

The patent mess was also on its way to a resolution. When RCA was formally chartered in October 1919, GE granted it reciprocal rights to all of its radio patents and inventions, and an immediate merger with American Marconi was undertaken. Within weeks, RCA had signed cross-licensing agreements with AT&T and its subsidiary, Western Electric, which allowed the companies use of each other's patents in the area of manufacture and sale of electrical appliances of all kinds. (About a thousand patents were involved.) RCA was made exclusive wholesale selling agent for the radio receivers manufactured by all three companies. Similar cross-licensing agreements were signed with other holders of important patents. The budding American radio industry had to all intents and purposes become an exclusive club, to be operated for the benefit of its members and in its directors' view of "the national interest."

In 1924, the niggling problem of what to do about remaining two-way radio in the hands of citizens—amateur radio—was dealt with by an international convention on the allocation of radio spectrum. Amateurs were henceforth to be denied access to radio frequencies below two hundred metres, which meant, in terms of contemporary engineering knowledge, they no longer had access to the only part of the spectrum usable for long-distance radio communication.[6] However, as radio amateurs began despondently tinkering with the "useless" chunk of spectrum to which they had been relegated, they soon perked up. It turned out that the higher they went in frequency, the farther they could transmit and the less power they needed to establish contact with distant stations. As they crept up the spectrum, cautiously at first, then with rising excitement, through the present-day AM radio bands and on to eighty- and fifteen-metre wavelengths that are now occupied by international shortwave broadcasters, they were soon setting distance records using power outputs that seemed infinitesimally small by commercial radio standards. Moreover, they discovered that at higher frequencies, static interference was no longer the bane of existence it had been on the low frequencies. And antennas, really efficient antennas, were much simpler to build since they were substantially smaller due to the shorter radio wavelengths involved.

The discoveries made by the amateurs on this new frontier for radio revolutionized the industry. Both RCA and British Marconi backed away from well-advanced plans to build worldwide radio networks based on massive low-frequency alternators, and returned to the drawing board to design a high-frequency system based on vacuum tubes and directional "beam" antennas that proved to be much cheaper and more reliable. Radio equipment became smaller, lighter and a great deal more effective as the general upward movement of radio services through the spectrum proceeded during the late 1920s and 1930s.[7] Today, the very low frequencies so popular in the days of Marconi and Fessenden are all but vacant—a static-ridden, abandoned landscape where amateurs, ironically, are once again beginning, in very small numbers, to tinker and explore, and where military doomsday communications systems for submarines confuse, disorient and sicken sensitive marine mammals.

But it is radio as a broadcast medium that mainly concerns us here, and we return to that subject to discover how it is that the radio spectrum, clearly a public resource, has in most places in the world come to be occupied principally by commercial operators, whose primary goal is to serve the private business interests of commercial sponsors.

The First Mass Medium

WHEN RCA was cobbled together following World War I, the Westinghouse Electric and Manufacturing Company had been left like a jilted lover on the outside of the cozy, monopolistic ménage involving RCA, GE and AT&T.[1] It was a snub that would change history, for it then fell to Westinghouse, by force of necessity, to introduce to the world the most powerful medium of mass communication it had yet seen.

Westinghouse naturally viewed the patent-sharing cartel in radio with alarm. It had entered World War I as a relatively minor player in radio, but emerged after two years as a manufacturing power to be reckoned with. Now it faced being frozen out of the post-war radio business. The company set out in hopeful pursuit of international radiotelegraphy agreements in Europe only to find itself beaten to the punch wherever it turned, by exclusive rights deals negotiated by the fast-moving RCA. Westinghouse briefly tried to turn a profit with its ship-to-shore stations by providing ships at sea with regular newscasts, but there were too few subscribers. It soon capitulated to RCA, giving up its ambitions in international radio-telegraphy in return for an agreement from RCA to purchase 40 percent of its radio components from Westinghouse. Westinghouse reluctantly became a major shareholder in RCA alongside AT&T and

General Electric, and the long-standing, debilitating patent mess was finally and definitively resolved.[2]

But the deal left Westinghouse with only the domestic market in which to offer radiotelegraphy services. It was a dismal prospect, since the country was already well provided with land-line telegraphy and telephone networks; radiotelegraphy would be a very small niche indeed where wired communications systems were so advanced. The only other way to make money at that stage of the industry's development was in the manufacture of radio components, an aspect of the business the RCA cartel had already thoroughly organized. It was in these circumstances that Westinghouse, almost by accident, first turned its attention to an entirely novel use for the medium—domestic radio broadcasting as a commercial venture.

The idea of using radio as a medium of mass entertainment had been in the air, however faintly, from the time of Fessenden's experiments of more than a decade earlier. The military buildup prior to World War I and the war itself had focused engineering attention on the military uses of radio, but as the war wound down, interest in civilian uses of the medium once again came to the fore. In Montreal, the Canadian Marconi Company experimented with scheduled broadcasts including recorded music, weather and news reports as early as the winter of 1918–19, making it North America's, and possibly the world's, first broadcast station.[3] The early programs were aimed at radio amateurs who had built their own receivers, most broadcasts beginning at about 7 p.m. and lasting for a couple of hours. On May 20, 1920, a special inaugural concert was broadcast from Montreal and monitored in Ottawa by a gathering at the Château Laurier hotel of the Royal Society of Canada, augmented for the occasion by Prime Minister Robert Borden and opposition leader Mackenzie King. The involvement of prominent political figures reflected the government's continuing active support of the industry, and of Marconi in particular. News of the broadcast caused the desired flurry of public interest, and Montreal stores began opening radio departments to sell home receivers.

Local cinemas played the radio programming during intermissions between films, further whetting the public's appetite for the new medium. The station's call letters, xwa, were changed to cfcf in November 1920, when it was granted official government permission to begin an advertised schedule of programming.

By 1921 the station was requesting permission to broadcast more hours, to satisfy burgeoning interest. Commercial sponsorship of programming began as early as April 1920, when the Canadian Berliner Gramophone Company began advertising its wares over cfcf with this announcement:

> His Master's Voice Records by Wireless Telephone! By arrangement with the Marconi Wireless Telegraphy Company of Canada, a His Master's Voice Victrola Concert, featuring the latest and most popular selections, will be given tonight and every Tuesday from 8 to 10 p.m. for the benefit of wireless students. Captains and officers of ships in port are invited to enjoy this entertainment aboard their vessels. Operators tune to 1200 meters.[4]

Early experiments in the United States were, by contrast, poorly funded and organized, lacking both the active support of a technically adept industrial powerhouse like Marconi and the encouragement of government. Only at Westinghouse was there any real interest, and even there it was only a sideline for one of the company's senior engineers, Frank Conrad. Conrad had for some time been experimenting by broadcasting music from the amateur station he operated from his garage in Wilkinsburg, Pennsylvania. He was deluged with mail from listeners all over the continent, many of them asking to hear particular tunes at particular times. It soon became an overwhelming job to fill the many requests, and he was forced to put his transmissions on a regular schedule, which ran from 7:30 p.m. to 9:30 p.m. on Wednesday and Saturday evenings. He called them "broadcasts," borrowing the term from agriculture: the spreading of seed over a wide area. The recordings were loaned to

Conrad by a local music shop, which in due course requested an on-air mention. Soon it was evident that recordings played on the programs were outselling others at the music store. Sales of radio receivers shot up in the area, and a local department store placed a newspaper advertisement that encouraged readers to buy one of their crystal sets in order to listen to Conrad's broadcasts.

It was the department store ad, placed by the Horne Company in the Pittsburgh *Sun*'s September 29, 1920 edition, that finally made the lights go on in the mind of Westinghouse vice-president Harry P. Young. He recalled the moment of inspiration in an address to the 1928 graduate business administration class at Harvard University:

> We were watching [Conrad's broadcasting experiments] very closely. In the early part of the following year [1920] the thought came which led to the institution of a regular broadcast service. An advertisement of a local department store in a Pittsburgh newspaper, calling attention to a stock of radio receivers which could be used to receive the program sent out by Dr. Conrad, caused the thought to come to me that *the efforts that were then being made to develop radiotelephony as a private means of communication were wrong, and instead its field was really one of wide publicity*, in fact the only means of instantaneous mass communication ever devised. [emphasis added][5]

A colleague of Conrad's, Samuel Kintner, provided a slightly different perspective on the moment in a 1932 memoir:

> Their advertisement in the Pittsburgh Sun . . . caught the eye of [Harry P. Young,] vice-president of Westinghouse. The next day he called together his little "radio cabinet," consisting of Dr. Frank Conrad, L.W. Chubb, O.S. Schairer and your speaker. He told us of reading the Horne advertisement and made the suggestion that the Westinghouse Company erect a station at East Pittsburgh and operate it every night on an

advertised program, so that people would acquire the habit of listening to it, just as they do of reading a newspaper. He said: "If there is sufficient interest to justify a department store in advertising radio sets for sale on an uncertain plan of permanence, I believe there would be a sufficient interest to justify the expense of rendering a regular service—looking to the sale of sets and the advertising of the Westinghouse Company for our returns."[6]

A little more than two weeks after the appearance of the Horne advertisement, in October 1920, Westinghouse had applied for a radio station licence and had been assigned the call letters KDKA by the U.S. Department of Commerce. Two weeks later, the station was on the air in time to carry the election returns in the presidential contest between Warren G. Harding and Charles Evans Hughes.[7] It was estimated that between 5,000 and 10,000 people were able to hear its signal.

Before broadcast radio could become universally popular, however, something would have to be done about the receivers of the day. The problem was that a typical radio set required two large batteries to operate, one a disposable dry cell of limited endurance and the other a lead-acid battery that needed to be periodically recharged and topped up with water, an inevitably messy process. There were two, sometimes three, variable capacitors involved in the tuning process, each of which had to be adjusted by a big knob on the front panel. Each of the vacuum tubes might also have a separate control. Changing wavelengths might involve removing one set of coils from inside the cabinet and replacing it with another. And some sort of outdoor antenna was usually required for all but nearby stations. Radio enthusiasts might enjoy fiddling with all those knobs, wires and adjustments, but the ordinary listener found it all far too complicated.

What was needed, then, was a user-friendly receiver, a simplified interface between the provider and end user of the broadcast information. The first AC-powered sets, developed by Canadian Edward S. Rogers and sold under the name Rogers Batteryless Radio Receiving

Sets, were shown at the Canadian National Exhibition in Toronto in 1925.[8] They were advertised with the slogan: "Just plug it in— then tune in—that's all!" Westinghouse followed with its own stripped-down, simple-to-operate set, as recalled by an early radio historian:

> No "forest of knobs" here; no complicated table of settings; merely one circuit and one handle to vary it. I can recall the personal scorn with which this single circuit receiver was viewed by "old-style" radio engineers, i.e., myself, for it was held that this was going back to the days of 1900 . . . Actual use showed that for handling by people who knew nothing of radio's technicalities the single circuit was just what had been needed.[9]

Westinghouse had stumbled on a new business plan for its faltering radio operations, one that seemed to hold some real promise. Within a year, three other Westinghouse stations were broadcasting, and national demand for the simplified receivers had outstripped the supply. Now other broadcasters began flocking to the airwaves.

Since the U.S. Radio Act of 1912 placed no restrictions on ownership of a licence beyond American citizenship, the new broadcasters were a colourful group. Several distinct categories emerged. First, there were the big manufacturing interests such as Westinghouse, GE and RCA. Then there were the department stores, like Gimbels and Wanamakers, that operated stations for self-promotion. Some hotels had stations. There were stations in laundries, chicken farms and a stockyard. In 1922, eleven American newspapers held broadcasting licences, mainly, one suspects, out of self-defence, just as newspapers today have been quick to populate the World Wide Web. Churches and universities operated stations. And there were many so-called ego stations operated by wealthy individuals in the spirit of noblesse oblige, or just for the hell of it.

In Canada, the year 1922 saw the issuing of thirty-six broadcast licences covering most major centres of population, from St. John, New Brunswick, to Vancouver. The very first was issued to the

Winnipeg Free Press, and most others were also granted to news-papers, including *La Presse* in Montreal, the *Star* in Toronto, the *Herald* in Calgary, the *Journal* in Edmonton and the *Province* in Vancouver. Canadian Marconi was issued licences in Montreal (CFCF), Halifax, Vancouver and Toronto. A common experience shared by all of these fledgling broadcasters in North America was their shock at discovering how expensive programming could be, especially once performers' unions began raising copyright issues and charg-ing for appearances.

In the U.S., RCA entered the broadcast arena in December 1921 with station WDY in Roselle Park, New Jersey, and an ambitious schedule of recorded music and live lectures, variety and drama. While RCA had to some extent inherited the slow-moving bureau-cratic propensities of its gargantuan parent, General Electric, there was at least one employee of the new company who had been deeply chagrined by the fact that Westinghouse had stolen a march in put-ting a broadcasting station on the air. David Sarnoff had, with the shotgun marriage, moved from being commercial manager at American Marconi to taking on the same position at RCA, where he was soon promoted to general manager. One of the more re-markable figures in the annals of American industry, Sarnoff, the son of penniless Jewish immigrants from Russia, had by dint of brains and determination and a knack for self-promotion risen from newsboy to telegraph messenger to Marconi radiotelegraph opera-tor, and finally was taken under the wing of the great Marconi him-self, to become a trusted adviser and protege.

Sarnoff's greatest personal asset was his comprehensive under-standing of the technology of radio and its practical applications. He had worked in every corner of the business. As early as 1916 he had seen such advances as Fessenden's Christmas Eve broadcast and better receiver designs converging to make an entirely new industry possible. In that year he had written for his boss at Amer-ican Marconi a memorandum on the subject that laid out the future development of broadcasting before anyone had even used the word.

"I have in mind," Sarnoff wrote,

> a plan of development which would make radio a "household utility" in the same sense as the piano or phonograph. The idea is to bring music into the house by wireless . . . The receiver can be designed in the form of a simple "Radio Music Box" and arranged for several different wavelengths, which should be changeable with the throwing of a single switch or the pressing of a single button . . . The same principle can be extended to numerous other fields as, for example, receiving lectures at home which can be made perfectly audible; also events of national importance can be simultaneously announced and received. Baseball scores can be transmitted . . . The manufacture of the "Radio Music Box" including antenna in large quantities would make possible their sale at a moderate figure of perhaps $75.00 per outfit . . . It is not possible to estimate the total amount of business obtainable with this plan until it has been developed and actually tried out but there are about 15,000,000 families in the United States alone and if one million or 7% of the total families thought well of the idea it would, at the figure mentioned, mean a gross business of $75,000,000 which should yield considerable revenue . . .[10]

With the world mired in the horror of Flanders, with Marconi operations under government control and the company focused on producing hardware for the military market in Europe, it was not a propitious time for Sarnoff's plan, and no action was taken. With the formation of RCA, he submitted it to his new boss, who, with a wary eye on Westinghouse, had given him the go-ahead.[11]

Broadcasting's growth in that year (1921) was nothing short of phenomenal, though it may seem less astonishing today from the perspective of those who have experienced the similarly breath-taking growth of the Internet. The number of new stations receiv-ing licences in the U.S. grew from 2 in August, to 23 in December, to 99 in May 1922; the number of radio receivers in the U.S. grew from 50,000 in March 1921 to 750,000 just fourteen months later. *Radio Broadcast* magazine, in its debut issue in May 1922, reported:

> The rate of increase in the number of people who spend at least a part of their evening in listening in is almost incomprehensible . . . The movement is probably not even yet at its height. It is still growing in some kind of geometrical progression . . . It seems quite likely that before the movement has reached its height, before the market for receiving apparatus becomes approximately saturated, there will be at least five million receiving sets in the country.

In fact, the 5 million mark was passed less than four years later, and by 1927 there were 6.5 million sets in use in the U.S., one for every seventeen persons. In 1940 there would be 50 million sets, one for every 2.6 persons. RCA, the major distributor of radio receivers, recorded awe-inspiring sales: 1921—$1,468,919.95; 1922—$11,286,489.41; 1923—$22,465,090.71; 1924—$50,747,202.24.

Another article in the same issue of *Radio Broadcast* gave this picture of the booming industry in 1922, a portrait that is eerily evocative of the early development of the modern computer industry:

> The manufacturers of radio receivers and accessories are in much the situation that munition makers were when the war broke. They are suddenly confronted with a tremendous and imperative demand for apparatus. It is a matter of several months at best to arrange for the quantity production of radio receiving apparatus if the type to be manufactured were settled, but the types are no more settled than were the types of airplanes in the war. The manufacturing companies are, therefore, confronted with carrying on their experimental work, devising new types and at the same time producing the best they can in such quantity as they can, and they must do all of this while building their organizations, working out their policies and

keeping an eye on the Government so that they can keep in accord with regulations.[12]

Despite, or perhaps because of, the rapid growth, the industry had yet to resolve the critical issue of how to pay for broadcasting. Westinghouse, RCA and other equipment manufacturers had an obvious economic interest in spurring the numbers of listeners: there was plenty of indirect revenue to be derived from receiver and component sales. Department stores employed their stations as advertising vehicles for their own wares. Newspapers opened stations with a view to cross-promotion, counting on increased paper subscriptions to pay the radio bills. But there was also a large number of new stations run by individuals who had no obvious source of financial support for their broadcasting efforts. The great debate of the day in the pages of radio periodicals and the more mainstream media was: how should radio broadcasting be financed?

Commercial sponsorship, although it was by no means unheard of (advertising had long since become the major source of newspaper revenue), was not the most popular approach to the problem; few thought it a likely source of substantial revenue. How much could one realistically charge for an advertisement that might be heard by a few hundred people, or at best a few thousand? RCA's David Sarnoff hated the idea on principle, believing it would destroy radio's potential for education and quality entertainment. He argued that radio should be financed by the big manufacturing companies like his own, and Westinghouse, as a public service. They would, after all, profit handsomely from appliance sales. (This sentiment may not have been altogether altruistic. The astute Sarnoff must have realized that introducing direct advertising revenue to broadcasting would make the field accessible to others who did not have the luxury of owning radio factories from which to derive indirect revenues.)

Sarnoff's public views on advertising were shared by Secretary of Commerce (soon to be President) Herbert Hoover. In a speech in 1922, Hoover declaimed: "The ether is a public medium and must be used for the public good. It is quite inconceivable that it should be used for advertising." *Radio Broadcast* magazine, fast becoming the unofficial bible of the industry, editorially supported public financing through an endowment model similar to that which had successfully built a system of libraries throughout North America and many fine universities in the U.S. Direct government financing was also proposed in the magazine, though somewhat gingerly, as befitted a mass-circulation outlet in an era of rampant anti-Bolshevist sentiment in America:

> A weird scheme this [government financing] will undoubtedly appear to many, but upon analysis it will be found not so strange, even to those who have no socialistic tendencies. In New York City, for example, large sums of money are spent annually in maintaining free public lectures, given on various topics of interest; the attendance at one of these lectures may average two or three hundred people. The same lecture delivered from a broadcasting station would be heard by several thousand people. Because of the diverse interests of such a large city as New York, it would probably be necessary to operate two or three stations, from each of which different forms of amusement or educational lectures would be sent out. The cost of such a project would probably be less than that for the scheme at present used and the number of people who would benefit might be immeasurably greater.[13]

Alas, commercial-free radio in America was an idea whose time had come and gone years earlier, when the first Westinghouse station, KDKA, drilled its modest Pittsburgh test well into the reservoir for advertising demand and came up with a gusher. In the paradox of conflicting values that has marked American history in the twentieth century, the distrust of the state in this case outweighed distrust of corporate monopoly power.

American political tradition views democracy as a triumph of the lone individual over the tyranny of government, and the threat of state censorship, raised at every opportunity by advocates of commercial sponsorship, sounded a deep chord. The overweening power of the modern twentieth-century business corporation with its vast financial resources, international reach, and armies of lawyers, lobbyists and public relations professionals was still largely unrealized, and the problem of corporate concentration of media ownership was too speculative to be taken seriously. The possibility of corporate censorship of media and what that might mean was never weighed against the less certain prospect of harmful government meddling.

Broadcasting's Pot of Gold

I N AMERICA, the ultimate solution to the financing conundrum was to come from what seems at first blush an unlikely
source: telephone industry giant AT&T, Alexander Graham
Bell's gargantuan child. The company had for years been interested
in vacuum tube technology, and its engineers had steadily refined
vacuum tube amplifiers to make transcontinental long-distance
telephony possible. And so, when AT&T announced in the spring of
1922 that it would open an experimental radio broadcasting station
in New York using the most advanced technology then available, it
had to be taken seriously.

It is a curious fact, and one that illustrates how little the future
of broadcasting was generally understood, that the patent cross-
licensing agreements between RCA and AT&T in 1920 and 1921 gave
AT&T the exclusive right to employ the pooled patents for radiotelephony. (RCA retained exclusive rights for radio*telegraphy*.) Voice
communication by radio was considered a natural extension of
AT&T's existing telephone interests; commercial radio clearly was still
being thought of primarily in terms of point-to-point communication as late as 1921. However, when new prospects for revenue were
scented, the telephone company was quick to extend its interpretation of the covenants to include all of commercial broadcasting. It

was AT&T's position for many years—one hotly contested within the industry—that any station engaged in broadcasting using any of the hundreds of patents tied up within the cross-licensing webs of RCA and its allies (which now included Westinghouse) owed a royalty to AT&T. Captured in this category was virtually every broadcast station in North America. And it was in large measure to protect its rights and potential revenues in this area that the company entered broadcasting when it did.

AT&T's broadcasting business plan was an interesting one. It was based on the economics of a long-distance telephone service, in which customers are charged by the minute for use of telephone company (telco) facilities. Extended to radio broadcasting, this meant that AT&T would be in the business of selling time on its transmitters, and advertisers would be invited to purchase a block of time and provide their own program content within that block. (This is similar to the commercial arrangements for infomercials on today's television channels.) Airtime that had not been sold to advertisers would be filled by AT&T's own programming resources to maintain audience numbers.

It is evident from the company's announcement of the new service in February 1922 that it had also hit upon the momentous idea of networking among stations to accumulate audience numbers large enough to be of interest to major sponsors. This deserves recognition as one of the most brilliantly imaginative business ideas of the twentieth century. The news release read:

> This is a new undertaking . . . and if there appears a real field for such a service . . . it will be followed as circumstances warrant by similar stations erected at important centers throughout the United States by the AT&T Company. As these additional stations are erected, they can be connected by the toll and long-distance wires of the Bell System so that from any central point, the same news, music and other programming can be sent out simultaneously through all these stations by wire and wireless with the greatest plausible economy and without interference.[1]

The first of the AT&T stations would be WBAY, which was soon folded into a second, technically superior station, WEAF. (General Electric weighed in at about the same time with its first station, WGY. It was a heavyweight that could be heard on the west coast, throughout Canada and in Alaska.) By 1925 the company was regularly assembling networks of up to twenty-five stations, linking them with its long-distance telephone lines.

Twelve days after it went on the air, AT&T's WEAF sold its first block of time to a Long Island real estate developer called Queensborough Corporation. A ten-minute segment was purchased by the company in each of the five days between August 28 and September 1, 1922, to sell its suburban condominiums. In keeping with the contemporary notion that content was king on radio and that listeners would not stand for a straight sales pitch, the advertisement was couched, though none too subtly, in a tribute to the American author Nathaniel Hawthorne, for whom part of the housing development (Hawthorne Court) had been named.[2] On September 21, 1922, WEAF carried three commercials: Queensborough Corporation, Tidewater Oil and American Express.

That same month, in *Radio Broadcast*, there appeared what may be the first published rant against radio commercials, under the headline "Should Radio Be Used for Advertising?":

> Anyone who doubts the reality, the imminence of the problem, has only to listen about him for plenty of evidence. Driblets of advertising, most of it indirect so far, but still unmistakable, are floating through the ether every day. Concerts are seasoned here and there with a dash of advertising paprika. You can't miss it; every little classic number has a slogan all its own, if it is only the mere mention of the name—and the street address, and the phone number—of the music house which arranged the program. More of this sort of thing may be expected. And once the avalanche gets a good start, nothing short of an Act of Congress or a repetition of Noah's excitement will suffice to stop it.

Later, when broadcast advertising had achieved the status of a fundamental engine of growth in the consumer society and the raison d'être for broadcasting itself, the idea of eliminating it would come to be seen as quaintly fantastic at best and downright unpatriotic at worst. In retrospect, though, it is difficult to find a point at which the idea of direct advertising on radio gained acceptance. Even in industry circles it was widely viewed with distaste. As late as 1925, a blue-ribbon committee of industry experts set up to mediate ongoing disputes between RCA, GE and Westinghouse, on the one hand, and AT&T, on the other, had this to say about advertising, in a report prepared for the companies involved:

> There is a natural conflict of interest between serving the broadcast listener [the purchaser of radio receivers] and serving the advertiser using broadcast facilities. The listener desires a program of the highest quality as free as possible from all extraneous or irrelevant material, particularly such as may be psychologically distracting from an artistic performance because of its commercial tinge . . . The tendency of advertising programs is toward direct advertising . . . the tendency of stations devoted entirely to pleasing the listener and without toll payment for advertising programs is to minimize to the utmost any inartistic or irrelevant text.

The committee recommended that RCA avoid direct sponsorship of programming by advertisers on grounds that "the Radio Corporation of America is the largest radio sales organization in the United States . . . [it] requires the good will of the broadcast listener and this might be jeopardized by the responsibility for the commercial success of toll advertising programs."

The committee also presented a concrete proposal for an idea that had been entertained in various forms since the advent of radio: a program-providing foundation, paid for by radio manufacturers and related industries on the basis of a percentage of their sales. The foundation would also accept advertisers' money, but would only permit indirect sponsorship of programming of the kind seen today in America's public broadcasting system.

The plan became a victim of the frenetic pace of evolution in the industry, overlooked rather than discarded, as issues of more pressing priority continued to demand attention. Nevertheless, as late as 1926, when Sarnoff and RCA launched NBC, the prevailing attitude on the boards of directors of both RCA and the new broadcasting network was quite clearly one of broadcasting as a public service, supported, but not driven, by commercial sponsorship. Unsponsored programming of special artistic merit, including broadcasts of symphony concerts, theatre and opera, was common, and educational programming held a prominent place in the network schedules. Historian Gleason Archer notes that in its initial months of operation, RCA's NBC recorded mounting deficits, and goes on to observe: "A deficit, however, was an expected development. The directors . . . were inclined to view the matter as a semi-philanthropic activity which the leading corporations of the radio industry were joining hands in supporting. It was regarded, and characterized by [Chairman] Owen D. Young, as 'an investment in the youth of America.'"[3] This was, perhaps, a point of view that could only be nurtured at the breast of a quasi-monopoly like RCA. The advisory board selected to guide programming on the new network reflected the "semi-philanthropic" attitude: it was decidedly heavy on university presidents, symphony conductors, clerics and philanthropists, and light on lawyers and businessmen.

However, the arrival on the scene two years later, in 1928, of the upstart Columbia Broadcasting System, with its ambitious young owner, William Paley, forced NBC to take a more aggressive stance. Paley was able to put CBS well into the black in its first year of operation by focusing on commercial sales, and by capitalizing on the networking experience won by NBC and its predecessor, the AT&T network, over such a long time and at such great expense. Before long CBS profits were matching those of NBC, on a small fraction of NBC's total revenues. CBS had demonstrated that there existed a greater public tolerance for commercials than NBC and its parent

RCA had believed possible. Paley very quickly became wealthy enough to support an extravagant Manhattan lifestyle, including a sumptuous townhouse and a private chef who had once worked for Enrico Caruso.

There was, as well, a shift in the nature of radio programming that arrived with the runaway North American hit show *Amos 'n' Andy*. In it, two white comedians, Freeman Gosden and Charles Correll, played black buffoons with unblushingly stereotyped parody. Even as an independent syndication distributed to a handful of stations on shellac recording disks, the show drew huge audiences that high-toned programmers at NBC could not ignore. Advertisers were dazzled by the numbers. NBC finally, in 1929, purchased the show for $100,000 a year. It was the network's first foray into pop programming, and within months *Amos 'n' Andy* was drawing 40 million listeners, or half the radio audience.

Over at CBS, the always-alert Bill Paley went on a crash program to shift his network's focus to popular programming as quickly as he could sign the artists. Paul Whiteman and his orchestra were hired for *The Old Gold Program* at $35,000 a week. Bing Crosby, a Hollywood crooner with a drinking problem, was rounded up and dried out for fifteen minutes a week on the network. The *True Story* drama series, based on a lurid pulp magazine, went into production. Soap operas ruled the afternoons. Comedians abounded.

With this kind of programming beginning to dominate the two early networks, advertising seemed less out of place than it once had in the context of more stimulating fare. Network programmers and advertisers had at last apparently located the pulse of mainstream America's cultural sensibilities, at least as they existed in the 1930s. Alternatively, one could say that they had discovered a formula in which commercial messages seemed less intrusive, more suitable and appropriate. For, while some of the "populist" programming was extremely popular, much of it was not, and yet virtually nothing of the original middlebrow format of plays, lectures, serious music and informed discussion survived.

Before long, the well-worn apologia for the draining of nourishment from mass programming would begin to be heard—that is, that commercial radio gives audiences what they ask for, what they want. It was, and remains, a specious argument based on an empty tautology: only programs that the public wants survive; if the program survives, the public must want it. Often, in reality, authentic public tastes had less to do with programming "success" or longevity than the skill of publicists and marketing specialists, network economic considerations, executive whims and, above all, the needs of advertisers. Furthermore, only part of the population got to "vote" for the programming—that part that frequently watched or listened to the programming offered. Those who chose to avoid it were, and are, effectively disenfranchised.

In the debate over how to finance radio programming, there was one obvious example of an industry that had apparently solved an analogous problem—the newspaper business. As described in chapter 6, American newspapers had in the late nineteenth century altered their business plans to give advertisers and the revenue they provided a much more prominent role. This involved a shift of publishers' allegiances from the subscriber and reader to the advertiser, so that readers became the bait to attract sponsorship. Though the impact of this shift was not well understood in the first decades of the twentieth century, it has become clear in retrospect. In the words of cultural historian Stewart Ewan,

> Newspapers, which throughout the nineteenth century had provided an arena for literary serialization and popular expression and whose diversity had provided for varied audiences, became increasingly commercialized and centralized in their direction. From 1900 through 1930 the number of daily newspapers in America declined steadily . . . more important, there was an even greater decline in the existence of a diverse press . . . By 1930, 80% of American cities had given way to a press monopoly. The role and influence of advertising in all of these

developments is marked. In the period 1900–1930, national advertising revenues multiplied 13 fold (from $200 million to $2.6 billion) and it was the periodicals, both dailies and others, which acted as a major vehicle for this growth.[4]

The model of the sponsored time-block or program had in a similar way placed radio content in the hands of advertising agencies, which acted as marriage brokers between the networks and potential sponsors. The ad agency naturally saw its first obligation as being to serve the interests of its client, the advertiser; serving the public was a secondary, peripheral consideration. While its early proponents had seen radio as a potentially powerful tool of public enlightenment and cultural enrichment, to the ad agency it was, rather, "a latchkey to nearly every home in the United States," a sort of psychological Santa Claus (or burglar) slipping through the radio into the home, leaving behind commercial messages. To quote a leading marketing specialist of the day:

> For years the national advertiser and his agency have been dreaming of the time to come when there would be evolved some great family medium which should reach the home and the adult members of the family in their moments of relaxation, bringing to them the editorial and advertising message. Then came radio broadcasting, utilizing the very air we breathe, and with electricity as its vehicle entering the homes of the nation through doors and windows, no matter how tightly barred, and delivering its message audibly through the loudspeaker wherever placed . . . In the midst of the family circle, in moments of relaxation, the voice of radio brings to the audience its program of entertainment or its message of advertising.[5]

And finally, the Great Depression appears to have softened public attitudes to advertising on radio. At a time when the new medium provided the only professional entertainment many North Americans could afford, there was a natural tolerance of, even gratitude for, the corporate spending on advertising that made so many programs possible. With the end of the Depression came all-consuming war, and by the time it had ended, the fact that radio had once had a genuine opportunity to be something other than a strictly commercially driven medium was but a fading memory of a hazy dream.

The ultimate victory for the advertising-financed model for radio came in 1927 when Congress passed a new Radio Act that effectively entrenched commercial sponsorship as the solution to the problem of radio's long-term profitability. It was a free-market model that responded to the neo-liberal mantra of "let the market decide." It is more than a little difficult to see how the public interest was best served in this decision, or how it is being served today by commercial radio. Combining commercial sponsorship with broadcast technology creates an irreversible slide toward the lowest common denominator in programming. It is inevitable, since broadcasting, by definition, makes no provision for addressing minority or niche interests. To be successful, a broadcaster had to satisfy as many people of as many diverse interests and backgrounds as possible, thereby maximizing the number of listeners. But he had just one vehicle with which to do that—his station or network and its programming lineup. Therefore broadcasters had no choice but to tune that vehicle to the satisfaction of the greatest number of listeners throughout the broadcast schedule. In other words, the broadcaster had no choice but to aim for the lowest common denominator, wherein lay profit and satisfied shareholders.

It is also of no small significance that commercially sponsored programming exists primarily and fundamentally as a means of selling the products or services of the sponsor. This fact inevitably shapes the content of the sponsored program: certainly the show will in no way be allowed to contain material that the sponsor might find objectionable for any reason, and where possible it will also be expected to further the commercial interests of the sponsor in some direct or indirect way. Thus, both blatantly and subtly, commercialization of the medium shaped the program content it delivered.[6] This applied even to news programming. Throughout the political tinderbox of the 1930s, NBC frequently cancelled programs that might "undermine the public confidence and faith." Cincinnati powerhouse station WLW had an explicit policy: "No reference to strikes is to be made on any news bulletin broadcast over our station." This was corporate censorship of real significance, since by 1939, 70 percent of the American populace reported that radio was their main source of news.

Nevertheless, faith in the market's "invisible hand," combined with an increasingly effective industry lobby, had, by the mid-1930s, "solved" the problem of funding. The technology of radio, and eventually television, would be configured to maximize profit, and "voting" on content would be confined to consumers rather than extended to all citizens. The gatekeeper function in cultural production would be delegated to business entrepreneurs to the exclusion of other elements of society. Commercial sponsorship would also lead to the transformation of American political processes, reshaping them to conform to the needs of commercial media, reducing politicians to the status of advertisers, forcing them to raise enormous sums of money to purchase commercials sandwiched between soft drink and detergent spots in order to reach the public, turning political contests into fundraising tournaments.

In a broader sense, the commercialization of radio had effectively taken what had been a shared public resource and made of it a tool for the furtherance of the interests of one segment of society, that is, business, and one social paradigm, the "consumer society." Whether or not that was in the interests of society at large may be a matter for debate; it is a debate, however, that one is unlikely to hear in a commercially sponsored broadcast.

In Britain, radio's development had taken a much different course following World War I. As in the United States, there had been the pressing problem of large radio manufacturing facilities built up during the conflict, with no peacetime market to serve. And, as in the U.S., the manufacturers were anxious to develop broadcasting as a means of supporting equipment sales.

However, from an overall strategic point of view, there were important differences between the two countries. Chief among these was the fact that while the U.S. was trying to develop a globally competitive industry, Britain was in the position of a world leader trying to defend the status quo. There were strong vested interests in both countries, but in Britain the more conservative among them would have the upper hand. The Royal Navy shared the view of American admirals that private radio would interfere with military communication. The Royal Mail had long had control over telephones, telegraphy and radiotelegraphy, and felt it only natural that its bureaucratic prerogatives should extend to the control of radiotelephony, or broadcasting, as well.

The British upper classes were generally disdainful of radio broadcasting. In G.E.C. Wedlake's SOS: *The Story of Radio-Communication*, the story is told of how the diplomat Sir Harold Nicolson came to hear Prime Minister Neville Chamberlain's declaration of war against Germany over the radio, on September 3, 1939. Nicolson was visiting friends in London's West End. "His host had no radio set, but the housemaid had one, and just after eleven she brought it into the room where they were sitting. It seems strange that as late as 1939 only the servant in a well-to-do household had a radio receiver. It showed, in fact, that in certain circles radio had still not been accepted. It was something for the masses; intelligent people did not listen to it."[7]

A handful of experimental broadcast stations appeared in Britain following the war, run by Marconi, Western Electric, Metropolitan-Vickers and others. Broadcasts from Europe, particularly the Sunday concerts from The Hague, were listened to avidly. British broadcasters were handicapped by a Royal Mail requirement that they go off the air for three minutes out of every ten so that an operator could check to see whether interference was being caused with any commercial radiotelegraph station. Despite this, the public response was only slightly less enthusiastic there than in North America, and it was clear that the government was going to have to allow broadcasting sooner or later. And so, in April 1922, a gathering

of interested parties was organized by the Royal Mail. The manufacturers were there, of course, as well as the armed services, the
Foreign Office, the Colonial Office and the Board of Trade. The
Royal Mail claimed jurisdiction over broadcasting based on the authority granted it in the Telegraph Act of 1869 and the Wireless
Telegraph Act of 1904. There was grumbling over the fact that neither act mentioned anything about radiotelephony, and the issue
was raised in the Commons, but it was never tested in court.

As it had been in the United States, the ownership of patents was
a crucial issue. Marconi, which controlled most of them, made it
plain that if other companies were to be given government permission to operate broadcast stations, they would not be given access
to the patents they would need to build either transmitters or the
receivers they hoped to sell to the public. The Royal Mail, for its
part, was opposed to giving Marconi or any other single company
a monopoly on broadcasting. It was decided that broadcasting in
Britain would be carried on by a corporation operated by a board
of directors drawn from the Royal Mail and the country's six biggest
radio manufacturers. Given the prevailing attitude among the ruling classes, there was never any doubt that it would be non-commercial radio; private companies would have to make their
money by selling receivers and other equipment. The broadcaster
itself would be financed by a licence fee of fifty pence charged with
every receiver sold. Half that money would go to the Royal Mail
and half to the broadcaster. When the company's charter expired
in 1926, it was reorganized as a Crown corporation (government
owned but independently managed) and given additional financing from the national treasury. Its staff by then had grown from 4 to
nearly 600.

The first BBC station opened on the roof of Marconi House in
the Strand, London, on November 14, 1922, with a newscast read by
an engineer into an ordinary telephone microphone (at two speeds,
fast and slow!) and a one-hour concert of recorded music.[8] Other
stations were quickly opened in Birmingham, Manchester, Cardiff,
Bournemouth, Newcastle, Glasgow and Aberdeen. The restrictions

under which the BBC had to operate give some idea of the latent hostility to the medium among those who governed it. For a start, it could broadcast only between 5 p.m. and midnight. Thanks to effective lobbying by the nation's newspapers—which were major customers of the Royal Mail's telegraph department—the BBC would not be permitted to broadcast news before it had appeared in print, which in practice meant before 7 p.m. The BBC could broadcast live speeches but not comment on them; it could broadcast the atmosphere and activities surrounding major sporting events but not the events themselves. It was, above all, forbidden to broadcast anything "controversial."

Hemmed in by all these rules, it is a wonder the BBC was able to build enough credibility with its audience to survive, and perhaps it wouldn't have if there had been competition from the private sector. But survive it did, to become the world's most respected broadcast organization. The competitive, innovative environment in American radio ensured that the U.S. would dominate world markets in radio manufacturing, but the quality of programming in Britain was unequalled. World War II was the BBC's turning point. Its wartime broadcasting gained it the respect and admiration of Britons of every class, and of people around the world. It never looked back. Today, when Japan and other Asian countries dominate the manufacturing sector in broadcasting, and the U.S. remains saddled with the abysmal level of quality in programming that is dictated by commercial considerations, it might well be argued that Britain made the wiser choice in the long run.

If any single individual can be given credit for the BBC's excellence, it would have to be John Reith, a minister's son and engineer who was appointed the first director-general of the newly formed corporation in 1927, a position he held until 1938. He had participated in the writing of the BBC charter, which granted it a monopoly over broadcasting and stated that it was to provide the highest-quality information, education and entertainment, operating at arm's length from government. Reith's ideas on broadcasting and social responsibility are set out in his 1924 book *Broadcast Over Britain*:

Till the advent of this universal and extraordinarily cheap medium of communication a very large proportion of the people were shut off from first-hand knowledge of the events which make history. They did not share in the interests and diversions of those with fortune's twin gifts—leisure and money. They could not gain access to the great men of the day, and these men could deliver their messages to a limited number only. Today all this has changed.

Reith believed that to use broadcasting for entertainment only would be to "prostitute" it. The BBC should "bring into the greatest possible number of homes . . . all that is best in every department of human knowledge, endeavour and achievement," and in doing so, he said, the broadcaster "obviously" had to maintain a "high moral tone." A monopoly was the only instrument that could achieve this high standard, because only a monopoly could "defy a cultural Gresham's law stating that bad drives out good."[9]

His views had their opponents, who called them elitist, but they also received widespread official and unofficial support. In 1934, *The Times* of London editorialized that it had been wise "to entrust broadcasting in this country to a single organization with an independent monopoly and with public service as its primary motive." Successive commissions of inquiry were to confirm that position. For the Fabian socialist W.A. Robson, it was "an invention in the sphere of social science no less remarkable than the invention of radio transmission in the sphere of natural science."[10]

The BBC adapted its wartime Forces Programme (a special format of variety and news broadcast throughout the world) to a peacetime audience, calling it the Light Programme. This supplemented the Home and Third programmes, successively more highbrow musically and intellectually challenging. Some saw this as fragmenting the "great audience" Reith had envisioned, but Director-General Sir William Haley instead spoke of an audience that could be encouraged to graduate from Light to Home to Third.[11]

The BBC's monopoly would eventually be broken by offshore

"pirate" commercial radio stations, some broadcasting from ships anchored in international waters, and by superstations such as Radio Luxembourg, which beamed rock music to a youthful British audience in the socially turbulent 1960s. Law enforcement initiatives to shut down the pirates failed, and to serve this audience the BBC created Radio 1, which followed the pirate format and even employed former pirate on-air talent. Radio stations serving local and regional rather than national audiences were set up at the same time. (There would eventually be five radio networks, regional services in Scotland, Wales and Northern Ireland, and about forty local stations in the BBC empire.) In 1973, new legislation permitted the launching of three national, commercially sponsored radio stations and more than 240 local broadcasters to compete with BBC outlets in all programming formats from news to pop and classical music.

Canadian broadcasting, destined to become in many ways the most technically sophisticated in the world thanks to the demands placed on engineers by geography and language (Canada is officially bilingual, and the CBC also broadcasts in Aboriginal languages), has had a schizophrenic relationship with commercial sponsorship. The first national radio network in the country was constructed by the publicly owned railway, the Canadian National, as a commercial enterprise. In 1932 it became the foundation for a new public broadcaster.

Since the earliest days of broadcasting, Canadian listeners had been drawn to the relatively high-budget, highly polished and extensively promoted programming on American radio. By the end of the 1920s, fully 80 percent of the programs listened to by Canadians originated in the U.S., and in 1929 stations in Montreal and Toronto joined American networks as affiliates. A concerned federal government, responding to this latest threat of cultural colonialism from south of the border (a burgeoning Hollywood film industry was similarly worrying), established a Royal Commission to examine the problem along with related issues, including the widespread public objections to commercial sponsorship on radio and spectrum interference from unregulated U.S. stations.

The inquiry recommended the setting up of a national, publicly funded broadcaster. Modelled on the BBC, it would be charged with carrying distinctively Canadian content to every community in the land. The commission's recommendations were energetically supported by an influential lobby calling itself the Canadian Radio League, which argued that the medium should be devoted to national public service rather than profit making. In 1932, after an unsuccessful two-year-long courtroom challenge by Ontario and Quebec to Ottawa's jurisdiction over broadcasting (a veiled attack on the idea of public broadcasting), Parliament passed an act establishing the Canadian Radio Broadcasting Commission. The CRBC was given broad powers both to establish radio stations and networks and to regulate the industry as a whole; its mandate was ultimately to take over all Canadian broadcast outlets.

But a penalty had to be paid for Ottawa's tardiness in dealing with the highly contentious radio issue, and it proved politically impossible to impose a public monopoly on an already entrenched commercial industry. The plan for an exclusively public domain for Canadian broadcasting was effectively stifled by the newly elected Conservative government of R.B. Bennett, which was operating under the financial constraints of the Depression years. Starved of the resources it needed to establish a countrywide network (despite charging a licence fee for all receivers sold), the CRBC set up stations in only five cities; in the rest of the country it worked out programming agreements with established private broadcasters, who were required to carry a prescribed number of hours of CRBC-produced content each day. This mixed private-public system was a model that would survive to the end of the twentieth century in both radio and television.

The industry was again reorganized in 1936, with the replacement of the CRBC by the Canadian Broadcasting Corporation (CBC). Thanks to increased funding provided by higher licence fees, the CBC greatly expanded the public network's coverage, with high-powered regional stations and a much longer schedule of original Canadian programming.[12] This domestic content was supplemented by some of the most popular American shows. While private stations were not allowed to form their own competing network (and objected loudly to this constraint), they managed to prosper on local and regional audiences and the advertising these attracted. The CBC itself became commercial-free (on radio) only in 1975.

Ottawa has consistently refused to grant the CBC the necessary funding to establish a third national radio network devoted to popular music and culture, attentive to fears of private broadcasters that such a service would undercut their audiences (and profits). Commercial radio in Canada is similar to its American counterpart, devoted largely to various pop music formats carefully structured by consultants to appeal to demographic niches of interest to advertisers. However, it differs in that the excesses of "shock" radio, fundamentalist religion and extremist political commentary have been avoided in Canada through comprehensive regulation of content imposed by a national broadcast regulatory authority—currently called the Canadian Radio-television and Telecommunications Commission, or CRTC.[13]

With the arrival of television in the 1950s, radio everywhere faced an enormous crisis. The prime-time evening audience in the U.S., for example, plunged from 17 million homes to just 3 million over the decade. It was not until the late 1960s and 1970s that highly portable transistor radios and universal adoption of automobile radios, along with revised program schedules and formats, restored much of this loss. The revised radio programming of both the BBC and the CBC spoke directly to listeners with a new informality, emphasizing radio's role as a companion. (Television, in contrast, is a tyrant, demanding complete attention.) The CBC got a further lift by eliminating commercial sponsorship in 1975. American radio, on the other hand, reacted to the challenge from television by going almost exclusively local, offering low-cost advertising for small businesses that couldn't afford TV spots. Production costs were pared to the bone, with formats featuring nothing but recorded music introduced by poorly paid "disc jockeys." The advent of subscription-based satellite radio and Internet "podcasting" posed a new set of challenges and opportunities, to which the industry is still adjusting.

Television: 1

T ELEVISION, particularly as it evolved on the North American commercially sponsored model, is the problem child of mass communications technologies. Anticipated as a natural and inevitable outgrowth of radio and motion picture technologies from the earliest days of radio experimentation, it was to incorporate radio's principal drawbacks as a one-way, top-down medium, and add several serious problems all its own. At the same time, it was seldom, if ever, able to attain the high standards of artistic merit reached in the cinema, thanks to its small screen and the adoption of radio's advertising-supported model. As a very "cool" medium, in McLuhan's terms, it demanded complete attention and created a vegetative subspecies of humanity aptly named the "couch potato." Far from bringing the best of culture to its audience, as it had the potential to do, it systematically debased public tastes as it sought out the lowest common denominator in order to maximize audience size.

Its executives argued that it merely gave people what they wanted. However, TV is not squalid because people are vulgar; it is squalid because people share the same primitive impulses and desires, though they are widely and wonderfully diverse in their higher interests and aspirations. Television exposed generations of children en masse to puerile, commercial-ridden pap and shocking violence, and then insisted that it was all good, harmless fun. There have been high points as well, most of them connected with TV's ability to bring important news into the living room, but even these have been ambiguous triumphs. The images carried on television news shortened the Vietnam War, but television conspired with the military to mask the horror of two Gulf Wars behind the telegenic myth of "surgical" smart bombs and civilian-friendly cruise missiles. TV shocked the United States out of its complacency toward Southern school segregation, but at the same time perpetuated racial stereotypes in dramas and sitcoms. TV helped speed the collapse of the Soviet Empire in Eastern Europe, but then promoted a consumer ethic emerging democracies could ill afford.

On balance, it is possible to argue—certainly in North America—that through most of its existence television has been more bane than benefit to society, a fact that makes it unique among the technologies of communication. It is only in recent years, as television has shattered into hundreds of specialty channels distributed on satellite and fibre optic cable, weakening the grip of the old network structure and providing viewers with a semblance of real choice in programming, that the medium has begun to show some net benefit to society. The social and political impact of both radio and television will be discussed in some detail in the next two chapters; the focus here will be on the technology behind television, a subject that holds the key to many of the medium's shortcomings.

In 1873, Willoughby Smith was a senior technician employed by the Telegraph Construction and Maintenance Company of Britain, the firm that had laid the first successful transatlantic cable eight years earlier. Smith had been assigned the task of finding a way to continuously test undersea cables while they were under construction. To work out an idea, he needed a material that had a high resistance to electrical current but was not a complete insulator, that he could use as a stand-in for many miles of copper cable. He decided to try bars of crystalline selenium. In his crowded lab, the counter space was fully occupied, so the selenium was placed on a windowsill. As his experiments progressed, Smith was surprised to notice that the current flowing through his test circuit seemed to be changing with variations in light outside: the sunnier the day, the more voltage his meters registered. Evidently, the resistance of selenium dropped markedly when it was exposed to light.[1]

It was an exciting discovery. Alexander Graham Bell was among the inventors who went to work on applications for it, and during a lecture in 1878 he told his audience that it ought to be possible to "hear a shadow fall" on a piece of selenium wired into a telephone circuit. He would develop that idea into what he came to consider his best invention, the "photophone," a wireless telephone. Bell mounted a mirror on a tightly drawn diaphragm of canvas and shone a strong light on it. Words spoken into a tube placed close to the mirror caused it to vibrate, in effect modulating the reflected light with the voice's vibrations. On the receiving end, a parabolic mirror collected the light reflected from the mirror and focused it on a selenium cell. As the received light varied, so did the current passing through the selenium from a battery attached to it. That variable current, when applied to a telephone receiver, perfectly reproduced the words spoken at the transmitter. The only drawback—and it proved to be fatal—was that the photophone worked only over short, line-of-sight distances, in perfect atmospheric conditions.

Bell's work on the photophone, however, was not wasted. The English physicist Shelford Bidwell, in tinkering with a replica of the photophone, had the inspiration that it ought to be able to transmit images. That is, changes in the intensity of light captured in a black-and-white photograph could be converted into a fluctuating electrical current by selenium, and that current could be sent down a telephone wire. At the receiving end, the photograph would be reconstructed by reversing the process and changing the fluctuating current back into varying intensities of light. He named it the "scanning phototelegraph"; we would call it a fax machine. In describing it to the Physical Society in London in 1876, Bidwell said with commendable modesty: "I cannot but think that it is capable of indefinite development, and should there ever be a demand for tele-photography, it may turn out to be a useful member of society."

The problem Bidwell had solved was a daunting one; normal telephony by comparison was simple. All a telephone had to do was carry a continuous stream of data as it emerged from the speaker's mouth in discrete syllables or bits. But what if what the speaker was saying had been presented all at once, as a page of dense text instead of a linear stream of bits? Clearly, the entire page could not be trans-mitted en bloc; it would have to be sent down the line letter by letter and word by word, so that the page could be reconstructed at the other end. That was essentially the difficulty in transmitting a picture, and the solution lay in finding a way to break it up into bits appropriate for transmission in a linear stream of electrical impulses and then reassemble them into a two-dimensional image at the other end. Bidwell's contribution was the idea of electrically *scanning* the image.

The phototelegraph can be considered in a direct line of descent toward television, in that it provided a method of converting pho-tographic information into electrical energy for transmission. It worked like this: A photograph was developed onto a glass plate. A strong light was shone through the plate onto a rotating cylinder about the size of a soup can, in the centre of which was a selenium cell. The cylinder was pierced by a pinhole, and as it rotated, it moved slowly from left to right, scanning the photograph onto the surface of the selenium cell. With each rotation, the pinhole tra-versed, or scanned, a narrow band of the photographic image directly adjacent to the line scanned on the previous rotation. The light falling on the selenium changed according to the shading of the photograph, and the selenium cell produced fluctuations in electri-cal current that were sent down wires to the receiving apparatus. The receiver used a stylus that mimicked the transmitter's scanning of the photograph, moving back and forth across a sheet of paper that had been chemically treated to make it sensitive to electricity, darkening when exposed to a current. Since the stylus was wired into the circuit carrying the fluctuating current from the transmitter, as long as it could be synchronized to move across the paper in exact concert with the motion of the scanning cylinder at the transmitter, the photograph would be accurately reproduced. Bidwell fudged a bit here: his desktop demonstration model had transmitter and receiver hooked up to the same motor, which ensured that they would be in perfect synchronization. This, of course, would have been impractical in a commercial model.

By 1905, Arthur Korn of Germany had perfected the idea. An ordinary photograph was wrapped around a cylinder and placed in the transmitter. As the cylinder rotated, a bright point of light moved along it, and the reflection of that light was captured by a selenium cell for transmission as fluctuating current down telephone lines. At the receiver, a sheet of photographic paper was wrapped onto a cylinder and loaded into the machine. The incoming current regulated the intensity of a small point of light scanning the spinning photographic paper, which was then developed in the usual way. The quality proved good enough for reproduction in newspapers, and the wire photo was born, a major boon to that image-hungry industry. In 1907, Korn set up a commercial fax network that linked Berlin with London and Paris over telephone lines.

It was only a small step to adapt the photo fax to wireless or radio transmission, and in 1924 the British Marconi Company and RCA staged a transatlantic swap of photos of President Calvin Coolidge and the Prince of Wales to publicize their new commercial transatlantic facsimile operation. Newspaper photos and weather charts were soon being transmitted around the world, though at such a high cost that for most ordinary purposes increasingly speedy international mail delivery was the preferred option. For the price of a single fax transmission, a three-pound package could be delivered by express mail.

It is a little-remembered curiosity that for a time the idea of the home facsimile machine for receiving broadcast manuscript newspapers in overnight transmissions from FM radio stations seemed poised to become the Next Big Thing in communications technology. By

1940, the industry's peak, there were forty radio stations offering this service in the United States, and more than ten thousand home fax receivers. A year later, only four stations were offering the service.[2] RCA was a leader in the field, and set its engineers the task of designing a home fax receiver that could sell for $50; the best they could do with the technology of the time was $500. Transmission times were relatively long, though it had shrunk from an hour for a four-page paper in 1938 to fifteen minutes a decade later. There was a brief revival of interest following the war when the *Miami Herald,* the *Philadelphia Inquirer,* the *New York Times* and other major newspapers got into the business, envisioning a future in which printing unions and newsprint producers would no longer hold them to ransom. But this revival, too, quickly faded. Cost and slowness of transmission doomed the industry; a newspaper could be picked up or delivered for a few cents, and radio (and later, television) could provide instant news with the flip of a switch.[3]

The problem of transmitting moving pictures, though it sounds daunting, was really only a little more difficult than still pictures. The earliest working televisions, in fact, had a lot in common with the facsimile machine. In 1884, Paul Nipkow of Germany patented a system that used a perforated disc spinning rapidly in front of a selenium cell to convert a moving image projected onto the disc into electrical information for transmission to a receiver. The perforations on the disc were arranged in a spiral so that the entire image would be scanned from top to bottom with each rotation. The perforation at the outer rim of the disc scanned the top few millimetres of the image as it passed over it, then the next perforation scanned a few millimetres lower, and so on. On the next rotation, the process was repeated. At the receiver, the fluctuating current from the selenium cell was reproduced as fluctuating light by an electric lamp wired into the circuit. A second spinning disc, identical to the first and revolving in perfect synchronization in front of the lamp, reproduced an image of the transmitted, moving picture. If the discs could be made to rotate fast enough, the eye would see the image as being in continuous motion rather than a separate series of pictures, thanks to the feature of human vision known as "persistence"—the eye retains an image for about 0.1 seconds after the light fades from it. Theoretically, if the image is refreshed more than ten times a second, the eye will perceive continuous motion. (In practice, to avoid flicker, the refresh rate needs to be 25 to 30 times per second.)

It was Nipkow's system, refined by J.L. Baird, that formed the basis for the BBC's earliest experiments in television, between 1929 and 1935. By then it had become clear that adequate picture definition would require a scanning rate much higher than 30 lines a second; 300 was closer to the magic number, and that speed of operation proved impractical for the mechanical system. The problem awaited an electronic solution.

Nevertheless, Baird remains an important figure in television history. An engineering colleague said of him:

> He was right at the end of the mechanical age. He thought in terms of wheels and sprockets and devices that spun around. He really wasn't with the electronics age at all. He hardly knew how a cathode tube worked. But he created a demand . . . If it hadn't been for Baird shouting and yelling and putting his crude 30-line pictures over London, we wouldn't have had television in this country before the war. He demonstrated that television could be done, if not the way it should be done.[4]

The electronic solution is commonly credited to a television research group at EMI (Electrical and Musical Industries) in Britain, and in the U.S. to a Russian-American émigré named Vladimir Zworykin. Zworykin had fled the Russian Revolution, taking with him an idea for an all-electronic television system, and had landed a research job with General Electric, where he worked on his scheme. But he was not satisfied with the level of support he was getting from GE, and when fellow émigré David Sarnoff of RCA offered him a position, he jumped ship. Sarnoff was convinced that television would eventually make radio obsolete—the "supplantive theory" of technology, he called it. He was wrong, of course, but his enthusiasm for the new medium was enough to secure Zworykin's loyalty. That, and a promise of $100,000 in development money. In 1932, Zworykin was able to demonstrate a complete television system at the RCA labs, using 120 scanning lines per second, which was quickly upgraded to 343 lines. (In 1936, the BBC adopted the EMI system, which used 405 lines per second.[5]) At the New York World's Fair in 1939, Sarnoff personally introduced the age of television with live broadcasts from the elaborate RCA pavilion, including a cameo appearance by U.S. president Franklin Roosevelt.

Until very recently, most reference works have given credit to Zworykin, Sarnoff and RCA for the invention of electronic television, and not without reason. Sarnoff was a consummate myth-maker and had a powerful radio and television network at his disposal to assist him in promoting RCA's achievements, real and fanciful. His personal mythology was an example of his talent: it included the "fact" that he had almost single-handedly taken care of radio traffic with the doomed *Titanic* and, later, the rescue ship *Carpathia* while a junior operator for the Marconi Company in 1912. His biography as prepared by the RCA public relations department contained this passage:

> On April 14, 1912, he was sitting at his instrument in the Wanamaker Store in New York. Leaning forward suddenly, he pressed the earphones more closely to his head. Through the sputtering and static . . . he was hearing a message: "S.S. *Titanic* ran into iceberg. Sinking fast." For the next seventy-two hours Sarnoff sat at his post, straining to catch every signal that might come through the air. That demanded a good operator in those days of undeveloped radio. By order of the President of the United States every other wireless station in the country was closed to stop interference . . . Not until he had given the world the name of the last survivor, three days and three nights after that first message, did Sarnoff call his job done.[6]

The paragraph contains several errors of fact that could only have been deliberate. April 14 was a Sunday and the department store was closed when the collision occurred at 10:25 p.m. Sarnoff donned his headphones the Monday morning following the sinking. Had Sarnoff remained at his post as described, he would have been there continuously for 100, not 72, hours, an unlikely feat in either case. He would likely have been unable to hear *Carpathia* and would have acted as a relay for stronger ships' stations and shore operations. In fact, the main role played by Sarnoff (and two other Marconi operators at the Wanamaker rooftop station) was to compile transcriptions of radio traffic for the Hearst newspaper *American*. Five days after the sinking and before *Carpathia* had reached New York, radio interference had grown so intense that Marconi shut down all but four of its own stations, and the Wanamaker store was among those closed. It is another fact of the historical record that a complete list of survivors and victims was not received onshore until the *Carpathia* docked, despite the fact that several well-heeled *Titanic* survivors were able to use the *Carpathia*'s radio to book rooms at New York hotels.

The true story of the invention of electronic television is that all of the important patents to the system eventually marketed by RCA were held by an independent mathematician and inventor from the unlikely state of Utah, who rejoiced in the name of Philo T. Farnsworth. Farnsworth conceived of the electronic image scanner and the picture tube as an awkward, lantern-jawed youngster of sixteen, and had patented these and many other associated circuits before he reached twenty. His genius put him on a direct collision course with the industry colossus, RCA, and its hard-driving president.

Thanks to the rather lenient terms of the antitrust "consent decree" of 1933, Sarnoff's RCA and AT&T continued to share virtually all of the important patents in the field of radio, and were thus able to decide who would and who would not be allowed to license rights to those patents. It was an important means of controlling competition, and Sarnoff, according to legend, would often assert, "RCA doesn't pay royalties; we collect them!" He had every intention of extending this arrangement to television.

Sarnoff sent Zworykin to pay a visit to Farnsworth's west coast lab to find out what he could about the television system the young man was developing. Zworykin left impressed by what he'd been shown, but confident he could engineer a way around Farnsworth's patents by building on his own ideas for the "iconoscope" picture tube. Farnsworth had in any case refused an offer to sell his invention to RCA, as he would continue to do, preferring to maintain control of its development himself. He was not the first (though he may have been the last) independent inventor to thumb his nose at the mighty RCA, and Sarnoff thought he knew how to deal with him.

The techniques were by now well established: flood the media with stories of RCA's leadership in the field to starve the competitor of capital investment and shake his morale; spend whatever it took to engineer alternative solutions to the technical problems at issue; attack the upstart's patents in court, using the full weight of RCA's awesome legal resources; continue offering the carrot of a patent buyout. Invariably, sooner or later, the lone inventor would crack or run out of money or both, and RCA would buy up his intellectual property.[7] It was a strategy RCA had used against Edwin Armstrong, perhaps the most brilliant and certainly one of the most prolific inventors in the field of radio, responsible, among many other breakthroughs, for FM (frequency modulation). Armstrong, following years of bitter, ruinously expensive litigation to protect his patents from RCA (and others), killed himself in 1954.

However, Farnsworth's patents were to prove legally impregnable, and Zworykin's attempts to engineer alternatives were unsuccessful with the iconoscope, which was too crude to be practical for commercial applications. When the RCA labs did come up with a successful camera tube in the "image orthicon" in 1937, Sarnoff felt confident enough to begin planning television's official inaugural for the 1939 World's Fair. AT&T had by then patented another crucial element of the TV network, coaxial cable capable of carrying television signals over long distances, and RCA could look forward with confidence to a patent-sharing in television on the model of the successful radio arrangement.

But AT&T, under increasing antitrust pressure from Washington, stunned Sarnoff and the rest of the electronics industry by offering a cross-licensing patent agreement to Farnsworth, in a dramatic public gesture during a hearing of the Federal Communications Commission (FCC). Farnsworth immediately accepted. Then came more bad news for RCA: lawyers preparing patent papers for the image orthicon discovered patents held by Farnsworth for the past four years that covered all of the tube's important functions. These patents were of course challenged, but with the distressingly familiar result of Farnsworth's priority being upheld in court.

Finally, RCA capitulated and agreed to negotiate a licensing arrangement with Farnsworth. The deal was signed without fanfare in a Radio City boardroom in New York in 1939. It was the only instance in which RCA had found it necessary to license rather than purchase intellectual property, and it was a bitter pill for Sarnoff to swallow. But it allowed television to finally reach the consumer market. Sarnoff consoled himself by winning the public relations war so effectively that not until late in the twentieth century was it widely recognized that Farnsworth, and not Zworykin and RCA, had been mainly responsible for inventing modern television.

Farnsworth himself, a Mormon of conservative values, supported by his brilliant and technically adept wife, Elma "Pem" Gardner Farnsworth, and other members of their extended family, had been a pillar of strength in his resistance to the manufacturing giant. But he was not immune to the stresses of RCA's legal challenges, and these, along with his workaholic habits, eventually led him to alcohol for relief. He sank into depression, had a nervous breakdown and was hospitalized for electroshock therapy. He had lost one brother in a car accident, and another lost an eye in an accident while working in his television lab. In 1947 the Farnsworths' house in Maine burned to the ground, taking many of their valuable papers with it. In 1954 he appeared on the television guess-the-guest show *What's My Line*. Asked by a panellist if he had invented some kind of machine that might be painful when used, he answered, "Yes. Sometimes it's most painful."[8]

Early electronic television was relatively simple compared with today's sophisticated colour technologies, but the operating principles remain much the same. The image to be transmitted was projected through a lens onto a small screen inside a long, cylindrical vacuum tube. The screen was coated with millions of tiny light-sensitive metallic particles. Where the Nipkow/Baird system had scanned the image using the clever mechanical expedient of a spinning perforated disc, electronic systems employed an electron gun. Similar in principle to the filament of a vacuum tube, the electron gun is an emitter of a focused beam of electrons. It was built right into the tube containing the photosensitive screen, and together they composed the principal element of television cameras for more than forty years. (Modern cameras use solid-state electronics.) The camera tube's electron gun was able to scan the image projected onto the photosensitive screen by means of electromagnetic collars, which deflected the electron beam back and forth across the screen from top to bottom several hundred times a second. As each individual segment of the screen was bombarded with electrons, it emitted electrons according to the brightness or darkness of the picture element projected upon it. These electrons were collected at the back of the screen as electric current. It is this current that was used to modulate the signal transmitted to the television receiver.

The receiver's picture tube (kinescope or cathode ray tube) was similar to the camera's. An electron beam was made to sweep across the luminescent material coating the viewing surface of the tube, in exact synchronization with the electron beam in the camera, replicating more or less exactly the brightness of each camera-scanned picture element. It sped back and forth from top to bottom of the screen, many times per second. (The synchronization between camera and projection tube was handled by a "synch code" transmitted along with the picture information.) Today's colour television works in a similar way, only with separate electron guns for different primary colours. (Newer flat-screen, high-definition television uses millions of tiny light-emitting semiconductors coating a flat display surface. Each semiconductor represents a pixel of the image digitally transmitted to the receiver.)

World War II shut down television broadcasting in the U.K. (though not in France and Germany) and severely restricted the schedule of NBC in the United States. The BBC had been broadcasting two hours a day, six days a week since November 1936 (noncommercially) and NBC had formally begun its TV operations three years later, in April 1939, broadcasting from the Empire State Building.[9] NBC programs were sponsored by advertisers from the outset. In 1940, there were about 10,000 TV sets in the London area and about 3,000 in New York. Following the war, interest in television skyrocketed in the U.S.: in 1949 there were a million receivers in use; by 1951, 10 million; and by 1959, 50 million, twice as many as in all other countries of the world combined. Audience numbers for movies and radio plummeted: average weekly movie attendance fell from 90 million in 1948 to 47 million in 1956. The number of cinemas in the United States fell from a high of 20,000 in 1945 to 14,500 eleven years later. Both industries slowly recovered profitability, if not cachet, with new content and promotion strategies.

Early American television, live or on film, drew on Broadway and vaudeville for much of its programming and performers, but with the introduction of magnetic videotape recording (developed by Ampex), beginning in 1956, the centre of gravity shifted to Hollywood, with its massive studio infrastructure and pool of acting, directing and scriptwriting expertise, and where programming sensibilities were more in tune with the commercial imperatives of the American industry. Starting with RKO in 1956, the major studios began to sell their libraries to television—embracing, after several years of stiff resistance to TV, the logic of joining that which cannot be beaten. At the same time, NBC and CBS began building major production facilities in Los Angeles.

In Britain, still suffering through post-war austerity, the BBC put

television programming in the hands of a cultivated Third programme broadcaster who later went on to be head of a university.[10]
Although programming reflected his elevated tastes, the early audience for British television was relatively uneducated: a 1951 survey
showed that 70 percent had left school by age fifteen. Nevertheless,
the new medium reached a million viewers that year. The coronation
of Queen Elizabeth II two years later gave it a further, substantial
boost.

In 1954, Westminster made provision for commercial stations to
compete with BBC television under the aegis of a new Independent
Television Authority, which had wide-ranging regulatory powers.
The result remains debatable. American-style newscasts with elaborate sets and high studio production values were immediately popular and drew the rather staid, content-oriented BBC news format in
that direction. On the ground, ITN was to build a first-class news
organization, in quality if not in reach and depth a match for the
BBC. The independent (commercial) channels produced and continue to produce some of the best TV drama on British screens, and
most of the worst. The competition, though, seems to have been
good for the BBC, which continues to be the world leader, and it was
certainly good for actors, producers, writers, technicians and all the
others employed in the television production business.

Long and sometimes bitter experience with radio and the private
broadcasting industry had taught authorities in Canada that with
the new medium of television, American content would inevitably
flood the Canadian airwaves unless a regulatory dike was built. The
first of these restrictions, introduced in 1961 after difficult consulta-
tions with private broadcasters, required about 50 percent of prime-
time broadcast schedules to be filled with Canadian-produced
programming. These rules have remained in place, though private broadcasters were able to circumvent their spirit due to an
overly broad definition of "prime time" (6 p.m. to midnight), which
allowed the scheduling of blockbuster American programming in
the hours when most viewers were watching (about 7 to 10 p.m.)

and the dumping of Canadian programming into the fringes on either side. The result has been that only in Quebec, with its insulating language and culture, does domestic programming thrive in the face of competition from south of the border.

Television: 2

OR MOST NORTH AMERICANS, inheritors of television as a medium of commercially sponsored information and entertainment, it may be perplexing how a technology with so much potential became such a letdown in practice. The American television comic Ernie Kovaks said television was a medium because it was neither rare nor well done. Architect Frank Lloyd Wright called it bubble gum for the eyes. FCC chairman Newton Minnow in 1961 famously characterized it as a "vast wasteland." When Kent Farnsworth, son of television's principal inventor, was asked what his father's attitude to TV had been, he replied, "I suppose you could say that he felt he had created kind of a monster, a way for people to waste a lot of their lives." The young Farnsworth added, "Throughout my childhood his reaction to television was 'There's nothing on it worthwhile, and we're not going to watch it in this household, and I don't want it in your intellectual diet.'"[1]

Television might be called the first entirely passive form of mass entertainment. It requires no involvement from its audience—certainly no serious intellectual engagement—and in fact demands all but complete immobility and mental disengagement in front of the glowing screen. Only the thumb moves, on the zapper. "When I was your age, we had to *walk* to the television to change channels," the

wisecrack goes. Radio, theatre, books, cinema all require the participation of the audience at one level or another, if only in applause
or the exercise of imagination; other media involve a conversation
between the user and the source. We bring to a book, for example,
our literacy, our imagination, our interpretive skills. The cinema,
at its best, engages the same talents in its audience, as well as stimulating their visual aesthetic sensibilities. (But movies shrunk to
the small screen lose the very immersive quality that so completely
engages the imagination and emotions in the cinema.) TV asks only
that the viewer show up, and it will do the rest. Even laughter is supplied. As audience stupefaction sets in, as it must, television must
create tricks and techniques to keep its audience from drifting off—
techniques such as the video jolt, the false climax, the flash of
nubile flesh, the shock of violence. In so-called talk programming,
civility and erudition are not effective; aggressive confrontation,
bald assertion, the rhetorical expletive is what's demanded.

There is another sense, however, in which television is not a
"passive" medium at all. It engages us by the millions, and brings us
back for more. It obviously is having some sort of impact on us as
we watch. An important clue to understanding this seeming paradox lies in McLuhan's cryptic dictum to the effect that we don't
watch TV, TV watches us. Or as New York ad executive and TV critic
Tony Schwartz put it: "TV is not a window on the world, it's a window on the consumer."[2] In other words, television should be seen
as a mental programming or conditioning agent, which is actively
invading us whenever we subject ourselves to its siren appeal. This
side of the equation is seen most explicitly in its advertising, of
which Neil Postman has written:

> The television commercial is not at all about the character of
> products to be consumed. It is about the character of the con-
> sumers of products. Images of movie stars and famous athletes,
> of serene lakes and macho fishing trips, of elegant dinners and
> romantic interludes, of happy families packing their station
> wagons for a picnic in the country—these tell nothing about

the products being sold. But they tell everything about the fears, fancies and dreams of those who might buy them. What the advertiser needs to know is not what is right about the product but what is wrong about the buyer . . . The consumer is a patient assured by psycho-dramas.[3]

Television advertisers, exploiting the findings of early twentieth-century behavioural science, developed the basic techniques for keeping the viewer glued to the screen: the burst of sound, the shocking or disturbing or sexy image, the quick cutting and frequent change of camera angle, the rapid zooms and pans. (Translated to the cinema screen, as they sometimes are by television-trained directors, these techniques tend to leave the audience nauseated, as if by motion sickness.) We've become familiar with it all, but it would have seemed wild and crazy to television's pioneers, back before advertisers had really got their hooks into the medium. Back then, you could film stage plays without adapting them for TV by kicking up the pacing, hiring "name" actors, dumping the "boring" bits and getting lots of close-ups.

Conventional wisdom tells us that, as bad as TV may be, nobody is forced to watch it; the box, we are frequently reminded, has an on/off switch on the front. But there is mounting evidence that the issue may be more complicated than we had supposed—that TV is addictive, and creates a dependence that is hard to shake.

What research has found is that the production techniques created for advertisers and borrowed by program producers provoke a physiological response in viewers akin to the "orientation response" first described by the Russian Ivan Pavlov in 1927. This is the "fight or flight" mechanism that prepares us to either flee or approach a strange object or creature. The body instantly quiets itself by slowing the heart rate and constricting blood circulation to key muscle groups while it focuses all its resources on the brain.[4] Research at Stanford University in 1986 showed that the quick cuts, rapid camera movements and sudden noises of typical commercial television programming can induce this primal orientation response, greatly increasing the attentiveness of viewers. "It is the form . . . not the content of television that is unique" in this regard, the researchers concluded.[5]

Other research has shown that TV watching results in a lower metabolic rate than other sedentary activities such as reading, writing, sewing or playing board games. This helps to explain the "veg-out" aspect of television viewing, confirmed by the research of Robert Kubey and Mihaly Csikszentmihalyi. As soon as viewers flick the set on, they feel more relaxed, physically. And of course their mind is diverted from whatever may have been nagging at them in the moments before sitting down to watch. But as soon as the set is turned off, viewers tend to feel a rush of returning stress and unease, often accompanied by guilt. (This may be due in part to the fact that when the orientation response—activated almost continuously in TV viewing—is relaxed, the heart rate soars before settling back to normal values.)[6] Habit-forming drugs work the same way, the two researchers point out.

> A tranquilizer that leaves the body rapidly is much more likely to cause dependence than one that leaves the body slowly, precisely because the user is more aware that the drug's effects are wearing off. Similarly, viewers' vague learned sense that they will feel less relaxed if they stop viewing may be a significant factor in not turning the set off. Viewing begets more viewing.[7]

Hence the central irony of television viewing: people watch a lot more than they want to, even though they report that the more they watch, the less satisfying it is.

The evidence for psychological and physiological addiction to television seems at least as convincing as the evidence of fast food dependence that began to emerge in 2004–5.[8] And the human damage caused is apparently of the same magnitude, even in purely physiological terms. After all, it is mainly TV that has become a substitute for the kinds of physical activities that kept our grandparents fit. Research into obesity and TV viewing has shown that even average watchers among men and women over forty are twice as likely as light viewers to contract type 2 diabetes. Along with lack of exercise, contributing factors noted are the poor eating habits and food choices promoted by TV advertising.[9]

Studies conducted by researchers at Case Western Reserve University School of Medicine and the University Hospitals of Cleveland indicate that television viewing in early and middle adulthood is strongly correlated with the likelihood of developing Alzheimer's disease in old age.[10] The research was reported by Dr. Robert Friedland. "Of all the activities we quantified—passive, intellectual and physical—Alzheimer's patients are in middle life less active in all of them except for one, which is television," he said. Dr. Friedland accepted that it is possible for television to be intellectually stimulating, "but probably that is not what is happening most of the time, especially in America, where people watch an average of four hours a day. I think it is bad for the brain to watch four hours of television a day . . . When you watch TV you can be in a semi-conscious state where you really are not doing any learning."[11]

And then of course there is the impact commercial television has had on our lives as citizens and participants in community affairs by its trivializing of politics and hogging of free time, not to mention the solid evidence for a linkage between TV violence and violence in schools and on the streets.[12]

With all its problems, it could be argued that television has constituted a kind of prison of the mind for several generations of viewers. But it has not been escape-proof. Television's blandishments have been strenuously resisted since the medium's birth, and technology has come to the aid of those who object to the total subservience the medium demands.

A key problem of linear, analog broadcast technology (a problem, at least, for the viewer) is that advertising on television has to be intrusive, has to interrupt the flow of programming. In a linear environment, it cannot be otherwise: viewers are forced to sit through the advertising in order to get to the next scene or program. A deceptively innocuous gadget called the wireless remote control—the "zapper"—first addressed that issue. The zapper has been a tool of enormous significance, because it does much more than make it possible to change channels or mute sound without having to rise from one's easy chair. The remote control put a crude editing tool in the hands of the viewer, giving him, after decades of enforced passivity, some rudimentary control over the content on the screen.

The problem of linearity of schedules and the "appointment viewing" it demands (the viewer must make herself available at the time the program is broadcast) was addressed in another way by the invention of the videocassette recorder, or VCR, and then by the development of the specialty channel on cable (or satellite) television. With the VCR, it was no longer necessary to be on hand in front of the TV at a specific time in order to catch a favourite show; it had become possible to record it and play it back later on, a process the industry refers to as "time-shifting." Programming functions of VCRs became synonymous with bad interface design, however, and were found to be so annoyingly complex by most owners that the device was seldom used for off-air recording. A majority of owners of VCRs used their machines primarily for watching prerecorded rental movies, a function for which they would soon be superseded by the digital video disc (DVD) player.[13] In most households, this meant that television viewing per se declined, since the playback machine is typically connected to the family's only (or main) set. This was of course an unpleasant development for television programmers and advertisers, but an even bigger headache resulted from the fact that the VCR made it possible to either delete commercials in the recording process or "fast-forward" through them during time-shifted viewing.

The availability of low-cost, digital storage media in the form of multi-gigabyte hard drives led to digital video recording (DVR) technology marketed as the PVR, or Personal Video Recorder. The PVR significantly improved on the VCR in both picture quality and storage convenience, and further enhanced the viewer's ability to watch programs at the time of his choosing. Not only can programming be recorded (eighty hours or more on current products), but live programming can be paused and "rewound" while still on the air. On recorded material, entire commercial breaks can be jumped at the touch of a button. And the user interfaces are uniformly superior to those of the VCR. The next step: an appliance that combines DVR technology with the ability to record on (and play back from) digital video discs—a combined DVR–DVD player in one box.

While broadcast television itself has been slow to change, the technology in the hands of its audience is revolutionizing the way television is consumed. The model is still top-down, point-to-multipoint, but the receiver is no longer quite as "dumb" as it used to be. The new digital storage and playback technologies are bringing television closer to the kind of random accessibility enjoyed by print media, with a consequent emphasis on editorial or dramatic content and a de-emphasis of the intrusions of advertising. This is good for the viewer, but obviously not good for the commercial sponsors.

With the new-found ability of the viewer to avoid commercials with the touch of a button, the old problem of how to pay for programming seems about to take centre stage once again. One response has been an enormous expansion in the practice known as product placement. Once restricted to the occasional discreet display of a soft drink can or cigarette package or automobile on the set of a TV show or movie, it has progressed to the point where entire productions are effectively product endorsements. Ad agencies that specialize in matching potential advertisers with program producers flourish in what has become a very big business wherever television and movies are produced, and producers are inevitably becoming more dependent on this kind of hidden subsidy. Manufacturers that provide props are routinely permitted to preview program scripts to ensure that their product does not appear in a bad light. Advertisers, who like to refer to product placement as "brand integration" into programming, see nothing wrong with advertising by stealth, and point out that, in television, broadcast regulators insist that products placed in a program be identified in credits at the end of the show. Few in the audience ever watch these acknowledgments, though—which typically roll by in tiny type at lightspeed.

Opponents say product placement in its many variations amounts to subliminal advertising, which is illegal in most jurisdictions. Advertising, they say, needs to be clearly delineated from programming on television, in the same way and for the same reasons that ads are separated from editorial content in newspapers. They also worry about the impact the practice has on the artistic choices made by program producers. It does seem clear that this is another case of corporate commercial interests penetrating ever more deeply into cultural production, and it is hard to see how such intrusion can have any net social benefit.[14]

One can easily imagine programs that are devised with the express purpose of providing placement opportunities for products. A 2005 American network "reality" show that featured a pair of ardent house cleaners tackling the filthiest living spaces imaginable—using the latest in cleaning products—came close to this ideal, as did a "makeover" show that offered free breast-implant operations to successful contestants. Programs like *American Idol* and its syndicated counterparts in other countries are not so much talent searches as a wildly successful means of pre-promoting the record sales of the winners, records in which the program producers hold an interest. The whole process is one of creating a commodity in the form of an instant celebrity. Talk shows fall victim to the placement trend when celebrity guests plug a product in apparently candid conversation in return for advertising contracts that can run high into six figures.[15]

Although newscasts are thought of as sacrosanct where product placement is concerned, and all reputable news organizations have specific prohibitions of the practice in their editorial guidelines and codes of practice, it happens regularly, though in a slightly different form. The newscasts of local stations affiliated with networks have for many years engaged in the practice of running news stories related to major network programming events, such as a made-for-TV movie or the debut or concluding episode of a series. Suggestions for such stories come from network programmers, and might include tie-ins to a local zoo for a major network movie "event" involving African wildlife, for example. The network program is promoted in a brief on-camera extro to the "news" story. This practice was set firmly in place in 1964, when NBC purchased the rights to be the lead broadcaster for the summer Olympics. NBC News made the Olympics its most-covered story that year, giving the Games 20 percent more airtime than the second highest-rated story. On the competing network newscasts, the Olympics didn't crack the top ten.[16] Fox News Channel's founding chairman, Roger Ailes, has been explicit in stating that its news content is shaped to serve the needs of advertisers and the upmarket, conservative demographic to which advertisers are attracted.[17] The old journalistic distinction between what people want to hear and what they need to know is lost to the demands of sponsorship.

A trend concurrent with the empowering of the individual viewer through new receiving and storage technologies is the continuing fragmentation of the television audience. Where once viewers had a choice of perhaps half a dozen channels, there are now hundreds available. This has proved a mixed blessing for advertisers, who like the ability to reach a highly specific demographic, as provided by the many specialty channels, while regretting the loss of the ability to reach virtually an entire nation, an asset once offered by the major networks. This trend will be emphasized with the eventual migration of television delivery to the Internet.

The decline of the monolithic network began with what we now call simply "cable," which got its start as CATV (Community Antenna Television) immediately after World War II. With the explosion of interest in the new medium, and the soaring affluence of the postwar economic boom, came demands for access to television signals in locations shielded from on-air transmissions by mountains or other geographic barriers. CATV coaxial cables linking homes to the cable operator's remote, very tall antenna system had bandwidth aplenty, and cable operators soon got the idea of adding their own channels to those picked up off the air. From this, the specialty channel developed, able to serve niche audiences because of its low operating costs (relative to broadcast TV) and dual revenue sources—advertising charges and subscriber fees.

Because it involved stringing cable into individual homes, like telephone lines, cable was a "natural monopoly," in the sense that it was wasteful to run cables of several competing companies into each area to be served. Thus, government regulators routinely granted cable companies exclusive access to geographical areas and/or urban districts. In return, they were required, in most jurisdictions, to establish "community access channels" in consideration of the highly profitable gift of monopoly.

Cable soon came to be seen as a competitor to over-the-air "free" television. Some historians suggest that had been the strategic goal of the cable operators from the beginning:

> Rather than rebroadcasting the signal to the entire community, they strung cables to carry the programming. These cables represent a major cost to the industry. However the purpose of the cables was not to deliver the product, but rather to exclude everybody who did not pay the cable operator for the same signal, which could [have been] retransmitted [over the air] at low cost . . . In short, the cable industry has spent an enormous amount of funds to convert an inexpensive public service into an expensive commodity.[18]

Whether intentional or not, the strategy proved immensely profitable: cable companies routinely sell for thousands of dollars per subscriber.

The so-called specialty channel, available *only* on cable, was conceived initially as a means of adding value to cable service and encouraging subscriber hookups. Among the first of these was Ted Turner's Cable News Network, or CNN, and it was followed by the all-music channel and channels devoted to travel, cooking, shopping, the courts, Parliament and Congress, science fiction, comedy, religion, animation, sex, movies (old and new, foreign and domestic), antique television shows, books, NASA, women's issues, history, the performing arts, interior decorating, renovations, gay culture, drinking, every variety of sports, foreign-language programming, rock videos, jazz, television listings, the weather, fitness and health, children's programming . . . and so on. Before long, the field had exploded from twelve or fifteen selections on an average cable system to hundreds. This greatly expanded both program choice (though a lot of the specialty content was simply recycled network programming) and viewing opportunities: most cable channels operated on a rotating schedule in which programs were repeated several times in a week. By 2000, prime-time viewing of television on cable had overtaken the American networks.

Delivery options, if not program choice, were expanded once again in 1995, when direct-to-home (DTH) satellite television came of age. Satellite TV had been available in North America for a decade, but market penetration had been severely limited by the problem of the eight-foot parabolic dish antenna required to receive signals from relatively low-powered satellites. Its customer base had been confined mainly to households in areas (mostly rural) where cable was not available, and suburban areas where lots were large and zoning bylaws lenient. Owning such a dish was an outward and visible sign of the importance of television in a family's life, and was, in the eyes of some, a reverse status symbol; in cartoons in the *New Yorker* the satellite dish was an essential artifact in any hillbilly landscape. But a new generation of powerful satellites using digital technology required only a discreet, pizza-sized receiving dish, and DTH television quickly became a direct competitor to cable, offering essentially the same services only in greater abundance and with superior (digital) technical quality. In Britain and Europe, where small-dish DTH technology had been in place for some time, North American–style cable access was introduced at about the same time, becoming a strong competitive factor and offering both cable TV and telephone service on the same line.

Telephone companies, for their part, began marketing their own television delivery services, which used the compression technologies developed for high-speed broadband Internet service. And all of this opened up the possibility of fully integrating television delivery services into the World Wide Web, with its potential for limitless sources of content.

But at this writing, for all the plethora of choice, and for all the Band-Aid patches on its problems, from the zapper to the specialty channel, television programming has remained, for the most part, stubbornly and disappointingly prurient, banal and trivial. In the new world of audience fragmentation across an increasingly broad base of program alternatives, the "vast wasteland" only seems to expand, as deserts will when there is overgrazing and deforestation along their rims.

The essential difference between the two television systems— the American commercial broadcasting networks and the public broadcasters like the BBC—can be illustrated by the fact that the BBC unabashedly, though by no means exclusively, catered to what North Americans might consider an elite audience, in both the arts and news and information programming. This focus would not, of course, have been practical for a commercial broadcaster. It was also possible for the BBC, as a public broadcaster, to mandate several different strata of programming, from highbrow to pop, on different television channels (and radio frequencies). This created a steady market for intelligent programming across the full range of tastes. Commercial television, permitted in Britain after 1952 (commercial radio had to wait until 1972), was limited for decades to a single channel while the BBC had two, and the result was that in a predominantly non-commercial environment, programmers at the advertising-supported outlets had to strive to meet the relatively refined tastes firmly established among viewers by the BBC. The effect was that Thames Television and Channel Four, to name two of the commercial outlets, often matched the BBC in program quality.[19]

The Canadian compromise of a CBC television network supported partly by commercial advertising revenue and partly by government subsidy provides ample proof, if any were needed beyond common sense, that public and private broadcasting cannot coexist within a single organization. CBC television's legislated commitment to the altruistic goals and principles of public broadcasting prevent it from wholeheartedly embracing the kind of content that would maximize commercial revenue. But the pressing need for substantial income beyond its government subsidy drives it to corrupt its cultural and public service programming, diluting it to standards acceptable to a very broad audience, both domestically and in potential foreign markets. The result is a schizophrenic program schedule that draws flak from both ends of the critical spectrum: some deride it as being fusty and elitist, others for being crassly commercial. Increasingly, it is being seen by tax-weary Canadians—and portrayed by corporate media competitors and their lobbyists—as simply irrelevant and therefore expendable.

The same is not true of CBC radio, which divides its widely diverse but always intelligent, commercial-free programming between two broadcast networks in each of the official languages (plus a variety of Aboriginal languages), and a third available solely on the Net and Sirius satellite radio. Its large audience is ferociously loyal.

Like other public broadcasters in an era of economic neo-liberalism, the CBC is subjected to increasing financial pressures from a federal government intent on minimizing expenditures. It reacts, quite naturally, by cutting back, not in revenue-generating areas such as professional sports coverage, but in precisely the non-commercial areas that give it what relevance as a public institution remains to it. Radio, despite its success, is placed on a starvation diet no less debilitating than television's. It is a recipe for frustration and, ultimately, failure; an ignoble experiment entered into by a series of Canadian federal governments unwilling to resist self-serving pressures from corporate commercial broadcast interests.

As it was with radio, commercial support proved to be a Faustian bargain for television. A commercial broadcast medium in a market economy, it is worth repeating, is inevitably little more than a vehicle for advertising in which all other content survives only to the extent that it furthers the primary goal of bringing an audience to the ads. Broadcasters like to say that advertising supports programming, but that is incorrect: programming supports advertising, and if it does not, it is cancelled. There was a time when this might have been an arguable proposition. Even Philo Farnsworth, who hated much of what he saw on television and often wondered aloud if his efforts had been worthwhile, was impressed when he joined millions of other viewers in July 1969 to watch Neil Armstrong take mankind's first steps on the moon. "This has made it all worthwhile," he is reported to have told his wife. But such unambiguously redeeming episodes are few and far between. Television in North America, like radio, was effectively hijacked by commercial interests early on in the game in the name of more and better sensation and spectacle, which it delivered, and audiences have been paying the Devil his due ever since.

The end of television's agonies, however, may be in sight. As the twentieth century closed, and the Internet loomed ever larger and inter-media convergence became a tangible reality (there will be more on that subject later), even television executives were waking up to the fact that their medium as they had grown up with it was not dying, but dead. In the U.S., the venerable NBC was the first of the early networks to realize that the future of all home information and entertainment media was digital, and that delivery would be in digital form by cable modem or satellite, over the Internet. Moving first into cable and then into cable–Internet hybrid content in partnership with Microsoft, NBC was followed closely by ABC and its parent Disney corporation.[20] The networks were preparing themselves for what now seemed a sobering inevitability, thanks to the continuing evolution of digital delivery technologies—a world in which every World Wide Web site and every blog has the potential to become a television station.

By the beginning of the new century, when U.S. household Internet penetration ranged from 60 to 75 percent in most urban areas, more than two-thirds of respondents to surveys affirmed they would rather give up their television sets than lose their Internet access.[21] By midway through the first decade, that choice was no longer necessary, because more and more television programming was available online through simulcasting by traditional outlets (the networks) and peer-to-peer file-sharing systems like BitTorrent. In 2005, BitTorrent downloads of movie and television programming accounted for fully one-third of all Internet traffic. The July 2005 Live 8 charity concert set a benchmark: more people watched the performances online on AOL than on ABC, MTV and VH1 combined. Music videos are watched more frequently on the Web than on television.

It seems likely that, in time, most television will be transmitted in digital mode via the Internet as IPTV (Internet protocol television). Viewers will select programming from a vast archive by searching its catalogue (Yahoo! and Google are currently gearing up), as opposed to checking TV listings for the day's offerings. Channels and network affiliation will mean little in this environment, and video—eventually in high-definition—will be available on all manner of portable devices. The distinction between television and cinema will be blurred, and then erased.[22]

By the end of the new millennium's first decade, television's vaunted 500-channel universe will seem charmingly quaint, as viewers contemplate content options in the thousands or even tens of thousands, delivered to their combination TV-Internet appliances by high-speed cable and telephone lines, or by satellite and other wireless technologies. There is no need to speculate about the range and depth of content that will be available: a few hours spent on the Web even today will demonstrate how truly extraordinary it can be. From this cornucopia of choice, doubtless a relatively small number of favourites will emerge to dominate in different markets. But the choices will have been more democratic in the sense that selections will be made from a much broader array of options than in the former media environment. It seems inevitable that television of the future will therefore be a more accurate reflection of the interests, aspirations and concerns of ordinary people.

The Politics of Media

P RESIDENT Woodrow Wilson, who had grasped radio's power as a new factor in world affairs, harboured serious reservations about it. In a speech in Des Moines, Iowa, in the autumn of 1919, he coined an insightful metaphor in describing the new medium's impact. "Do you not know," he asked his audience, "the world is all now one single whispering gallery?" He added:

> Those antennae of the wireless telegraph are the symbols of our age . . . All the impulses of mankind are thrown out upon the air and reach to the ends of the earth; quietly upon steamships, silently under the cover of the Postal Service, with the tongue of the wireless and the tongue of the telegraph, all the suggestions of disorder are spread throughout the world.

With the revolutionary tumult then engulfing Russia vivid in his mind, Wilson warned of the spreading "poison of revolt, the poison of chaos."

Wilson was acknowledging the enormous power of radio broadcasting as an instrument of propaganda, a power the world had scarcely begun to exploit at the time of his speech, and which few others had recognized. Today, among the democracies of the world, communications technologies tend to be accepted as tools of liberation, weapons against oppression, guarantors of freedom. But not all communications technologies have the same impact on democratic institutions, and the broadcast technologies such as radio can serve any master, democratic or authoritarian.

In actively promoting the growth of radio, governments the world over were motivated to a greater or lesser degree by the fact that the medium allows them to communicate directly with their citizens and so to influence, persuade and instruct them. Radio's importance as an instrument of social and political control is attested to in the fact that the first target of insurrectionists everywhere since about 1925 has been the country's radio (and now television) stations. The problem, on the other hand, for those who wish to exercise control, is that radio is not confined by political boundaries, and broadcasts of foreign origin can sometimes have as much impact as those from domestic authorities. In Germany prior to World War II, the penalty for passing on news heard on a foreign radio station was five years in jail, and the government reduced the odds of this happening by manufacturing a *volks* radio that was capable of receiving only those frequencies occupied by German stations. As well, every district in the country was assigned an official called a *Funküberwachthund*, whose job it was to wire up public squares and other meeting spaces with loudspeakers whenever radio programming deemed important by the government was aired. The Soviet Union severely restricted private ownership of radios and instead wired much of the country (and the rest of Eastern Europe) with loudspeakers attached to central party-controlled receivers. The Soviet household radio appliance had the virtue of being simple to operate: it had only a volume control.

Television, like radio, has never been content with servicing exclusively local or domestic markets. The power of television as an agent of change has made it impossible for either government or business to ignore the medium's potential for opening new markets and promoting friendly attitudes worldwide. Until recently, however, the fact that it was confined to the VHF region of the radio spectrum, where signals travel by line of sight and are thus confined to distances within the antenna's horizon, made TV an almost exclusively domestic medium. The global era of television was foreshadowed by AT&T's Telstar, which successfully relayed pictures from the United States to Britain and France in brief experiments in 1962. The new era got under way in earnest in the mid-1960s with Syncom and Early Bird, the first geosynchronous communications satellites, stationed, respectively, over the Pacific and Atlantic oceans. Despite the enormous cost involved, television networks on both sides of the Atlantic began using "the Bird" regularly, driven by the same imperative that forced widespread business use of the telegraph in the 1850s: if they didn't, their competitors surely would. Today, there are hundreds of commercial communications satellites in orbit, many of them carrying television signals.

The impact of satellite technology was felt most immediately in the area of live news telecasting. By 1989 a planet-wide force of undeniable power and influence, satellite television, with its new ability to ignore political boundaries and flout local censorship, was in a position to claim a major role in accelerating the collapse of the Soviet Empire in Eastern Europe simply by facilitating access to news. Soviet premier Mikhail Gorbachev's science adviser reported that the Gorbachev administration in the final days of the Soviet Union had a deliberate policy of providing wide public access to foreign satellite television as a means of thwarting expected coup attempts by hard-line Communists. With foreign television news freely available, Gorbachev believed, no palace revolt could achieve the backing of the populace. He was proved correct on more than one occasion.[1]

Nevertheless, even in the democracies, it is misguided to call radio as it evolved following the 1920s, or television, which adopted an identical regulatory and administrative model, "democratic" media. In principle, they are quite the opposite. The most cursory look into what is involved in owning a broadcasting station, the sheer cost and the onerous regulatory requirements, is sufficient to

demonstrate that while everyone is free to listen to radio or watch
TV, only a select few are able to broadcast. And in no way can those
who are granted that privilege be said to be representative of those to
whom they transmit their programs; the de facto economic and regulatory screening processes see to that. The public at large has never
had more than nominal direct input into the process by which
licence holders are selected, that input usually consisting of the
opportunity to file an objection once every few years when a licence
is up for renewal by the regulatory authority. Nor does the public
have any formal means of influencing the nature of broadcasters'
programming in any but the coarsest, least discriminating ways—
through boycotts of advertising and letter-writing campaigns. Positive programming suggestions must be offered in the deferential
spirit of Oliver Twist, and are anyway likely to be politely ignored.

The issue of access to the technology is one that defines the history of broadcast communication and has returned to haunt us in
the era of the Internet. It is illuminating to look back at how it has
been handled, and how it came to be that access to radio, which
began as a two-way or bilateral medium available to the public, was
organized so that the public retained the privilege of receiving
programming but lost the right to originate broadcasts.

From the beginning, access was a concern among legislators
wherever radio was introduced. As we saw earlier, the U.K. gave the
Royal Mail a monopoly over broadcasting. In the United States, on
the other hand, the first act to regulate radio, passed by Congress in
1912, prohibited the secretary of commerce from withholding a
licence from any U.S. citizen who applied; radio was to be open to
all. By 1923, so many stations were crowding the two frequencies
then allotted for broadcasting that they often had to double up,
sharing airtime in their coverage areas. Disputes were inevitable and
frequent. Something had to be done, though no one quite knew
what. Commerce Secretary Herbert Hoover reacted by making more
bandwidth available, that is, by increasing the number of frequencies on which stations would be allowed to broadcast.[2]

This eased the pressure, but it soon built up again since a feature of the receivers of the era was poor selectivity among adjacent signals. However, that was an engineering problem that had already been solved. One of the great inventive geniuses of radio, Edwin Armstrong, had capped a long series of technical triumphs with the design for a "superheterodyne" receiver, which was vastly superior to anything then on the market in terms of both sensitivity, the ability to detect weak stations, and selectivity, the ability to tune out interference from nearby signals.[3]

So while the technical issues affecting access had in part been solved by 1924, it was also true that the medium's commercial possibilities and political power were better understood. That inevitably changed attitudes to access as well. By that year, fourteen hundred broadcast licences had been issued in the United States. Secretary Hoover, acting with the insistent advice of industry lobbyists, announced that all available broadcast frequencies were now filled and that no further licences would be issued. Interference among stations—"chaos" on the airwaves—was given as the reason for this fundamental shift in policy, but it tilted the balance away from public access and toward commercial control. Not only were new licences no longer available, existing licences immediately acquired a substantial scarcity value; and universities and altruistic individuals and organizations, which owned hundreds of small, public service, non-commercial radio outlets, reaped a cash bonanza as their licences were bought up by the big commercial broadcasters. Radio would henceforth be first and foremost a *business*, and a medium of advertising, in which non-advertising content played the role of attracting audiences for commercial messages. Access to broadcasting facilities was proscribed in the way already described.

Nevertheless, in the glow of optimism that often accompanies new technologies, it was widely seen as a triumph for democracy that, in 1925, President Calvin Coolidge was able to deliver his inaugural speech to an assembled radio audience estimated at more than five million. There were high hopes for the impact of radio on

political discourse in general, for reasons outlined in an August 1932
Saturday Evening Post report on the Democratic National Convention of that year:

> The Democratic Convention was held in New York, but all
> America attended it . . . [radio] gives events of national impor-
> tance a national audience. Incidentally, it also uncovered another
> benefit radio seems destined to bestow upon us, the debunking
> of present-day oratory and the setting up of higher standards in
> public speaking . . . Orators up to the present have been get-
> ting by on purely adventitious aids: a good personality, a musi-
> cal voice, a power of dramatic gesture have served to cover up
> baldness of thought and limping phraseology . . . The radio
> is even more merciless than the printed report as a conveyor of
> oratory . . . It is uncompromising and literal transmission. The
> listeners follow the speech with one sense only. There is noth-
> ing to distract their attention. They do not share the excitement
> and movement of the meeting, nor does the personality of the
> speaker register with them . . . Silver-tongued orators whose
> fame has been won before sympathetic audiences are going to
> scale down to their real stature when the verdict comes from
> radio audiences.

There is little need to point out the irony in this argument,
which paradoxically seems logically bulletproof. Of course radio
must force on politicians a more reasoned, substantive style of discourse! Then why didn't it? The answer is in the phrase, "The listeners follow *the speech* . . ." In early experimental radio, speeches
often were broadcast in their entirety. The commercialization of
radio and the resultant assigning of monetary value to airtime soon
put an end to that, and before long there was no "speech" for listeners to follow. Commercials placed a value on airtime that hadn't
been there before. Time became money; airtime became a commodity, and as such it could most efficiently and conveniently
be sold in regular blocks. Commercials forced a new approach to

programming, in which content had to fit into a rigidly adhered-to schedule so that advertisements could appear in the time slots for which they had been sold. Content had to fit the format, rather than vice versa.

News programming was no exception, and that meant that everything within a newscast had to be weighed for its information value in relation to everything else that was newsworthy at that moment. Excerpts from speeches became more and more truncated, as did excerpts from interviews. Only in the most extraordinary of circumstances was the politician given unmediated, uninterrupted access to the public on commercial radio. The glib phrase, the oft-misleading metaphor, the dramatic expostulation—the sound bite—was commercial radio's replacement offering for oratory. In time, oratory itself would become a lost art, replaced by sloganeering.

Broadcasting's proponents have consistently argued that the unilateral or point-to-multipoint media serve the important function of bringing society closer together through shared experience provided by broadcast programming. The vision of the American or Canadian or Brazilian or Australian family settled around the living-room television set, sharing with millions of other families the same network programs, learning the same things, experiencing the same emotions, is a portrait painted by this notion. It is a cozy picture—until one stops to consider what it is they are learning, and from whom, and to what end. The short answer is that broadcast outlets are designed to further the goals of those who run them. Those goals may be entirely laudatory and wholly constructive, as they can sometimes be in a developing nation in which society lacks the necessary cohesion to form an effective nation-state. Under these circumstances, the power of broadcasting can be used very effectively in advancing socially useful goals.

But the cohesion provided by uniformity of experience is not the only, or even the preferred, form of socially useful solidarity. The great sociologist Émile Durkheim identified two kinds of solidarity in society.[4] The first was "mechanical solidarity," by which he meant the kind of cohesion imposed by criminal law and paternal authority of various kinds—the type of solidarity that leads to conformity, regimentation, hierarchies and strict discipline. The second was "organic solidarity," by which he meant the cohesion that is enforced by civil law, custom and consensus, and which grows out of continuing conversation among individuals of different training, beliefs and understandings. Either can hold a nation together, and both are present in any society. Most of us would agree that we'd like to see rather more organic and less mechanical cohesion in our countries. Durkheim also made the obvious point that broadcast technologies such as radio, TV, newspapers and movies tend to promote mechanical solidarity, while bilateral media such as the telephone and mail (and now the Internet) encourage the organic variety. Compare the role of the (bilateral) fax and Internet in the collapse of the Soviet Empire or in the civil liberties movement in China with the role of (unilateral) broadcast radio in Nazi Germany and in Rwanda during the Tutsi genocide.

The social solidarity, the so-called democratizing impact, claimed as a benefit of broadcast technologies clearly falls into the mechanical category, while bilateral technologies such as the telephone and the Internet just as obviously promote organic solidarity, as facilitators of conversation and self-organization. Plato would have recognized the distinction: he pointed (especially in the *Gorgias*) to the antagonism between communication in the form of dialogue, which is the speech adequate to philosophical truth, and "rhetoric," the one-way speech by which the demagogue seeks to convince the masses. Hannah Arendt saw a massive shift having taken place in media-saturated Western culture, away from truth and in the direction of opinion:

> In the world we live in, the last traces of this ancient antagonism between the philosopher's truth and the opinions of the market place have disappeared. Neither the truth of revealed religion, which the political thinkers of the seventeenth century still treated as a major nuisance, nor the truth of the philosopher,

disclosed to man in solitude, interferes any longer with the affairs of the world.[5]

More recently, Jurgen Habermas has drawn a distinction between "system integration," in which people are held together by rules, procedures and regulations, and "social integration," in which they stay together by virtue of shared understanding that is worked out continuously through communication among themselves (see chapter 9). He warns of a disturbing late-twentieth-century "uncoupling" of the two. "It is not a matter of indifference to a society," Habermas says, "whether and to what extent forms of social integration dependent on consensus are repressed and replaced by anonymous forms of system-integrative association."[6] Habermas fears that in future, people will co-operate, not because they have reached consensus based on the understanding that arises out of true communication with one another, but merely because they are conforming to the demands of a system. There will, in fact, be no spaces left in which true communication can take place. All of life will be bureaucracy. We will live in an authoritarian world.

Regardless of whether Habermas's projections are on the mark, it is possible to argue that broadcast technologies have a more important role to play in politically immature or developing societies than in mature ones; that "mature" societies such as the developed Western nations are on balance better served by bilateral media such as computer and telephone networks than by broadcasting, whether by satellite and cable or over the air. Certainly it seems sensible to re-examine the roles of broadcast technologies and the resources dedicated to them in the technically advanced democracies, now that bilateral media are widely available.

A useful insight into the operations of contemporary mass media, particularly in light of the continuing trend toward consolidation of ownership in fewer and fewer corporate hands, can be gained from Noam Chomsky's propaganda model, which forms the core argument of his famous *Manufacturing Consent*. His position is that American democracy is something very different from the myth of government of, by and for the people; it is rather government by a ruling elite that operates with the "manufactured" consent of the people. The historical basis of his argument is summed up in a phrase of the influential American editorialist and historian Walter Lippmann: "A mass cannot govern," he said. Lippmann, commenting approvingly on the philosopher Thomas Hobbes and the democratic theory of post-revolutionary England in the seventeenth century, argued that the affairs of government are too complex for average citizens, and that governing of necessity must be undertaken by a sophisticated ruling elite who were trained to the task. Ordinary citizens should be fed a simplified, predigested version of the important issues, around which their consent can be organized. Chomsky points out that this approach to "democratic" rule was explicitly endorsed by the founders of the American republic and argues that it has persisted to the present day.

According to Chomsky, the manufacturing of this citizen consent is the role of mass media. He lists five "filters" which form the basis of the strategy used by the power elite to ensure that media content reflects their views. They are:

- the size, concentrated ownership, owner wealth and profit orientation of the dominant media;
- advertising as the primary income source;
- the reliance of media on information provided by government, business and "experts" funded and approved by these sources and agents of power;
- "flak," or the ability of agents of power to harass and punish dissenters within the media;
- anti-Communism as a "national religion and control mechanism."[7] (The basic mechanism of control is fear: anti-Communism has been replaced by "anti-terrorism" since 1989.)

Although Chomsky refers to his model as "an institutional analysis" (not a hypothesis, but fact) and provides exhaustive examples of its workings, it has been consistently criticized as a simplistic "conspiracy theory." Critics find it impossible to imagine that the men and women who control the dominant media outlets conspire to control America's (and the West's) media agenda with a success as spectacular as that ascribed to them by Chomsky. Media professionals violently object on the grounds that they are the people Chomsky is talking about, and they ought to know whether or not they are involved in a conspiracy on behalf of an elite power group. But corporations do not exhibit uniform behaviour because they are conspiring with one another, but simply because they are kindred creatures whose sole object is profit. The observed effects of the propaganda model are less those of a conspiratorial cabal than of a hive mind at work: employees must subscribe to the corporate goal or face dismissal. Individual media workers are seldom required to address the explicit issues raised by Chomsky's filters; they are expected rather to conform to corporate standards, regulations and goals, both implicit and explicit. The filters are, as it were, concealed behind the curtain of corporate compliance.[8]

PART TWO

THE DIGITAL ERA

"Reasoning Is But Reckoning"
The Philosophic Underpinnings
of the Electronic Computer

AT THIS POINT in the story of the evolution of communications media, a great watershed occurs. It has been alluded to throughout the preceding chapters; now is the time to look into this transformative change in detail.

The watershed is the widespread adoption by communications media of the shared symbolic language of digital systems. The change began slowly, with the construction of the first electronic digital computers during and immediately following World War II, and has continuously gathered momentum since then. The phenomenon is often referred to as "convergence," meaning the intersection at a single point of the technical development trajectories of TV and other visual media; radio; the telephone and telecommunications; text-based publishing; graphics; still pictures; and interactive media. That focal point is characterized by the shared use of the simplest and therefore most universally applicable language imaginable, the binary language of ones and zeros as it is employed by digital computers.

Just as Swahili, the lingua franca of Africa, allows people from many linguistic backgrounds to communicate with one another all over that continent, binary code allows for communication between otherwise separate and distinct information media. A major portion of the world's vast and growing computing power is devoted to the business of translation of print, video, audio and graphic illustration from their original analog forms into digital, binary code for editing and other forms of "value-adding" manipulation, and for transmission and distribution of the enhanced product, and then translation of that product back to the analog or wave-based structures our human senses are equipped to respond to. In this context we can think of the digital computer as a sort of universal translating appliance of the kind that turns up from time to time in science fiction.

The story of where this remarkable machine came from and how and why it works is woven like a compelling subplot through the history of Western civilization. The digital computer, far from being an alien and bloodless tool of impenetrable complexity, is, more than any other artifact of human invention, an extension of our most impressive capabilities and a reflection of some of our most profound insights. It is impossible to comprehend the trajectory of modern communications technologies and the new economy they have spawned without understanding what makes the computer, above all, a very human instrument.

We should begin with the observation that not all computers are digital—some are analog. The difference between the two is significant. Digital computers operate by counting, while analog computers operate by measuring, that is, by *analogy*. An old-fashioned pocket watch *measures* time by mechanically translating the distance covered by spinning wheels and cogs in its works into the changing position of the hour and minute hands in relation to the numbers around the watch face. A modern digital watch *counts* vibrations of a crystal which is excited by a tiny battery, and that is converted into a numeric readout by a microchip. Early bicycle speedometers registered speed by spinning a friction wheel against the bicycle wheel rim. Their more accurate digital replacements count the number of times a magnet attached to a wheel spoke passes a sensor attached to the fork. In practical terms, the distinction means that digital computers can be much more precise than analog computers, since measurement can never be 100 percent accurate whereas counting can. What is measured, apparently accurately, with a yardstick may be significantly too long or short when measured with a micrometer. No two bushels of wheat or gallons of gasoline are precisely the same in weight or volume. The tiniest of inaccuracies at one scale are magnified into significance at another. Scale always matters in measurement, whereas it does not in counting. Digital computers are therefore excellent preservers of the integrity of the information they deal with; there is, in principle, no loss of information no matter how many manipulations or iterations it may go through.

Of course, counting only works if there are separate and distinct entities to be counted (one cannot very well "count" the water coming out of a hose!), and the trick that makes digital systems perfectly accurate is a requirement that such entities be well defined in the system's "operating rules." A digital water meter counts the number of revolutions made by a wheel placed in the flow of water. The meter can be perfectly accurate in its own terms because it has in effect divided up the flow into discrete volumes required to cause a revolution of the wheel. It has, in Nicholas Negroponte's image, turned *atoms* of water into *bits* of information.

The alphabet is a digital system in which the letter *A* can be represented a number of different ways—in different fonts, in different media and in different handwriting styles—but a convention of the alphabetic system is that all such variations, so long as they are legible, are accepted as *A*s. In arithmetic, another digital system, a digit can "legally" be represented by symbols as diverse as characters written on paper or an assemblage of marbles. In this way, wide variations in the content of individual units can be tolerated while preserving the accuracy of the digital system. The text in a book is created within a digital system; a painting is not. Which helps to explain why it is possible to reproduce a four-hundred-year-old

Shakespearian sonnet with complete accuracy in a book published in our time, while it is not possible to reproduce a Rembrandt portrait of the same era in the same book (or in any other medium) with anything approaching complete accuracy. To fully understand the Rembrandt, you must see the original.

How, then, do digital technologies reproduce sounds and images that are intrinsically analog in nature? They do it by measuring values of sound and colour and light such as amplitude and wavelength, and assigning numbers to those values. Those numbers can then be translated into binary form, and transmitted or manipulated or reproduced by the machinery of digital electronic systems. A digital recording of a solo cello suite is made by sampling the sound waves produced by the instrument many times a second, and assigning binary numbers to the pitch and amplitude of the sound at each sampling. A digital representation of a painting is made by dividing the image field into many small sectors and assigning numbers to the various qualities of the light in each sector. Digital technologies become more accurate in their translations of analog media in direct proportion to their *sampling rates*—that is, the frequency with which they sample sound, for example, or the number of discrete segments into which they divide a picture. Thus, a digital reproduction of an analog sound or image can be extremely accurate, but never an *exact* replica since that would involve an infinite number of samples.

Digital systems, however, are much more interesting than their utilitarian role as analog surrogates would suggest. They have the distinction of being a fundamental metaphysical category, which proposes that meaning can be captured in symbols (such as numbers or combinations of letters), which are then capable of manipulation according to prescribed rules.

The combination of a digital system and its formal rules of operation—the complete package—is usually referred to as a "formal system." Formal systems, because they are digital, are independent of the medium in which they are embodied. It is the *form* of the system and not the physical nature of the tokens or symbols employed that matters. The game of checkers, like chess, is a formal system. It could be played with hay bales and bedsheets in a cow pasture just as well as on a conventional checkerboard with plastic discs. Baseball, although also a game, is not a formal system. To try to play baseball in a swimming pool would radically alter the game and how it proceeds. For the same reasons, as the Shakespeare/Rembrandt example above indicates, we can reproduce Shakespeare on the JumboTron in a football stadium as accurately as on parchment, but not the Rembrandt.[1]

The hidden power of formal systems reveals itself when the tokens or symbols being used are assigned meanings. Then the operations of the system become subject to interpretation, and if a formal equivalence between the operations of the symbols and the things they represent in the real world is maintained, those interpretations will have *meaning* in the real world. A formal system is therefore a way of abstracting real-world problems, resolving them at the abstract level and interpreting the results back into real-world terms. If this sounds complicated, it is not: arithmetic is such a system, in which five oranges contained in one basket can be added to three oranges contained in another basket using the symbolic, digital language of numbers (which are not oranges but are capable of representing oranges). Without ever having to physically count all of the oranges at once, we know there are eight of them in total, because the result of our calculations using the formal system called arithmetic ($5 + 3 = 8$) tells us so.

The insight that language, with its rules of grammar and syntax, can in some respects be seen as a formal system led to speculation as early as the sixteenth century that thought itself, inasmuch as it is based on language, may follow some of the same rules as other digital systems such as arithmetic. The English philosopher Thomas Hobbes (1588–1679) made the case in 1651 with characteristic bluntness: "Reasoning is but reckoning," he stated. By this he meant two things. First, thinking is "mental discourse." The only difference between thinking and talking out loud or working out arithmetic problems with pencil and paper is that thinking is conducted internally, thoughts being expressed not in written symbols or spoken words but in special brain tokens Hobbes called "phantasms" or thought "parcels." Second, reasoning at its clearest follows rules that lead to correct outcomes just as accounting does. In other words, reasoning is a mechanical procedure akin to operating a mental calculating machine: it is a digital process.

Hobbes expressed his notion of the formal nature of reasoning in *Leviathan*:

> When a man reasoneth, he does nothing else but conceive a sum total, from addition of parcels; or conceive a remainder, from subtraction of one sum from another . . . These operations are not incident to numbers only, but to all manner of things that can be added together, and taken out of another. For as arithmeticians teach to add and subtract in numbers; so the geometricians teach the same in lines, figures . . . angles, proportions, times, degrees of swiftness, force, power and the like; the logicians teach the same in consequences of words; adding together two names to make an affirmation, and two affirmations to make a syllogism; and many syllogisms to make a demonstration.[2]

It is a rather mechanical notion that is unlikely to have occurred to earlier thinkers produced by a less mechanistic era, before Galileo, before Spinoza. But it was perfectly in keeping with the contemporary views being expressed by René Descartes (1596–1650), who is generally credited with inventing both modern mathematics and modern philosophy.

No philosophical trifler, Descartes set out to rebuild the edifice of knowledge from first principles. In order to establish those first principles on a firm foundation, he attacked the enterprise by systematically doubting everything that can be doubted. Can I doubt that I am sitting in front of the fireplace in a dressing gown? he asked. Yes I can, because I have dreamed that I was here when in fact I was asleep in bed. I also know that people may have hallucinations which seem remarkably real. If the material world cannot be trusted, Descartes then asked himself, how about the more abstract world of arithmetic and geometry? Surely it should be more reliable. But what if there were an evil demon bent on misleading me in my computations, causing me to make a mistake whenever I add two plus two or calculate the area of a circle? If there were such a demon, it could be that everything I see is only an illusion concocted as a trap for my credulity. How can I know anything for sure?

As it turns out, there is one thing we can all know for a certainty, Descartes said. I may not have a body; it may be an illusion like everything else in the physical world. But thought is different. "While I wanted to think everything false," he reflected in his *Meditations*, "it must necessarily be that I who thought was something; and remarking that this truth, I think therefore I am, was so solid and so certain that all the most extravagant suppositions of the skeptics were incapable of upsetting it, I judged that I could receive it without scruple as the first principle of the philosophy that I sought."[3]

Here is the same argument in another form: I can doubt that my body, or my brain, exists. I cannot doubt that I see and hear and feel and think. Therefore, I who see and hear and feel and think cannot be identical to my body or my brain, otherwise in doubting their existence I would doubt the existence of myself—which would be a contradiction.

This approach to first principles had the effect of placing mind above matter in the hierarchy of things, since one could only know about the latter through the workings of the former. Descartes expanded on this theme to propose two distinct substances in the universe: mind and matter. This dualist philosophy had the attraction of being more intuitively believable than either a strictly materialist point of view in which everything, mind included, is just a form of matter, or an idealist point of view in which there is nothing *but* mind and its creations. But it stirred up one of philosophy's longest-running and most vehemently contested debates. The question it raises is: How do mind and body interact if they are indeed different "substances"? How can a mental event with no physical mass, no charge, no location or anything else physical, make a physical difference in the brain, or anywhere else? It is a debate that was to have obvious interest for the computer scientists who would arrive on the scene three hundred years later, eager to develop artificial intelligence based on silicon chips and electrons. Could such a creation ever be authentically intelligent in human terms if Descartes was correct about mind and matter being fundamentally different stuff? How do you build a mind? What is it made of? How is it connected with the machine? Where Descartes and his contemporaries had started with mind as a given, artificial intelligence as a discipline (AI) arose out of the idea that mind could be seen as an emergent property or product of sufficiently complex systems of logic processors. That is, mind spontaneously *grew out of* the operations of certain kinds of formal systems.

Descartes himself had a number of answers to the question of how mind interacts with the body, none of them very convincing. The one that had the most currency over the years was that the mind and body operated like two perfectly synchronized clocks; what appeared to be cause and effect in their interactions was really just synchronicity. In a time when the mechanical clock was the chief technological marvel, the argument had a certain authoritative ring to it.

Descartes's major contribution to mathematics was the invention of analytic geometry, which he developed as a means of converting geometric problems of lines and volumes into algebraic notation, a way of solving geometric problems using algebraic methods and formulae. In a sense, he had applied digital (arithmetical) techniques to a field that had grown out of analog measurement. Perhaps even more important than the invention itself was the way Descartes abstracted the notion behind it. What analytic geometry did was concentrate on the *relationships* between various elements of a problem, rather than on the elements themselves. The same approach, he realized, could be used in solving problems in physics as well—in fact, in any rule-based system.

The fact that real-world problems could be examined and solved using the abstract symbols of algebra led Descartes to further examine the relationship between symbols and the things they symbolize. In particular, he concluded that thoughts were symbols just like mathematical notation, in that they were representations of things that existed in the real world, an idea which further reinforced the essential dissimilarity between mind and matter. Just as mathematical notation need have no direct connection with the objects it described in order to be of practical value, so too with thoughts. Thought was in fact a digital system. Rationalism, the philosophy that grew out of Descartes's speculations and which was to have such an enormous impact on Western society over the next three hundred or more years, takes the position that reason is in fact the only secure path to knowledge—more reliable even than sensory experience.

The question remained: if thought was a digital system, what were the rules that governed the operations of that system? The German philosopher and mathematician Gottfried Wilhelm von Leibniz (1646–1716) is best remembered as the inventor of the mathematical system called differential calculus, but he also put a lot of energy into answering that very question. He believed it should be possible to design a "universal calculus" by which all human reason could be abstracted, codified and reduced to digital notation. In pursuing this goal he invented symbolic logic, which, while regarded as a curiosity in his day and for many succeeding generations, would turn out to be a mathematical innovation of incalculable importance.

A contemporary and rival of Newton (each had discovered differential calculus independently), Leibniz agreed with the great English scientist that the only reliable route to unimpeachable knowledge was through mathematics, the apotheosis of Reason. But he saw application for this view in fields far removed from science. It seemed to Leibniz that if one could identify the fundamental elements of experience, and the bottom-line or irreducible forms of relations among them, one could by successive combination of symbols representing these experiences and relationships describe all possible knowledge with mathematical accuracy. The laws of reasoning were to be converted to mathematical formulae and all logical deduction would be reduced to algebra. A new universal language of great precision and power would be at work; it would be the pinnacle of achievement in the rationalist, determinist philosophy that saw the world as a clockwork mechanism engineered to perfection by God.

The idea of reducing thought to algebra could only have occurred in the environment of supreme confidence in human reason that characterized the era of emerging modern science, a time when it seemed as if all of nature's mysteries were about to be resolved through the application of mathematics to carefully observed natural phenomena. Newton's achievement of a universal formula for describing the operations of gravity was only the most outstanding of these results; the book of nature really did seem, as Galileo insisted, to have been written in the language of mathematics, and thus be open and accessible to complete understanding through the application of reason. As Leibniz himself confidently predicted, "the time will come, and come soon, in which we shall have a knowledge of God and mind that is not less certain than that of figures and numbers, and in which the invention of machines will be no more difficult than the construction of problems of geometry."[4]

A person of prodigious mental energy and stamina, Leibniz was confident that his universal calculus could be put together in short order: "I believe that a number of chosen men can complete the task within five years: within two years they will exhibit the common doctrines of life, that is metaphysics and morals, in an irrefutable calculus." He foresaw his system being widely adopted as a means of resolving disputes of all kinds, his assumption being that once the correct answer had been produced by his logical formulae, the disputants would have no choice but to accept the result. He proposed that it be used initially to test the body of Christian doctrine and establish a core of knowledge that all the multifarious branches of post-Reformation Christianity could agree on.

There is a famous quotation that nicely captures the spirit of Leibniz's enthusiasm for the idea. "All inquiries which depend on reasoning would be performed by the transposition of characters and by a kind of calculus," he said, "and if someone would doubt my results, I should say to him: 'Let us calculate, Sir,' and thus by taking pen and ink, we should soon settle the question."

Though obviously misguided in his belief that constructing a universal logic—a *lingua characteristica*—would be a simple chore, Leibniz sensed the power of digital, formal systems to amplify information: "Once the characteristic numbers of many ideas have been established the human race will have a new *Organon* [Aristotle's rules of logical reasoning], which will increase the power of the mind much more than the optic glass has aided the eyes, and will be as much superior to microscopes and telescopes as reason is superior to vision." His logical calculus was based on another discovery, which he credited to the Chinese. In studying the hexagrams of the ancient *I Ching*, he found the vestiges of a binary notation system: "The sixty-four figures represent a binary arithmetic . . . which I have rediscovered some thousands of years later . . . In binary arithmetic there are only two signs, 0 and 1, with which we can write all numbers . . . I have since found that it further expresses the logic of dichotomies, which is of the greatest use."[5] He imagined (though did not build) a binary computer employing a mechanical logic gate.[6]

He did, however, construct a mechanical calculator based on decimal arithmetic, which he demonstrated before a meeting of the Royal Society in London in 1673. He had been inspired, he said, by a device built in 1642 by the French religious philosopher and mathematical prodigy Blaise Pascal (1623–62). Pascal, then nineteen years old, had hoped his machine, which he later patented and which is thought to have been the first geared digital computer, would be of use to his father in his business of tax collecting. Leibniz, characteristically, was uninterested in such mundane applications: his calculator "was not made for those who sell oil or sardines," he said. He had in mind, rather, a means for delegating the drudge work of mathematicians, astronomers and others much engaged in calculation to underlings made reliable by their machines, "for it is unworthy of excellent men to lose hours like slaves in the labour of calculation, which could be safely relegated to anyone else if the machine were used."7

While decimal arithmetic calculating machines based on Leibniz's design would undergo more or less continuous development, his ideas of binary arithmetic and a calculus of thought were not paid much attention for the next two hundred years. But then George Boole (1815–64), the self-taught nineteenth-century English mathematician, set out to construct "a mathematics of the human intellect" in the spirit of Leibniz, in which logic is expressed not in words but in precise mathematical symbols. Boolean logic proposed that all logical argument could be translated into a series of "yes" or "no" responses, which in turn could be represented in binary terms. The numbers one and zero were used by Boole to indicate existence or non-existence when referring to classes, and truth or falsehood when applied to propositions. Boole showed that symbols of this kind obey the same laws of combination as symbols in algebra, which meant that they could be added, subtracted, multiplied and divided in almost the same way as numbers, to give a result that was either true (1) or false (0). Letters of the alphabet were used to represent objects or qualities of objects.8 The symbols +, −, × and = represented the logical operations *or*, *not*, *and* and *identity*.

Without straying too far into the thickets of the subject, a couple of examples may serve to illustrate the general thrust of Boole's scheme. If the symbol x represents the class of "all white objects" and if the symbol y represents the class of "all round objects," Boole used the compound symbol xy to represent the class of objects that are both white and round. He saw that since the class of objects that are white and round is exactly the same as the class of objects that are round and white, it is possible to write: $xy = yx$. Similarly, the notation $1 - x$ can be used to represent all objects that are not white, and $1 - y$ all objects not round, so that $(1 - x)(1 - y)$ = all objects neither white nor round.

If, on the other hand, x and y are mutually exclusive classes (in other words, no member of one class can at the same time be a member of the other), the notation $x + y$ can be used to represent all objects that belong to class *x* or to class *y*. So, if *x* represents all men and *y* represents all women, *xy* represents all people. It must therefore be true that *x* + *y* = *y* + *x*. Furthermore, if *z* represents the class of all Canadians, then *z(x + y)* = *zx* + *zy*—in other words, the class of Canadian men and women is exactly the same as the class of Canadian men and Canadian women.

It may seem that these examples are merely a complicated way of stating the obvious. But there is a power in symbolic logic that allows it to be helpful in reaching conclusions that are not immediately apparent when a problem is stated in ordinary language. In fact, insurance companies faced with elaborate policies that needed interpreting in the face of complex claims have used Boolean logic to determine when they were liable and when they were not.[9]

There are few more abstruse fields of intellectual endeavour than formal symbolic logic in its modern manifestations. And so it may seem all the more astonishing that this most abstract of disciplines has turned out to have an enormous impact on the day-to-day lives of virtually everyone on the planet. The explanation lies in the fact that Boole and Leibniz had made of logic a digital system operating by formal rules; in other words, a formal system. In today's terminology, they made logical problems accessible to solution by algorithms, an algorithm being simply a set of steps through which a mathematical solution can be reached. Boole's system, moreover, was a binary one that needed only the digits 1 and 0 to function, no matter how elaborate the question asked of it. As an algorithm for logic, when the appropriate time arrived, the Boolean system would be ripe for adoption by computer scientists.

The Amazingly Precocious
Charles Babbage

I T WAS THE NOT ENTIRELY HAPPY lot of the English inventor Charles Babbage (1792–1871) to become the first person to seriously attempt to employ the ideas of symbolic logic in constructing a digital computer.[1] He was one of those prodigies of intellect who populated nineteenth-century Europe, and Great Britain in particular. He is the father of operational analysis, or time-and-motion studies, producing the first text on the subject in 1832, nearly eighty years prior to the work of the better-known Frederick W. Taylor. He was a leading mathematician of his time. He investigated the British post office and made recommendations that led to the establishment of the penny post. He invented the railway cowcatcher and occulting beacon lights for marine navigation. As one fascinated by complex mechanisms, he was an accomplished lock-picker and an expert on ciphers. Not surprisingly, he knew most of the principal scientists of his era, and counted among his literary friends John Stuart Mill, Charles Dickens, Robert Browning, Thomas Carlyle, Lord Tennyson and Captain Frederick Marryat. He explored live volcanoes and wrote authoritatively on dating of archaeological finds, and published a paper on surface features of the moon, where a crater is now named for him.

The scion of a wealthy banking family, Babbage was able to make of himself a gentleman amateur of natural philosophy and technology in an age when all relevant knowledge was accessible to any intelligent man or woman, regardless of academic background. Babbage, as it happened, was schooled at Cambridge, but at a time when English universities studiously eschewed instruction in applied sciences (engineering, as we would say today) as being beneath them. Oxford and Cambridge played negligible roles in the Industrial Revolution. In Babbage's youth, compartmentalized studies or "disciplines" had yet to be imposed. "Physics, chemistry, science and engineering, literature and philosophy, art and industrial design, theory and practice—all constituted a continuum of knowledge and skill, within which men roamed freely," says historian Paul Johnson.[2]

As Babbage's century closed, academic turf would be divided and subdivided within universities, as knowledge and information became commodities—hard-won possessions to be jealously guarded within the individual disciplines. It was a rare economist who would know anything of chemistry; few chemists would have more than a passing knowledge of astronomy. Specialization led to rapid advances in many fields of science and technology thanks to the focused effort it produced, but it also led to development of arcane dialects and impenetrable terminology, which served to deny knowledge to non-specialists and protect the specialist's territory from outsiders. It crippled interdisciplinary communication for the next 150 years.

It was also a feature of Babbage's world that the state of the contest between medicine and disease was such that enormous tragedy was a commonplace in the lives of even the privileged. In 1827, when Babbage was hard at work on his famous Difference Engine, the most advanced calculating machine the world had ever seen, he had to deal in a single year with the deaths of two of his children, his father and his wife, Georgiana. Some biographers speculate that the stress unhinged him, with the result that he was from then on constitutionally unable to finish his machines, always finding a way to improve them that delayed the work of fabrication until new drawings had been prepared.

It is not surprising that he should have been attracted to a much-discussed challenge that was impeding the progress of all the physical sciences—the need for swift and accurate computation of large numbers. The problem of error-riddled mathematical tables used by astronomers, navigators and engineers to simplify their calculations was a real and lively issue as the Industrial Revolution gathered momentum in England, and Babbage showed an early interest in the possibility of mechanizing their production to ensure accuracy. In 1818 he travelled to France to have a first-hand look at recent advances in mathematics there, and it was during this visit that he encountered the remarkable work of Gaspard de Prony. Prony was a leading civil engineer in Napoleonic France, and a prominent advocate of the country's conversion to the metric system as part of the republic's program of rationalization of all things. Prony was assigned the unprecedented task of producing for publication logarithms of whole numbers from 1 to 200,000 and trigonometric values for 3,600 divisions of a circle—a job that could normally be expected to take teams of skilled mathematicians many years to complete. As a first step, the mathematicians would have to calculate an algebraic formula called a polynomial that would approximate each value required. Then, long and tedious arithmetic calculations would have to be done, based on the polynomials, to derive each number included in the tables.

Prony's solution allowed him to complete the job in a fraction of the time it would otherwise have required. He decided to divide up the labour, creating an assembly line of mathematicians of varying levels of skill, a notion he'd picked up quite by accident, according to Babbage's account,[3] while browsing through a copy of Adam Smith's economic treatise *The Wealth of Nations*. In a famous passage, Smith had illustrated the idea of division of labour as a key to enhanced productivity by describing a pin factory in which each step of the process was handled by a different worker, rather than the workers producing complete pins on their own. Smith had visited such a factory, and had concluded that dividing up the labour increased overall output by several orders of magnitude. In a flash of inspiration, Prony determined to employ a similar attack on his own problem of the tables.

In Prony's calculating factory, a handful of highly skilled mathematicians created the polynomials. Arithmetical calculations arising out of them were divided into two tiers of difficulty and assigned to teams of calculators of appropriate skill levels. According to Babbage, most of the hordes of calculators on the lowest tier knew nothing of mathematics beyond simple, mechanical addition and subtraction. Prony had created a human precursor of the yet-to-be-invented programmable computer. Babbage, well primed in the theories of mechanical computation, recognized the analogy, and set about converting the human analog into mechanical form. It would be one of the epic journeys in the annals of technology, replete with Victorian melodrama and genuine tragedy.

Naturally, Babbage had to work with the techniques and materials available to him in the early to mid-1800s, and so his amazing computation machine was designed to be constructed of thousands of carefully machined brass gears and cogs arranged in incredibly complex patterns and powered by a steam engine. Work proceeded for a decade beginning in 1822, financed by an increasingly restive British minister of finance. The government had initially shown interest in the project because more accurate mathematical tables would have significant economic and military benefits, not to mention the fact that errors in marine navigational tables were frequently responsible for the loss of lives at sea. However, a characteristic quip from Prime Minister Sir Robert Peel, one of several politicians from whom Babbage sought support in his requests for government backing, neatly sums up the difficulty faced by governments then, as now, in funding arcane scientific research. "I should like a little previous consideration," he remarked to a friend, "before I move in a thin House of country gentlemen a large vote for the creation of a wooden man to calculate tables from the formula x^2+x+41. I fancy Lethbridge's face on being called to contribute."[4]

Babbage was in some ways his own worst enemy, a victim of the French proverb that says the best is often an enemy of the good; he was continually revising and simplifying his plans, with the result that nothing got finished.[5] Had he chosen to freeze development work at any time during the years he worked on the Difference Engine, it is entirely likely that he could have produced a working model within a reasonable time at a figure acceptable to the government. The machine was designed to multiply or divide two 50-digit numbers, to 100 decimal places, in less than a minute. In 1991 a team of engineers and technicians at the Science Museum in London constructed a portion of his Difference Engine #2, assembling some four thousand components from the original drawings. It worked.[6]

Government funding for the Difference Engine was eventually halted, never to be renewed. Meanwhile, Babbage's fertile mind had come up with radical new designs for an Analytical Engine, a machine that would automate not only arithmetic processes but also the logical control of those processes. He had found a way to mechanize the idea *if/then*. Data would be fed into the machine by means of punch cards similar to those being used in the newly invented jacquard loom, which was revolutionizing the textile industry through wide-scale automation. Input provided by punch cards would be processed by a "mill," or calculating and decision-making unit, operating under instructions from a "store," or memory, another bank of finely machined gears and interconnected shafts. Thanks to the adjustable nature of the memory function, the machine could be programmed to handle all sorts of computational chores, and those processes could be altered or adjusted automatically, with decisions based on its own calculations. The machine was in fact capable of doing simple, autonomous deductive reasoning; for example, *If* the answer is *x, then* add *y* and proceed to operation *z*. An answer could be automatically fed back into the machine as data for finding another answer in a complex problem.

It was, in every important respect, a modern digital computer, except that it was designed to be constructed of brass and mahogany. If completed, it would have occupied most of an aircraft hangar (had such a thing existed) and required six steam engines to power it. The Analytical Engine was so far out of its time that it might have been the fictional product of the fertile imagination of an H.G. Wells or Jules Verne; one expects a Disney adaptation to reach the cinemas at any time.

In his constant quest for improved methods of machining and other industrial processes necessary to the production of parts for his calculating machines, Babbage visited factories and workshops all over Europe. The knowledge he gleaned was assembled in his *Economy of Machinery*, an update of Adam Smith's account of the benefits of the division of labour in a pin factory. For Babbage, the great benefit of dividing labour was that low-skilled components of any job could be separated out and assigned to low-paid workers. Karl Marx was to lean heavily on Babbage's analysis, finding in it evidence of the factory organization as the means by which profit was maintained through the exploitation of labour. Babbage's interests took him in a different direction when studying the same body of information: he concluded from his analysis that human thought was as amenable to mechanical organization as the weaving of cloth on a jacquard loom. In a chapter entitled "The Division of Mental Labours" he said: "There is no reason why mental as well as bodily labour should not be economized by the aid of machinery."[7]

He was fascinated by mechanical automata of the kind produced by craftsmen of the previous century, and had restored a dancing naked lady, a wind-up figure he kept in his parlour. It disappointed him that visitors were invariably more interested in his "silver lady" than in the fragment of his Analytical Engine in the next room, and he concluded that he would have to find a way to have his machine perform some sort of human feat in order to get people interested in it.

This was more than a trivial concern—he needed public enthusiasm if he was to continue receiving government support. Babbage concluded that a game requiring intellectual skill might do the trick: "I selected for my test the contrivance of a machine that should be able to play a game of purely intellectual skill successfully; such as tic-tac-toe, drafts, chess, etc. . . ." He immediately saw that in fact "every game of skill is susceptible of being played by an automaton." Babbage made elaborate plans to build game-playing machines and charge the public to match wits with them, as a way of raising money for continued development of his Analytical Engine. But, like so many of his schemes, the plans were never acted on—at least, not in any public way.

As a younger man, Babbage was the toast of England, and counted as friends and acquaintances the leading lights of the day. He held Isaac Newton's Lucasian Chair at Cambridge University from 1828 to 1839, and Charles Darwin writes that he "regularly attended his [Babbage's] famous parties." But in old age his frustrations with funding and bureaucracy and the limits of machine technology mounted, and he became a well-known curmudgeon, notorious for his energetic campaigns against organ grinders and other "street nuisances" in London. In return, they pitched stones through his windows and jeered at him in the streets. Despite his incipient grumpiness, he had the good luck to attract the benevolent attention of Lord Byron's only legitimate daughter, Lady Ada Augusta, Countess of Lovelace, who was not only a brilliant mathematician, but beautiful and well heeled to boot.[8] She wrote a number of routines for the Analytical Engine, becoming the world's first computer programmer in the process. (The modern programming language Ada is named in her honour.)

The relationship between Babbage and Lady Lovelace is both poignant and deliciously shrouded in intrigue. She was the age his only daughter would have been had she not been taken from him by illness; he was slightly younger than her dead father would have been. In a world in which his inventions were ridiculed even by eminent scientists (the Astronomer Royal called the Difference Engine "humbug" and the Analytical Engine "worthless"), she understood perfectly how and why they worked and what they were capable of, and produced the single most authoritative book on the subject. Indeed, Babbage might have escaped history's appreciation altogether were it not for her careful documentation of his work.

Their increasingly intimate friendship took a bizarre twist some-time in 1848: the otherwise rich and well-preserved correspon-dence between them contains a large lacuna in this period, with only tantalizing hints of the reasons why so many letters should have been destroyed, presumably by Babbage himself. As the story has been pieced together, it appears that Lady Lovelace enlisted Babbage's help in a scheme to use the partly completed Difference Engine to beat the odds at the racetrack. The scheme appears to have carried on for a period of four years, until Lady Lovelace's death in 1852. It is a fact that the countess was heavily involved in betting on horses at the time, indeed, had pawned her jewels twice in order to pay her debts. Each time, they were redeemed by her mother, Lady Noel Byron.

The surviving record indicates a blackmailer named Crosse was paid a small fortune by lawyers engaged by Lady Byron after her daughter's untimely death of cancer. The agreement stipulated that he was to destroy in the lawyers' presence "all of Lady Lovelace's let-ters and all her husband's, including 'the all-important letter from him to her, assenting to and authorizing her betting proceedings, and which letter she had handed over to Crosse.'"9 Babbage had appar-ently acceded to Lady Lovelace's deathbed request that he make the payoff himself, but eventually agreed to the lawyers' involvement. One of Babbage's servants, Mary Wilson, had been mixed up in the scheme: Babbage had seconded her to the Lovelace household, where she appears to have acted as an accomplice, possibly a go-between for Lady Lovelace and the bookmakers who placed her bets. She was fired by an outraged Lady Byron when the whole messy story emerged with Ada's death. Babbage insisted Mary Wilson be given a settlement of £100, and he left her £3 a month for life in his will, the only person outside his immediate family to be recognized.

The death of Ada had its own horrific overtones: her sickroom had to be padded with mattresses to prevent her from injuring her-self when she was in the paroxysms of agony caused by her disease. She was just thirty-seven when she finally succumbed, the same age her father had been when he died.

Lady Lovelace's descriptions of Babbage's machines remain clear and readable today. The Difference Engine, she said, was to the Analytical Engine as arithmetic is to analysis. The Difference Engine could do nothing but add, and problems had to be reduced to a series of additions. The Analytical Engine, on the other hand, could add, subtract, multiply and divide directly. The Difference Engine could only tabulate results; the Analytical Engine could develop more complex solutions by *feeding back* its results into the system for further computation. Because it was programmed using punched cards, it could be used for a wide variety of computations without altering its physical structure.

The idea that his Analytical Engine could manipulate symbols other than numbers was well understood by Babbage, particularly in the case where the machine reached into its "store," or memory, to change its own program. Lady Lovelace spoke of the machine as "weaving algebraic patterns just as the Jacquard loom weaves flowers and leaves," and she envisioned it being used to write music and play chess.[10] Both knew they were tinkering on the fringes of artificial intelligence, as this particularly perceptive passage suggests:

> The bounds of *arithmetic* were, however, outstepped the moment the idea of applying the cards had occurred; and the Analytical Engine does not occupy common ground with mere "calculating machines." It holds a position wholly its own; and the considerations it suggests are most interesting in their nature. In enabling mechanism to combine together *general* symbols in successions of unlimited variety and extent, a uniting link is established between the operations of matter and the abstract mental processes of the most abstract branch of mathematical science. A new, vast and powerful language is developed for the future use of analysis, in which to wield its truths so that these may become of more speedy and accurate practical application for the purposes of mankind than the means hitherto in our possession have rendered possible.[11]

As anyone who has endured a computer crash will know, a computer that does not function is a remarkably unimpressive device. Babbage's blueprints and half-finished pile of wheels and cogs could not change the world. His vision was hopelessly beyond the reach of the technology of the day. In general, the clockwork machine he had blueprinted was just too complicated, and in particular, machine tools of the day could not produce gears to the fine tolerance required, certainly not at a cost that could be borne by Babbage and his backers.[12] He had demonstrated, however, that the great power of formal systems such as mathematics and symbolic logic could be tapped by mechanical means—in effect, automated. The implications were profound, because once automation had been achieved, the remaining challenge of speeding up the process was a straightforward engineering problem.

Babbage died in his eightieth year in 1871, virtually forgotten; only one old friend outside his immediate family attended his funeral, and the Royal Society of which he had long been a member did not think to print the customary obituary. He suffered the final indignity of having his brain removed and pickled for study. Of course, nothing of value was learned from it. The curious, however, can still see it for themselves at the Museum of the Royal College of Surgeons in London.

An unexplored footnote to his career is his influence on the work of his more famous contemporary, Charles Darwin. In his *Ninth Bridgewater Treatise*, Babbage ruminates on miracles and how they might be explained in the context of the kind of thoroughly mechanistic, deterministic universe he and most of his scientific cohort believed in. Babbage proposed that what are thought of as miracles are sudden variations in long machine programs or routines caused by an abrupt switch to another algorithm. Charles Darwin was reportedly impressed with these thoughts, and they had some bearing on his conception of the origin of species as an outcome of natural law, with no need for divine intervention.[13]

Babbage's influence was also felt in the evolution of economics, most directly through the great theorist of price and marginal utility,

William Stanley Jevons, who saw in the Analytical Engine a model of the operations of the market economy.[14] He also saw in Babbage's machine a model of the human mind, the two insights leading to a vision of economic systems as autonomous, self-regulating, machine-like entities. Liberal laissez-faire economic theory was thus able to aspire to a precision equal to that of any other branch of engineering, a circumstance that helped to conceal for 150 years the fact that it was actually more ideology than science.

The Secrets of Automatic Formal Systems and the Enigmatic Alan Turing

AMONG Babbage's greatest insights was the realization that the ultimate power of formal systems is realized through their automation. The formal systems of arithmetic and geometry can be used to abstract real-world problems into relations between symbols (through symbolic logic) and, by slavishly following the rules of the formal system, provide reliable answers with relevance for the real world. The step-by-step methodology is tedious and no doubt mind-numbing, but it is at the same time very powerful due to the fact that it is error-free. That it is tedious in human terms doesn't really matter because formal systems can run on machines, whose "minds" presumably cannot know numbness.

As Babbage also knew, to his eternal frustration, to be of any practical value an automatic formal system needs an appropriate medium—a machine of some sort—within which it can be executed. Babbage pushed the machine technology of his era to its limits and well beyond, without ever being able to realize his designs. The formal system called symbolic logic had to wait for the discoveries of Faraday and the other inventors of electronics, and in

particular for Fleming's vacuum tube, before it would find a medium in which it could be embodied in a practical way. It needed an
embodiment appropriate to its capabilities.

Two key conceptual notions were lacking as well, to bridge the
gap between Boole's theorems of symbolic logic and a device to
manipulate them in useful ways. Both arrived just prior to World
War II.

The young British mathematician Alan Turing (1912–54) was
doing work on symbolic logic when, in one of the twentieth century's most impressive intellectual achievements, he provided the
first of the needed concepts by working out on paper the complete
details of how an electronic computer might function. In 1934 he
was twenty-two years old, a newly installed graduate fellow at
Cambridge with a £300-a-year stipend and free room and board.
Although the fellowship involved no formal duties, he was expected
to work on some mathematical problem of significance. He chose
to take up where Kurt Gödel had left off, tying up a loose end left
unresolved by Gödel's theorem, which was still causing consternation among mathematicians the world over (see chapter 4). The
dangling question was: is there any means by which it might be possible to distinguish between provable and non-provable mathematical statements, that is, short of actually proving or disproving them
(which Gödel had demonstrated was not possible)? Might there be
some formula or other that could be applied to give an answer of
"provable" or "not provable"?

The reader may well smile at the angels-on-the-head-of-a-pin
nature of such a question. It would be reasonable to ask of what
possible use it could be to spend one's time trying to answer it. A
taxpayer might be prompted to demand whether a financial grant-
in-aid for such a project was a sane way in which to spend public
money. Turing's experience, though perhaps somewhat more dramatic than others, was a prime example of how rarefied science
can—in spite of its insistence on purity of motive—advance the
cause of civilization in very concrete ways.

Turing tackled his problem by trying to conceive of a machine that could provide the required "provable/not provable" answers— a machine, because it would by definition operate without the intervention of human imagination or judgment to affect its decisions. To solve a problem mechanically, a machine must obviously be able to accomplish its goal within a finite number of steps. The finite operations used to solve a problem are collectively called an algorithm, and the question Turing was really asking is: are there any kinds of problems in logic or mathematics that cannot be solved using algorithms? It is a question that could also be seen as a clarifying query about Boolean logic: what can and cannot be achieved with this kind of formal system? Turing was able to demonstrate that there was indeed no way to test for provability or non-provability of mathematical statements, thus providing a definitive reply to the question he'd set out to answer. But much more important was what he'd learned about the machine he had invented as a by-product of his analysis. He could show conclusively that *any* computation that could be carried out by algorithms could be done on his "Turing Machine."

He found, in other words, that he had invented something quite miraculous: a machine that could do the work of *any other* machine. The Turing Machine was capable of duplicating the operations of any formal system whatsoever, that is, any system that operated according to identifiable rules or algorithms—as do all machines, not to mention many natural systems. Put another way, if one could set out an algorithm for the operations of a process, that process could be simulated by a Turing Machine. (Today's "Turing Machines," in the form of supercomputers, can, for example, accurately model the dynamics of a nuclear explosion or the growth of a cellular structure.) It was this brilliant achievement that led to the digital revolution which is in the process of changing our world. Turing's 1936 paper "On Computable Numbers" described in complete detail the theoretical structure of all digital computers to the present day; it is one of science's most significant documents.

The essential operations of the computer as understood by Turing are astonishingly simple. To accomplish its tasks all any digital computer does is write one of two symbols (1 or 0), one at a time. Which one it writes is determined by the existing state of the system as the computer finds it (or "reads" it) and a finite set of formal operating rules. Whether it is playing chess or crunching national tax accounts or navigating a space vehicle, any task being performed by a computer can be explained in terms of this simple, step-by-step reading/writing procedure. Strings of ones and zeros are used to represent numbers, letters and other symbols, according to agreed-upon conventions or protocols. Among the best known of these is the ASCII protocol, which lists 256 characters as completely representing the alphabet and its punctuation marks, and assigns a binary code, or string of ones and zeros, to each character.

With different algorithms, or sets of rules, different tasks can be done by the same machine. As we've already seen, while this may seem a tedious way to go about solving a problem, it is also extremely precise and thus powerful. The straightforward engineering challenge is to find ways to make the machine perform its humdrum operations more and more rapidly.

The second conceptual breakthrough that was required before the digital computer could become a reality was made by a master's student in electrical engineering at the Massachusetts Institute of Technology at about the same time as Turing was writing his seminal paper. The young American, Claude Shannon, had landed a research assistant's job at MIT working with Vannevar Bush on his electromechanical analog computer, the "differential analyzer," one of the most advanced computers on the planet at that time. His experience with Bush led Shannon to do his 1938 master's thesis—sometimes called the most influential ever written—on the relationship between the computer and another interest he had pursued earlier in his academic career, symbolic logic. In his thesis he showed how complex arrangements of electrical switches behave according to the rules of—Boolean logic! A switch, in being open or closed, is in effect saying "yes" or "no" to an electrical current, or, in Boole's terms, "true" or "false." Therefore, any logical relationship that could be translated into Boolean algebra could also be expressed in an array of electrical switches.

The Boolean expression $a \times b = c$ (a or b is equal to c, where *or* is represented by the multiplication symbol x in Boolean notation) would be represented by two switches in parallel, either one of which could be closed to allow current to flow. This was termed an "or" circuit because it conformed to a Boolean expression in which two propositions are joined by the conjunction *or*: if either is true (if either switch is closed), then the sum is true (the current will flow). Two switches in series, on the other hand, is analogous to an *and* expression: both must be closed for current to flow, and if one is open and the other closed, current will be blocked (since it must pass through both switches to reach c), just as in the Boolean expression $a + b = c$, both a and b must be true for c to be true (for current to flow). Shannon found that any conceivable arrangement of switches had a corresponding expression in Boolean logic. The converse was an even more powerful idea: any proposition that could be expressed in Boolean logic could also be expressed in an arrangement of electrical switches. Since arithmetic problems are problems in symbolic, or Boolean, logic, Shannon had also showed how electrical circuitry could be wired to solve arithmetical problems.

Minds such as Shannon's and Turing's were not to be overlooked in pursuance of the war effort against Hitler. (In fact, the two mathematicians were to meet as senior technical advisers to their respective governments and discuss their mutual interests halfway through the conflict, when Turing crossed the U-boat-infested Atlantic on the *Queen Elizabeth* to inspect American efforts at code making and code breaking.) In 1939, Turing found himself attached to a motley group of tweedy classics scholars and unkempt chess champions housed in a series of cottages at the British Code and Cypher Unit in Bletchley Park, an estate northwest of London in Buckinghamshire. This was the modest beginning of what would become a very large and very secret part of the war effort, one that was to be a decisive factor in the defeat of Germany. Throughout the war, Turing was a senior figure in astonishingly successful British efforts to break the German communications codes in all theatres of action.

The German cipher machine, which the Nazis believed with absolute assurance to be failsafe, was called Enigma. The British effort to second-guess the machine was called Ultra. Turing's insights into the logical workings of machines were literally invaluable, in that the Achilles heel of Enigma proved to be the very fact that it *was* a machine, and therefore its operations could be simulated by a Turing Machine, or digital computer. By the end of the war, thousands of men and women were involved in the decoding and interpreting effort run out of Bletchley Park. And they were being assisted by super-secret, high-speed digital computers—at first electromechanical using mechanical relays, but later fully electronic—in which Turing had played a key design role.[1]

While his was undoubtedly one of the most important individual contributions to the winning of the war, it went unacknowledged for more than two decades because the work that had been accomplished at Bletchley Park was (and in some respects still is) highly secret. And at the height of the espionage and Red paranoia excesses of the Cold War, in the summer of 1954, Turing was found dead in the bedroom of his suburban Manchester home, a victim of cyanide poisoning. There was a hasty inquest, and the coroner pronounced it a "straightforward suicide."

The background to Turing's death suggests that final judgment on the coroner's verdict of 1954 should perhaps be reserved. Turing, an amiable, gentlemanly and thoroughly eccentric genius of scruffy professorial habits and with a passion for marathon running, was a homosexual whose innate honesty compelled him to inform any close friend of the fact. He was also in possession of a full mental catalogue of the secrets of Ultra, which Britain and the United States then regarded as of the highest strategic value. At Manchester University, where he spent his last years working, he had access to a Ferranti computer on which other scientists were doing work for the British atomic bomb program.

Two years before his death, he was arrested and charged with gross indecency following a consensual homosexual encounter in the privacy of his own home with a young man. (The police learned of it while investigating a burglary Turing had later reported: he suspected the young man and told the police so.) Homosexual relations between consenting couples were then illegal in Britain, as in most of North America, and the relaxed tolerance of homosexuality that Turing had found at pre-war Cambridge had largely vanished after the war. Homosexuals were considered by the governments of Britain, the United States and Canada to be obvious security risks, unfit for military service of any kind and dangerously unsuitable for work of a strategically sensitive nature. In all three countries, loyal citizens with unimpeachable records were hounded from their jobs and sometimes to their deaths during the 1950s by government security agencies because they were homosexual.

Turing was tried in open court, convicted and put on one year's probation, during which time he was forced, as a condition of his sentence, to take a drug that was supposed to help cure him of his "deviant" tendencies by causing temporary impotence. It also caused him to develop breasts.

Shortly before his death he confided to a long-time friend that he had been providing continuing help to a government decrypting effort but had lately been told that there was no longer any place for homosexuals in such top-secret work.[2] Whatever these facts may say about Turing's death, in no sense does it seem just to call his suicide, if such it was, "straightforward." It was a disturbing and ignominious end for a person who deserves to be celebrated as one of the great men of the twentieth century.

The Computer Comes of Age

T URING'S MACHINE, no matter how brilliant in conception, would not have had much impact on society had it not found a physical embodiment appropriate to it, as poor Babbage had discovered. Babbage died a disappointed man in 1871; in 1942, seventy-one years later, the world's first working analytical engine began operating at Harvard University. The IBM Automatic Sequence Calculator, Mark 1, was a fully automatic digital computer that used mechanical switches operated electrically to solve equations described in Boolean logic. Like Babbage's machine, it was controlled by punched media, in this case tape instead of cards. Its speed and capacity greatly exceeded anything achieved to that date by even the most sophisticated analog calculating machines.

The impetus behind IBM Mark 1, as with so much of computer research and development, had come from the military. One of the more serious problems of computation with which the United States Navy needed help was calculating the trajectory of various shells and missiles. This is a relatively straightforward task if the shell is to be fired in a vacuum; in the real world, it is enormously complicated by such considerations as atmospheric humidity, air density, the shape of the projectile and its velocity. Gunnery crews were forced to operate by trial and error, using approximations supplied by the best mechanical calculators then available. More precise calculations and faster compilation of tables, as provided by the IBM machine, were of important strategic value.

In 1942, Britain was deeply involved in a desperate program to construct a fully electronic digital computer. With the German cipher system having been broken at Bletchley Park, there was now an urgent need to speed the process of computation involved. Banks of super-secret electromechanical machines, themselves far in advance of anything the world at large had ever heard of, were falling behind the flow of available information. Important messages were being decoded too late to be of use. Built between February and November 1943, Colossus, as the electronic computer was called, was so deeply shrouded in military secrecy that it was an antique before the world knew it existed. It operated using binary arithmetic, which allowed it to get away with a relatively small complement of 1,500 vacuum tubes. Later models used 2,400 tubes.[1] Eleven of the machines were built during and immediately after the war, evidence of a truly staggering effort of technical skill, administrative determination and inventive genius.[2]

Across the Atlantic at the University of Pennsylvania, hundreds of operators were being kept busy computing artillery trajectory tables, using the biggest and fastest of the last generation of electromechanical analog calculating machines. Meanwhile work had begun, on another part of the campus, at the Moore School of Electrical Engineering, on an electronic version of the Mark 1 IBM machine called the Electronic Numerical Integrator and Computer (ENIAC). It was not completed until the war was over, but it was by far the fastest computer in the world when it was up and running.

ENIAC had a front panel a hundred feet long, contained 17,468 vacuum tubes (it used the decimal rather than binary system, which would have called for fewer electronic switches), required a dedicated power line to supply its demand for 174 kilowatts of electricity, occupied eighteen hundred square feet of floor space and weighed thirty tons. It cost $800,000 to build in 1945. Teams of engineers and technicians were required to operate it. Replacement of tubes alone was a challenge: one burned out, on average, every few hours. It could do 38 nine-digit divisions in a single second, a fact that seemed incredible at the time.[3] In one of its first tests, it performed in twenty seconds an atomic energy calculation that was taking human-operated calculating machines of the Manhattan Project forty hours to complete. It was programmed by changing the wiring on a complex control panel, which looked like an early telephone switchboard with its hundreds of patch cords. To change a program was a tedious and frustrating labour of many hours. It was made even more frustrating, legend has it, by cleaning staff who would occasionally accidentally knock one of the plugs out of the board and, to avoid discovery, stick it back into a hole at random.

As often happens with frontier technologies, the designers of ENIAC made discoveries in the course of their work that rendered the machine obsolete even before it had been completed. With war still raging in 1944, they approached the army's Ballistics Research Laboratory for more funding, to produce a more advanced machine called EDVAC (Electronic Discrete Variable Automatic Computer). Then fate gave them the opportunity to recruit one of the brightest minds of twentieth-century science, a man whose stature would, they knew, add immeasurable prestige to their project. Mathematician John von Neumann was brought onto the team, to join ENIAC veterans J. Presper Eckert and John Mauchly. As a group, they developed a breakthrough in computer architecture that has since borne von Neumann's name.

John von Neumann had been a child prodigy in mathematics in Hungary. At twenty-three, he had earned a degree in chemical engineering in Zurich and a Ph.D. in mathematics from the University of Budapest. In 1930 he joined the faculty of Princeton University, where he became a member of the Institute for Advanced Study along with Albert Einstein; contemporaries placed them in the same intellectual class. (In 1936–37, Alan Turing was also at the Institute, on a visiting fellowship.) Von Neumann pursued an astonishing range of interests, publishing work on quantum theory, mathematical

logic, continuous geometry, meteorology, aerodynamics, economics, automata theory and the theory of hydrodynamics. It was this
latter interest that would lead to his involvement in the Manhattan
Project. There, he contributed the implosion method of detona-
tion, which was used in the atomic bomb exploded over Nagasaki.

Von Neumann's initial exposure to advanced computers, we
are told, took place on a railway platform in Aberdeen, Maryland,
home of the army's Ballistics Research Laboratory, to which he was
a consultant. There, on a crisp wartime evening, he met Herman
Goldstine, who was the chief liaison officer between the Ballistics
Lab and the ENIAC project at the University of Pennsylvania.
Goldstine recognized the great mathematician and introduced
himself. Though both men held top-level security clearance, their
conversation was guarded at first, until Goldstine made reference to
progress with ENIAC. He later recalled: "When it became clear . . .
that I was concerned with the development of an electronic computer capable of 333 multiplications per second, the whole atmosphere of our conversation changed from one of relaxed good
humor to one more like the oral examination for the doctor's degree in mathematics."[4] In September 1944, von Neumann visited
the ENIAC project and soon after became a consultant.

His impact on the EDVAC proposal was profound. Leaving technical aspects of the machine to Eckert and Mauchly, he focused on
the abstract problem of the relationships between the logical components. He wrote a paper on the team's developing ideas, which
Goldstine circulated and which was immediately recognized as a
breakthrough in computer architecture. Unfortunately, it bore only
von Neumann's name, and the design it proposed became known as
"von Neumann architecture." This did not endear him to Mauchly
and Eckert, though in hindsight he appears to have been innocent
of any intent to co-opt the team's work.

There were major ramifications: the Moore School team dis-
solved in acrimony and bitterness. Mauchly and Eckert had early on
realized the commercial potential for the machine they were developing

and were already embroiled in a dispute with Moore School officials over patent rights. Publication of von Neumann's paper scarcely helped matters for them: the army argued the paper had placed EDVAC architecture in the public domain, making it unpatentable. Mauchly and Eckert angrily resigned their university positions, intending to develop a commercial version of EDVAC on their own. They filed for patent protection in 1947; Bell Telephone Laboratories and IBM vigorously intervened, and the case dragged on and on until 1964, when the patent was finally issued.

By then, Mauchly and Eckert had sold their interests in the patent to Sperry Rand for $600,000. It was another bitter disappointment for them; they had hoped to carry on in business for themselves. But though they had both been deeply involved in the top-secret military projects to build ENIAC and EDVAC, new military contracts were inexplicably denied them. Finally, Mauchly learned that an army/FBI security check had found him to be "communistically inclined." The main basis for this allegation was an anonymous colleague's recollection that Mauchly had once signed a petition (along with several hundred other scientists) calling for civilian control of atomic energy in the United States. The petition had been sponsored by the American Association of Scientific Workers, which army intelligence regarded as having been a Communist-front organization.

It was an egregious example of the McCarthyist excesses of the Cold War. Mauchly himself, not knowing the exact nature of the charges against him, thought he might have come under suspicion for having been a member of the Consumers Union, which the House Un-American Activities Committee had also identified as a Communist front.[5] It would take six long years for Mauchly to clear his name and regain high-level security clearance, but in the meantime his company had withered on the vine, forcing the sale to Sperry Rand.

In 1967, Honeywell Inc., with IBM watching with interest, brought suit against Sperry Rand, alleging that the EDVAC patent, granted after such laborious litigation, was invalid because the design had been appropriated from an obscure Iowa State University physicist whom Mauchly had met back in 1940. The physicist himself had long ago lost interest in computers and, until the idea was planted in his mind by Honeywell's lawyers, had never thought of Mauchly as having borrowed his ideas. He had never sought a patent on his own work, indeed had never bothered to announce it in public. In the grand swashbuckling tradition of the Western Union suit against Bell, it was a thin thread on which to hang a lawsuit, but Honeywell's legal resources were formidable.

Pretrial proceedings took three and a half years, during which time thirty thousand exhibits, including the autobiography of Charles Babbage, were identified. The hearing itself ran from June 1971 to March 1973. Seven months later the court ruled that the ENIAC patent was invalid. It also ruled that Eckert and Mauchly had waited too long to apply for protection in the first place. Under U.S. law, inventors have one year after making an invention to apply for a patent. The judge ruled that ENIAC had been in "public use" since December 1945 (thanks to the von Neumann paper), but the patent hadn't been applied for until June 1947.

Whatever its other merits, the lawsuit effectively demolished any serious patent barriers to ongoing development of the nascent computer industry, which was plainly one of the goals of Honeywell and its collaborators. Sperry Rand, having sunk more than a million dollars in legal fees, declined to appeal. For them, it was strictly a financial decision.

John von Neumann did not live to see the resolution of the legal wrangling. He died in 1957 when he was just fifty-four, of bone cancer probably resulting from exposure to radioactivity during his work on atomic weapons. Since 1955 he had been a key member of the U.S. Atomic Energy Commission, which at that time had as its main responsibility the development and stockpiling of nuclear weapons. Not long before his death, he crystallized his virulent anti-Communist views for an article in *Life* magazine in which he advocated pre-emptive warfare against the Soviet Union: "If you say why not bomb [the Soviets] tomorrow, I say, why not today. If you say today at five o'clock, I say why not one o'clock."[6]

The key to the success of von Neumann's legacy, the so-called von Neumann computer architecture that most computers employ to this day, lay in its use of a large internal memory that could be accessed directly. It was large enough to hold both data to be manipulated *and* operating instructions, or "programming." The fact that the operating instructions could be accessed directly, and at electronic speed, rather than the machine having to read through punch cards or tape to find its next command, meant it ran much faster than ENIAC. It was also much more flexible, because there could be continuous feedback between the operating instructions and the computer's computational routines, which gave the machine a new power and autonomy, the ability to "bootstrap" itself into higher levels of performance and complexity without the need for continuous human intervention. (It was this ability that would lead to comparisons with the human mind.) The fast, randomly accessible memory would come to be called "random access memory," or RAM.

The world's first computer using stored programs in RAM, however, was put into operation not in the United States but at Cambridge University in England, in 1949. The design, largely by Turing, took full advantage of his Bletchley Park experience, and as a result placed great emphasis on speed of operation. Pilot ACE (Automatic Computing Engine) was built to run at a "clock speed" of one megahertz (one million cycles per second), much faster than EDVAC. It also incorporated the idea of a large memory, an idea that was in fact implicit in Turing's original conception of the Turing Machine; RAM storage within ACE was in the order of 100 kilobits, an enormous sum for the time. Unfortunately, and tragically for Britain's computer industry, the development of ACE was placed in the hands of government bureaucrats, where it languished. Turing himself withdrew from the project in frustration in 1947. Britain's substantial head start in computer development was squandered while nimbler private companies in the United States, operating with rich financial incentives from Washington, first caught up and then, by the early 1950s, established an irreversible lead.

The first *commercial* computer with a stored program, or RAM, was made by the Remington Rand company (later Sperry Rand) on a design of Eckert and Mauchly. The Universal Automatic Computer (UNIVAC I) was delivered to the U.S. Census Bureau in 1951.[7] UNIVAC represented a tenfold jump in speed over ENIAC, though it was still slower than ACE. It contained only five thousand vacuum tubes, shoehorned into a cabinet 14 feet long by 7 feet wide by 9 feet tall, and it operated at a clock rate of 2.5 megahertz. It used magnetic tape storage instead of punch cards for its instructions and had about one kilobyte of RAM.

The sale to the Census Bureau was a fitting one for the first of the commercial mainframe computers, because the Census Bureau had been the first modern customer for practical mechanical means of calculation. Required by law to conduct a full census of the American population every ten years, by the 1880 census (when the U.S. population had reached 50 million) the Bureau found to its dismay that it took more than seven years to process the data that had been collected. It was clear that unless some method was found to speed up the system, the Bureau would be unable to fulfill its legal mandate. Hence the department's continuing interest, beginning as early as 1890, in mechanical calculators. In that year it purchased a machine built in Belgium and modelled directly on plans taken from an article written by Charles Babbage about his Difference Engine.

Eventually, forty-six UNIVAC machines were sold by Sperry Rand, despite the conventional wisdom of the time that insisted there was enough demand in the United States for perhaps two or three computers of its power. A 1950 *Business Week* article said, "Salesmen will find the market limited. The UNIVAC is not the kind of machine that every office could use." Even more revealing of the challenge of selling the computers of the day is Lord Bowden of Chesterfield's description of the job in a comment to British communications theorist Colin Cherry: "I had to sell the wretched things, if I was to earn my living and keep my firm in business. I decided that I had the most peculiar job in the world, until I met a man on the *Queen Mary* who sold lighthouses on commission and he told me about some of his problems!"[8]

The profound shock caused by the Soviet Union's test explosion of an atomic bomb in August 1949 provided the impetus for a new burst of creativity in computer design in the United States. The explosion, coupled with the knowledge that Soviet long-range bombers were capable of reaching U.S. targets via the Arctic, caused near-panic in the Truman administration's defence establishment. American air defences were in no way capable of dealing with such a deadly threat, one that seemed palpably real at a time when China was falling to the Communists, the Berlin blockade had only just ended, and insurgent nationalist, anti-colonial movements supported by the Soviets were springing up all over Asia and Africa.

The response to the Soviet atomic threat was a crash program to build a state-of-the-art network of early-warning radar stations around America's perimeters—scores of stations capable of picking up low-flying aircraft and tracking them until interceptors could scramble to shoot them down. Canada was willingly co-opted into the scheme through the North American Air Defence Command (NORAD), as many of the stations would have to be built in that country's High Arctic regions. What made the plan feasible was the emerging power of computers to coordinate information flooding in from the many radar stations.

The U.S. military turned once again to MIT, where it had been financing a major computer project called Whirlwind. Initially envisioned as a program to develop a flight simulator that could train pilots on a number of different aircraft, Whirlwind had evolved into much more than that. Its speed was such that it was capable of tracking several aircraft in real time and relaying intercept coordinates to attacking fighters. It grew into a huge project, employing seventy engineers and technicians and another hundred support staff, with a budget of more than a million dollars a year. Scientists Robert Everett and Jay Forrester were in charge; Forrester is credited with inventing, for Whirlwind, the first magnetic core memory system, which further boosted the machine's speed by a factor of four.

With the promise of bottomless funding, MIT computer scientists turned to the development of SAGE, or Semiautomatic Ground Environment, the heart of the new computerized air defence system. Whirlwind became the prototype backbone computer, and Forrester and his team invented a whole new family of technologies to enable radar stations to communicate directly with the mainframes. In tests in 1953, SAGE, which weighed 250 tons, was able to successfully track as many as forty-eight targets simultaneously. Continually updated and refined with new computer technology (much of it co-designed by IBM) and new weapons of interception, SAGE remained in service until 1984. The system's eventual cost was $61 billion. But many of those who worked on SAGE now believe that despite its cost and sophistication, it would never have been able to fend off a full-scale Soviet onslaught. It was the best system possible at the time, but it was excruciatingly vulnerable to being swamped by large numbers of attacking aircraft. To conceal its technical inadequacies, it was extensively promoted in public statements as virtually infallible. It was, in the words of Paul Edwards, "more than a weapons system: it was a dream, a myth, a metaphor for total defense."9

Whatever its shortcomings as a defensive weapon, SAGE provided a host of spinoffs that were of seminal importance, especially in the field of computer networking and communication. Robert Everett gave Whirlwind an interactive graphical interface: a technician could touch a blip on a radar screen with a light pen (invented by Everett) and information on the object would appear on the screen. Touching the dot and typing *T* on a keyboard would designate it as a target. So that the twenty-three SAGE control centres across the U.S. and in Canada could communicate, SAGE engineers developed the modem (modulator-demodulator), which translated the computer's digital information into analog form for transmission through the telephone system, and then converted it back into binary form at the other end for computer consumption there. SAGE technology also formed the foundation for applications as diverse as air traffic control and airline ticket reservations systems. Contracts for its development put IBM solidly in the forefront of the international commercial computer industry. The original Whirlwind computer's sixteen-bit architecture also provided the foundation engineering for a new generation of smaller, faster, less expensive machines called minicomputers, which are the direct ancestors of today's ubiquitous personal computers.

IBM went on to design and market a range of business-oriented computers culminating in the Model 650, which rented for $3,000 a month and was tended to by a priesthood of clean-shaven, close-cropped, white-shirted, black-shoed IBM service personnel. Company officials felt they were taking an enormous risk with the new line and planned for a production run of only 250 machines; they were astonished when business snapped them up in the thousands. The Model 650 made IBM the world's undisputed leader in computer manufacturing.

The early notion that there was no widespread market for computers, and that only a handful could fulfill any nation's requirements, was widespread and deep-seated. In 1951, the British physicist Douglas Hartree remarked: "We have a computer here at Cambridge; there is one in Manchester and one at the [National Physical Laboratory]. I suppose there ought to be one in Scotland, but that's about all."[10] In 1956, Howard Aitkin, builder of the pioneering Harvard Mark I electromechanical computer, told a German symposium on the future of computing: "If it should ever turn out that the basic logics of a machine designed for the numerical solution of differential equations coincide with the logics of a machine intended to make bills for a department store, I would regard this as the most amazing coincidence that I have ever encountered."

The failure of the nascent industry's top post-war scientists to foresee the future that machines of their own design were helping to bring about can only be attributed to a failure to understand the implications of von Neumann's innovation, the large random access memory, or RAM. Von Neumann of course understood that having enough internal memory to store both data to be manipulated and the operating instructions as to how to manipulate it meant that a computer would be able to perform arithmetic on its own instructions and thereby modify them. He saw this as a way of making the machines operate faster and smarter; they would be able to tackle more complex problems with less overall memory. What he apparently did not see, and what none of his contemporaries appear to have seen, was that his architecture also allowed computers to write their own programs on the fly, and it was this ability that would lead to a world in which computers would become almost as commonplace as electric motors and be used for a thousand purposes other than computation. It was this ability that permitted computers to be programmed—to be given their instructions—in "higher" languages, in assembly and compiler languages and interpreters that were easily understood by people, and that the computer itself translated into its own machine language of ones and zeros. It was also this ability that allowed computer interfaces to be designed that would further simplify human–machine interaction through the use of menus, the mouse, joysticks, video display terminals and even voice recognition.

The scientists, engineers, corporate strategists and military procurement experts failed to get beyond the narrow idea of the digital computer as a replacement for platoons of human computers working with calculating machines. It would take a generation of undisciplined student hackers, incorrigible phone phreaks, inveterate video game players and barely post-pubescent entrepreneurs to begin to realize the true potential of the do-everything machine Alan Turing had invented. By simply *playing* with what was after all the most miraculous toy of all time, they uncovered its hidden cultural dimensions. It was this anarchic mob of unkempt social misfits who conceived of the personal computer and brought it into being.

Information and Cybernetics

W HILE THE AIR DEFENCE DEMANDS of World War II and of the post-war era prodded computer hardware designers to ever greater efforts, they also led directly to one of the major theoretical insights of the century and a cornerstone discipline of the Information Age. It is called information theory, and, as its name implies, it is central to the development of the various communications media because it is the discipline that deals with the problems of how best to transmit information in the presence of noise, or non-information. It has been broadened, as well, to deal with more abstract problems, as indicated in this quotation from Norbert Wiener, the MIT mathematician who is credited with working out the major problems in the field:

> The commands through which we exercise our control over our environment are a kind of information which we impart to it. Like any form of information, these commands are subject to disorganization in transit. They generally come through in less coherent fashion and certainly not more coherently than they were sent. In control and communication we are always fighting nature's tendency to degrade the organized and to destroy the meaningful; the tendency . . . for entropy to increase.[1]

Information theory developed out of the military's requirement for better gunsights as the speed of air combat rose dramatically toward the end of World War II. The key to shooting down an enemy airplane (or a partridge!) is to "lead" the target so that the bullet or missile will intersect the flight path of the target. When the target is being piloted by a human, this becomes a difficult proposition, since he will normally take evasive action if he knows he is in danger. However, using position-indicating technology such as radar, combined with statistical data on the evasive manoeuvres permitted by aerodynamics, on physics, and on physiological considerations that limit the enemy pilot's choices, useful predictions can be made. When the known parameters of evasive action are blended with the observed motion of the target being fed back into a sufficiently powerful computer, it becomes possible to "lead" even an intelligent target with remarkable accuracy.

The key is providing continuous "feedback" on the enemy's position to refresh the computer's calculations and sharpen its estimates. And the reason that works is that each choice made by the enemy pilot determines to some extent what his next manoeuvre will be. The choice of actions is limited by previous actions; he cannot, for instance, immediately turn west if he is flying east. By continuously eliminating impossibilities and improbabilities, the computer leaves an ever-narrowing range of probable placement of the target over time. Projecting this only a few seconds into the future gives time to aim an intercepting shell or missile at a point in space where the target is predicted to be.

Norbert Wiener realized that his general theories developed during the war were mathematically related to one of the thorniest problems of modern electronic communications: how to deal with spurious interference to intelligent data, caused by noisy transmission channels. It turns out that the problem of how best to encode data in a noisy environment is closely related to the problem of predicting its value or content at some time in the future, a mainly statistical issue like that of "leading" an enemy aircraft. Telephone and telegraph engineers had been stymied by interference problems for decades. Wiener's work showed the way to solutions.[2]

Out of his wartime studies Wiener developed ideas of feedback and how it can be used to control technical systems, which he published in his seminal work *Cybernetics* in 1948. Closely related papers were published at about the same time by electrical engineer Dennis Gabor and MIT alumnus Claude Shannon, who was now working at Bell Labs. Together, the work of these three men, all influenced to some degree by the ubiquitous mathematical genius of John von Neumann, founded the new science of information theory, sometimes called communication theory.

At its most basic level, the discipline recognizes that there is much redundancy in most communication, and that *useful* communication exists exclusively in new or novel data contained in any transmission. Television pictures, for example, are routinely compressed for delivery to cable outlets, or "head-ends," using a digital process that transmits only elements of the picture that have changed, leaving the receiver to replicate those elements that have not changed. The difference between pictures compressed by ratios as high as 10:1 is impossible to distinguish with the naked eye. Or perhaps a less technical application will make the concept clear. We all know that communication between friends goes more smoothly than between strangers, and that one can convey information to friends using just a few words that contain new information, whereas to get the same thought across to a stranger might take an elaborate explanation. This is obviously because friends have stored a great deal of information about us in their memories, and this stored information helps them in interpreting what we are saying to them. As Claude Shannon proposed in his groundbreaking book *Mathematical Theory of Communication* in 1948, information is really "the resolution of uncertainty."[3]

It is not much of a stretch to see how this notion relates to the problem of targeting an enemy aircraft. The more you know about the target, the better able you are to predict its next move. Or, put another way, the more you know about the target, the better able you are to reject spurious or inaccurate predictions of that move. Applied to the problem of noise on a telephone line, the theory states that the more you know about the data coming down the line, the more able you are to predict what the next character or string of bits is likely to be, which means that you are able to filter extraneous "noise" out of the system with increasing efficiency. Here *know* is understood not in the sense of knowing the message's content, but understanding its makeup from a statistical point of view. The closer you come to being able to predict the next character with complete accuracy—in other words, the closer you can come to rejecting 100 percent of the noise or interference—the closer you can come to completely error-free transmission. And in the case of the interceptor pilot or anti-aircraft gunner, the closer he will come to being able to shoot down the enemy with complete certainty.

In the case of the gun-sighting or fire control problem, the challenge was to incorporate the human and mechanical elements of the gun–aircraft system into a single mathematical model, and this Wiener and his colleagues did by treating the human pilot as a servo-mechanism of the aircraft, operating on the basis of negative feedback in the same way that a boat's helmsman steers according to the effect his actions have on his compass bearing, continually correcting and re-correcting. It was not a case of a human piloting a machine, but of a single integrated machine in which the pilot was one more mechanical component. Here was the beginning of the science of cybernetics, which Wiener defined as the scientific study of systems whose behaviour is regulated by feedback mechanisms which allow the output of the mechanism to control the action producing that output. (An ordinary wall thermostat is a cybernetic device.) In its purest form, as proposed by Wiener, a cybernetic machine could be seen as striving for and maintaining goals; moreover, human goal-seeking behaviour could be explained in terms of feedback. As Wiener said, "the nervous system and the automatic machine are fundamentally alike in that they are devices which make decisions on the base of decisions they have made in the past."4 It was a view that "collapsed the differences between the animate and inanimate, organism and machine, signal and message, the Natural and the Artificial."5

It was clear to Wiener that if cybernetics was a technology of control and communication, it would be used in the military and on the factory floor: "From the very beginning of my interest in cybernetics, I have been well aware that the considerations of control and communication which I have found applicable in engineering and in physiology were also applicable in sociology and economics."6 But he was deeply conflicted by what he saw as the social sciences' too-enthusiastic adoption of cybernetic insights. He resigned from the Econometrics Society over his "misgivings regarding the possibilities of employing more than elementary statistical methods to economic data." It was as if his theories on the identity of machine and mind, of which he was convinced, led to conclusions he could not accept, a world of which he could not approve. "[T]he social sciences are a bad proving ground for the ideas of cybernetics," he said.7

Wiener's anti-aircraft system was tested on an electromechanical analog computer that had been designed by Vannevar Bush twenty years earlier, but when it was compared with other, less complicated predictive sighting devices in 1943, it lost out to one developed by Hendrick Bode of Bell Labs. Working with Bode at that time was none other than Claude Shannon, who had come to Bell by an indirect route from MIT, following a year of residence at the Princeton Institute for Advanced Study. At the Institute, he had inevitably come under the influence of John von Neumann, through whom he came to serve on the National Defense Research Committee, working on anti-aircraft fire control. But his main work at Bell was in the area of cryptanalysis, or code breaking, and he collaborated there in 1943 with Alan Turing on that subject, and on shared notions of the human brain as digital computer.

Wiener had declined to participate in the Manhattan Project, a career highlight for most of his wartime colleagues at the elite levels of American science and mathematics, and was profoundly shaken when he heard of the A-bomb obliteration of Hiroshima. He vowed at that time never again to contribute his talents to military science, or to accept military funding for his research. This effectively marginalized him for the rest of his career. His cybernetic view of humans and their institutions was eventually to lose its initial popularity in sociology and anthropology, but it exerts a continuing, profound influence in economic theory and in branches of cognitive science.

Following the war, leadership in information theory fell largely to Claude Shannon at Bell Labs, who, in 1949, proved a theorem of information which stated that for a channel of any given capacity, it is possible, with suitable coding, *and despite interference from random noise*, to transmit information at any rate up to the channel's capacity with an error rate approaching zero.[8] It was a stunning proposition: information could be transmitted, free of error, through even very noisy channels, so long as some small portion of the information made it through in undegraded form. The key was in the way the information had been coded: knowing the code, it would always be possible to use bits of received information to locate and reconstruct the bits missing or degraded by noise. It was an idea that perhaps only someone who had been involved in cryptanalysis could have spawned.

The error-correcting codes that allow computer networks to function effectively are developed on statistical models of the probability of a given bit of information being next in line to be received. In making these predictions, the model ignores the content of a message, and treats information as a simple commodity, as a choice of one message from a set of possible messages. The messages chosen by the sender each occur with a certain level of probability—in other words, some choices are made more frequently than others. For example, an English sentence is a choice of the first word, then the choice of the second word, which is influenced by the first; then the choice of the third word, which is influenced by the preceding two choices; and so on. And all of this is done within a known, formal framework called grammar.

It turns out that making predictions about transmissions of the English language is not as difficult as it might seem, because there is actually, on average, very little new information carried with each succeeding letter. This is because there is a wide range in the frequency with which letters occur in English usage: some letters, such as *e* and *a*, are very common, while others, including *z*, *q* and *x*, are used only infrequently. Were all the letters to have the same incidence of use, prediction would be more difficult. If you know for certain what the next letter in a sequence is going to be, it actually carries no new information at all because you knew in advance what it would be.

Information content is measured in bits. If all of the letters in the English alphabet had an equal probability of being used in a sequence, the information rate would be about 4.76 bits per letter. In fact, the information rate calculated for English is closer to one bit per letter. English is about 50 percent redundant, a fact that can be verified by observing vanity licence plates on cars, in which information is often compressed while remaining intelligible: LT AGN; HVY METL; RLY RISR; UPN ATM.

The code developed by Morse and Vail known as Morse code is a crude example of how information theory works to compress data. Morse code begins with an understanding of the frequency with which each letter of the alphabet is used in English text. To figure this out, Vail used the clever expedient of checking printers' type trays to see how many of each letter they kept in stock. The letter *e*, the most commonly used in the language, is thus coded as a single dot. The letter *t*, also frequently used, is coded as a single dash. The rarely used letter *z*, on the other hand, is coded as two dashes and two dots, a considerably longer sequence. Coding of data as complex as digitized television pictures or animated graphics obviously requires much more elaborate algorithms than Morse code, but the principle is the same.

Shannon's theorem immediately led to a great deal of research on devising suitable ways of encoding information for transmission. This research would prove enormously fruitful in a range of applications, from compression algorithms to error-correction routines to encryption. Perhaps its most important applications would come with the networking of computers, a development that grew out of the North American air defence project and moved into the civilian world of time-sharing on mainframes, and has continued through to our own era and its proliferating World Wide Web. On any computer network, in fact on any *information* network, bandwidth is the bedrock issue—that is, how much data can be crammed into a given transmission space, be it a television channel with bandwidth limited by government edict, or a length of copper wire or fibre optic cable with bandwidth limited by the laws of physics. Information theory is the tool used to get optimal results.

As useful as information theory has become in the transmission of data, it is important to keep its limitations in mind. In treating all information as neutral data, ignoring its content, it confines itself to what Jurgen Habermas calls instrumental communication (see chapter 9). This is one of the things that concerned Norbert Wiener about the wholesale adoption of his cybernetic ideas by the social sciences, especially economics. It should not be assumed that because the problem of noise in a communication channel or forum has been solved by one of Shannon's algorithms, it necessarily follows that *understanding* occurs. True communication among people involves not only grammar or rules of transmission, but also syntax, the relationship of the data to the real world—in a word, its in-context *meaning*. It is thus a mistake to confuse Shannon's information theory with a theory of communication.

Modelling brain functions on information theory will not, in other words, produce a complete theory of human intelligence, because intelligence involves not only grammar but also syntax. Shannon himself seems not to have accepted this, a form of myopia shared by many of those involved in the early days of cybernetics and information theory, and passed along later to their young colleagues in artificial intelligence research.

The Prodigal Semiconductor

THE BELL LABORATORIES in New Jersey were humming in 1948. It was the year Claude Shannon published his groundbreaking work on information theory, and it was also the year of the announcement of the first transistor, an invention for which John Bardeen, Walter Brattain and William Shockley of Bell Labs were to be granted the Nobel Prize eight years later. It was with the transistor that warp-speed development in the electronics industry got under way. The little device could do everything the vacuum tube could, but it was much smaller, much faster, much more reliable, used very little electricity and generated very little heat.

The transistor is one of a whole family of electronic components that developed out of continuing research into materials called semiconductors. These are minerals whose ability to carry an electric current lies somewhere between that of a good conductor and an effective insulator. Semiconductors and their peculiar electrical properties had been known since 1906, and, as we've seen, some of the earliest practical radio receivers, crystal sets, made use of the rectifying ability of lead sulphide (galena) crystals tickled by a fine silver wire or "cat's whisker." Advances in understanding of the subatomic world brought about by continuing developments in quantum theory made possible great strides in the practical application of these puzzling devices. Behind the scientific curiosity was

the compelling impetus of an urgent need for something to replace the vacuum tube, which World War II had pushed to the limits of its practical applications. A typical large aircraft of the period,
for example, contained as many as three thousand vacuum tubes,
a serious weight and power drain consideration, and, on the civilian side, telephone switchboards using vacuum tubes for improved switching speed presented major reliability headaches due
to the limited lifespan of the tubes.

At Bell Labs, Shockley and his colleagues were fascinated by the
mysterious electrical phenomena occurring at the junction where
the "cat's whisker" made contact with the semiconductor surface.
They probed the area with a second and then a third wire, discovering that the current between wires 1 and 2 varied with the voltage
applied to wire 3. The semiconductor thus had a lot in common
with Fleming's vacuum tube. Not only would it act as a rectifier, but
it could be made to act as an amplifier, just as the three-element vacuum tube did: a weak incoming current or signal was reproduced at
much greater strength in the output current.

The U.S. military was immediately interested in furthering the
development of the transistor, and funded it lavishly through contracts for the Atlas intercontinental ballistic missile, airborne computers for the air force and improved radar-tracking equipment for
the navy.

What exactly *was* it that Shockley, Bardeen and Brattain had
found so fascinating about the point where the cat's-whisker wire
touches the surface of the semiconductor crystal? Something mysterious was going on at that fragile interface, something that allowed
the crystal to act as a detector of radio waves and a rectifier of alternating currents.

What Shockley and his colleagues hypothesized was this: The
crystal structure of silicon and other semiconducting solids is such
that even at room temperature there is enough heat energy to allow
some of the electrons in the individual atoms' outer orbits to break
loose from their electrical bonds and roam freely. Where those electrons have departed the crystal structure, a vacant space is left. Since

electrons carry a negative charge, the newly vacant slot has the appearance, to nearby electrons, of a positively charged space, and the Bell Labs group called it a "hole" for lack of a more descriptive term. A "hole" is best imagined as a bubble in a pot of simmering water: the bubble is actually an absence of water in that small region. By virtue of their positive charge, holes are able to attract nearby electrons. When an electron succumbs to that attraction and jumps to fill the hole, it creates a new hole in the atom from which it jumped. Consequently, it appears as if the hole is migrating from one atom to another, while the electron is seen to be moving in the opposite direction. Imagine two atoms side by side, the one on the left with a loosely bound electron, the other with a hole. When the electron jumps from left to right to fill the hole, the hole appears to jump from right to left, showing up in the spot vacated by the electron. Electrical current, in other words, is flowing in both directions: positive current in the direction of the holes and negative current in the direction of the electrons.

Holes do not exist in most metals because they are a feature of the crystalline structure of minerals. It is their existence that makes semiconductors strange and unique and allows for their many useful applications. Prior to the discovery of holes, it was believed that only electrons conducted current, which, as a consequence, flowed only in one direction. The new notion of two-way electrical flows proved crucial to the understanding of semiconductor devices.

Having discovered this much, the Bell group speculated about what would happen if the crystal were deliberately contaminated with impurities, to change its electrical properties by giving it more holes, or more free electrons. Could a "supercrystal" be made? Pure silicon crystals were melted in furnaces and "doped" with tiny amounts of arsenic and antimony, gallium and indium. Two different effects were noted. In the case of arsenic and antimony, doping added to the number of free electrons available in the crystal, and since electrons are negatively charged, this was called n-type silicon. In the case of gallium and indium doping, the effect on the crystal bonding within the silicon was to increase the number of holes, since the impurities robbed the silicon of electrons. Because holes are positively charged, this was called p-type silicon.

This is where the experiments got exciting. If a thin slice of p-type silicon was layered over a slice of n-type silicon, it was discovered that a current would flow only in one direction through the unit. It was an entirely solid-state semiconductor that had the electrical properties of a diode, or two-element vacuum tube. It could therefore serve as a rectifier of alternating current, or a detector in a radio receiver. The explanation for what was happening was that when the two doped wafers were layered together, an orgy of attraction between oppositely charged holes and electrons occurred at the interface, or junction region. This immediately created a band of space on both sides of the junction where electrons and holes had neutralized one another, an area where both positive and negative charges were depleted. Common sense might have expected the transfer of charges to continue between the two wafers until they became electrically neutralized, but this was not what the scientists observed. The process proved to be self-limiting, with only a narrow band on either side of the junction being affected. The researchers called this the "depletion zone," and it turned out to be just wide enough to make a stable barrier against any further transfer of charges from one silicon wafer to the other. There was nothing left in the depletion zone to attract either electrons or holes.

When a battery or other source of electrical current is connected across the diode formed by the two silicon wafers, the equilibrium in the device is upset and holes and electrons will now have enough energy to bull their way across the neutral depletion zone. But here is the critical distinction: if the battery is connected one way, current will flow, but if the battery connections are reversed, current will *not* flow. The device is either a conductor or an insulator, depending on the direction of current flow in the circuit into which it is wired.[1] Shockley's team had created a practical, rugged, mass-producible replacement for Fleming's thermionic valve, or vacuum-tube diode, which had been the workhorse of the electronics industry for a generation. Not only was the new solid-state diode more reliable, it was much, much smaller and lighter, and it did away with the power-consuming and heat-producing filament required by the vacuum tube.

More excited experimentation demonstrated a phenomenon that seemed as magical as alchemy. If a wafer of either p- or n-type silicon was sandwiched between two wafers of the other kind (i.e., p-n-p or n-p-n), the resulting device would amplify an electric current presented to it! This tiny sandwich of doped silicon crystal was capable of taking a weak current, such as a faint radio or audio signal, and reproducing it in amplified form, just as the three-element vacuum tube of Fleming and De Forest had done.[2] As if that were not amazing enough, the device could be made to conduct current or not, by changing a tiny voltage applied to the filling in the sandwich. It was a solid-state switch that could be turned on or off *in a picosecond* by remote control! A device worthy of the wizardry of the emerging technological revolution, it was ten times easier to manufacture than the vacuum tube; it was about a hundred times smaller, used a thousand times less energy and would become ten thousand times more reliable. And of course, as a switch, it was orders of magnitude faster than anything else on the planet. The device was dubbed a "transistor" because the inherent job done is *trans*ferring a current across a res*istor*.

With the development of the transistor and the avalanche of other solid-state devices that quickly followed, the race to miniaturization and subminiaturization was under way. More than half a century later it has not ended. Equally as important as the triple virtues of reduced size, reduced power consumption and reduced weight were the gains made in the speed of operation of electronic circuits due to the unbelievable rapidity with which these devices were able to switch their state from conductor to non-conductor and back again.

At first monopolized for military purposes, the transistor went into commercial use in hearing aids in 1953 and in portable radios the following year. The first transistorized digital computer was assembled in 1965 at the Massachusetts Institute of Technology's

Digital Computer Laboratory, with the support of IBM, on a military contract. Its job was to replace a 55,000-vacuum-tube machine that was the cornerstone of the contemporary air defence system. By the decade's end, transistorized computers were available in the civilian market: the Control Data 1604 of that era contained 25,000 transistors in its central processing unit.

In 1955, Shockley left the scene of his triumphs at Bell Laboratories to set up his own company in the Santa Clara Valley near Palo Alto, California, about halfway between San Francisco and San Jose. Nearby Mountain View was his hometown, and Stanford University was close at hand. His plan, in the spirit of Marconi and Bell and Edison, was to manufacture products based on his own inventions, to become an amalgam of scientist, engineer and entrepreneur, and, not incidentally, to get rich in the process. He set up shop in a concrete block building in an industrial park and hired a dozen Ph.D. electrical engineers and a handful of clerical and administrative staff. They set to work melting silicon in electric furnaces, doping it with traces of exotic minerals and testing the results for improved semiconductor characteristics.

Brilliant though he was at the business of research, Shockley was by all accounts an insensitive and overbearing calamity as a manager of people. In the summer of 1957, less than two years after he'd founded Shockley Semiconductors and less than a year after he'd received his Nobel Prize in physics, eight of his key engineers mutinied. They got together to form a company of their own; it had occurred to them that all they needed to succeed in this new business was their own intellectual capital—their brainpower and experience—and some money to rent another empty manufacturing space. Fairchild Camera and Instrument Company staked the start-up money in return for an option to buy back the new company, Fairchild Semiconductor, for $3 million any time during the next eight years.

The defectors had picked a propitious time to go it alone. IBM, Hewlett-Packard and others were preparing designs for electronic computers employing semiconductors rather than vacuum tubes, and demand for transistors from the radio industry was beginning to boom. Nineteen fifty-seven was also the fateful year of Sputnik 1. The news that September that the Soviet Union had placed a basketball-sized artificial earth satellite in orbit rattled the American nation to its entrepreneurial roots. The launch a month later of Sputnik 2, a 1,200-pound payload including a dog, Laika, galvanized the U.S. military-industrial defence establishment into desperate action to catch up. Just two years earlier, and with the U.S. and Soviet hydrogen bomb testing programs newly under way, John von Neumann had been able to announce that the Americans were able to "pack in one air plane more firepower than the combined fleets of all the combatants during World War II." As chairman of the Strategic Missiles Evaluation Committee set up by the Pentagon, he was also a key participant in the race to develop intercontinental ballistic missiles (ICBMs) to deliver thermonuclear warheads, which he referred to as "nuclear weapons in their expected most vicious form."[3] The launch of Sputnik 1 seemed to indicate that the Soviets had attained a lead in launch capabilities. The transistor was the foundation on which new American missile technologies, including smaller and more powerful computers, would be built.

As the perceived "missile gap" was closed, it blended into a "space race" with the Soviets (who put space pioneer Yuri Gagarin in orbit in 1961), a race to place ever more sophisticated military surveillance and communications satellites in orbit. The dual need for miniaturization and increased computing horsepower for onboard guidance and navigation gave further impetus to research and development in the strategically vital American electronics industry.

Before Fairchild Semiconductor was two years old, its research director, Robert Noyce (one of the Shockley defectors) had designed an entirely new way to fabricate circuits that did away with the need to wire individual components together on circuit boards. It takes a nanosecond for an electric current to travel through a foot of copper wire; at the computational speeds computers were achieving, circuit slowdowns due to connection length were already becoming a problem. Noyce's idea was to etch both the circuitry and the transistors and other electronic components, such as resistors and capacitors, directly onto fingernail-sized wafers of silicon, using a process similar to photolithography. The significance of the new process for producing these "integrated circuits" or "microchips" was clear to everyone, including Fairchild Camera and Instrument, which immediately exercised its option to purchase, making Noyce and his fellow defectors wealthy men. Noyce was just thirty.

Within a decade of its formation, Fairchild Semiconductor had grown from the original group of ex-Shockley employees and a handful of support staff to employ some twelve thousand people. Revenues soared to $130 million. By the early 1960s, competing microchip businesses were springing up like mushrooms in the rain, most of them next door to Fairchild in the Santa Clara Valley. So many of them were there that people began calling it Silicon Valley. And most of the start-ups were formed by defectors from— where else?—Noyce's own Fairchild Semiconductor, getting into business on their own with their intellectual capital and a bit of money from venture financing. About fifty of them launched their own firms to produce microchips, and they came to be called Fairchildren. Thus was an industry born of sand and scientific insight. Without it, the communications revolution could not have happened.

Shockley, the pioneer, never lost his bitterness over the defections from his company. It struggled thereafter and was eventually bought out by Clevite Transistor. He had been teaching at Stanford, and was elevated to an endowed professorship of engineering and applied science in 1963. In the late 1970s, he figured importantly in the counterculture turmoil of the time—unfortunately, as a focus of anti-establishment enmity. He had begun campaigning about the threat of something he called "dysgenics," by which he meant the retrograde evolution of the human species caused by the unregulated mating of people who, in his view, were flawed by subnormal intelligence or physical defect. It was an idea Samuel Morse might have found appealing; many saw it as closet racism. Shockley proposed a private foundation that would reward hemophiliacs,

epileptics and people with low IQ who would agree to be steril-
ized. He sued the *Atlanta Constitution* for a million dollars when
the newspaper likened his ideas to Nazi eugenics, and was awarded
a token one-dollar payment, which amounted to a stinging moral
rebuke. Undaunted, he entered the Republican primary of 1982
seeking a California Senate seat as a single-issue candidate warning of dysgenics; he placed eighth with eight thousand votes. He
continued thereafter to be more interested in talking about his
bizarre theories of race and intelligence than semiconductors, for
which he nevertheless eventually held more than ninety patents.

Robert Noyce and
the Integrated Circuit

I N 1968, Apollo 8 circled the moon with three American astronauts on board and returned safely to earth, an extraordinary
feat of navigation and piloting made possible by the integrated
circuits Robert Noyce had pioneered.[1] The on-board computer was
more powerful and far faster than ENIAC, but was about the size of a
suitcase. In the same year, Noyce, now forty-one, caused a sensation
in Silicon Valley by quitting Fairchild Semiconductor to set up his
own company. With another of the original Shockley defectors,
Gordon Moore, he rounded up about $2.5 million in capital
(including half a million of their own money), rented another non-
descript Silicon Valley multi-purpose concrete building and
launched Intel Corporation.

Intel would specialize in manufacturing memory chips. The
company's first commercial product, the 1103 chip, was about the
size of the O on a computer keyboard and contained four thousand
transistors. Intel's workforce leaped from 42 at start-up to more
than a 1,000 four years later, in 1972. The next year, 1973, the workforce ballooned to more than 2,500. Sales in 1972 were $23.4 mil-
lion; in 1973, they hit $66 million.

There was more to come. A thirty-two-year-old Intel engineer named Marcian E. (Ted) Hoff Jr., fresh out of Stanford, invented the "microprocessor," which, amazingly, put all of the logic and arithmetic functions of a complete computer on a single silicon chip. Intel had been commissioned by the Japanese company ETI to construct a programmable desktop calculator, but Hoff was unhappy with the design they'd submitted. It called for thirteen separate chips containing different logic functions. In a leap of imagination, Hoff saw that it should be possible to create a chip that would be a complete programmable computer, and link it with a few memory chips that would contain its operating instructions. The computer-on-a-chip would be a generic product that could be mass-produced and would be usable in all sorts of applications, from traffic lights to cash registers and video games to nuclear missiles and telephone switchboards. After all, as Turing had shown, all computers are essentially the same—they are in fact do-anything machines—so why design complicated, one-off devices for every application that came along? It didn't make sense. It was much more efficient to program a generic processor chip with software, which was a lot less expensive to produce than custom hardware. The programming would go on a separate memory chip.

The calculator that Intel eventually produced for ETI (marketed as Busicom) had just four chips, mounted on a circuit board. The processor chip itself contained 22,000 transistors.[2] Intel began marketing the new chip, designated 4004, late in 1971. It was the size of a fingernail, sold for less than $100, and matched the performance of IBM machines of the early 1960s that had sold for upwards of $300,000 and required a forklift truck to shift. Industry historian Stan Augarten notes:

> Although Intel did not realize it at first, the company was sitting on the device that would become the universal motor of electronics, a miniature analytical engine that could take the place of gears and axles and other forms of mechanical control. It could be placed inexpensively and unobtrusively in all sorts

of devices—a washing machine, a gas pump, a butcher's scale, a jukebox, a typewriter, a doorbell, a thermostat . . . Almost any machine that manipulated information or controlled a process could benefit from a microprocessor.[3]

Just four months after the 4004's release, in April 1972, Intel announced the 8008 chip,[4] which was followed a year later by the 8080. The 8080 was twenty times faster than the 4004, a robust and flexible platform that would form the foundation of the nascent microcomputer industry.

Intel stock tripled in value. By 1982 the company's sales had grown to almost a billion dollars a year. Along the way, Noyce had attracted renewed attention, not as a scientist and inventor, but as an influential business manager, whose corporate style was decidedly informal and (superficially) democratic; Noyce was by now undeniably a plutocrat. The management hierarchies Noyce set up at Intel were as thin as the silicon wafers he manufactured. The Noyce style was lean and efficient, well adapted to constant change, and it managed to wring maximum effort and commitment out of the young engineers it employed. The rate of burnout, divorce and family breakdown in Silicon Valley would become legendary.

In a colourful biographical essay on Noyce, writer Tom Wolfe pointed out that the principal players in the microchip revolution that began in the 1960s had remarkably similar backgrounds: most had grown up and gone to college in small towns in the American West and Midwest. Wolfe attributed their successes to the shared background of dissenting Protestantism in these American towns and universities, and the egalitarian, hard-working approach it fostered to getting things done. Although generations removed from the pious men and women who founded the small towns they came from, these homesteaders in Silicon Valley had unaccountably carried with them the Protestant work ethic that valued achievement through labour and eschewed ostentatious displays of wealth and position (though not wealth and position themselves). Wolfe concludes:

Surely the moral capital of the nineteenth century is by now all but completely spent . . . And yet out in Silicon Valley some sort of light shines still. People who run even the newest companies in the Valley repeat Noycisms with conviction and relish. The young CEOs all say: "Datadyne is not a corporation, it's a culture," or "Cybernetek is not a corporation, it's a society," or "Honey Bear's assets"—the latest vogue is for down home non tech names—"Honey Bear's assets aren't hardware, they're the software of three thousand souls who work here."[5]

Wolfe might with equal persuasiveness and perhaps greater accuracy have assigned Silicon Valley's successes to the less pious engineering ethic that had developed through the late nineteenth and early twentieth century, in which engineering is explicitly and heroically at the service of capitalist enterprise (see chapter 7). This would account for the glaringly anomalous fact that the private lives and social intercourse of Silicon Valley denizens are, famously, anything but morally righteous in nineteenth-century Protestant terms. Corporate capitalism is not concerned with moral issues, or even with private lives. Even Noyce's vaunted collegial approach to management has less to do with moral uprightness than with engineering efficiencies; it is simply the most productive and profitable way to organize creative people. At the manufacturing level in the semiconductor industry, it should be noted, affluent collegiality is as hard to find as it is in a Philippine T-shirt factory.

Working out the manufacturing processes for integrated circuits deserves recognition as one of the all-time triumphs of engineering in any field. Where the engineers of the mechanical era strove to test the limits of scale with the biggest ships, the longest canals and tunnels, the tallest iron structures, the deepest underwater cables, the most powerful steam locomotives and the longest railways, the new field of electrical engineering focused more and more on the other end of the continuum, on the world of microscopic and then submicroscopic structures and processes. The structures electrical engineers have succeeded in building are so tiny as to be invisible to the naked eye, and are also the most complex artifacts ever made by humans.

At Bell Labs, where the transistor was invented, the idea of integrated circuits had been investigated and dropped. The Bell engineers had reasoned that if the circuit was to function, all of the transistors, capacitors, resistors and other electronic components within it must work. If a circuit containing even as few as twenty transistors was to have a 50 percent probability of working, the probability of each individual component working would have to be 96.6 percent. This, Bell scientists believed, was an impossible success rate to achieve.[6] They were, of course, wrong, as Robert Noyce and others were to demonstrate in such dramatic fashion. Miniaturization in integrated circuits quickly proceeded to a state where, as early as the 1970s, researchers had begun to examine the fundamental limits to size and power dissipation imposed by the laws of thermodynamics and the new science of information theory. Though chips were by then so small that a microscope was required to see individual components, it appeared they were still many orders of magnitude away from the absolute physical limits to size. Since 1968, the density of transistors on a single chip has doubled about every two years. Intel's flagship product in the late 1980s, the 386 chip, contained 375,000 transistors. In 1989 it was superseded by the 486 chip, which contains more than 1 million transistors. In 1990, Motorola announced a new chip containing 4 million transistors. Today, the number of transistors being routinely fabricated on a single chip exceeds 100 million. The size of individual components has shrunk at a comparable rate, from about 10 microns (millionths of a metre) in 1968 to less than 65 nanometres (billionths of a metre).

Much of the early impetus for this amazing progress came from persistent and pressing demand from the military for ever more sophisticated computing and communications devices for increasingly complex Cold War armaments and defence systems. The space race provided added push. But the economics of integrated circuit fabrication have a logic of their own that promotes miniaturization. Each wafer of silicon must go through a series of steps in the manufacturing process that are the same whether the wafer is to contain one or one thousand components. Obviously, the unit cost of components drops dramatically with the number that can be squeezed onto each wafer. Likewise, there is a very strong natural economic incentive for manufacturers to find ways to achieve very high levels of reliability in individual chips, in other words to minimize the number of defects creeping into the manufacturing process. In practice, wafers of silicon are commonly about twenty centimetres in diameter, and each is divided into many small chips containing identical circuitry. If each wafer contains 100 chips that sell for $50, and if the rate of discarded chips due to defects is 70 percent (a typical figure in the late 1960s and 1970s), then the factory is producing gross income of $75 million a year. If the defect rate can be reduced to 50 percent, the factory can increase its earnings to $125 million a year, and almost all of the gain will be pure profit.[7]

A modern integrated circuit, when viewed under an electron-scanning microscope, has an eerily half-organic, half-mechanical look to it, with its many layers of oxide and metal deposits, its etched-in geometric shapes and gently curving slopes. Seen in cross-section, it resembles a profile of geological strata laid open by a highway engineer's road cut, with overlapping layers of sediment and rock formations, lava flows and mineral deposits. In truth, it can be hard to believe it is a man-made artifact.

The manufacturing process takes place in stages, and is almost completely automated. The first step is to design the circuit, a process facilitated by design software. Then the circuit must be translated into a series of screens, as many as twenty or thirty for a typical integrated circuit, which will be used in the photoengraving process. This extremely complex drafting process too is highly automated through the use of computer-assisted design (CAD) software that can produce detailed drawings based on input of various design and fabrication criteria. These screens are the "blueprint" that the engineer hands over to the manufacturer. They represent about a third of the total cost of chip manufacturing, but fortunately can be used over and over to pattern many thousands of wafers.

The actual fabrication involves growing large silicon crystals of exceptional purity in a furnace within a sealed chamber filled with argon or some other inert gas. The electronic-grade silicon melted in the crucible is 99.999999999 percent pure, and is refined from common quartz, one of the earth's most abundant minerals. A seed crystal of silicon is carefully lowered into the melt and then slowly pulled back out as a much larger crystal grows. The product of this computer-controlled process is a crystal of pure silicon that may be as much as 30 centimetres in diameter and one to two metres long; it looks a lot like a big sausage.

Next, the crystal is sliced into thin wafers with a steel saw blade that has been dusted with diamond chips. Once a wafer has been washed and cleaned and polished, it is ready for the photographic process. Typically, a layer of doped silicon is applied to the wafer, followed by a thin layer of a "photo resist" material that will dissolve in an etching liquid wherever it has been exposed to light. Here is where the screens come in. The first of them is placed over the chip, and the chip is exposed to a flash of bright light. The screen is removed, and the chip is washed to dissolve away the exposed photo resist. A layer of doped silicon is applied, filling the exposed areas, then another layer of photo resist and another screen. Many succeeding layers of doped silicon, quartz insulation and various metals are applied until the process has been completed, and the individual chips can be separated, tested and packaged. All of this takes place in some of the most expensive manufacturing plants on earth, which are also among the cleanest environments on the planet, to limit the defects caused by stray dust particles. Technicians, clad from head to toe in special dust-free fabric, quietly monitor computer-controlled machines of incredible sophistication and complexity beneath their unassuming metal cabinetry.

The challenge currently facing integrated circuit manufacturers is the approaching limits of the optical lithography processes, in which the wafers are exposed to light through the various screens so that the surface can be etched. Component size has become so vanishingly small that it is close to matching the wavelength of light used to expose the resist material. The search is on for a new process that uses non-optical techniques for etching. X-ray lithography works much like optical lithography and at comparable through-put rates, though with its shorter wavelength it can produce much smaller features. Other promising technologies are quantum dots and nanotubes, each as exotic as its name would suggest. There seems no end in sight to the progress predicted in 1965 by Intel co-founder Gordon Moore, who correctly forecast that the number of transistors placed on a chip would double about every two years into the foreseeable future.

While chip technology has been evolving, parallel, similarly spectacular advances have been made in the capacity and speed of access for long-term data storage in computers. UNIVAC made a major step forward with the use of magnetic tape, an enormous advance over punch cards, but data still had to be sought out in a linear process that involved moving the tape back and forth over reading and writing heads. The magnetic disk, in which data is recorded in concentric rings on a constantly rotating platter, was introduced in the 1950s. The read/write head skimmed the surface of the rotating disk, dropping to the surface to do its job as required. The physical distances involved in accessing data were greatly reduced, speeding the process significantly once again. Concurrently, the density of data being stored was steadily increased. The now-familiar "hard drive" is a stack of such high-density disks, with read/write heads for each surface, mounted in a hard shell or box. As with integrated circuits, no limit to advances in this area of computer technology has yet appeared.

The Personal Computer

I T WAS JUST one pleasant surprise after another at Intel. The first integrated circuits had brought the company overnight wealth almost beyond comprehending. Now its 8080 microprocessor, the "computer on a chip," was about to launch an industry that would spark a revolution in communications that would in turn change the world.

We've seen that, thanks to the exigencies of World War II and the interminable Cold War that followed, the development of the electronic computer up to and including the 8080 chip had been financed and supervised largely by the military in Britain and the United States. No technology is "value-free" or "value-neutral," least of all communications technologies; they carry within them the values of the social structures and institutions out of which they develop. Take the humble family washing machine. Electric and automatic, it is such a commonplace that it may seem value-empty. However, to someone from another culture, say, an Eritrean Bedouin, it is as value-laden as a mechanized Tibetan prayer wheel is to a North American. The washing machine has built into it all the values of a modern, industrial, consumer society. It tells us that cleanliness is important; that clothes should be washed in the home rather than outside; that they should be washed by a family member rather than a servant (otherwise why bother to make it so easy); that menial work is something to be avoided if at all possible (or why have the machine at all); and so on. As Michael Shallis observes in *The Silicon Idol*, "The [washing] machine requires electricity, piped water and drainage services. It is dependent on a detergent industry and systems of transportation . . . It has also been produced with a certain attitude to work built into it. It is not neutral at all; to accept a washing machine is to accept a specific attitude to nature, to man's place in the world."[1]

As a child of the military, the computer circa 1975 bore unmistakable traits of military organization and priorities. A 1978 study of the U.S. computer industry estimated that between 1958 and 1974 the U.S. federal government, through the Department of Defense and NASA, had funded computer development to the extent of $1 billion. By then, IBM, the main commercial beneficiary of this funding, boasted revenues of more than $11 billion; the computer industry at that time was characterized by the wryly descriptive name "IBM and the Seven Dwarves."[2] The computers the military bought and paid for, whether made by IBM or, infrequently, other companies such as Sperry Rand, were massive, hugely expensive, highly secret in their operations, protected by elaborate security measures, pampered by air conditioning and attended by an anointed priesthood of white-coated minions who mediated between actual users and the machine itself, taking delivery of the batches of punch cards that constituted programs and placing them reverently in the machine's maw. Mainframe computers of the era, whether military or commercial, were a reflection of the military's obsession with hierarchical structure, control and order. They could be nothing else.

But that was not the whole story. A computer counterculture was emerging among people who believed that computers could and ought to be placed in the hands of ordinary people. Its members were mainly very young, almost exclusively male, and most were more or less loosely affiliated with university engineering schools where they had privileged access to the few computers then in existence. They were influenced both by their shared fascination with electronic technology and by the wider "flower power" counter-culture movement swirling around them. Stephen Levy has documented their story admirably in *Hackers: Heroes of the Computer Revolution*. Although he warns that it is essentially incapable of being codified and is best understood by observing its adherents, he nevertheless lists the salient elements of the "hacker ethic": access to computers, and anything that might teach something about how the world works, should be unlimited; all information should be free; authority is to be mistrusted, decentralization promoted; hackers (people) should be judged by their hacking (accomplishments) rather than by bogus criteria such as degrees, age, race or position; you can create art and beauty on a computer; and, finally, computers can change your life for the better.[3]

It has been noted by more than one jaundiced observer that the hacker ethic sounds a lot like plain old-fashioned youthful rebelliousness, idealism and irresponsibility, something apparently programmed in our DNA. That, however, is an observation of the ethic's derivation, not a judgment of its value or utility. While much of it may seem trite today, the ideas behind the ethic were anything but commonplace when they evolved, during the era of the mainframe computer, the primacy and infallibility of IBM, and the dominance of military funding. Computers at that time were an explicit extension of the traditional social control mechanisms fostered by the institutions responsible for the computer's development.

Hackers simply believed that this was not the most appropriate use of the technology; that computers ought to be placed in the service of change in society. The hacker ethic states, in essence, that by providing access to information and the power to manipulate it, computers can be powerful tools for liberation of the innate creativity of the individual in society. It is a view that owes a great deal to the German-American philosopher Herbert Marcuse, whose 1964 *One-Dimensional Man* was much discussed on university campuses everywhere. Marcuse argued that automation could ultimately lead to egalitarianism, by allowing workers to wrest control of the means of production from the corporate power structure. The proletariat in both capitalist and socialist countries had been so thoroughly co-opted by materialism and philistinism that it would require the leadership of far-sighted individuals on the fringes of society to bring about this shift in social structures. Marcuse saw the hippie counter-culture and the anti-war protest movement of the time as playing this catalytic role, and might have included the hackers had they not been so nearly invisible. Once ordinary people had assumed control of the means of production, their natural goal would be to liberate the human spirit rather than simply maximize profits. In more mundane terms, the productively self-employed were bound to have other priorities beyond simply making money. True free-dom, he believed, can emerge from automation, though not before corporate capitalism and bureaucratic communism both had done their worst.[4]

The Intel 8080 microprocessor, an artifact of total, unfathom-able mystery to the intellectual humanist establishment in 1975, was excitedly seized upon by hackers as the means to realize their humanist goals. It was the tool that would put the enormous power of computers into the hands of the ordinary individual. It was the anti-authoritarian silver bullet. While the hippies sought to pro-mote change through passive resistance, grassroots organization, art and good vibrations, and the more militant yippies fought pitched battles with authority as represented by the police and the military all over North America and Europe, the hackers, virtually unnoticed at the time, were busily working toward similar social goals through management of technology. It remains debatable which of these groups of avowed revolutionaries ultimately had the most impact. Hippie icon Stuart Brand, founder of the *Whole Earth Catalogue* and, more recently, the Electronic Frontier Foundation, has this to say:

I think that hackers—dedicated, innovative, irreverent com-puter programmers—are the most interesting and effective body of intellectuals since the framers of the U.S. Constitution . . .

No other group that I know of has set out to liberate a technology and succeeded. They not only did so against the active disinterest of corporate America, their success forced corporate America to adopt their style in the end. In reorganizing the Information Age around the individual, via personal computers, the hackers may well have saved the American economy . . . The quietest of all the '60s subcultures has emerged as the most innovative and powerful.[5]

In the late 1960s the computer industry began to diversify in a small way, producing a range of machines that were much more compact than the big IBM-style mainframes, and also less powerful. Often, however, they made up for their lack of brute strength with extra speed and flexibility. These were called "minicomputers." Produced by companies such as DEC and Data General, they typically sold for less than $15,000 or $20,000 and were used mainly in business and industry, for process control and accounting. They also found their way into university computer labs, where they were inexpensive enough to be made directly accessible to students. It was hands-on experience with minicomputers such as Digital's PDP line that inspired many hackers to explore the possibilities of the truly personal computer, if only as an abstract concept.

The notion took on concrete potential when, in January 1975, the American hobbyist's magazine *Popular Electronics* published a cover story about a shoebox-sized computer called the Altair 8800. Built around the Intel 8080 chip, it was available either in kit form or assembled from a tiny Albuquerque, New Mexico, electronics hobby firm called Micro Instrumentation and Telemetry Systems, or MITS. Fully assembled, the MITS computer sold for $650; in kit form it cost just $395. In its editorial that month the magazine said: "For many years, we've been reading and hearing about how computers will one day be a household item. Therefore, we're especially proud to present in this issue the first commercial type of minicomputer project ever published that's priced within the range of many households . . ." It was, in fact, the first personal computer.

The president of MITS and the Altair's designer was Edward Roberts, a former U.S. Air Force captain who had run MITS at first out of his garage and later from a couple of rooms in a nearby shopping mall.[6] Prior to publication of the magazine article, MITS was $300,000 in debt and on the ropes; two years later, Roberts sold it to a large computer peripherals manufacturer for $6.5 million, and retired to a farm in Georgia.

The Altair was a machine only a dedicated computer aficionado could love. To get it to do anything, you had to enter a program bit by bit using a series of front-panel toggle switches. Its internal memory (RAM) was just 256 bytes, and it had no external memory (or ROM), so that whatever program had been laboriously loaded into it would vanish whenever it was turned off. There was no display screen, just a few rows of tiny red lights by which a user was able to divine what was going on inside the box. It sold like hotcakes. MITS was overwhelmed by demand, much of it in the form of prepaid orders. Shipments fell weeks, then months, behind. Promised peripheral equipment such as memory boards, terminals and paper-tape readers for entering data wasn't available for almost a year, and then only in limited supply.

Much of the extraordinary demand came from members of computer hobbyists' clubs, principally in the United States, the most famous of which is the San Francisco Bay area's Homebrew Computer Club. Its meetings were attended by well over a hundred enthusiasts, some of whom had taken delivery of Altairs, many more of whom were impatiently waiting for their orders to be filled. They showed one another programs they had written that performed such miraculous feats as adding together two digits. One member brought the entire club to its feet in wild applause by programming his Altair to play the song "Daisy" by causing raspy noises on a portable radio. The feat was a tip of the hat to the 1968 movie based on Arthur C. Clarke's novel *2001: A Space Odyssey*. As HAL, the malevolent computer that has murdered most of a Mars-bound spacecraft's crew, is systematically lobotomized by the surviving crew member, the last thing it utters is a phrase from "Daisy."

Homebrew Computer Club members helped one another with advice, components and peripherals. But what was most intensely lusted after by a majority of them was a BASIC interpreter for the machine. BASIC was an "assembly language" that would reside within the computer memory; its purpose was to translate plain English instructions, entered via a keyboard or punched paper tape, into machine language of ones and zeros. That would eliminate the tedious, time-consuming and error-prone procedure of programming directly in machine language using the front-panel toggle switches.

MITS had such a BASIC interpreter for the Altair, but the chaos within the overburdened company was such that it too failed to ship on time. It had been written by a computer-savvy Harvard Law School freshman and computer prodigy named William Henry Gates III and his programmer friend Paul Allen. They had seen the *Popular Electronics* article and realized immediately that there was an opportunity for anyone who could put together a BASIC interpreter tiny enough to fit into the Altair's minuscule memory. Six weeks later, they had finished the job and Allen flew to Albuquerque to show Ed Roberts what they'd achieved. MITS bought the program and made Allen the company's software director. Bill Gates dropped out of school and began programming full-time.

The knowledge that an Altair BASIC existed but was not being made available was enough to drive the average hacker crazy, and it led to the inevitable: the program was pirated at one of MITS's marketing demonstrations. It was copied and distributed at computer club meetings and through the mail all over the world. To the hobbyists involved, it seemed like simple justice; after all, many of them had already paid MITS for their copies and hadn't received them. And in any case, software heretofore had always been free. It was part of the hacker ethic: if you wrote a program, you distributed it free to others in the expectation that they would work on it themselves and, one hoped, improve it. At worst, you might let people use it and suggest to them that if they liked it and found it useful, they could send you a few dollars just to cover your costs. The idea of making software specifically to sell at a profit . . . well, there was something *not right* about it.

For Bill Gates, though, piracy was theft, pure and simple. As president and co-owner (with Allen) of the fledgling Microsoft Corporation, he wrote an open letter saying as much, and it was widely published. "As the majority of hobbyists must be aware, most of you steal your software," he wrote. "Hardware must be paid for, but software is something to share. Who cares if the people who worked on it get paid?" The letter was perfectly in character for Gates, who, it would soon become apparent, had the business instincts of a wolverine. But reviews were scathing; one computer club in California even threatened to sue Gates for calling hobbyists thieves. It was the beginning of Gates's career as the Richard Nixon of the computer industry, the ambitious over-achiever whom people love to hate. Some have compared him to radio pioneer David Sarnoff, another man whose overweening ambition and cutthroat competitiveness often put him on the wrong side of U.S. federal antitrust regulators bent on keeping the industry competitive. Gates, like Sarnoff before him, had the brilliance to see that the real money to be made in his industry was not in hardware, but in software. For Sarnoff, that meant networks and radio programs; for Gates, it meant computer applications. This insight would make him the richest man in the world.

Other personal computer companies sprang up, many in California garages and vacant warehouses. By 1977 there were thirty or more products on the market, including Heathkit, Cromemco, IMSAI, Radio Shack and Commodore. And there was Apple Computer, the creature of Homebrew Computer Club enthusiast Steve Wozniak and his chum Steve Jobs. Their company and its products were destined to have a profound impact on the budding industry.

Where Ed Roberts of MITS had been more or less in the mould of the classic American small businessman and entrepreneur, right down to the overstuffed, short-sleeved cotton-polyester shirt with pocket protector, and Allen and Gates were typical owl-eyed, skinny computer nerds, Wozniak and Jobs were anything *but* conventional. Jobs, a self-described "freak" with shoulder-length hair, sought spiritual insight in soft drugs, vegetarianism and Eastern mystical philosophy. He preferred bare feet to shoes and drove a Volkswagen minivan. Wozniak, "Woz" to his friends, had a penchant for corny practical jokes and cultivated wildly erratic work habits. As a scruffy college dropout who was a spectacularly good programmer, he managed, but only just, to hold down a steady job in the calculator division of Hewlett-Packard in Palo Alto.

Jobs and Wozniak had met in 1971, when Jobs was sixteen and Wozniak twenty-one. Despite the age difference, they had much in common, including the same high school alma mater. That year they could be found lurking in the halls of UCLA Berkeley, selling Wozniak-designed "blue boxes," gadgets for making free long-distance phone calls. A fellow student from that era recalls:

> I was happy to be at UC, Berkeley, in 1972, but unlucky enough to be a resident of one of the dormitories, filled with freshmen away from home for the first time. One night, acting on a lead from a mutual friend, two young men known by the names "Hans" and "Gribble" came to my room for a visit. ["Gribble" also went under the name Oaf Tobar.] They were really named Jobs and Wozniak, and they were selling blue boxes.[7]

When he finished high school, Jobs spent two years at Reed College in Portland, Oregon, before dropping out, returning home and landing a job as a programmer with a start-up computer game company called Atari. A few months later he took what savings he had been able to accumulate and headed for India as one of the generation's "dharma bums," returning in 1974,

just about when the Homebrew Computer Club was getting
organized.

Jobs and Wozniak formed the Apple Computer Company in
1975 to sell a computer kit "motherboard" Wozniak had designed
around an integrated circuit chip being produced by a company
called MOS Technology. Their kit was less powerful than some of
the competing products from Atari and IMSAI and others, but it
had the virtues of a low price ($666.66) and the built-in ability to
be hooked up to a television screen. Jobs landed an order with a
hobby shop for a hundred of the boards at $500 each, and the two
suddenly had a viable business. To raise operating capital, Jobs sold
his VW van and Wozniak his HP calculator. That brought in $1,350,
and they were able to borrow $5,000 from a friend. They got the
components they needed on thirty-day credit.

In all, Apple sold about 175 of the boards, enough to convince
the two Steves that they should continue on in business. While
Wozniak turned to designing a new and better computer that would
become the famous Apple II (he hung on to his day job at Hewlett-
Packard), Jobs looked to organizing the business end of things. He
asked one of Silicon Valley's newly minted millionaires, a thirty-two-
year-old former Intel marketing manager named A.C. Markkula, to
help him draft a business plan. Before he had got very far into the
project, Markkula realized that Apple was sitting on a potential
gold mine, and bought a third of the company for $91,000. Then
he arranged a $250,000 line of credit with a bank and raised another
$700,000 in venture capital.

On a firm financial footing, and with professional management
on tap, Apple was positioned to handle the wild success that its
Apple II machine became. It was the Volkswagen Beetle and the
Austin Mini of the personal computer industry, a fun, friendly
machine selling for an affordable $1,195. It sported a floppy disk
drive when many of its competitors were still using slow and unreliable cassette tapes for memory storage. It would support a colour
monitor. Most important of all, it left open expansion slots so that

third-party inventors could come up with hardware to enhance the machine. The young company also made a point of working with software developers, sharing machine specifications they needed to develop programs. This openness was one of the keys to the rapid early development of the personal computer industry, and was a dramatic departure from the policy in place at IBM and other established manufacturers, which preferred a strategy of locking in market share to their closed, proprietary systems.

Jobs had hired an industrial designer to do the plastic case for the Apple II—not just any designer, but Harmuth Esslinger, creator of the Porsche 928 fuselage—and had seen to it that the machine had a warm and friendly look and feel about it. Wozniak, an inveterate computer gamer, had made it a great game machine. Even more significantly, it was the only computer of its time that ran the breakthrough spreadsheet program called VisiCalc, an application that was authentically revolutionary in its time in opening the public's eyes to the potential of these little machines. Jean-Louis Gassé, who would become product development manager for Apple, has written of his first encounter with the program in 1981:

> So VisiCalc offered itself to me on the screen: a sheet of ruled paper with rows and columns. Little by little I noticed that this program, which looked like nothing in particular, allowed three budget simulations (something every company head needs but never has the time or courage to do) to be executed in two steps . . . a single item changes and everything is recalculated . . . I couldn't believe my eyes . . . That was the day I realized that you didn't have to be a programmer anymore to use a computer.[8]

The Apple II was just right for the market when it was introduced in 1977, a near-perfect match between consumers' dreams and builder's vision. Apple became the fastest-growing corporation in the United States, its sales soaring from $775,000 in 1977 to

$35 million in 1981 and nearly $1 billion in 1983. When the company went public in 1980, its stock hit a market value of $1.2 billion on the first day it was offered. Markkula had parlayed his $91,000 investment into $154 million; Jobs was now worth $165 million and Wozniak $88 million.

In a classic case of hubris in large corporations, IBM ignored the personal computer market for three long years after the Apple II and its competitors from Commodore, Radio Shack, Atari and others were introduced. But when it decided to move, it surprised nearly everyone with the sophistication of its entry. The IBM PC was startling—astonishing even, considering the reputation of its maker for secrecy and proprietary technologies—because the company had decided to open up the computer's architecture. Open architecture meant that any third-party developer could get a copy of the computer specs and go to work on designing add-ons, peripherals, software, or even clone the motherboard itself. IBM PC clones did in fact begin to appear almost immediately. The company had made it possible for small ventures to compete with its PC on an equal footing, and that led to rapid development of the product line.

When it came to writing an operating system for its personal computer, IBM turned to Bill Gates's Microsoft. It was, for Gates, the opportunity of a lifetime: whatever operating system the IBM PC used was sure to become the industry standard, which would mean that most personal computers sold around the world would use it, and that was bound to make Gates a very, very wealthy man. The operating system Microsoft designed for the IBM PC was called, simply, MS-DOS, for Microsoft Disk Operating System. It was robust, flexible and workmanlike, but it was decidedly unfriendly to anyone not already familiar with computers and their languages. Nothing about it was intuitive; it came with thick manuals that needed to be studied before the simplest operations could be performed. The IBM PC was a grey, buttoned-down accountant's tool kit. It offered the power of the microchip to a broad public at a reasonable price, but on *its* terms, not theirs. Despite its open architecture, it was very much a product of top-down thinking.

Thus, while the IBM PC was built for, one might even say imposed on, the market, the Apple II had grown out of its market. The distinction was apparent in virtually every aspect of the two machines, from operating systems—especially operating systems— to cabinet design to clarity of monitor presentation to the size of their respective owner's manuals (Apple's was slim and graphically appealing), right down to the way the motherboards were designed. Its open architecture was the IBM product's eventual salvation: it became more friendly as third-party designers and software developers gradually changed it to suit the needs of ordinary human beings. But it was a long, slow process.

Whatever its initial shortcomings when compared with the Apple II, the IBM PC served to legitimize the personal computer industry in the minds of many ordinary users and business people, and to take it into the mainstream in the same way as Western Union's entry into the telephone business had almost overnight greatly expanded the market initially developed by the then-unknown Bell Telephone. The IBM product's introduction was a key step in making the personal computer a commonplace appliance in homes, and in businesses of all kinds.

In 1984, Apple introduced a new model that was to make the distinction between the IBM-compatible PC and its own products crystal clear. The Macintosh, a product of the vision of Steve Jobs and his messianic desire to make computing accessible to everyone, introduced two innovations that radically simplified the interface between user and machine: the now-ubiquitous "mouse" and the icon-based "desktop." The Mac was a further development of Apple's earlier and unsuccessful Lisa business machine, which failed principally because it was aimed at the wrong market. Corporate business purchasers were not ready for a machine that made computing fun, and the home-business computer market had not yet developed to the degree that it could support a product as expensive and sophisticated as Lisa.

The Lisa interface was developed over a period of nearly three years beginning in 1978, by Apple designers who were working with

an explicit set of goals that detailed Jobs's vision.⁹ Instead of an
inscrutable blank screen and a flashing cursor, the new interface
presented the user with a picture of an electronic desktop with icons
the user manipulated to tell the computer what to do. A menu bar
across the top of the screen offered further options with pull-down
submenus. Documents were displayed in windows that could be
sized to suit the user. The general layout of the interface could be
altered to a user's individual tastes and preferences.

Some of the guidelines that the Apple designers worked with
were listed in the project's Marketing Requirements Document
(1980), which opened with the declaration:

> Lisa must be fun to use. It will not be a system that is used by
> someone "because it is part of the job" or "because the boss told
> them to." Lisa will be designed to require extremely minimal
> user training and hand holding. The system will provide one
> standard method of interacting with a user in handling text,
> numbers, and graphics . . .¹⁰

The Macintosh transferred these guidelines to their logical environment, the personal computer market, and the result was a radical machine that had been designed from the ground up with the
idea that computers ought to be easy to use—playable, in fact, like
a musical instrument—by anyone who knew a few rudimentary
rules. You could use it for spreadsheets and word processing, but
you could also draw with it, make music with it, design page lay-
outs. The hardware itself was a giant step forward, with its all-in-
one plug-and-play format and attention to design aesthetics, small
footprint, auto-eject floppy disk drives and loudspeaker. An Apple
engineer recalls,

> Even the packaging showed amazing creativity and passion; do
> any of you remember unpacking an original 128K Mac? The
> Mac, the unpacking instructions, the profusely illustrated and
> beautifully written manuals, and the animated practice program

with audio cassette were packaged together tastefully in a cardboard box with Picasso-style graphics on the side. Never before had a computer been delivered with so much attention to detail and the customer's needs.[11]

This was a computer designed to be an extension of its user, in direct contrast to the IBM product, which treated its operators as living peripherals who were required to know pages of machine-like DOS command codes and obey machine, rather than human, logic. Anyone who has been puzzled over the years by the fierceness of the loyalty of Macintosh users will do well to keep in mind this crucial distinction. If Bill Gates was the Richard Nixon of software developers, then the IBM PC was Nixon as cyborg: it had the power, it had the authority, it had the market success, but nobody *loved* it. It is also true that there was a certain macho appeal to the very complexity of MS-DOS in the business and technical communities. It gave those who had mastered it a special cachet and improved their job security. The DOS-literate had a vested interest in opposing anything that would reduce the economic scarcity of their special knowledge. They had reason to like the fact that DOS was difficult.

By the 1990s, Apple Computer had seen the MS-DOS operating system devour the lion's share of the personal computer market, thanks in part to the availability of bargain-priced IBM clones. What was even more worrying than the gap in hardware prices, however, was Microsoft's success in emulating the very features of the Macintosh operating system that had accounted for its strong appeal. With each succeeding iteration of its Windows operating system, Microsoft drew closer to mimicking the Macintosh interface. A long and expensive lawsuit charging Microsoft with infringement of copyright had failed.

By the mid-1990s, Apple seemed to have lost its nerve, and its direction. It toyed with licensing its hardware, and licensed Macintosh clones made a brief appearance in 1997–98. By then, in attempting to be all things to all people, the rudderless company had introduced a bewildering plethora of models designed to compete head-to-head in the Windows/IBM marketplace, in which the core virtues of the Macintosh were increasingly obscured. Work on a "revolutionary" new Mac operating system dragged on endlessly; meanwhile Macintosh computers were promoted as being capable of running the Windows operating system under emulation. The distinction between the two was becoming perilously indistinct to all but the most knowledgeable users, and yet Macs remained relatively expensive. By 1997, Apple was facing the dangerous prospect of steadily shrinking market share combined with a loss of market identity.

In desperation, the company asked Steve Jobs to return to the helm. (He had been squeezed out in the early years of expansion in a boardroom putsch, a not-uncommon fate among the industry's founding geniuses.) In one of the more remarkable business achievements of the decade, within a year of his return Jobs had put Apple firmly back on the rails, principally by refocusing its efforts on its traditional areas of strength: elegant operating systems, intuitive software, brilliant hardware design within a limited product line, and technical superiority. To this list he was able to add, for the first time, strongly competitive pricing. With the Internet and World Wide Web markets extending Macintosh's acknowledged superiority as a communications and publishing platform into the vast new world of online interactivity, the company's prospects seemed once again secure.

Perhaps more than any other single event, the introduction of the Macintosh had helped to clarify the future direction of personal computing, had helped to make clear the possibilities latent in the phenomenon of computing power widely distributed among the general populace. The Mac had been designed to be used as a communications tool, and it was eagerly adopted as such. While it did poorly in the mainstream business market, it was snapped up by writers, artists, musicians, educators, architects, designers, mathematicians—creative people in general and communicators in particular.

The phenomenon of desktop publishing was a case in point. With its strong built-in graphics capabilities, the Macintosh quickly became the cornerstone of a new cottage industry in which it was possible to publish virtually anything, from newspapers to handbills to books, at relatively low cost. Text and images could be prepared, edited and even typeset on the computer. With the introduction of the laser printer, high-quality printing too became a desktop operation. Every aspect of the traditional publishing industry had been made accessible, except the mechanisms of distribution, which remained largely in the hands of bookstore chains and their buyers and periodical distributors. With the advent of the World Wide Web in the mid-1990s, this final hurdle to personal publishing would be overcome as well, giving any individual with a computer and a modem, in principle at least, access to the communications power of a newspaper editor or network television producer. The democratic revolution in textual communication, launched but only partly realized by the printing press, was taken a giant step closer to fruition by the personal computer.

What was true of publishing was also true in the fields of music production, sound editing and the graphic arts, and, eventually, video editing and production. In each case, the personal computer dramatically extended access to the field by drastically reducing both capital costs and the cost of materials. In television, for example, lightweight digital cameras costing a tiny fraction of the price of a standard professional video camera, matched with low-cost desktop editing software, made it feasible for the freelancer to enter the field of TV news and documentary production. Until the computer chip made these products available, extremely high equipment and operating costs had maintained this as an exclusive preserve of the corporate media businesses and the networks. As with desktop publishing, however, distribution remained a problem for freelance video producers; traditional television news and current affairs operations have historically been loath to accept outside contributions for reasons related mainly to professional pride, union contracts, consistency of style and legal liability. And of course setting up one's own TV station was out of the question for all but the very wealthiest in the community. The World Wide Web, once again, has begun to offer accessible, low-cost alternatives for distribution, and these will proliferate as Internet bandwidth and high-speed access expand. As television and computer merge through technologies such as the PVR and high-definition digital TV formats, an era of "personal media" is upon us, not just in the sense of personal appliances such as the iPod and BlackBerry, but in the sense of small-scale production of content in all its forms.

It was with the advent of the computer network, then, that the personal computer's ultimate destiny as a powerful communications appliance began to crystallize. Like the telephone before it, the personal computer had been thought to be essentially a business tool; the Macintosh computer itself was dismissed by business as a toy, just as Bell's telephone had been dismissed a century earlier by the president of Western Union as a "scientific toy" not worth serious development, and certainly not worth purchasing the rights to manufacture.

Today's personal computers are vastly more powerful and orders-of-magnitude faster than the early prototypes of the breed. A typical laptop of today boasts more computing horsepower than was available to the entire U.S. defence establishment at the height of the great air defence panic of the 1950s. And that power is being amplified enormously, and with unknown consequences, as the world's computers are linked in their tens of millions on the worldwide network that is the Internet. So it is to the Internet that we turn our attention next.

A Digital Mardi Gras

T HE INTERNET is a technology without precedent. It was not invented so much as imagined. It was not built—it just grew, as if instructed by some deeply embedded coding. It is not so much the product of individual minds as the realization of the collective vision of small groups of men and women, mainly academics and computer enthusiasts, all over the world. It was born into the deeply psychotic world of Cold War nuclear gamesmanship, yet transcended it magnificently. It mirrors human needs and aspirations, playfulness and genius, creativity and depravity better than any other technology ever devised. A visitor from another galaxy could learn a great deal about humanity from the Internet. Science fiction writer Bruce Sterling said of the Net, in a wonderful image:

> No one really planned it this way. Its users made the Internet that way, because they had the courage to use the network to support their own values, to bend the technology to their own purposes. To serve their own liberty. Their own convenience, their own amusement, even their own idle pleasure. When I look at the Internet . . . I see something astounding and delightful. It's as if some grim fallout shelter had burst open and a full-scale Mardi Gras parade had come out.[1]

The implications have been concisely described this way:

It took a hundred years and billions of dollars to wire the world into a switched telecommunication network. It took half a century and billions of dollars to create computers you could afford to put on your desk. A ten-year-old kid with a hundred dollars can plug those two technologies together today and have every major university library on earth, a bully pulpit, and a world full of co-conspirators at her fingertips.[2]

It all began in the 1960s, when schoolchildren all over the northern hemisphere were receiving regular instruction on how to survive an atomic attack by sheltering under their desks in a fetal crouch, and when building contractors were doing a land-office business in backyard bomb shelters. The RAND Corporation,[3] Washington's best and most frightening Cold War think tank, applied its formidable brainpower to what had been identified as a pressing strategic problem: How could some semblance of civil and military authority be maintained in the United States after nuclear bombs and warheads had laid waste to the country?

It was well understood that no conventional communications network, wired or radio, no matter how well fortified and armoured, could survive an all-out nuclear attack.[4] And presuming that an Armageddon-proof network *could* be built, how would it be organized and managed? Any central authority hunkered in concrete-hardened headquarters would be an obvious, high-priority target for enemy missiles, and no bunker could hope to survive a direct hit from a hydrogen bomb. It would be the first place to be obliterated. The think tank wrestled with this grotesque puzzle, and arrived at an audacious solution.

RAND's Paul Baran, in a landmark report, "On Distributed Communications," eventually made public in 1962, proposed a network that would have no central authority. Furthermore, it would be built from the ground up to operate while in shambles.[5] It was to be a system so full of redundancies that it could survive horrible mutilation and still keep functioning. What's more, it would be able to grow back dismembered limbs.

The son of Polish immigrants, Baran attended Drexel University engineering school and got his start working for the ill-fated Eckert–Mauchly Computer Corporation in 1949 at age twenty-three. He moved from there to the Hughes Aircraft Corporation, studying nights to get his master's degree at UCLA. In 1959 he joined RAND's computer science department. He has described the challenge he faced at RAND this way:

> Both the US and USSR were building hair-trigger nuclear ballistic missile systems. If the strategic weapons command and control systems could be more survivable, then the country's retaliatory capability could better allow it to withstand an attack and still function; a more stable position. But this was not a wholly feasible concept, because long-distance communication networks at that time were extremely vulnerable and not able to survive attack. That was the issue. Here a most dangerous situation was created by the lack of a survivable communication system.[6]

RAND had been able to acquire successively the latest IBM computers, and Baran, with his Mauchly–Eckert background, was in a position to imagine an all-digital solution. In the best Cartesian fashion, he threw out all pre-existing notions of what a communications network should be. "An *ideal* electrical communications system can be defined as one that permits any person or machine to reliably and instantaneously communicate with any combination of other people or machines, anywhere, anytime, and at zero cost," he wrote. "It should effectively allow the illusion that those in communication with one another are all within the same sound-proofed room—and that the door is locked."[7] And later: "If war does not mean the end of the earth in a black and white manner, then it follows that we should do those things that make the shade of grey as light as possible."[8]

The principles on which he based his solution were simple but revolutionary. The network would be assumed to be unreliable at all times, and would be designed to work around its own breakdowns. All the nodes in the network would have equal status, each with its own intelligence and storage capability, and authority to originate, relay and receive messages. They would consist not of standard telegraphy equipment, but high-speed digital computers for switching and storage. There was no limit, in principle, to the number of these nodes. In other words, it would be a *distributed network*, and there would be no attack-vulnerable central hubs.

The messages themselves would be divided into packets of binary code, each packet equipped with the address of its destination, its originating address, the information needed to place it in correct sequence with other packets, and a "handover tag" that recorded the address of each node it had passed through on its way to its destination. Packets would speed their way through the network on an individual basis, beginning at a source node and ending at a specified receiving node, the one in the address. The particular route taken would be unimportant: each packet would be bounced like a pinball from node to node to node, in the general direction of its destination, until it ended up in the right place. Once there, it would be reassembled with other packets to reconstitute the original message. If whole chunks of the network had been vaporized, that wouldn't matter; the packets would find their way via whatever nodes happened to survive. It was, in retrospect, a solution that seemed to rely as much on the lessons of biology as physics. New high-speed computers made it feasible.

The Los Angeles freeway system provides a useful metaphor for what goes on in a packet network. Just like a packet, each vehicle on the freeway knows where it is going (or at least its driver does) and where it has come from, and if one exit ramp is blocked by traffic or construction, police posted there will wave it on to the next, allowing the vehicle to find a detour by which to reach its destination. Vehicles of many kinds originating from many different locations and with as many different destinations can share the same freeway at the same time. (On a standard telephone network, the analogous situation would be for authorities to open the most direct "freeway route" from sender to receiver to only one vehicle at a time, in other words to create a dedicated circuit.) As traffic thickens, the vehicle's speed decreases, but it will always (barring mechanical breakdowns and drive-by shootings!) eventually get to its destination. In fact, packet networks are more efficient than the freeway system because they have a way to handle the equivalent of an LA drive-by, which is the occasional corrupted or damaged packet. Error-correcting protocols resident at each node report "bad" packets back to the sender and they are immediately retransmitted. It is also important to note that the more complex the freeway system becomes, the more on- and off-ramps and interchanges it has, the more likely it is that a given vehicle will be able to get where it wants to go despite widespread damage to the system. There are simply more options for detours in a more complex system.

Packetized data has other advantages: packets may be compressed in accordance with the rules of information theory to increase transmission speed and take maximum advantage of limited network bandwidth, and they can also be individually encrypted for security. Error-detecting codes work most efficiently on short strings of code, checking each packet individually for errors and re-sending only those that fail.

Baran himself credited his initial inspiration to Claude Shannon, whom we met earlier in connection with information theory. Shannon had in 1950 devised a mechanical mouse that was capable of negotiating a simple maze on its own, and Baran saw that the logic used by the mouse, with its tiny electromechanical computer, was the same as would be required to route a message through a distributed network. He had also had long talks with Warren McCulloch, a psychiatrist at MIT's electronics research lab who had co-authored an influential paper speculating on similarities between the brain and computers. While von Neumann and Shannon had seen in the paper evidence for their notion of brain-as-machine, Baran was more interested in how the brain can sometimes recover lost functions by bypassing a damaged region, and wondered if a communication network could be made to function in the same way.

It all seemed a far-fetched, horribly inefficient, almost chaotic system by traditional telecom engineering standards, and the whole idea of it drove telephone company engineers crazy just to contemplate. They were most comfortable in a straightforward world of dedicated circuits carrying analog signals. AT&T personnel conscripted to the project did their best to kill it before it was ever made public. Their objections carried weight, because it was over the telephone network, that intricate, switched web that had been built and paid for over the preceding hundred years at a cost of billions of dollars, that the packet network planned to piggyback. Trunks here and there would need to be beefed up to provide a reliable, high-capacity network backbone, but the plan was feasible mainly because so many millions of miles of switched telephone lines were already in place. In the end, there was just no denying that the switched packet network idea perfectly matched the specified military requirements in that it was about as close to an indestructible piece of communications machinery as could be imagined.

Paul Baran's RAND report on distributed networks was released to the public in 1962. In his discussion of security aspects of his doomsday communications network he drew the obvious conclusion that "if one cannot safely describe a proposed system in the unclassified literature, then, *by definition*, it is not sufficiently secure to be used with confidence."[9] In a later interview he said, "We chose not to classify this work and also chose not to patent the work. We felt that it properly belonged in the public domain. Not only would the U.S. be safer with a survivable command and control system, the U.S. would be even safer if the USSR also had a survivable command and control system as well!"[10]

In the same year that Baran's RAND report was released, the U.S. Department of Defense's Advance Research Projects Agency (ARPA)—part of the fallout from the trauma caused in American military and scientific circles by the Soviet Union's successful Sputnik satellite launches in 1957—was asked to organize research into how best to take advantage of the nation's growing inventory of computers, in particular those advanced machines that had been developed for air defence and other command and control functions. This project, like Baran's doomsday project, involved high-security computer networking, and so it was rolled in with the RAND research, broadening its scope and objectives beyond strictly military applications, into pure research on inter-computer communication. Dr. J.C.R. Licklider, know universally as "Lick," was appointed to head up the project in October of that year. It was a felicitous choice: Lick was exactly the right person for the job, his background in psychology and engineering giving him a rare degree of insight into the potential of computers as well as a refreshing openness in his handling of research associates.

Among Licklider's first initiatives was to shift the project's research contracts away from the corporate world into the best university computer research programs. ARPA's far-sighted mandate was to fund research that was likely to result in advances of at least an order of magnitude over the current state of development, and his assessment of the industry at that stage was that further major gains in computer applications would be made only by "out-of-the-box" thinking, that is, research into areas that had no obvious or immediate commercial applications. According to the completion report filed on the ARPANET project,

> the computer industry, in the main, still thinks of the computer as an arithmetic engine. Their heritage is reflected even in current designs of their communication systems. They have an economic and psychological commitment to the arithmetic engine model, and it can die only slowly . . . Even universities, or at least parts of them, are held in the grasp of the arithmetic engine concept . . . [whereas] the ARPA theme is that the promise offered by the computer as a communication medium between people, dwarfs into relative insignificance the historical beginnings of the computer as an arithmetic engine.[11]

Licklider was especially interested in the area of interactive computing, as opposed to the "batch processing" methods that were then in vogue. He was, in short, a hacker at heart. From the beginning, he seems to have understood that communications was computing's destiny. In a moment of prophetic whimsy, he dubbed his team of computer specialists the "Intergalactic Network," and he focused research on developing software that would allow computers to talk to one another, and thus allow humans to talk to one another through computers. His insight had arisen out of his observations of a phenomenon connected with time-sharing on mainframe computers, that is, allowing several users access to the same computer at the same time rather than scheduling batch processing of stacks of punch cards. A colleague notes that "Licklider was among the first to perceive the spirit of community created among the users of the first time-sharing systems . . . In pointing out the community phenomena created, in part, by the sharing of resources in one time-sharing system, Lick made it easy to think about interconnecting the communities, the interconnection of interactive, on line communities of people . . ."[12]

By 1967 the basic conceptual structure of what would become ARPANET, the predecessor to the Internet, had been established by the team. The problem of communication between computers running on different operating systems (i.e., speaking different languages) would be handled by constructing a network to which entry would be gained through nodes consisting of minicomputers programmed to handle the translation issues. The idea was that these gateway computers would translate incoming data from users and their polyglot computers into a universal Net language, and would also translate data stored on the Net back into the language being used by the accessing computer. This strategy has survived in the current system of using Internet Service Providers for dial-up and/or dedicated access to the Internet. ISPs now constitute a sizable industry, with subscriber revenues in the hundreds of millions of dollars.[13]

In December 1969, there were four nodes on the infant American network, which was named ARPANET after its sponsor. (These were all at universities with large defence research establishments: University of California at Los Angeles, University of California at Santa Barbara, Stanford Research Institute and University of Utah.) Scientists and researchers were now able to share one another's computer facilities by long-distance telephone lines.[14] By 1971 there were fifteen nodes in ARPANET; by 1972, thirty-seven.

As early as its second year of operation, the technicians who minded ARPANET noticed it was changing. ARPANET's users had transformed the computer-sharing network into a kind of electronic post office. The main traffic on the network was no longer long-distance computing; instead, it was news and personal messages. Researchers were using ARPANET to collaborate on projects, to trade notes on their work and, increasingly, to just chat about whatever interested them. Clever software routines were being devised almost daily to make this informal communication easier and more efficient. User surveys reported great enthusiasm for these non-regulation network services with their automated mailing lists, newsgroups, digests and other nifty, time-saving wrinkles—far more enthusiasm than was felt for long-distance computing, which in any case was fast being made obsolete by plummeting computer hardware prices and the increasing power of minicomputers and the new PCs.

Next to its speed and efficiency, it was the Net's colloquial informality that most endeared it to users. Licklider noted:

> One of the advantages of the message system over letter mail was that, in an ARPANET message, one could write tersely and type imperfectly, even to an older person in a superior position and even to a person one did not know very well, and the recipient took no offense. The formality and perfection that most people expect in a typed letter did not become associated with network messages, probably because the network was so much faster, so much more like the telephone . . . Among the advantages of the network message services over the telephone were the facts that one could proceed immediately to the point without having to engage in small talk first, that the message

services produced a preservable record, and that the sender and receiver did not have to be available at the same time.[15]

In its early days, ARPANET use was confined to those students and faculty lucky enough to be affiliated with one of the host universities in the U.S. However, those who did not share that good fortune, but nevertheless understood something of the communications potential of computers, did not sit idly by. In 1970 the first of many so-called store-and-forward nets was launched. These were essentially e-mail discussion groups in which letters or "postings" were available to anyone who was a member of the group. Nowadays the process is called "conferencing" and the groups involved are called "newsgroups." Early store-and-forward nets tended to be clumsy to use and slow, but by the late 1970s and early 1980s these had evolved into much more friendly environments based on user-developed software with names such as Usenet, BITNET and Fidonet, and they were now capable of catering to the burgeoning numbers of personal computers. They would make up the "network of networks" that eventually became the Internet.

Fidonet proved to be the precursor of the BBS, or bulletin board service, of which there were soon tens of thousands, including some very big ones, including Prodigy, CompuServe and America Online (these will be discussed further in the following chapter). Many catered to special interests, including, inevitably, pornography. Others attempted to offer a selection of topics catering to subscriber interests, along with online conferencing or "chat" on different subjects.

Other forms of networking sprang up. Usenet, short for Unix User Network, was based on a software protocol that allowed computers running the Unix operating system popular on university campuses to communicate with one another. It was another example of a client/server arrangement: a user connects to a computer, which connects to a main server on which are stored all Usenet postings, ready for retrieval. In its earliest incarnation, Usenet was used mainly by university students and faculty as an area for discussion of academic issues and the sharing of new information about everything from research grants and papers to conference dates and proceedings. Soon, however, thriving discussion groups, or newsgroups, sprouted around such non-academic topics as science fiction, movies and food.

Usenet was a haywire, ad hoc electronic post office that had grown up without any planning. To try to put some order into the mounting chaos of proliferating newsgroups, its early volunteer administrators had established two categories, "mod" for those newsgroups that used a moderator (who filtered out spurious postings and generally kept the discussion on track) and "net" for those groups that were unmoderated.

By the summer of 1986, Usenet had become so big and rambunctious, it seemed at times like a wild and woolly frontier town. There were newsgroups on hundreds of subjects, and postings were becoming less polite, orderly and disciplined, though at the same time more diverse and in many ways more interesting, if one could afford the time to separate the wheat from the chaff. The administrators decided a radical restructuring was needed. Seven new subject hierarchies were proposed: .com (for computers); .misc; .news; .rec (for recreation); .sci (for science); .soc (for society); and .talk. The last of the groups, ".talk," was designed as a repository for all the unsavoury, salacious, politically incorrect and sociopathic newsgroups that had appeared like banana slugs among the Usenet flora. If they were all confined to a single hierarchy, they would be easier for network administrators to remove from their Usenet feeds, should they wish to do so. There was, significantly, no serious talk of attempting to ban or in any way censor the groups, beyond making them easy to avoid.

The reorganization is remembered in Net lore as the "Great Renaming," and it caused a flame war—a spate of e-mail argument and vituperation—of unprecedented proportions. Everybody seemed to have a strong opinion on whether it was necessary or unnecessary, a good or a bad thing, high-handed and autocratic or just businesslike. It was clear as never before that the Net's users

regarded it as their community property, and were actively hostile
to any attempt to impose a hierarchy of management upon it. The
volunteer administrators who had organized Usenet and its backbone of servers and who carried out the Great Renaming were vili-
fied as the "Backbone Cabal."

The pot boiled over when a gadfly named Richard Sexton proposed two deliberately provocative new discussion groups under
the "rec" umbrella: rec.sex and rec.drugs. Following normal protocol, Usenet denizens were given a chance to cast e-mail votes on
whether the groups should be officially listed. The vote passed, but
in a decision that became a watershed in the cultural history of the
Net, the Backbone Cabal refused to create the groups or to carry
them on backbone machines.

What happened next does much to explain both how and why
the Net has remained an ungoverned, unstructured, organic entity.
First "drugs" and then "sex" were granted status in an alternative
Usenet set-up using routings that were separate from the official
backbone. Alt.drugs along with alt.gourmand and a handful of
other alternative discussion groups were created by student Brian
Reid, who had become an unhappy camper when the Backbone
Cabal commanded him to change the name of his own rec.gour-
mand recipe exchange to rec.food.recipes. The cheek! Surveying
his new alternative creations and noticing an oversight, Reid sent
the following impertinent message to Usenet administrators: "To
end the suspense, I have just created alt.sex. That meant that the alt.
network now carried alt.sex and alt.drugs. It was therefore artisti-
cally necessary to create alt.rock-n-roll, which I have also done. I
have no idea what sort of traffic it will carry. If the bizzaroids take it
over I will . . . moderate it; otherwise I will let it be."[16]

In reminiscing online about his exploits, Reid would confess
five years later: "At the time I sent that message I didn't yet realize
that alt. groups were immortal and couldn't be killed by anyone. In
retrospect, this is the joy of the alt. network: you create a group,
and nobody can kill it. It can only die when people stop reading it.
No artificial death, only natural death." He added, in an insightful

aside: "I don't wish to offer an opinion about how the Net should be run; that's like offering an opinion about how salamanders should grow: nobody has any control over it, regardless of what opinions they might have."[17]

As early as 1970, computer networks similar to Usenet had begun emerging all over the world, and it was recognized from the start that if a way to interconnect them could be found, it would be a boon to academic life and communication. The Internet, the global network of networks, was formally proposed in 1972. In October of that year, the first International Conference on Computer Communications was held in Washington. A public demonstration of ARPANET was offered as a working model of how the international net might work, using forty computers set up in one of the conference halls. Scientists from Canada, France, Japan, Norway, Sweden, Great Britain and the U.S. discussed the need for agreed-upon protocols that would allow computer networks in various countries to be tied together.

An InterNetwork Working Group (INWG) was created to shepherd the protocol project, and Vinton Cerf, who was involved with UCLA's ARPANET node, was chosen as the first chairman. The vision proposed for the architecture of the network of networks was, as Cerf would later recall, "a mess of independent, autonomous networks interconnected by gateways, just as independent circuits of ARPANET are interconnected by IMPs [Information Message Processors—gateway computers]."

Figuring out how to program those magic Internet gateways was more easily said than done. It would be two more years before Vinton Cerf and his UCLA colleagues completed writing and testing some code they called TCP/IP. In an act of profound pragmatic and symbolic significance, the protocol was placed immediately in the public domain by its inventors, freely available to everyone.

The tradition of public disclosure had been firmly established by Licklider and the graduate students involved in the ARPANET project from the beginning, in the best hacker tradition. All ARPANET developments, including beta or "trial" versions of software, had been posted and commented upon via the Net itself in a system called Requests for Comment, or RFCs. By dramatically broadening the range of people involved in software development, the project had extended the hacker ideal of "bottom-up" development into the realm of government-sponsored, high-level research, and the results were to be spectacular. It was, moreover, a distinct departure from the prevailing mode of secrecy in research as practised by corporate laboratories and the university research establishments they sponsored; and it reflected the mood of anti-establishment radicalism on university campuses that was dramatized in the free speech movement and the occupations by students of university administrative offices on several campuses.[18] That mood can be sensed in an early RFC posted by graduate student Steve Crocker, a member of the team working on ARPANET:

> The content of a note [RFC] may be any thought, suggestion, etc., related to the [development of gateway software] or other aspect of the network. Notes are encouraged to be timely rather than polished. Philosophical positions without examples or other specifics, specific suggestions or implementation techniques without introductory or background explication, and explicit questions without any attempted answers are all acceptable. The minimum length for a note is one sentence . . . These standards (or lack of them) are stated explicitly for two reasons. First, there is a tendency to view a written statement as ipso facto authoritative, and we hope to promote the exchange and discussion of considerably less than authoritative ideas. Second, there is a natural hesitancy to publish something unpolished, and we hope to ease this inhibition.[19]

Robert Braden, another student participant in both the ARPANET and Internet projects, reflected years later:

> For me, participation in the development of the ARPANET and the Internet protocols has been very exciting. One important

reason it worked, I believe, is that there were a lot of very bright people all working more or less in the same direction, led by some very wise people in the funding agency. The result was to create a community of network researchers who believed strongly that collaboration is more powerful than competition among researchers. I don't think any other model would have gotten us where we are today.[20]

TCP/IP, the universal language of the Internet, is arguably one of history's most important linguistic developments. TCP, or Transmission Control Protocol, codes messages into streams of packets at the source, then reassembles them at their destination. IP, or Internet Protocol, handles the addressing, seeing to it that packets can be routed across multiple nodes and networks using computers of many different makes and models. Still, getting TCP/IP adopted by the Internet (which had been launched with primitive ARPANET software called Network Control Protocol, or NCP) took some finessing by Cerf and other ARPANET developers. By now, habitués of the Net had taken a proprietary, even chauvinistic interest in it and were reluctant to see it changed. However, without a universal protocol, the Net would be effectively hobbled and prevented from reaching its full international potential. In the end, as Cerf recalls, the new standard was simply imposed by *force majeure*:

In the middle of 1982, we turned off the ability of the network to transmit NCP for one day. This caused a lot of hubbub unless you happened to be running TCP/IP. It wasn't completely convincing that we were [serious about the changeover], so toward the middle of fall we turned off NCP for two days; then on January 1, 1983, it was turned off permanently.[21]

The Internet grew. The network's decentralized or "distributed" structure made expansion as easy as building with Tinkertoys. The original Usenet and other networks like it in the U.S. had gradually migrated to the ARPANET backbone throughout the 1980s, and in other countries a similar consolidation under national backbones had been long under way. From a handful of hosts in 1983, the Internet grew to 2.5 million computers linked to 10,000 hosts in 1993, to 30 to 50 million computers and 4.5 million hosts in 1995. A decade later it was estimated that the number of Internet users worldwide was close to a billion, and growing rapidly.

Cerf, looking back in a 1995 Internet forum posting, was bemused by his success:

> I had certain technical ambitions when this project started, but they were all oriented toward highly flexible, dynamic communication for military application, insensitive to differences in technology below the level of the routers. I have been extremely pleased with the robustness of the system and its ability to adapt to new communications technology . . . But I didn't have a clue that we would end up with anything like the scale of what we have now, let alone the scale that it's likely to reach by the end of the decade.[22]

In a watershed development in April of that same year, the U.S. government withdrew its support of the country's Internet trunks, the high-capacity backbones of the Net that had been built on government subsidy. In a carefully planned transition, the Internet in the U.S. switched seamlessly over to commercially operated backbones—with no noticeable interruption to service, despite the fact that the main load-carrier, the National Science Foundation's NSFNET, was at the time handling nearly twenty terabytes of data per month (a terabyte is a thousand million bytes). The Net, in the United States at least, had cut the maternal apron strings and now stood alone and independent.

How the Net Became a Mass Medium

Hypertext and Browsers

T HERE ARE THREE MILESTONES in the evolution of the Internet that are so significant as to merit examination as breakthrough technologies in their own right: the World Wide Web, the graphical-interface Web browser and the search engine. The World Wide Web gave the Net a usable index with hypertext links when it had previously struggled along with only a table of contents; the graphical interface provided a colourful, friendly, point-and-click interface to replace bleak text and arcane keyboard commands; and the search engine automated the search process and made manageable the mountains of information available on the Net (see chapter 29). Together, they made of the Internet a mass medium in the truest sense—a medium of, by and for ordinary people. And in doing this, they played a critical role in deflecting attempts to control the medium for purely corporate purposes, as had happened with radio and television. When commercial interests did come to the Net, they found it necessary to adapt to an implacably embedded technical environment and protocol regime that had been designed to give priority to the interests of the individual user. The story of how all of this came about is the tale of two competing paradigms for online services, one that views users as consumers and the other that sees them as citizens.

Nineteen seventy-four, the year that TCP/IP was released to the public, was also the year in which a parallel form of computer-based communications emerged with the first of what were called Bulletin Board Systems, or BBSs. At first mainly academic or interest-related and non-commercial, the idea of online communities was quickly taken up as a business opportunity by commercial BBS operators. CompuServe, which would become one of the giants of this new industry, went online in that year. The business plan of the commercial BBS was to provide fee-paying subscribers with services such as e-mail, databases of various kinds (depending on the interests of subscribers) and forums for real-time chat on all manner of topics. Almost anyone with a home computer with sufficient storage could host a BBS ; subscribers needed only a modem and password, which came with the subscription fee. Some BBSs were to grow very large.

By the end of the 1980s, the conspicuous success of CompuServe had attracted attention and giant commercial interests began moving into the field, offering continent-wide and eventually worldwide access to a greatly expanded menu of databases and services, including a form of online shopping in which customers placed orders with BBSs based on selections made from CD-ROMs. The accounting firm H&R Block purchased CompuServe; General Electric launched GEnie; IBM, Sears and CBS got together to establish Trintex, later to become Prodigy; and America Online (AOL) was put together by a group of young entrepreneurs who soon made it the biggest and most successful of the lot.

Until about 1990, few people outside the scientific and academic establishments knew anything about the Internet itself, although the notion of online services of the kinds provided by BBSs had begun to receive some attention in the traditional media. (A Massachusetts Institute of Technology text called *Technology 2001: The Future of Computing and Communications*, published in 1991, makes no mention of the Internet.) The larger BBSs such as CompuServe and AOL had by now established substantial subscriber bases thanks to heavy promotional expenditures, and they had begun to exploit new revenue opportunities by offering online advertising. (In 1994, CompuServe claimed 3.2 million users in 120 countries; AOL reported 3.5 million subscribers, Prodigy 1.4 million.) The commercial BBSs had largely co-opted consumer online communication and made it their own, by virtue of their easy-to-use interfaces to databases geared to satisfying business customers while providing a wide range of entertainment and information services. E-mail and online chat[1] also developed into major selling points for potential new subscribers. Chat, which tended to devolve into online flirting, helped to bring down the median age of those using the services, while significantly broadening the subscriber base beyond its early business and computer aficionado stalwarts.

Throughout this period of evolution, the telephone industry had been slowly supplementing its worldwide copper-wire infrastructure with fibre optic cabling, linked by satellite radio transponders of very wide bandwidth. Staggering amounts of data can be moved down fibre optic pipelines—hundreds of thousands of simultaneous phone calls, hundreds of TV channels.[2] The telephone companies soon found themselves, in principle, with virtually unlimited bandwidth on their hands, an embarrassment of riches. All that was required to realize the potential was heavy investment in infrastructure to bring the bandwidth now available on intra- and intercity trunks right to the customer's doorstep. With that done, almost any conceivable mix of programming and content could be delivered. The telcos began to show an active interest in fields that before 1990 had been the exclusive preserve of television. In short, they saw new revenue opportunities in owning and providing what they called "content" or "video dial tone" and what the television industry calls programming. At the same time, cable television had reached levels of household penetration throughout much of the industrialized world that encouraged cable companies to entertain thoughts of providing telephone service in competition with the telcos. The trend toward deregulation in industrial economies everywhere was making it possible for those corporate dreams to be realized, first in Britain, then in the U.S. and Canada, where most legislative restrictions on competition between cablecos and telcos were removed in the 1990s.

By the middle of the decade a major turf war had erupted, with cablecos and telcos jockeying for position in what was thought by industry mavens to be the new frontier of the multi-billion-dollar home entertainment business, the so-called information highway. This was to be a high-bandwidth delivery system to homes for what was envisaged in corporate boardrooms as digital, pay-per-view television with an interactive component. The interactivity would be confined mainly to games, and to searchable databases for news and various kinds of information, including financial services and shopping. It was perceived from the start as a television-based rather than PC-based enterprise. Almost no thought was given to adapting the innovations in interactivity already in use on the Internet; indeed, the number of senior executives in either the cable or telephone industry who had had Internet experience was vanishingly small.

On the proposed information highway the "brainpower" needed to make television sets digital and interactive was to be added in the form of set-top boxes containing microprocessors. Sale, rental and support of these devices would provide one more revenue stream for the service providers. In competing for this perceived information-highway market, cable companies had the advantage of an installed subscriber base served by high-bandwidth coaxial cable capable of carrying hundreds of digitized and compressed television channels. However, these cables had been installed with millions of one-way traps and amplifiers, which would prevent data from being sent back down the line. This was not thought to be a serious handicap at the time: the only return data the cable companies were interested in receiving was pay-per-view orders and payments, and, if need be, these could be handled by telephone links. The telephone companies, although they had built intercontinental fibre trunks of enormous capacity, had to contend with the fact that individual subscribers were still linked to the system with twisted pairs of copper wires, which, even with the best of contemporary digital compression, could only carry a single television channel along with some data and one or two voice channels. On the plus side was the fact that the telephone network was truly symmetrical, allowing data to be sent in both directions, to the capacity of the lines. This was an asset that was all but ignored, however, in the early stages of the broadband competition.

Major capital investments would be required by both the telephone and cable industries if they were to begin delivering the kind of bandwidth-consuming "interactive" video fare each believed held the cherished key to the home entertainment vault. Both industries sponsored expensive trials of so-called video-on-demand in Britain, the United States and Canada, and these received widespread journalistic coverage. Among the most ambitious were those undertaken by Time Warner in Orlando, Florida, and Viacom in Castro Valley, California. Typically, a demographically correct subdivision or urban neighbourhood would be rewired with high-capacity, two-way cable connected to a bank of computer servers. The video-on-demand servers would contain dozens of digitized movies along with other video entertainment, video games, prepackaged news and online shopping services, all available on demand. It was, in reality, an attempt to adapt commercial broadcast television to the digital environment in a way that would maintain TV's one-way control structure while exploiting new revenue opportunities offered by digital media and limited interactivity.

But a funny thing happened on the way to the bank. Lucky consumers who had been given free or highly subsidized broadband services in these market tests fooled around with them for a few days and then lost interest. On-demand movies, which the cableco and telco planners had expected to provide a revenue bonanza, were a bust. People were already comfortable with making their selections from the much bigger catalogues available at video stores, or watching those movies provided by specialty cable channels or on-air TV, and they were unwilling to increase the time previously devoted to watching movies at home. The news services, which were inferior to conventional TV news, were ignored. In 1996, the last of these market tests threw in the towel and wrapped up operations. Losses were huge: Time Warner swallowed a reported $200 million on its Orlando trial alone.

In one of the classic miscalculations of modern business history, both the entertainment and communications industries had failed to grasp the important values of digital, computer-mediated communications networks, had failed to understand the fundamental nature of their appeal. These industries conceived of interactivity only narrowly, in terms of the ability to select and pay for content. They saw their so-called "interactive" broadband services as enhanced broadcasting, rather than envisioning an entirely new medium in which every subscriber is both a consumer and a provider of content. They failed to understand the lesson of the telephone, which was that people, given the opportunity, will choose not simply to *get* content but to *be* content as well. Or the broader historical lesson that it is dangerous in the extreme to offer people a little freedom where none had previously existed: given a little, they will quickly rise up and demand a lot.

The place where those lessons *were* understood was the Internet. The Net had, after all, been built from the bottom up by its users, built to serve their interests exclusively, in a network environment that resists top-down management. The Net viewed its users as citizens (or "netizens" in the argot) while the information-highway sponsors saw users as consumers. Citizens have rights and expectations that consumers do not share. And chief among these is the right to have one's say, and to be heard. The Net was structured in its very hardware and software to respect that right; the broadband video-on-demand systems were set up in ways that denied it, their content being the exclusive domain of their owners.

And so it was that sometime in 1995 the highly publicized and excruciatingly expensive wars for online dominance between the telcos and cablecos became irrelevant, consigned to history by a broad flanking movement on the part of the Internet, a sudden and surprising manoeuvre that settled the issue definitively by crushing both contenders. Even AOL (1996 revenues approximately US$1 billion) and the other hugely successful BBSs were shaken to their foundations.

Until the spring of 1993, the Internet had experienced continuous, though modest growth of about 10 percent a month, which reflected the intimidating nature of its interface. Already an enormous, even overwhelming, resource, it required expert knowledge to reveal its treasures, despite the free distribution by university computer science labs of several rudimentary search tools with such whimsical names as ARCHIE and Veronica. Researchers at the European Particle Physics Lab (CERN, for Conseil Européen pour la Recherche Nucléaire) were among those who found that the sheer volume of valuable information available to them was getting to be hopelessly unmanageable. Oxford graduate student Tim Berners-Lee and some colleagues at CERN tackled the problem in an imaginative way by creating universal standards for data to be posted in their network and a universal addressing system with which to retrieve it. The first was HTML, or Hypertext Markup Language; the second HTTP, Hypertext Transfer Protocol. They called the network the World Wide Web, and in the tradition of the Net they made the protocols freely available at no charge. Any Internet document formatted according to World Wide Web protocols was ipso facto a part of the Web.

The World Wide Web is an innovation that can be compared to the invention of the alphabetical index for books, or the development of the various indexing systems for libraries that allow us to zero in on the material we're looking for and quickly retrieve it. But it is also much more than that, thanks to its employment of hypertext linking. Any word or passage on a web page can be highlighted (usually by underlining) and the coding behind the page allows the creation of a link between that word or phrase and any other word, phrase or document on the Web. Simply clicking on the underlined text (with a mouse) will activate the link and carry the reader to the linked data automatically, wherever in the world it might be. The idea was to connect relevant material in a way that would facilitate both vertical and lateral exploration of an area of information. From its earliest implementation, the Web spawned a new recreation called surfing, which is somewhat akin to browsing in an encyclopedia (if one can imagine an encyclopedia of *billions* of pages!). Early surfers found seemingly limitless pleasure and stimulation in aimlessly following World Wide Web hyperlinks wherever they might take them in the labyrinthine world of interlinked websites.

To access the Web from a personal computer required a software program called a "browser," which translated the HTML programming of a website into readable text, pictures and clickable links. The earliest browsers were efficient but uninspiring and somewhat complicated to use. Very soon, however, the synergy between developers of the Web infrastructure and designers of browsing tools led to a stage of evolution in which web pages were presented in colour and a variety of typefaces, complete with photographs and graphic images and even rudimentary animation. And then came live audio and full-motion video: the Web was clearly destined to become a highly sophisticated multimedia environment, awaiting only adequate bandwidth to deliver its limitless potential.

The remarkable phenomenon of the "personal home page" developed early and spontaneously, as Web users succumbed in their thousands and eventually millions to the temptation to add their own content to the network. It was a simple matter for anyone with a computer and modem to program a web page in the standard HTML, add some digitally scanned photographs, and publish a calling card that announced his or her existence and uniqueness to the world. (Software soon emerged to automate the HTML programming.) Most contained hyperlinks to favourite websites. These personal home pages were the precursors of the blog (Web log or diary), which has individuals from all walks of life venturing into territory once occupied exclusively by professional journalists and opinion makers. The blog, in text, audio and eventually video, was destined to fulfill the Web's promise of becoming a sophisticated medium of many-to-many broadcasting.

Despite these innovations, the Internet and the World Wide Web remained well below the horizon of public consciousness. Then, in August 1993, Marc Andreessen, a greenhorn programmer working for peon's wages with the U.S. National Center for Supercomputing Applications (NCSA) in Urbana-Champaign, Illinois, wrote a web browser program called Mosaic. Of course, he made it available for downloading on the Net, free of charge. Thanks to its elegant interface and point-and-click ease of use, Mosaic was an instant hit, and its impact was every bit as significant for the Internet as VisiCalc's had been for the personal computer industry. Anyone who spent half an hour surfing with Mosaic came away from the experience understanding that a new and important medium of mass communication had been born in the World Wide Web. The impact was every bit as powerful and intuitively exciting as had been the first public demonstrations of the telegraph or telephone or motion pictures; it was the reaction one might imagine of someone whose sense of hearing or vision had suddenly become vastly more acute, opening up the potential of greatly enhanced interaction with the world. It was, in a word, thrilling.

With the release of Mosaic in mid-1993, the World Wide Web began a period of breathtaking, exponential growth that was to change the communications landscape, confounding the plans of some of the world's biggest telecommunications and cable television companies in the process. It was the Web, more than anything else, that had made the Internet a giant-killer and doomed to oblivion the monopolistic dream of a broadcast-style "information highway."

For Andreessen and a handful of young programmers attached to the Mosaic project, success was not an unmixed blessing. With the soaring numbers of Mosaic downloads on the Net came an equally impressive number of requests for help in implementing the program, at all times of the day and night, from eager users all over the world. And then there were increasingly insistent offers from investors who saw potential in Mosaic and wanted to either buy it outright or license it. Andreessen was in way over his head, as he confessed a year later in an interview, and he abruptly quit his NCSA job, intending to drop the Mosaic project and return to a quiet life of programming. He later told a reporter, "At the NCSA, the deputy director suggested that we should start a company, but we didn't know how. We had no clue. How do you start something like that? How do you raise the money?"[3]

The answer was, if your idea is good enough, the money will raise you. In March 1994, Andreessen was tracked down at a small California software company by a savvy Silicon Valley veteran on the rebound from an unpleasant breakup with Silicon Graphics, the computer animation powerhouse he'd founded and where he'd been chairman of the board. Jim Clark understood Mosaic's commercial potential, and he also knew how to set up and run a business. Clark and Andreessen formed Mosaic Communications Inc., flew back to Illinois and in a single afternoon hired all of the key Mosaic developers away from NCSA. To avoid paying licensing fees to NCSA for Mosaic, they set about writing a new browser incorporating Mosaic's most popular features, and improving on them. It was called Netscape, and within a few weeks of its release it had taken over more than 80 percent of the worldwide browser market. The business strategy was unusual, and its success led to later adoption by many other software developers: Netscape was made available free for downloading on the Net, and the company made its money licensing it to corporate users and selling Internet service providers (ISPs, the companies that offer Internet hookups to subscribers for a monthly fee) the software needed to implement its features on their servers. The new company gave away the "reader" and sold the "publisher."

There was a deeper significance to Netscape's successful game plan than initially met the eye. By the time of the program's release, the World Wide Web had evolved through several generations of increasing sophistication, and some far-sighted observers were beginning to have inklings of its potential to become much more than a way to construct, index and link databases. Software was being developed by Sun Microsystems and other companies that allowed web pages to behave in interesting ways by rapidly downloading small applications to the browser's computer. These so-called applets (called *Java* applets in Sun's case) might, for example, animate a graphic, or cause lettering to scroll, or any number of other things. It seemed a small step to extend this technique to larger applications, and before long Net visionaries were talking about the Web of the future as a gigantic "hard drive" full of applications, available for instant access whenever, wherever and by whomever they were needed. The Net would indeed have become the computer, and users would plug into it with cheap appliances that needed only enough processing power and storage to run a browser. (Among the first of these Web-based applications, and the most successful, was Hotmail.)

In this scenario, the browser was seen to take on new significance, because it had the potential of becoming the operating system for the Internet-as-computer. In other words, it would be the vehicle through which the user is able to retrieve information and use applications such as e-mail and basic business tools. Microsoft had proved with MS-DOS how crucial market domination in operating systems can be in terms of controlling the industry and its standards. Whoever dominated the Net browser market would be in a position to shape the development of this new medium while effectively keeping a lid on competitive threats. This would be especially true as the full panoply of Web offerings migrated to cell phones, pocket organizers and other wireless devices. As a vision of the future of the Internet and personal computing, however, this idea was either before its time or simply mistaken. (Time will tell.) But the rise of Netscape did in fact force the mammoth Microsoft Corporation to radically rethink its corporate strategy during the early months of 1996, in order to avoid being leapfrogged by the anticipated new generation of Web-based applications and Web-centred computing. It did this with surprising alacrity.

In late 1995, Bill Gates circulated a memo at Microsoft entitled "The Internet Tidal Wave" in which he announced that the Net was "the most important development in computing since the debut of the IBM PC" and declared it the company's "Number One priority." He pulled out of an expensive interactive TV trial with Time Warner,

Creative Artists Agency and Tele-Communications Inc. called Cablesoft. Among other highly visible and highly significant changes made by Microsoft was a drastic revision of its plans for the Microsoft Network, which had been initiated as a vehicle to compete with the likes of America Online, Prodigy and CompuServe, the big commercial BBSs. In making the changes, Microsoft had finally come to accept what had been foreseen by others in the industry months or even years earlier—that the new, graphic-enhanced, user-friendly World Wide Web was a serious if not fatal threat to the proprietary BBSs. As the Web continued to expand its database at a rate of 20 percent a month, there was very soon almost nothing offered by the BBSs that could not be had for free on the Web, and access to the Net through local ISPs was significantly less expensive than typical BBS subscriber fees.

Even in early 1996 there was a staggering volume of information available on the Web that was not to be had on any BBS, as the Web went from a few thousand to tens of millions of sites worldwide in astonishingly short order. In terms of volume and range of content, there was simply no way any BBS could compete with the Web. The reason was structural, in that the BBSs typically paid for their content from "content providers" (mainly traditional media outlets that returned a portion of any earnings to the BBS in the form of "rent"), while on the Web content was provided free and, with only a tiny number of exceptions, was available equally free. Since no one owned the Web, no one could own its content (except on individual sites) or charge for it en bloc. But the very fact that it was accessible to hundreds of millions of people all over the world, twenty-four hours a day, made it of immense strategic interest to business, and to social institutions of all kinds (as we will see in succeeding chapters). Content of every conceivable description was being placed on the Web in stunning, almost incomprehensible quantities. Internet "newbies," or new users, were invariably astounded by the fact that so much genuinely valuable information was available free of charge. It was as if a department store in their neighbourhood had decided to stop charging for its merchandise! How could it all work if virtually everything was free?

Answers to that question can be offered at several different levels. (See also chapter 31.) It can be noted, for instance, that the cost of information is determined mainly by the expense involved in its collection and organization on the one hand, and its publication and distribution on the other. There is at any given time a great deal of information, both public and proprietary, whose collection and organization costs have already been sunk and that would be made freely available if there was no cost attached to the distribution process. Take, for example, a government report on an issue of public concern, or a professional organization's monthly journal, or stock market data more than a few minutes old and therefore of no further use to the commissioning trader. In each case the cost of preparing the information for publication is an expenditure borne by commissioning users. Distributing the information traditionally involved printing thousands of copies of the publication and paying for their delivery, or, in the case of stock market data and other electronic information, the creation and installation of private telecom networks. Thus, the cost of distribution is what would typically determine how widely the information was circulated. The Internet dramatically lowered the publication cost threshold by allowing anyone, anywhere in the world, to have access to information "published" only once on a website and thus made permanently available, and it rendered private telecom networks redundant. It is as if a single copy of a book or magazine could be read by virtually everyone in the world, more or less simultaneously. Internet publishing released enormous quantities of textual information that was ready and waiting for wide distribution. This included everything from literary masterpieces whose copyright had expired to product information to scientific and medical databases to gallery contents to government documents of all kinds. And the Internet opened the possibility of redistributing time-sensitive data previously confined to private networks and simply discarded after its initial use.

Tapping into this dammed-up reservoir of information accounted for an initial flood of information of historically unprecedented dimensions.

A less obvious fact is that information is unlike other commodities in that distributing it does not deprive the provider of its future use. When you part with your automobile, it is gone; when you distribute some information you have, you still have it. Information is thus shared rather than consumed. One need not manufacture the commodity anew for each client or customer. This fact also helps to keep its cost down.

Finally, as the Web matured, it came to be understood that value could be created out of thin air, as it were, simply by attracting visitors to websites in large numbers, just as population densities and traffic patterns or access to commuter rail service determine the value of real estate in the traditional economy. The way to attract them was to provide useful or entertaining content free of charge. As Kevin Kelly reported in *New Rules for the New Economy*: "In the first 1,000 days of the web's life, several hundred thousand webmasters created over 450,000 web sites, thousands of virtual communities, and 150 million pages of intellectual property, primarily for free. And these protocommercial sites were visited by 30 million people around the world, with 50% of them visiting daily, staying for an average of 10 minutes per day."[4] All those visitors were potential sources of information, or potential customers, or potential voters, or potential supporters of a cause, or potential travellers to your country or city, and so on; they constituted far greater value than the cost of attracting them in the first place.

The commercial BBSs with their hefty subscriber fees were left facing what appeared to be a gaunt future in the mid-nineties. In response to the Web's popularity, they first dramatically lowered subscription fees and then reluctantly began offering access to the Web through their own facilities, hoping to hang on to subscribers by providing a "safe" and friendly interface through which to explore the Net, along with access to their familiar and popular proprietary features such as online versions of popular newspapers and magazines. To add insult to injury, however, many of those proprietary features withdrew from BBSs to set up shop independently on the Web, where they had complete control of their sites and where they did not have to return tithes to the BBS owner on whatever income they might generate.

This was the situation facing the industry in 1996 as Microsoft prepared to launch its lavishly funded Microsoft Network BBS (MSN, for short). The plan was withdrawn, revised and relaunched as an elaborate website, charging no subscription fees. The hope—and it proved to be justified—was that by producing an engaging and informative "portal" site, the company would be able eventually to capitalize on large numbers of visits by selling advertising.[5] It was one more indication that the Net was likely to become the metamedium of the coming century. A year or two later only America Online remained of the once-flourishing consumer BBS industry, and it had survived only through the drastic expedient of transforming itself into an Internet service provider, while at the same time swallowing up its only surviving competitors (including the mammoth CompuServe).

In a dramatic wave of large-scale consolidation of Internet business in late 1998, AOL purchased Netscape in a $4.2-billion stock swap that also involved Sun Microsystems, aiming to become the world's dominant ISP, and positioning itself to take advantage of emerging markets for hand-held Internet access devices and other new technologies on the horizon. Netscape's long feud with Microsoft was at an end: AOL announced it would continue to use the Microsoft Internet Explorer software as its proprietary browser, which it had agreed to do originally as the price Microsoft had demanded in exchange for a clickable AOL icon on the "most valuable real estate in the world," the Microsoft Windows desktop display. Within months Netscape's share of the browser market had slipped to single digits.

Eventually, the biggest threats to Microsoft's market dominance in both browsers (Explorer) and operating systems (Windows) would come not from another corporate competitor, but from freeware products whose code was open, and whose evolution involved, in true hacker-ethic tradition, the volunteer participation of thousands of programmers worldwide. Linux and its variations challenged Windows, and browsers like Firefox threatened Explorer, which was plagued by an apparently unending series of security breaches.

Meanwhile, the inventor of the World Wide Web, Tim Berners-Lee (now Sir Tim), and colleagues affiliated with the World Wide Web Consortium were working on what they hope will be a giant leap forward in the Web's evolution. It is called the Semantic Web, and it involves a series of coding protocols that tag existing Web information with identifiers that allow computers to draw inferences and make connections and correlations that are currently left to the human user. Protocols named XML, RDF and OWL respectively establish a basic syntax, set up rules for categorizing objects and provide a sort of multilingual dictionary that allows computers that are programmed differently to understand each other. The Semantic Web is intended to turn Web browsers into intelligent agents capable of setting up appointments, booking travel, routing merchandise deliveries, assembling a bibliography and doing any number of other logic-based chores. It could, potentially, simplify Web searches and at the same time make them enormously more fruitful in terms of assembling relevant information. It is a project Leibniz would have admired.

Skeptics, however, suspect that the Semantic Web project is the pursuit of Artificial Intelligence by other means, yet another dead end destined to have minimal impact. The problem with asking a machine to navigate the world of human language and experience is that every fact or statement in that environment exists within a context of related facts or statements, and that context in turn exists within a wider context with its own facts and statements, each with its own context, and so on, ad infinitum. Humans, because they have grown up immersed in those overlapping contexts, understand them intuitively. But they have to be programmed into a computer, and that has turned out to be so large a task as to be virtually impossible. After fifty years of work, the quest for artificial intelligence that would mimic or exceed human abilities has been an acknowledged failure largely for this reason.

The Semantic Web seeks to sidestep these problems by, in effect, making a parallel world of the Web, a universe in which all meanings are plain and all thinking is done in logical syllogisms. Machine browsers or "agents" would be able to operate "intelligently" in such a world. Or, as Internet technologist and commentator Clay Shirky notes, "Since it's hard to make machines think about the world, the new goal is to describe the world in ways that are easy for machines to think about."[6] This, readers may recall, is the "instrumental reason" of which philosopher Jurgen Habermas has warned.

Semantic relationships may or may not be its future, but there is no doubting that the World Wide Web has, in the few short years of its existence, transformed our world in ways that surprise even its inventors. As was the case with earlier bilateral technologies, it has demonstrated that when people, as opposed to corporations and other bureaucracies, are granted open access to and effective control over their means of communication, the results will be limited only by the boundaries of human creativity.

By the late 1990s, the Web browser had made a cornucopia of information available, but before all that newly available information could work its magic, a major technological challenge needed to be met: how could the riches of the Web be made not just available but truly *accessible*? And a commercial problem persisted: how to pay for Web content.

How the Net
Became a Mass Medium
Directories and Search Engines

I F THE EXPLOSION of public interest in the Web is strongly
reminiscent of the great enthusiasm for radio in the 1920s and
1930s, there is a remarkable parallel on the commercial side
of things as well. It lies in the fact that those pioneer businesses that
eagerly staked claims in the cyberspace of the Internet seventy years
later had no more idea how to make those claims pay off than did the
early radio entrepreneurs. The Big Question was exactly the same:
where will the money come from to pay for the content? Charging
fees for Web access beyond the basic ISP tariffs was not feasible for
reasons we've already discussed (how can you charge for access to
something you don't own?), and it was soon made painfully clear to
several high-profile websites that subscriber fees for access to individual sites were unacceptable to the vast majority of Web users, if
for no other reason than there was such an enormous wealth of
directly competing material available free of charge. As with radio,
the business model that eventually gained favour was commercial
sponsorship. But on the Web, sponsorship was a whole different ball
game for both the sponsor and the user.

In the beginning, advertising was not among the "approved uses" for the Internet permitted by its early sponsor in the U.S., the National Science Foundation (NSF), which provided major funding for the American Internet backbone. But by the mid-1990s this was a rule obeyed more in the breach than the observance, and it seems clear that the NSF recognized that advertising could no more be censored on the Net than pornography or political extremism or anything else. Beyond that, there was good reason to allow experimentation with commercial applications to this new medium, particularly since government sponsorship was understood to be only an interim arrangement designed to assist in start-up operations. When the NSF eventually did withdraw its support of the Internet in 1995, the issue of advertising and other "approved uses" became moot.

As a random-access, interactive medium, the Web operates on the principle that content is selected by users rather than being broadcast at them. This means that commercial messages can be skirted, ignored or eliminated in any number of ways, both manual and automatic. For example, a Web surfer can simply turn off the graphic enabler of her Internet browser, and advertisements, which invariably are downloaded as graphics, will no longer be visible. There is, in fact, a positive incentive to do this as a matter of routine, particularly on dial-up connections, since text-only web pages load far more quickly than those with pictures or animation. (And the pictures remain accessible, just a mouse click away on the "missing image" icon that replaces the missing picture.) The same technique can immobilize irritating animations, pop-up windows and unwanted audio. For an advertisement to be effective in an interactive medium like the Web, it must be of some use, otherwise it is likely to be ignored, since it cannot intrude or impose itself on the user in the way a radio or television commercial can.

At first confounded by a medium so seemingly advertising-averse, businesses soon began to see a silver lining, in that the Web was a two-way street where commercial sponsorship was concerned. While it was true that users could and would ignore advertisements that held no interest for them, advertising sites could also count on those who did visit to have a genuine interest in their product— why else would they visit? Virtually every visitor was a sales lead. Advertising as it evolved on the Web was thus tightly targeted and highly informational, to a degree where it could be argued that it provided useful content to the Web as opposed to littering it with noisome clutter. It would prove a successful strategy: Americans were spending as much as 70 percent of their time on the Web searching for product information related to planned purchases. There are now few businesses of any kind in the wired Western world that do not have a website providing information on their products and services.

Advertising on the Net was a fundamentally different phenomenon than it had been in the linear broadcast media of radio and television, and posed no inherent threat to the quality or integrity of content, simply because the Net is endlessly expandable, whereas the radio and TV spectrum had been strictly limited. In the broadcast media, advertisements displace and intrude into non-commercial content. On the infinitely expandable Net, there is, in principle, unlimited room for both commercial and non-commercial sites, and users can choose among them freely. Commercial and non-commercial content exist, as it were, in the same space but in different dimensions.[1]

Having said that, it needs to be acknowledged that advertisers have been trying very hard to bend the Web to their needs. Many large websites now carry banner ads designed to attract attention, and studies show that in terms of simple brand recognition they are as memorable as television commercials even when there is no "click-through" by the user. ("Clicking" on the ad typically takes the user, via a hypertext link, "through" to the advertiser's website.) The Web's technical flexibility in this regard led marketers to come up with a strategy impossible in any other medium: when a user sought a particular website by entering its name in a search engine, the engine's "returns" page would feature an automatically inserted banner ad for a related product or service along with the standard list of Web addresses. Advertisers had to rethink the idea when they were sued for copyright infringement by several companies, notably Playboy and Estée Lauder. Playboy objected to its name being juxtaposed with banner ads for X-rated porn sites, and Estée Lauder executives hit the roof when they discovered that searching for their company's name brought up ads for Fragrance Counter. These were teething pains.

Eventually Overture, quickly purchased by Google (see below), refined the idea so that "Google ads" became ubiquitous on the Web. A search using keywords in Google automatically generates small text advertisements, which, on sites adapted for them, appear alongside related site content. Websites have an incentive to make room for the ads (although they don't have to) because they are paid a fee ranging from a few cents to a few dollars for each click-through. On large sites with heavy traffic, revenue generated this way can be substantial. "Contextual" search engine ads of this sort quickly became a major economic driver on the Web. By 2005, annual expenditures on Internet advertising would outpace all outdoor advertising, reaching a staggering $9.6 billion in the U.S., and topping £1 billion in the U.K.

An attempt to adapt tried-and-true broadcast strategies to the Net was responsible for the huge investments made in portal sites such as Netcenter, Microsoft, Yahoo! and SNAP at the twentieth century's close. Just as radio station owners invented the broadcast network to accumulate the large audiences wanted by sponsors, portal sites attempt to persuade large numbers of users to make the portal the page that opens first when the user's browser is launched, and leadership in the portal sweepstakes translates directly into enormous advertising revenue. The means of persuasion varied: Microsoft placed the button linking users to its portal prominently on the Windows desktop; Netscape browser software defaulted to Netcenter unless the user entered a custom default page. Doubtless many more advertising strategies will be tried and discarded, or adopted as part of the marketing repertoire. One thing is certain, however—the Net "audience" can never be considered captive or passive in the way audiences have been captive to limited numbers of outlets in the broadcast media. Net surfers, unlike the television viewer, will always be able to tailor their experience on the Net to their own tastes.[2]

From the World Wide Web's earliest days, the most visited sites were the search services that sprang up in bewildering profusion before settling into a series of consolidations. Their popularity quickly made them the most valuable properties on the Web. For if the Net's staggering and ever-expanding resources are its principal attraction, they are also its Achilles heel. Any information repository as diverse and dynamic as the Web is only as good as its index, and the Web does not have an index, at least not in the ordinary sense. What it does have are search engines, and catalogue-like directories.

The best-known and most widely used directory, Yahoo!, is the creation of a pair of Stanford University graduate students named Jerry Yang and David Filo, who wanted a way to organize their personal interests on the Web. In 1994 they converted Yahoo! into a massive database of Web links designed to serve the wider Internet community, inviting website developers to submit their URLs for inclusion. With the help of artificial intelligence specialist Srinja Srinivasan, they set up an operation in which websites are catalogued according to a very large and continuously expanding hierarchical classification system that strives to cover the entire field of human knowledge. Addresses of new sites began arriving in the form of e-mail requests for registration from website developers, and from Yahoo!'s robotic Web crawler or "spider," a software program that automatically roamed the Web from link to link, searching for new sites. Each was visited and assessed by a human classifier (initially, Yang and Filo), who decided whether the site was worthy of inclusion in the directory, and in what categories it ought to be listed. The site grew so quickly that it threatened to disrupt computer operations at Stanford, where it resided on Yang's and Filo's workstations: Yahoo! was racking up million-hit (100,000-visitor) days by the autumn of 1994. In early 1995, Marc Andreessen invited them to move the directory to the newly incorporated Netscape's computers.[3]

Yang and Filo knew they had a potential business on their hands, and in April 1995 they were able to secure nearly $2 million in venture capital. Professional managers were brought on board, from Motorola and Novell. There was a second round of venture financing that autumn, and in April 1996 the company went public with an IPO (initial public offering of shares) that raised about $1 billion. By then a staff of nearly fifty classifiers were working at the company headquarters in Sunnyvale, California, looking at each site and deciding on the appropriate slot for it within the catalogue.

As catalogues do, Yahoo! provides a context for every website it lists, and this is its major virtue. Looking through the Yahoo! listings is akin to browsing a library's stacks, where books are shelved side by side according to topic. Its drawback is that, given the Web's rate of growth, there is little or no hope that Yahoo!, or other directories like Answer.com, will be able to keep their catalogues either up-to-the-minute or comprehensive. That does not mean that directories become irrelevant, any more than a year-old set of the *Encyclopaedia Britannica* is useless. It does suggest that Yahoo! and other catalogues fill a role as trusted and familiar sources of advice rather than know-it-all indexes.

Yahoo! had very quickly parlayed its initial successes into becoming one of the top portal sites in much of the world, and one of the top money-makers on the Web. It began a round of purchases, eliminating competition and adding new services such as Web-based e-mail, radio streaming and website hosting. It became a major hub for e-commerce sites and online shopping. In the process of becoming an online business empire, however, Yahoo! also shed the idealistic vision of its young founders, who had started out to build a service that would accept and rank sites strictly on merit, so as to add value to the Internet experience.[4] From the beginning, one of the reasons why Yahoo! was so widely admired was that it helped to realize the initial promise of the Web by offering a way for small entrepreneurs to advertise their existence at no cost, and in a context that put them on the same level as major corporations. On Yahoo!, a mom-and-pop dog biscuit company was, in principle, no harder to find than Purina. This pleased not only the small businesses but also the many ordinary people who half hoped, half believed that the Web was going to cause fundamental changes in American capitalism by challenging the hegemony of mammoth corporations.

Not long after going public, however, Yahoo! began charging a fee for admission to its directory, and another, higher, monthly fee to get favourable placing at the top of search returns. This of course transformed the directory concept, in a way analogous to the changes the penny press revolution brought to the reader–publisher relationship in newspapers (see chapter 6). Yahoo!'s primary focus is no longer on adding value to the Net by providing information in the form of a free directory service. Its interest now lies in maximizing revenue from the directory by charging for premium services that necessarily distort any notion of a level playing field for big and small businesses.

With the change of focus came a slow slide into financial doldrums for the company. Recovery began in 2003 when Yahoo! bought several search engines: Inktomi ($235 million), Overture ($1.6 billion), Altavista and Alltheweb. It had now become more search engine than directory, a business option that, while it may have disappointed Yahoo!'s legions of loyal users, opened wider opportunities for advertising revenue. Yahoo! Inc. Senior vice president Ted Meisel now presented the business this way: "Our mission is to be essential to marketers of all types around the world" and "to integrate and simplify online advertising, allowing businesses of all sizes to take advantage of the Yahoo! search marketing solutions that best fit their marketing goals."[5] Not a word here about the Web user or the value of the Web itself.

In the know-it-all Web index (as opposed to Web catalogue) field, a number of contenders for the biggest, fastest and best Web search engine were to emerge as the Net matured. They were initially launched for one of two reasons: because there were challenging

technical problems to be experimented with, in the process showing off state-of-the-art computer hardware and software (for which
there was a strong corporate network market), or because they held
the potential of earning their makers a lot of money. The basic principle behind their operations is an information grid in which rows
list web pages and columns list words and phrases. Some engines list
every word on a page; others list only keywords likely to be searched
for. The pages themselves are located by automated Web spiders
that systematically drop in on websites to check for new data. When
a user initiates a keyword search, the engine scans its grid for inter-
sections where there is a match between keyword and web page.
The addresses to those pages, and sometimes a brief description, are
retrieved and presented to the searcher as clickable hyperlinks. As
the most visited sites on the Web, search engines were soon handling
millions of requests a day—and charging premium rates for advertising banners. In a wave of consolidations in 1999, several of the
most successful search engines were purchased for incorporation
into portal sites.

Of these second-generation, commercial search engines—Lycos,
Excite!, Alta Vista, Inktomi, Infoseek, HotBot, to name just a handful—Google was to emerge in 2000 as the runaway market leader.
Not only was it amazingly fast, it seemed almost preternatural in its
ability to return the most helpful links. Its secret lay in the fact that
it catalogued far more websites than any of its competitors—
billions of pages—and it used a unique technology for selecting the
returns. Google ranked web pages not simply by the frequency with
which they used searched-for keywords, but with an algorithm that
checked how many other sites linked to the page being returned—
the number of so-called "back-links." Thus it provided a rough-and-
ready screening for popularity among Web users, the pages with the
most back-links being displayed at the top of the returns. The company describes its page-ranking technology this way:

> PageRank evaluates all of the sites linking to a web page and
> assigns them a value, based in part on the sites linking to them.

By analyzing the full structure of the web, Google is able to determine which sites have been "voted" the best sources of information by those most interested in the information they offer. This technique actually improves as the web gets bigger, as each new site is another point of information and another vote to be counted.[6]

(However, it also favours older, established sites over newcomers, with little regard to merit.)

The strains on hardware—the simple need for mammoth processing capacity to handle the sheer size of the Web—was an obvious potential problem, but Google had also developed an innovative approach to hardware, using thousands and eventually hundreds of thousands of low-cost, consumer-grade PCs linked together rather than a handful of hugely expensive supercomputers. The approach brought rewards in ease of expansion and in the reliability that comes with massive redundancy.

Google's corporate history, like Netscape's and Yahoo!'s, is a textbook example of the kind of spectacular financial success that can accompany a good idea in an emergent field of technology like the Web. Company founders Larry Page and Sergey Brin got together in 1996, aged twenty-four and twenty-three respectively, to work on search engines as graduate students in computer science at Stanford University. Their project to explore the use of back-links in search algorithms was dubbed Backrub. Within a year it was causing a buzz among engineers in the know. By 1998 they had a terabyte of hard-drive storage stacked in cheap housings in Page's dorm room, and Brin set out in search of portal sites and directories that might be interested in licensing their very promising search technology. There were no takers; one portal CEO told them, "As long as we're 80 percent as good as our competitors, that's good enough. Our users don't really care about search."

Page and Brin decided to set up a company, raise some start-up capital and go it alone. In September 1998, Google Inc. opened for business in a garage in Menlo Park, capitalized at about $1 million, most of the money having come from family, friends and acquaintances. Google.com was answering about 10,000 queries a day. It began attracting media attention: *USA Today* did an article, and *PC Today* named it one of the top 100 websites for 1998. By February 1999, Google had more than doubled its staff to eight, and moved into a larger space in a Palo Alto office building. It was now handling 500,000 search requests a day. Four months later, the company announced it had secured a second round of financing from two local venture capital firms, for $25 million. New financial and engineering staff arrived. Once again the computers were packed up and moved, this time to the company's permanent headquarters in Mountain View, California. When AOL/Netscape licensed Google to be its Web search engine, the number of queries handled each day leaped to more than 3 million. By 2000 there were some sixty employees, a disproportionate number of them Ph.D.s, enjoying the kind of pampered working conditions the company had already become famous for—the gym, the comfy furniture, the free snacks, the fine dining in the cafeteria, the parking lot roller-hockey games.

Licensing of Google technology to client sites was booming, and in mid-year the company introduced what would become the real money-maker, the sale of keyword-related advertisements, a technique pioneered by Overture (now owned by Yahoo!). Google ads, with a little fine tuning, were to become a roaring success. Advertisers loved them, because they were charged only for click-throughs. For its part, Google strove to increase click-through rates by ensuring that ads appeared only alongside closely related web-page text in search returns. Google searchers did not seem to mind the advertisements, because they were text-only and relatively unobtrusive—indeed they often provided useful supplementary information. By year-end Google was fulfilling 100 million search queries a day, from all over the world. *Google* had become a verb, as in, "I googled my own name," soon to be incorporated into new editions of dictionaries.

The company became profitable for the first time in 2001. In 2003 it was chosen by AOL to provide search services and ads to the

ISP's 34 million subscribers. In 2004 it went public with an IPO that raised $1.7 billion. Its revenues that year were over $800 million, half of it from Google ads. The company continued aggressively to expand its search capabilities, still driven by the idealistic goals of its founders to provide a service that would index the world's information, wherever it could be found, and make it available on computers.

Now a multi-billion-dollar, publicly traded enterprise, the company insisted that it would remain "a core value" at Google "that there be no compromising of the integrity of our results. We never manipulate rankings to put our partners higher in our search results. No one can buy better PageRank®. Our users trust Google's objectivity and no short-term gain could ever justify breaching that trust."[7] This was an obvious and unflattering reference to Google's main competitor, Yahoo!, initially every bit as idealistic as Google but where one can now buy preferential page ranking.

Whether and for how long Google can continue to live up to its stated "core values" is a real question. The history of corporations during the past century would suggest that, now that the company has gone public, it will be difficult, if not impossible, to maintain as a core value *any* goal that might conflict with maximizing profit. In other words, the founders' idealism will remain an operational premise only so long as it underwrites the universal corporate goal of maximum profitability. Thus, in 2006, Google agreed, in return for direct access to the world's biggest potential market—China—to censor its search returns for Chinese users, eliminating anything to do with human rights, independent news (including the BBC) and anything else the Chinese authorities deemed unsuitable. Yahoo! had already acceded to similar demands for the same reason: the potential for profit was simply too large to be ignored, and neither company was breaking any laws in censoring its content.

The next phase in the commercial development of the Web will be played out in the search and directory arena, and the results are impossible to predict. (Advertising revenue prospects inevitably lured the lumbering Microsoft into the search engine market in

2005.) This should be a cause for concern to anyone who appreciates the Web as an almost unbelievably rich source of information available to ordinary people at modest cost. Google and other search engines are free to change their search algorithms at will, and frequently do just that. No prior warning is given, and no information on the new algorithms is released. The reason for the secrecy is that if the algorithms were known, programmers would be able to develop websites that had no purpose other than to achieve high search engine rankings and thus (potentially) make a lot of money from contextual ads. This would devalue the usefulness of the search engines, which earn their reputations, and their money, from their reliability as sources of authentic information.

But the secrecy has a serious downside. The lack of information makes the Web economy a very unstable, risky business environment. For anything but the biggest corporate websites, which generate high traffic through traditional advertising and promotion methods (CNN, CNBC, Disney, etc.), it can take thousands of person-hours of coding work devoted to "search engine optimization" (SEO) to develop even a modest income from what have become known generically as "Google ads." Small businesses that depend on that income for survival lead a precarious existence, their continued welfare dependent on decisions over which they have no control and about which they have no information. Given that large, publicly traded corporations must place the wider public interest in the shadow of the financial interests of their shareholders, it would be dangerous to assume that *any* such company will, in the long term, continue to provide search access to the Web that is designed first and foremost to serve the public, to add value to the shared resource that is the Web.

It is time, perhaps, to return to the earliest days of radio broadcasting to revive some old ideas about financing content (in this case, search engine returns) through government levies, or foundations, or endowments. The ability for individuals to search the Web's vast resources quickly and efficiently, on the one hand, and for entrepreneurs and organizations of all kinds to make themselves known to the world in the face of massive corporate advertising expenditures, on the other, have become too important to global society to be left solely in the hands of for-profit enterprises. If the Web is to fulfill its dazzling potential as a vehicle for information, education and entertainment, as well as commerce, the public interest needs to be represented directly, through search and directory services that will reflect something akin to the altruism of the public broadcasting ethos.

Anarchy and Public Space

The Internet Grows Up

JOURNALISTS often refer to the Net as "anarchic," and that's not an inappropriate description, although, clearly, the Internet does not exist in a political vacuum: in principle at least, the laws of nations apply on the Net as they do in ordinary life. One can harass or be harassed, defraud or be defrauded, libel or be libelled, pander or be pandered to, threaten or be threatened, exploit or be exploited on the Net just as in the real world, and the same criminal and civil protections and penalties apply. They may, however, be difficult to enforce because of the boundary-less, transnational character of the Net, and because of the difficulty of establishing the identity of users who wish to be anonymous. Early on in the history of the Net, lawyers began to worry that "the rise of an electronic medium that disregards geopolitical boundaries throws the law into disarray by creating entirely new phenomena that need to become the subject of clear legal rules but that cannot be governed, satisfactorily, by any current territorially based sovereign."[1] The Net is public space that is shared by millions of "citizens" but lacks a government. It survives and flourishes thanks to the fact that the vast majority of its users mind their manners and obey the Golden Rule. It owes much of its staggering resources to simple altruism and goodwill, a desire to share. As an experiment in anarchism, it can only be described as an encouraging success.

This seems especially true in contrast to the media environment provided by the commercial dictates of the almost entirely profit-centred industry we think of as the traditional media. The German-American philosophers Max Horkheimer and Theodor Adorno provided a bleak account of the traditional capitalist "culture industry" at about the time the TCP/IP protocols were being drafted in 1975. For them, mass culture is a deliberately constructed propaganda system that aims to reach every nook and cranny of society with its message of the blissful necessity of capitalism and consumerism. Its overall purpose, writes Adorno, is to "reproduce the status quo within the mind of the people,"[2] and in doing so it "impedes the development of autonomous, independent individuals who judge and decide consciously for themselves."[3] In *Dialectic of Enlightenment* they write that the twin goals of the culture industry are social control and profit in the service of "the absolute power of capitalism." Its role is to "defend society" and it provides something for everyone, "so that none may escape" its blandishments. "The stronger the position of the culture industry becomes, the more summarily it can deal with the consumer's needs, producing them, controlling them, disciplining them, and even withdrawing amusement."[4]

The sociologist and media critic Herbert Schiller extended Adorno and Horkheimer's analysis of traditional media to present a view of a worldwide cultural imperialism that has developed around "a rapid, all encompassing communications technology (satellites and computers)," and serves the needs and objectives of the corporate capitalism of America, Great Britain and Western Europe. American media, in particular,

> create, process, refine and preside over the circulation of images and information which determine our beliefs and attitudes and, ultimately, our behavior. When they deliberately produce messages that do not correspond to the realities of social existence,

the media managers become mind managers. Messages that create a false sense of reality and produce a consciousness that cannot comprehend or willfully reject the actual conditions of life, personal or social, are manipulative messages.[5]

No doubt these are excessively pessimistic perspectives, but they cannot be dismissed as entirely without foundation. A question worth asking is to what degree the public space of the Net is in danger of being subverted in the same way. In this context "public space" as it relates to the Net is an idea worth exploring a little more deeply.

Public space is first and foremost an architectural concept. In the official lexicon of urban designers, space devoted to streets, parks, squares, boulevards and so on is public space. But so is a mall concourse or the lobby of a hotel, in that they are ordinarily accessible to the public. This ambiguity makes it a controversial definition. At architecture schools, students bemoan the loss to private interests of what once was public space, as happens when construction of a shopping mall shifts the focus of a town from the central square or main street to the enclosed commercial spaces of the mall. While the main concourse of a mall may *seem* to be public space, it is not; pamphleteers, panhandlers, buskers and boisterous teenagers all learn this lesson definitively when they are given the bum's rush by private security guards. Furthermore, the public has no control over the amenities or lack of same in such pseudo-public spaces.

The online environment in which the Net operates is, and must be seen to be, public space analogous to the airwaves that carry broadcast signals—that is, *real* public space, and not the as-if, shopping mall variety. There is nothing in this recognition that precludes the physical structures of the Net—the copper and optical fibre lines and the switching devices and digital-coding machinery—from being owned and operated for profit by private enterprise. It is the space that is created when those lines are humming with data, the cyberspace, that has to be acknowledged as public space. The Net exists in that space and is, by definition, owned and controlled by its millions of users. It was designed and built to be that way, and the design works. The public nature of the Internet is lodged deep in its defining technologies.

Legal scholar Lawrence Lessig has compared the code (programming) that defines the architecture of the Net to a *constitution* that sets out rights and responsibilities of citizens and institutions in the physical world.[6] His point is that it should not be blithely assumed that the Net will forever remain the kind of public space it was carefully designed to be, because whether it does or not depends on programming and protocols. The Net was defined by a set of open and non-proprietary protocols that allow free and open access without any need for licensing or identification or fees or permissions, because it was designed for research and communication, not commerce or control.

That this architecture is far from optimal in serving the interests of business is clear: the corporate vision of interactive commerce involves collecting as much consumer data as possible and wherever possible while controlling the choices made online so as to maximize sales opportunities. Corporate business has no interest in dispensing information freely when it can be charged for, or when it will in any way interfere with sales. It prefers the old information highway model promoted by the telcos and cablecos prior to the blossoming of the Web, in which browsing is restricted to proprietary sites, user identity must be disclosed, usage is tracked and recorded, everything has a fee attached, and site design is aimed at maximizing sales and advertising opportunities. This is the model that best serves the interests of the corporation, and corporations have a fiduciary responsibility to place their own interests before all others.

Lessig contends that government, too, naturally leans to the architectures of control and surveillance because they simplify the exercise of power. This may be a peculiarly American viewpoint, in that it sees government and the interests of the individual as inherently adversarial. In other nations, where a different balance is sought between the rights of the individual and collective rights, the issue will be interpreted differently. But there will be wide agreement with Lessig when he argues that law enforcement agencies of all kinds constitute a powerful private lobby within government that strongly favours architectures which permit identification and tracking of users. The extent to which law enforcement surveillance is desirable or necessary will always be controversial. Should the public have access to encryption algorithms that are for all practical purposes impossible for national security agencies to crack? This would be like having a telephone system that made it impossible to tap conversations, ever. Where is the proper balance here between the individual's right to privacy and the community's collective right to security?

While it is true that Internet architecture as it currently exists makes it difficult for government to regulate behaviour on the Web, it is not the case that it is difficult for government to regulate the architecture itself. When telephone networks in the United States switched to digital technologies, it became much harder to predict the routing of telephone conversations and therefore to tap them. In 1994, Congress passed the Communications Assistance for Law Enforcement Act, which directed telephone companies to use digital architectures that would simplify the task of court-authorized eavesdropping for law enforcement agencies. This legislative approach has not, so far, been widely adopted where the Net is concerned. For example, in cases of law enforcement, where authorities have chosen to force Internet Service Providers to reveal the identity of suspected criminals, they have typically done so through the traditional expedient of obtaining a warrant to search the ISP's payment records. The alternative—legislating changes to Internet protocols that would have the effect of automatically identifying users—has so far been avoided. But it could be done.

One area where government intervention is clearly needed is in combatting those most egregious defilers of public space, the spammers, source of billions of unsolicited commercial e-mails each day. In the words of Internet pioneer Vinton Cerf, "Spamming is the scourge of electronic-mail and newsgroups on the Internet. It can seriously interfere with the operation of public services, to say nothing

of the effect it may have on any individual's e-mail mail system . . .
Spammers are, in effect, taking resources away from users and service suppliers without compensation and without authorization."7
By some accounts, spam makes up more than half of all e-mail traffic. The cost to legitimate users is, in collective terms, astronomical.
Each spam message eats up bandwidth and server time, not to mention the time taken to delete it from the recipient's inbox. Much of
the junk mail is fraudulent, attempting to get recipients to reveal
credit card and PIN numbers ("phishing"), or selling quack medical
remedies, or promoting worthless stocks and other get-rich-quick
schemes. Much of it is pornographic, or advertises pornography.
Most spam originates in the United States, where, as one might
expect, anti-spam activism is widespread and well organized. However, attempts to pass rigid anti-spam legislation in Congress and in
state legislatures have faced an uphill battle thanks to interventions
from the nation's enormous marketing industry and even (ironically) from lobbyists for the anti-spam software industry. Marketers
argue that any interference with unsolicited junk mail amounts to
an infringement of the sender's First Amendment free speech rights.
Their opponents insist that an individual's e-mail address—especially when purchased from an ISP—is not and should not be "public information" to be "harvested" by spammers and flooded with
advertising, and that spam, in that sense, is an invasion of privacy.

To the degree that it degrades a public resource, and wastes a
great deal of time and money, spam amounts to theft and vandalism.
Spammers—and there are only a handful who are responsible for
most of the problem—clearly ought to be prosecuted, and increasingly they are being sued, fined and jailed all over the world.[8] But
the spam continues. Perhaps it is time to consider those companies
and individuals who knowingly hire the services of spammers to be
accessories in crime, and vigorously prosecute them as well.

The Information Economy

I NFORMATION is always an important component of any economic system, and in that sense the information economy has always been with us. What is new and potentially revolutionary is the advent of high-bandwidth digital networks enveloping the globe, multiplying many thousandfold our ability to move information from place to place, and the approaching ubiquity of the silicon chips that allow access to those networks. It is as if we had advanced from primitive irrigation systems to the ability to make rain, from dryland farming to hydroponics.

As information has risen to a position of dominance in the economy, we have begun to realize that it is like no conventional commodity—indeed, it cannot properly be defined as a commodity at all. Commodities, as economists define them, have the property of being rivalrous—that is, if I consume some of one, there is less for you. We are rivals in that respect, and the commodity is the subject of that rivalry, and thus rivalrous. Bread is rivalrous: if I eat a slice, there is one slice less for you. Information is not like that. If I consume some (by "knowing" it), there is just as much left for you. Information is non-rivalrous. In fact, it may well be that in consuming information I am enabled to add new findings, shed new light, develop new insight, which will *add* to the corpus. My consumption of information will in that case have led to an *increase* in the resource.

This creates several problems for economists. First, how should information be priced? Normally, economic goods are assumed to be scarce, and are priced according to the cost of producing one more unit of production, that is, according to their marginal cost. While vast resources may have gone into producing a breakthrough or an insight or a finding, the marginal cost of sharing that knowledge with others is, typically, trivial. You can publish it on the Net, for instance, for all to see.

Second, information is not naturally a scarce commodity. It is therefore difficult to justify exclusive or restrictive *ownership* of information. In economic doctrine as it has come down to us from the eighteenth-century savants, private property is a means of husbanding scarce resources, the idea being that if you own a thing, you will take care of it. (This logic was even applied to slaves, as a justification for the practice of owning workers rather than just "renting" them, for wages. According to the theory, slaves would be treated better than ordinary workers.) If information is not, by its nature, scarce, and thus not in need of careful husbanding, how can private ownership be justified? Information, however, can be *made* scarce, through copyright or patent laws that restrict its use to those who can afford to pay royalties. And that is in fact the purpose of such laws, to bring information into line with market rules. Copyright and patent law amounts to a system for making information artificially rivalrous, and thus subject to market pricing mechanisms.

A further headache for economists is the fact that markets are presumed to operate on the basis of informed consumers. It is consumers consciously seeking out the best value for money that, in theory, makes the market an ideal distributor of goods and services. By making informed choices, the consumer ensures that the good will survive and the bad and the ugly will disappear. But with information, the product and knowledge of it are one and the same. If I have knowledge of the product, I have the product.

It can be argued that, because the marginal cost of information is effectively zero, information should be free. Moreover, even if a price were to be attached to it, the market could not operate effectively because it is not possible to give consumers the information they need to make wise choices without giving away the product, or important parts of it, itself.[1]

Because of these peculiarities, the continuing debate over copyright and under what conditions it ought to be permissible for anyone to make use of artistic or intellectual property (information) created by someone else has been politically charged. Much of the discussion has taken place outside the parameters of economic theory because, in some respects, the issues involved are really moral questions, which market dogma is ill equipped to answer satisfactorily. If the marginal cost of my hearing the Montreal Symphony Orchestra's rendition of *The Planets* is zero, once the costs of production have been covered and a reasonable profit margin has been reached, why shouldn't it be available free? The same question might be asked of a movie downloaded over BitTorrent or a pop tune from Napster or other peer-to-peer systems for sharing files. How, and for how long, can maintaining artificial scarcity over artistic and intellectual products be justified, especially when it is clear that the more they are consumed, the better off we are as a society? Where is the correct, just balance between the interests of the producers of the intellectual property and its consumers?

Anyone who has been observing this conflict will have noticed that the most vocal elements are not the producers, or even the consumers, but the distributors, which are almost exclusively large, multinational corporations. While these companies claim to be advocates for the interests of their "stables" of writers and artists, there is no doubt that their own interests are, in the end, what really matter to them. This is simply the nature of the corporate beast. Thus in an important sense the debate resolves itself into one between the interests of business and the corporation, which are centred on secrecy and the creation of scarcity and thus profit, and the interests of the public, which are best served by the free flow of information.

One solution to the conundrum of how to reward developers of intellectual property for their efforts, without at the same time needlessly restricting the flow of information in society, is to organize payment on an actuarial model. This would involve everyone's paying a small amount into a publicly managed fund, which would then be used to pay creators a prescribed amount each time their creation was downloaded or accessed in some other way (perhaps borrowed from a library). The reasoning behind the actuarial proposal is that, even though not everyone who pays into the fund will make use of all the information being supported in this way—some won't use any at all—everyone in society benefits from its use in the way I've described above: when information is used (shared) it tends to create more information, which enriches society. The actuarial principle is one way of having the public—society at large—pay for that which has obvious value but no obvious price. (The model can be adapted to apply to society at large or to specific communities of interest.)

Another possible solution is the idea of charging very small amounts for access to content through one of a myriad of proposed "micropayment" schemes. Where this has been tried, it has generally failed, for the simple reason that there is always so much free content on the Web of comparable quality. In such an environment, even the tiniest of payments creates a psychological (though not financial) barrier to purchasing. For artists, authors, bloggers and other Web creators, this is a very real problem.

The "marketspace" created by the Net is a historically unique commercial environment. It exists nowhere and everywhere at the same time, and can be accessed from anywhere in the world. It provides a rich, multimedia communication environment exceptionally well suited to commercial transactions of all kinds, from initial contact, through sales, to service and customer retention. The closeness with customers that it affords by making communication cheap and easy allows for marketing of an entirely new kind, in which the customer gets involved in the product cycle as early as in the design stage. The Net is radically superior to any other medium for serving niche markets around the world. While it is now possible to purchase just about anything on the World Wide Web, some of the most encouraging success stories involve niche products and services for which the market is substantial but geographically dispersed. Specialty food products, arts and crafts, designer and special-purpose clothing, rare cars and antiques, specialized books and instruction, unique resorts and accommodation, and specialized consulting services all find a much-enlarged and constantly expanding market in the Net, either through their own websites or on auction sites such as eBay.

George Gilder is an outspoken, optimistic American technophile whose prognostications are often on target. In the heady days of Netscape 1.0 he called the Internet "the most egalitarian force in the history of the world economy," because, he said,

> the Internet creates jobs by making workers more productive, and thus more employable, regardless of where they live. By engendering more investable wealth, it endows new work, providing the key remedy for the job displacement entailed by all human progress. By aggregating distant markets, the Internet enables more specialization, and more productivity and excellence. It will help all people, but most particularly the poor, who always comprise the largest untapped market for enterprise. And the Internet will continue to grow, transforming the global economy with its power and building a new industry even larger than the PCs.[2]

Similarly euphoric was the Canadian futurist Don Tapscott, author of *Paradigm Shift* and *The Digital Economy*:

> The Age of Networked Intelligence is an age of promise. It is not simply about the networking of technology, but about the networking of humans through technology. It is not an age of smart machines but of humans who through networks can combine their intelligence, knowledge and creativity for breakthroughs in the creation of wealth and social development . . .
> It is an age of vast new promise and unimaginable opportunity.[3]

From the perspective of a decade later, one can only say the jury is still out on the economic impact the Net is having on individual human lives. Certainly a great many jobs have been created through the emergence of Internet-based businesses. But because these jobs tend to be technologically assisted to a high degree and therefore, as Gilder points out, highly productive, they are necessarily fewer in number than the less productive jobs they replace. New info-tech jobs that do not require high skill and education levels, such as call centre support work, are now routinely farmed out to low-wage regions of the nation and the world. While this undoubtedly represents a desirable redistribution of the world's wealth, it nevertheless reduces employment opportunities for those who have lost jobs in developed nations due to the new technologies of communication that have made the new global corporation feasible. And many of the jobs that are provided are poorly paid, lacking in benefits and less than fulfilling.

Nevertheless, it is still early days for the Net and for computer automation. The Stanford University Center for Economic Policy in California has done intriguing research into the economic impact of the electric motor as a kind of template for what we might expect with the microprocessor. In examining the transition from steam to electric motive power in the U.S., the study concludes that it takes fifty to seventy-five years to thoroughly exploit the productive potential of a new technology. During the first half of the transition, economic performance and prosperity collapse before they go up. The really substantial benefits from new fundamental technologies do not show up until two-thirds of the way through the transition. Projecting these findings onto the integration of information technologies, which has been under way for some time now, the Stanford study suggests:

> Since the early 1970s U.S. productivity has improved very slowly and real wages have been falling as the nation's employers have struggled to get undertrained workers to generate improved performance with immature technologies. But by 2010 to 2015,

the U.S. will become a mature information-intensive economy and surpass the levels of general prosperity and upward mobility experienced during the 1950s and 1960s.[4]

Just how that prosperity (measured statistically as growth in GDP) will be distributed is a question the Stanford study does not address.

Network Society

Α S ALL TRANSFORMATION TECHNOLOGIES DO, the Internet is changing more than our economic environment— it is changing the way we perceive the world and our place in it. From the point of view of understanding the social change being provoked by new information technologies, "network society" may provide a better paradigm than "the information economy." The term was coined by sociologist Manuel Castells, who has spent many years looking into the social impact of information networks.[1]

Some of the features of network society are:

Globalization. While worldwide trade has been with us for centuries, it is only within the past thirty years or so that the backbone of the economy has been made up of corporations and institutions that carry on business on a planetary scale. Globalization means more than being able to get a Big Mac and watch CNN anywhere in the world; it is about a reordering of time and space made possible by communications technologies that permits complex action-at-a-distance in real time.[2]

Capital is by now thoroughly globalized through financial and currency markets and the operations of multinational corporations. While much labour remains local, in the form of factory and service work, an increasing number of jobs are also becoming globalized, as in the case of call centre operators and software technicians of all kinds. As Castells points out, this aspect of network society is characterized by an extremely uneven distribution worldwide. Whole regions and even continents are left out, as capital and jobs flow to areas of cheap skilled labour and welcoming tax structures and regulatory regimes. This is not simply a case of First World versus Third World; many of the areas excluded from the economic processes of network society are located cheek by jowl with centres of prosperity and power in the network economy. This is a "Fourth World," dominated by women and children. He warns of the "schizophrenia between two spatial logics," the virtual space created by instantaneous worldwide communication networks and the real space of places. In the first, anything seems possible; in the second, hope is replaced by despair.

The network enterprise. This includes, but is not confined to, the multinational corporation with subsidiaries, suppliers and workers all over the world. It takes in, as well, strategic alliances between corporations that form around a specific project and then dissolve. General Motors, for example, purchases key components of its small cars from Toyota; Apple Computer works with IBM to develop a new chip. It is the network enterprise—and in particular the modern business corporation—on which, increasingly, all other aspects of society are being modelled.

Wal-Mart is a prime example of the network enterprise. The world's largest retailer, it is also, in its own right, China's eighth largest trading partner. Its use of information technology is legendary: the temperature of every one of its more than 3,500 American stores is controlled from its headquarters in Bentonville, Arkansas; each cash register's purchases prompt inventory systems to reorder stock; logistics software keeps track of hundreds of thousands of shipments at home and abroad; and computers monitor workers' hours and productivity.

As global operations, network corporations can and do shift work from continent to continent in search of optimal cost/productivity locations. This has transformed the power relationships between capital and labour, dramatically weakening the organized labour movement and its impact on politics. Workers in industrialized societies who are self-employed, temporarily employed or part-time—who have, in other words, none of the security of income employment taken for granted by most twentieth-century workers—now account for roughly half the workforce. At the same time, however, the power and influence of network corporations has reached the point where they are able to successfully promote the rollback of traditional social security measures such as unemployment insurance and social assistance, and at the same time prevent implementation of new social welfare measures (such as, in the U.S., universal health care).

The result is that "most societies in the world, and certainly OECD countries, with the US and the UK at the top of the scale, present powerful trends towards increasing inequality, social polarization, and social exclusion. There is increasing accumulation of wealth at the top, and of poverty at the bottom."[3] The trend rides on a wave of ideology, but it is realized through information technology.

The transformation of work and employment. All manufacturing technologies, whether steam-driven or microprocessor-based, displace labour in one way or another; that is what they are designed to do. In displacing labour, they reduce costs to manufacturers, and these savings are eventually passed on to consumers as lower prices and to investors as increased earnings. In the past it has always been possible to argue, at least in principle, that everyone has benefited from labour-saving technologies, because the workers displaced were able to find new, often better jobs working in a new industry created by, or ancillary to, the technology that eliminated their former job.

For example, the introduction of electricity greatly reduced the need for manual labour throughout the economy, but it also created entire new industries directly related to electrical production (dam building, power distribution, turbine design, domestic and industrial wiring, and so on), as well as ancillary industries to manufacture electrical tools and appliances. The advent of the automobile and the consequent revolution in personal transport brought with it not just the car factory with its assembly-line jobs but also a boom in road construction and tourism and the development of the petroleum manufacturing and distribution industries. Jobs were lost in one sector but replaced, and then some, in others.

What makes network society's computer-based technology unique in this context is that it operates at a different level than the machine technologies of earlier industrial transformations. Like the mechanical clock, the computer is a technology that embodies an abstract idea—in this case, logic—and is able to operate autonomously. Get either device up and running and it will continue doing what you've asked of it indefinitely, until it runs out of energy. Like the clock, too, the computer operates in production processes at the level of *control*: control of processes and administrative control. But unlike the clock, the computer operates not just as a tool but as a *factor of production* as well. It does more than assist humans in controlling processes; it very often replaces humans. We are accustomed to machinery that replaces people in process jobs, for example the new robot on the assembly line, but we have very little experience with machines that replace people in administrative and control positions. Even the infamous time-and-motion specialist, with clipboard and stopwatch in hand, can be replaced by computer systems which automatically monitor workers' performances, and which can go beyond that to adjust the working environment in accordance with this input, to maximize productivity in a dynamic way.

No matter how sophisticated earlier labour-saving technology has been, it has always required human oversight to ensure its efficient operation. No longer. Computers and automated systems of today can often get the job done without human supervision, either on their own or by empowering customers. In the first case, think of telephone operators displaced by voice recognition technology, which can dispense information and handle long-distance telephone transactions; in the second, think of telephone auto-attendant systems which empower (or require, more properly) the caller to find the person being called without the intervention of a telephone receptionist ("If you know the person's name, press the first three letters . . ." etc.). Online banking, which allows the customer to fulfill the role of the bank teller, is another example of so-called customer empowerment, as is Federal Express's pioneering use of the Internet to allow customers to track their own parcels through the system without having to call FedEx telephone operators. Online shopping services are yet another. All of these computer-based technologies displace workers by getting customers, with a little help from microprocessors, to do the workers' jobs.

Computers, as we've seen, can control virtually any process for which formal operating procedures (algorithms) can be described and put down in a manual. And their cost goes down month by month. The clock in its time provided a necessary tool for the development of capitalism, permitting the efficient organization of the various factors of production, but today's computer-based information technology is the capitalist's ultimate dream. It is a key factor of production, whose price is more or less continuously falling in relation to performance.

There is no practical, foreseeable limit to the numbers of jobs that can be displaced by this new metatechnology. This is not to say that computers can handle any human function you can name; that is obviously not the case. What it does mean is that we cannot draw any meaningful boundary around the areas in which we can expect computer technology to be able to take over human job functions. There is no area of human endeavour in which computer-based technologies cannot fulfill at least some of the functions currently being handled by humans. "The role of humans in capitalist enterprise is clear," states Noah Kennedy.

Humans fill the roles in productive processes that are uneconomical to mechanize. This should not be a shocking statement, for if any of our jobs could be done at a lower cost by a machine there is no doubt that this would come to pass. Similarly, there is no doubt that each day technology closes in on new intellectual tasks that previously required human intelligence, which is just another way of saying that the task is being rationalized to the point that it can be reduced to formal description and performed by an algorithm. If there is not at this very moment someone formulating a plan for displacing all or part of your labor with machinery, then the sad fact is that you make too little money to make it worthwhile.[4]

British sociologist George Spencer, writing in the journal *Futures* before China exploded onto the consumer goods market and India became a major tech employment centre, linked concern about automation with trends in job migration to low-wage areas of the world:

This provides a perspective on the high-level policy initiatives to combat structural unemployment, and it opens the question of how radical such initiatives must become, if they are to have any real effect. Put crudely, we can try to make our labor as cheap as its competitors' overseas, but there is no hope of making it as efficient as many processes permeated by [computer-assisted technologies] already are, and as many others promise to become in a range of areas that defies quantification. And, in the context of the changing global division of labor, our chances of winning against the emerging combination of cheap labor *with* [computer-assisted technologies] are not good.[5]

Kennedy too finds cold comfort in the observation that, in past technological revolutions, displaced workers have always been reabsorbed into the economy.

Though admittedly it has always been difficult to imagine new types of labor that would rescue society from the technological displacement of the age, does anyone really have any reassuring concept of what meaningful role in production hundreds of millions of laborers can serve if the very pace and capacity of their thought is obsolete?[6]

The information technology programs that increasingly manage network society's business has a name; it is called Enterprise Resource Planning software (ERP). Two major developers are America's Oracle and Germany's SAP. It is designed to automate the management structures of large corporations, ensuring conformity to strict productivity guidelines. Thomas Davenport, author of corporate re-engineering texts, writes in *Mission Critical* that with ERP "there is no more hiding when performance is poor, and so no more *ex post facto* revisions."[7] Not only workers but managers, too, can be monitored through their interaction with their computer workstations.[8]

ERP software bears some striking similarities to an invention of the Utilitarian philosopher Jeremy Bentham (1748–1832). Bentham's "panoptic prison" was a twelve-sided polygon framed in iron and sheathed in glass, creating what Bentham called "universal transparency." Its design principles were widely adopted by prison builders of the nineteenth century in Europe and North America. In principle, a single guard in the hub of the wheel-like structure would be able to see into each of the cells radiating like spokes from the centre; prisoners would have no privacy, ever. That in turn would assure the automatic functioning of authority. As the French philosopher and sociologist Michel Foucault pointed out in his classic work *Discipline and Punish* (1979), the genius of the design is that, for the power of authority (management) to be exercised effectively, it is not necessary that the inmates (workers) be under constant surveillance, only that they know they *might* be being watched. In Foucault's words, "He who is subject to a field of visibility and who knows it, assumes responsibility for the constraints of power; he makes them play spontaneously upon himself . . . he becomes the principle of his own subjugation." The effect of this, in turn, is that authority (management) can evade the appearance of coercion. "It is a perceptual victory that avoids any physical confrontation and which is always decided in advance."9 For workers in ERP-enabled corporations, "the empowered computer that confronts the employee at the beginning of every working day is nothing less than Foucault's 'tall outline of the central tower from which he [the employee/prisoner] is being spied upon.'"10 Discipline is integrated into the "architecture" of the work environment, and by that means internalized and inscribed in the worker without the unpleasantness of overt punitive measures.

In the acres of cubicles of the call centre and other modern corporate workplaces "are digital assembly lines in which standardization, measurement, and control come together to create a workplace of relentless discipline and pressure."11 According to the sociologist Simon Head, in ERP we find "the outlines of a project truly Orwellian in its ambitions. The project is to develop technologies that are essentially human-proof in their operation, technologies whose control over employee behaviour is so powerful that, no matter how ill-trained, alienated, or transient a workforce may be, technology can still be relied upon to deliver strong and improving levels of employee productivity."12

In discussions of the broad sweep of historic changes in the economy, such as this one, the impact on individual human lives can easily be missed. Economist Heather Menzies has provided one representative story:

> Carol Van Helvoort works for the Pizza Pizza chain, processing orders from a computer and modem hooked up in the bedroom of a one-bedroom apartment on the fringes of Metro Toronto. It doesn't bother her that the computer monitors everything she does. What bothers her is that what she does is so little worth monitoring. For two four-hour chunks every day, she repeats the same few phrases again and again, and goes through the same few actions on her keyboard.
>
> She talked about the inconvenience of having the family phone line taken over for eight hours a day, as Pizza Pizza turns her home into a virtual workplace. She talked about how young mothers have had to get their kids to keep quiet. "But why should they? What does it do to family life?"
>
> She also worried about women's increased vulnerability in abusive relationships, going nowhere when they go to work; being trapped inside the home all the time.
>
> It was the loneliness and isolation that bothered her the most. She used to do her hair all the time; she used to do her nails, but now why bother? "You don't even bother getting dressed half the time," she said, as though she's disappeared that much as a social being.
>
> She'd quit tomorrow, she told me, "but there's nothing out there. If I want to work, I have to pay the price."[13]

Virtual culture. Culture in network society is increasingly organized around electronic media, from the cell phone, with its text messaging and photographic capabilities, to television. On one hand, this results in an incredibly diverse variety of offerings, available on demand. On the other hand, and for reasons dealt with earlier, broadcast media tend to degrade quality.

Interactivity is another feature of virtual culture in network society, and nowhere is it as welcome, perhaps, as in the dissemination of news and information where social and political elites have traditionally held a monopoly on delivery. There is clearly a continuing need for broadcast-style news delivered by professional journalists working under well-understood codes of conduct and style. But the ability to interact in something close to real time with information sources (to query, comment, challenge, suggest) encourages conversation as opposed to monologue, and in doing so promotes the communication of understanding as opposed to purely instrumental communication (see chapter 9). As "audiences" become less passive receptors and more active participants in shaping dialogue, understanding can only be improved.

Politics. Ever since universal distribution of television was achieved, sometime in the mid-twentieth century, the arena of politics has been defined by the media. In the era of broadcasting, this fact placed non-mainstream political expression at a severe disadvantage, because it was difficult to gain access to media. At the same time, the cost of doing politics, even for mainstream parties, became enormously inflated as political campaigns came to rely more and more on paid advertising. This need for political advertising, especially on television and radio, was driven in part by the failure of commercial broadcast media to give more than cursory coverage to campaign issues (See chapter 18). An environment had been created in which political parties were increasingly spoken of as "brands" to be "marketed" to the voters. In such an environment, the thirty-second commercial spot makes sense.

The Internet has provided substantial relief from these costs, offering a far less expensive and more flexible vehicle for political messaging. Moreover, the interactivity that characterizes the Net tends to promote forms of communication that facilitate understanding through dialogue. The other side of this coin is that scurrilous and inaccurate information is also more easily circulated on the Net than through traditional journalistic outlets. But on balance it would seem that there is more to be gained than lost. Costs associated with political organizing and fundraising are also dramatically reduced in the network environment. All of this has a tendency to increase political involvement, which is to say the ability of people to give political expression to their ideas and beliefs.

To the extent that increased political participation begins to resemble politics by referendum, it becomes a matter for concern. Traditionally, in liberal democracies, participation has been through elected representatives. Network society offers at least the possibility of a more direct democracy through continuous polling and flash votes, for example, which may or may not be a good thing. The U.S. constitution, it is worth recalling, was framed on the assumption that, in Walter Lippmann's phrase, "a mass cannot govern"—not without the mediation of an informed elite dedicated to public service. It can be argued that since the unprecedented pressures of work in network society leave little time for most citizens to reflect on complex political issues, the need for representation becomes more, not less, important, as a means both of explaining political issues to constituents and of representing the opinions of constituents in parliamentary assemblies.

Timeless time. Manuel Castells has proposed that a feature of network society is a new attitude to our understanding of time, which, after all, is a socially constructed concept. Time may be ordered according to laws imposed by the nature of the physical universe—by the phases of the moon, for instance, or rotation of the earth on its axis—but our perceptions of time are culturally conditioned by social institutions and technology. While we all have the subjective experience of time passing more slowly or quickly depending on our circumstances and activities, our technology (clocks) tells us otherwise. In the "timeless time" of the network society, Castells says, experience is ordered not as a stately progression of things but in the manner of randomly accessible information on a hard disk, there being nothing to distinguish past from present from future.

All dominant processes in network society tend to be ordered in this way, he says. "I find it certainly in the split-second financial transactions of global financial markets, but also I find it, for instance, in instant wars, built around the notion of a surgical strike that devastates the enemy in a few hours . . ." New medical technologies blur the human life cycle, with plastic surgery, drugs and reproductive technologies that extend the age and conditions for bearing children. Anti-aging nostrums line pharmacy shelves. Hospital machinery keeps death at bay indefinitely. In many jobs, hours of work are extended around the clock, 24/7. Seasons are obliterated in supermarkets, where fresh strawberries and asparagus can be had in the depths of winter. The wealthy avoid seasons altogether, following the sun. Entertainment of all kinds is available any time, on demand. "We live . . . all our tenses at the same time, being able to reorder them in a composite created by our fantasy or our interests."[14]

The space of flows. The proliferation of networks reduces to insignificance the space of places, or geographical space. Of significance now are flows of information, materials, products and people around the world. If we can think of space as being defined by the coexistence of things in time, then flows are what creates space in network society. "Things" still exist *together*, in the sense that they share time, but they may be located physically on opposite sides of the globe, interconnected in real time by network technology. When someone in France chats over the telephone or on the Net with a friend in New Zealand, where exactly does the conversation take place? Somewhere in the flow—in cyberspace.[15]

The geography of cyberspace is markedly different from that of physical places. It shrinks those places that are of no interest to network society, whose assets are not required. Flows of capital seek or avoid different physical locales and in so doing shape the space of places, by enriching or marginalizing them. Flows of other kinds of information tend to follow paths blazed by capital, further reshaping the physical world. The geography of cyberspace is the reality in which large corporations tend to live.

Castells believes that the major conflicts of our time are likely to involve the restructuring of time and space by network society and the conflicting world views that result. On the one hand we have the self-obsessed networks of capital and consumerism with their seemingly randomly accessible time; on the other, the linear, evolutionary time sequences of traditional peoples, the poor and environmentalists. Similarly, we have the space of flows of the information economy, inhabited largely by business corporations and financial institutions, versus the space of places, the physical spaces where most of us live, where culture is rooted and history is made. These tensions can and do result in conflict within cities, between countries and across continents. "We may be heading toward life in parallel universes whose times cannot meet."[16] There is a marked similarity here to the warnings of Jurgen Habermas about the drift in information society toward "the system" and its fundamentally inhumane ethic of mechanistic productivity and efficiency, in which function is preferred over meaning and instrumentality over experience.

One of the newer sources of resistance to the space of flows is a growing realization that networked globalism, while it can and does produce economic efficiencies, may also be creating instabilities that can lead to cascading technical breakdowns which spell disaster to societies dependent on these systems. An economic system in which all the slack has been squeezed out by efficiencies such as just-in-time delivery from suppliers is highly vulnerable to a myriad of technical glitches, any one of which can disrupt flows and, since there is no slack or excess capacity in the system, cause an immediate, domino effect in the closing of factories, supply shortages in the market and so on. As Thomas Homer-Dixon has pointed out, "as a system becomes more complex, it can become opaque to its managers. They might understand the bits and pieces they work on, but not what happens when all the bits and pieces interact together." This applies to both human and robotic, or software, managers. He uses as an example the 2003 blackout that left much of eastern North America without electricity, in some cases for days.

> Deregulation of the grid in the 1990s caused long-distance electricity sales to skyrocket, vastly increasing the connectivity and complexity of the whole electrical system. At the time of the blackout this system included six thousand power plants run by three thousand utilities overseen by 142 regional control rooms . . . In this environment, as one expert said, they needed the reflexes of "a combat pilot managing an aircraft that has been badly damaged" to cope with the grid's complexity and speed. Little surprise, then, that it eventually crashed.[17]

While such complexity may seem a natural application for sophisticated information software, and is, the point is that at no level of foreseeable sophistication will software programs be able to anticipate and head off *all* problems. And in a globally interconnected environment, the results of even one unforeseen accident can and frequently do have catastrophic consequences.

At some stage, and under any management regime, the benefits of the interconnectivity made possible by information technologies are outweighed by the potential for disaster. "Risk" is often defined by the formula *risk equals probability (of an accident) multiplied by consequences (of that accident)*. Thus, according to the formula $R = P \times C$, at some stage it becomes clear that no matter how small Probability is, the value assigned to Consequences will be high enough to make Risk unacceptably large. Determining that threshold level is a moral rather than a technical question, and therefore a matter not for experts but for the citizens who, after all, have to live with the consequences.

Looking back at the nineteenth-century machine age, Lewis Mumford painted a picture that is startling in its relevance to our own time of obsessive concern with the quantitative. He wrote:

> The leaders and enterprisers of the period believed that they had avoided the necessity for introducing values, except those which were automatically recorded in profits and prices. They believed the problem of justly distributing goods could be side-tracked by creating an abundance of them; that the problem of applying one's energies wisely could be cancelled out simply by multiplying them; in short that most of the difficulties that had hitherto vexed mankind had a mathematical or mechanical— that is a quantitative—solution. The belief that values could be dispensed with constituted the new system of values.[18]

In the age of information, the changes technology will bring to society will be determined by each of us, both by our deliberate actions and by our passive acquiescence in the actions of others, be they individuals or institutions, such as corporations and government agencies. We must never lose sight of the fact that information systems, for all their subtlety and flexibility, are built on machine logic, and that this logic is purely instrumental in its goals. The richness of human existence begins with the instrumental but extends far beyond it, into the realms of creativity and imagination, of conversation and learning, of charity and compassion. To the extent that we control our machines, we can use them to help create a world in which each of us has the time and space in which to pursue his or her uniquely human destiny. To the extent that we allow them to control us, we will slide into a world in which humans have become extensions of their machines, where productivity and consumption are the ultimate, and only, values.

Notes

Prologue: Extensions of Man

1. The terms "information technology" and "communications technology" are used more or less interchangeably throughout the book. While I recognize that there are important semantic differences between the two, in practical terms they amount to the same thing, for most purposes. I note as well that in academe, information theory and communication theory have identical roots. There can be no communication without information, and information, which is socially constructed, cannot exist without communication. Hence, the Age of Information might just as well be called the Age of Communication. Simple convention has persuaded me to use the former.

2. Neil Postman, *Amusing Ourselves to Death: Public Discourse in the Age of Show Business* (New York: Penguin Books, 1986), 161.

3. Postman, *Technopoly: The Surrender of Culture to Technology* (New York: Vintage Books, 1993), xii.

4. Ibid., 189–90.

5. Ibid., 161.

6. G.J. Mulgan, *Communication and Control: Networks and the New Economies of Communications* (Cambridge: Polity Press, 1991), 251.

7. Gene I. Rochlin, *Scientific Technology and Social Change* (New York: W.H. Freeman and Co., 1974), 149.

Part One: The Analog Era

Chapter 1: The Meaning of the Age of Information

1. This subject will be dealt with in more detail in chapter 29. A valuable source is N. Katherine Hayles, *How We Became Posthuman: Virtual Bodies in Cybernetics, Literature, and Infomatics* (Chicago: University of Chicago Press, 1999).

2. This reached its height with the fall of Byzantium (Constantinople), the surviving Eastern Roman Empire, to the Turkish army in 1453.

3. See Wade Rowland, *Galileo's Mistake* (Toronto: Thomas Allen & Son, 2001; New York: Arcade Publishers, 2003). The dispute centred on science's claim to definitive knowledge of the world, rather than Copernican orbital mechanics.

4. Nevertheless, Newton hung on to the ideas of divinity and the soul, and his God was not merely an impersonal First Cause or an indifferent creator—he was the God of the Bible, "the effective Master and Ruler of the world created by Him." It is God, by existing always and everywhere, who constitutes time and space.

5. Arthur Koestler, *The Trail of the Dinosaur* (Toronto: Macmillan, 1955), 245.

6. J.N.W. Sullivan, *The Limitations of Science* (New York: North American Library, 1949), 147.

7. Lewis Mumford, *Technics and Civilization* (New York: Harcourt, Brace and Co., 1930).

8. Ibid., 50–51.

Chapter 2: The Need to Communicate

1. For more on language as an innate ability, see Noam Chomsky, *Language and Problems of Knowledge* (Cambridge, MA: MIT Press, 1988).

2. Greek writing can be shown to have evolved from Semitic alphabets, which in turn grew out of Egyptian prototypes, but by incorporating phonetic indicators and vowel signs into the letters themselves, it made a leap so far beyond its predecessors that it is clearly different in kind rather than merely in degree.

3. Eric Havelock, *Preface to Plato* (London: Basil Blackwell, 1963), 200.

4. Northrop Frye, *The Great Code* (New York: Harcourt, Brace, Jovanovich, 1982), 7.

5. See also Lewis Mumford, *The Condition of Man*, ". . . the person is an emergent from society, in much the same fashion that the human species is an emergent from the animal world"; W.G. Greene, *Moira*, ". . . the

whole trend of Greek thought is from an external toward an internal conception of life"; Werner Jaeger, *Paideia*, ". . . other nations made gods, kings, spirits: the Greeks alone made men."

6. Eric McLuhan and Frank Zingrone, *The Essential McLuhan* (Toronto: Anansi, 1995), 241.

7. Ibid., 242–43.

8. Quoted in Elizabeth Eisenstein, *The Printing Press as an Agent of Change: Communications and Cultural Transformations in Early-Modern Europe*, vol. 1 (Cambridge: Cambridge University Press, 1979), 66.

9. See, in this connection, his *The Structural Transformation of the Public Sphere* (1962).

10. It is interesting to note that issues of format and industry standards were as important in the emerging railway networks as they are in modern communications technologies such as the videocassette recorder, the Internet, and digital radio and television. The earliest railways adopted a rail gauge of 4' 8", a distance probably inherited from early rut roads and adopted for coal wagons used in mines. The Great Western line from London to Bristol was built on a seven-foot gauge in 1841, for what were then, and remain, sound and sensible engineering reasons: it provided a smoother, more stable ride for rolling stock and could accommodate more powerful engines. But the need for networked railways to operate on the same rail gauge, and the fact that the narrower gauge had already become the industry standard, doomed wide-gauge to oblivion in Europe and North America despite its technical merits. The narrower gauge was granted legal status in Britain in 1846 and in the U.S. in 1885.

11. Jane Austen, *Emma* (Oxford: Oxford University Press, 1971 [1815]), 266–67.

12. Paul Johnson, *The Birth of the Modern* (London: Weidenfeld and Nicolson, 1991), 167.

13. Charles Babbage, the patron saint of modern computers, provided consulting services and may be responsible for the insight that the cost of delivering letters was influenced more by processing than by distance.

14. Harold A. Innis, *Empire and Communications* (Toronto: University of Toronto Press, 1972), 159. This represented an early victory for liberal, laissez-faire economic theory.

Chapter 3: Prelude to the Telegraph

1. George B. Dyson, *Darwin Among the Machines* (Cambridge, MA: Perseus Books, 1997), 132.

2. Geoffrey Wilson, *The Old Telegraphs* (New York: Philmore and Co., 1976), 20.

3. "Like spirits in the guise of mechanism" is strongly evocative of a later phrase often adduced in writings about communications technologies and the computer in particular: "The ghost in the machine." The latter was coined by British philosopher Gilbert Ryle, who used it in a discussion of claims for a human soul, the "ghost" in the "machine" of the human body. The strong sense that intelligence is somehow operating within complex technologies is especially prevalent where communications technologies are concerned, and might be attributed to the notion that these inventions are, in more than merely a metaphorical sense, "extensions of man," and are therefore closely identified with human attributes such as consciousness and intelligence.

4. Johnson, *The Birth of the Modern*, 166.

Chapter 4: The "Invention" of the Electron

1. Bern Dibner, *Ten Founding Fathers of the Electrical Science* (New York: Burndy Library, 1981), 37.

2. *The Book of Knowledge*, vol. 7 (New York: The Grolier Society, 1911), 2117.

3. It doesn't take a nuclear physicist to recognize that the properties of time and space are so intimate to an understanding of the universe that tinkering with them will require wholesale changes elsewhere in the theoretical construct. Thus, by the time Einstein had finished working through his idea of special relativity, he had come to the breathtaking conclusion that mass and energy were interchangeable, that one could be converted into the other, and that the relationship between them could be summed up in the famous equation $E=mc^2$.

4. *New York Herald*, May 30, 1844.

5. John Gribben, *Schrödinger's Kittens* (London: Weidenfeld and Nicolson, 1995), 18.

6. Werner Heisenberg, *Physics and Philosophy* (New York: Harper and Row, 1958), 41.

7. Niels Bohr, *Atomic Theory and Human Knowledge* (London: John Wiley, 1958), 62.

8. J.A. Wheeler, K.S. Thorne and C. Misner, *Gravitation* (New York: Freeman, 1973), 1273.

9. Quoted in M. Capek, *The Philosophical Impact of Contemporary Physics* (New York: Van Nostrand, 1961).

10. W. Thiring, "Urbausteine der Materie," *Almanach der Osterreichischen Akademie der Wissenchaften* 118 (1968): 160.

11. David Bohm and B. Hiley, *On the Intuitive Understanding of Non-locality as Implied by Quantum Theory* (London: Birkbeck College, University of London).

12. It will not have escaped the notice of some readers that quantum field theory bears a striking resemblance to the idea of *ch'i*, or life force, in Chinese traditions of Confucianism, Taoism and Buddhism. The neo-Confucian philosopher Chang Tsai said: "When the ch'i condenses, its visibility becomes apparent so that there are then the shapes [of individual things]. When it disperses, its visibility is no longer apparent and there are no shapes. At the time of its condensation, can one say otherwise than that this is but temporary? But at the time of its dispersing, can one hastily say that it is then non-present?" Those wishing to delve further into this area of convergence are directed to Fritjof Capra's *The Tao of Physics* and Gary Zukav's *The Dancing Wu Li Masters*.

Chapter 5: The Electric Telegraph

1. It is in this connection that the Internet, as a superior medium of communication among scientists and academics, has been called the greatest scientific tool of the twentieth century.

2. A fascinating variation on the telegraph was patented in 1843 by the Scotsman Alexander Bain. A predecessor to the scanning fax machine, it employed clockwork pendulums in the transmitting and receiving apparatus. The transmitting pendulum swung back and forth over raised metal type of the kind then used in newspaper printing, progressively scanning down the page. Whenever a needle attached to the pendulum was in contact with metal, current would be sent down the telegraph line. At the receiving end, this current would be transferred to a needle or fine brush on a second pendulum, which moved progressively down a sheet of paper treated with potassium iodide. The chemical turns brown when exposed to an electric current, and in this way the image presented by the type at the transmitter was faithfully reproduced. In 1865 the Italian physics professor Giovanni Caselli established the first commercial fax system, linking Paris with other French cities, using a modification of Alexander Bain's original device. He transmitted nearly five thousand faxes in the first year.

3. Letter from Samuel Morse to U.S. treasury secretary George M. Bibb, December 12, 1844. Morse was trying to convince the U.S. government to purchase rights to his invention.

4. Ibid.

5. Letter from Samuel Morse to U.S. treasury secretary McLintock Young, June 3, 1844.

6. G.W. Brock, *The Telecommunications Industry* (Cambridge, MA: Harvard University Press, 1981), 63.

7. Asa Briggs and Peter Burke, *A Social History of the Media: From Gutenberg to the Internet* (Cambridge: Polity Press, 2002), 143.

8. The San Francisco to New York rate was soon moderated to six dollars for the first ten words (which included place of origin, time and date), 75 cents per additional word.

9. An equivalent logic drives the current expansion of business on the World Wide Web: what is possible becomes necessary.

10. Daniel Czitrom, *Media and the American Mind* (Chapel Hill: University of North Carolina Press, 1982), 8.

11. Charles Briggs and Augustus Maverick, *The Story of the Telegraph and a History of the Great Atlantic Cable* (New York: Rudd and Carleton, 1858), 13.

12. Annie Ellsworth, daughter of the U.S. commissioner of patents, and a romantic interest, who was first to tell Morse that Congress had passed the bill supporting his test line from Washington to Baltimore.

13. Numbers 23:23.

14. Taliaferro P. Shaffner, "The Ancient and Modern Telegraph," *Shaffner's Telegraph Companion*, February 1854, 85.

15. Czitrom, *Media and the American Mind*, 11.

16. H.L. Wayland, "Results of the Increased Facility and Celerity of Inter-Communication," *New Englander*, November 1858.

17. David F. Noble, *Religion and Technology: The Divinity of Man and the Spirit of Invention* (New York: Penguin, 1999) and *Beyond the Promised Land* (Toronto: Between the Lines, 2004). See also Margaret Wertheim, *The Pearly Gates of Cyberspace* (New York: W.W. Norton, 1999).

Chapter 6: A Worldwide Web

1. W.F. Butler, *The Wild North Land*, quoted in Rosemary Neering's *Continental Dash* (Ganges, B.C.: Horsedal and Schubart, 1989).

2. *New York Times*, August 6, 1858.

3. Ibid.

4. Field's trials were not at an end. He lost most of his cable fortune speculating in stock of New York's Elevated Railway Company. His wife died soon after, and a son and daughter both succumbed to insanity. He died in his sleep in 1892.

5. Oliver Gramling, *AP: The Story of News* (New York: Farrar and Rinehart, 1940), 34.

6. Postman, *Amusing Ourselves to Death*, 65.

7. It must be admitted, however, that it is very difficult to know with certainty which pieces of random information will end up being of use to an individual and which will not. What seems irrelevant today may be relevant in the changed circumstances of tomorrow. Maine and Texas, *pace* Thoreau, certainly did have much to talk about on the eve of the American Civil War.

8. Postman, *Amusing Ourselves to Death*, 69.

9. "The Intellectual Effects of Electricity," *Spectator*, November 9, 1889.

10. W.J. Stillman, "Journalism and Literature," *Atlantic Monthly*, November 1891.

11. Czitrom, *Media and the American Mind*, 21.

12. A similar transformation had begun in Germany nearly twenty years earlier, and had spread through much of Europe.

Chapter 7: The Invention of the Modern Inventor

1. J.D. Bernal, *Science in History* (Cambridge, MA: MIT Press, 1971), 35.

2. Sir Desmond Lee, "Science, Philosophy and Technology in the Greco-Roman World," *Greece and Rome* 20 (1973): 70–71.

3. Arthur Koestler, *The Act of Creation* (New York: Pan Books, 1971), 267.

4. David F. Noble, *America by Design: Science, Technology and the Rise of Corporate Capitalism* (New York: Alfred A. Knopf, 1977), 34.

5. Ibid., 34.

6. Langmuir received the Nobel Prize for research into molecular films on solid and liquid surfaces. He was also responsible for significant improvements in both the light bulb and the vacuum tube.

7. Noble, *America by Design*, 118.

8. George Basalla, *The Evolution of Technology* (Cambridge: Cambridge University Press, 1988), 128.

9. I have dealt with corporate personhood and its ramifications in detail in *Greed, Inc.* (Toronto: Thomas Allen & Son, 2005; New York: Arcade Publishers, 2006).

10. Theodore Vail, quoted in N.R. Danielien, *AT&T: The Story of Industrial Conquest* (New York: Vanguard Press, 1979), 98.

11. L.H. Baekeland, "The U.S. Patent System, Its Uses and Abuses," *Industrial and Engineering Chemistry*, December 1909, 204.

12. Noble, *America by Design*, 108–9.

13. Rochlin, *Scientific Technology and Social Change*, 102.

Chapter 8: The Telephone

1. Elisha Gray to A.L. Hayes, Nov. 2, 1876; quoted in David A. Hounshell, "Elisha Gray and the Telephone: On the Disadvantages of Being an Expert," *Technology and Culture*, April 1975, 157.

2. Lloyd W. Taylor, "The Untold Story of the Telephone," *American Physics Teacher* 5 (1937).

3. The Western Union directors were not the only potential investors suffering from myopia. George Brown, founder of the *Globe* newspaper in Toronto (forerunner to the *Globe and Mail*), passed up an offer from Bell to purchase patent rights outside the United States. And Sir William Preece, the chief engineer to the British post office, reported to a House of Commons committee in 1879 that there was little need for telephones in Britain: "Here we have a superabundance of messengers, errand boys and things of that kind . . . if I want to send a message—I use a sounder or employ a boy to take it."

4. The Edison transmitter also used a small induction coil or transformer to step up the current leaving the carbon button before passing it along to the telephone line.

5. A similar authenticating effect was experienced a century later by the pioneering Apple Computer when the giant IBM decided, more than a little tardily, to enter the personal computer market.

6. Herbert Casson, *The History of the Telephone* (1910; reprint, Freeport, N.Y.: Books for Libraries Press, 1971), 66.

7. Quoted in Carolyn Marvin, *When Old Technologies Were New: Thinking About Electric Communication in the Late Nineteenth Century* (Oxford University Press, 1988), 80.

8. Ibid., 226.

9. Francis Jehl, *Menlo Park Reminiscences*, vol. 1 (Dearborn, MI, 1937), reprinted in *The Telephone, An Historical Anthology* (New York: Arno Press, 1977).

10. Western Electric operated a Canadian branch plant, called Northern Electric (incorporated in 1895), which provided the same services to Bell Canada as Western Electric did for the parent Bell company in the United States. In the 1920s and 1930s, Northern Electric branched out into consumer electronics, radio broadcasting apparatus and other lines of electrical equipment. In a 1956 consent decree negotiated with the U.S. Department of Commerce, Bell divested itself of its 40 percent interest in Northern Electric, which continued to grow. It would eventually be reorganized as Northern Telecom, and then Nortel Networks, one of Canada's largest corporations and one of the world's largest manufacturers of telecommunications equipment.

11. R.B. Hill, "The Early Years of the Stowger System," *Bell Labs Record* XXXI, 3 (March 1953): 95ff. The system, as developed by Stowger's Automatic Electric Company, required five wires, four for switching and one for talking. This was later reduced to three wires and ultimately two.

12. Communications from another planet seem to have been a persistent, if discreet, theme in turn-of-the-century engineering circles. Marconi is reported to have listened for signals from Mars aboard his yacht *Elettra*, no doubt provoked by spurious low-frequency radio signals that had many of the same qualities as telephone-line noise. H.G. Wells, who had begun his science fiction career in 1895 with *The Time Machine*, followed up in 1898 with *The War of the Worlds*, in which Mars invades Earth. It is now understood that the mysterious radio signals are generated by high-energy solar radiation acting on the earth's outer atmosphere.

13. Casson, *The History of the Telephone*, 121.

14. Much of the work done in clearing up distortion owes its success to early research done by the British scientist Oliver Heaviside, a brilliant but socially inept mathematician whom Norbert Wiener has described in *Invention* (Cambridge, MA: MIT Press, 1993) as "sincere, courageous, and incorruptible"—which no doubt accounts for the fact that he "was born poor, lived poor and died poor." Heaviside also made important discoveries in the propagation of radio waves by atmospheric phenomena.

Chapter 9: A Convivial Technology

1. As distinct, of course, from the telephone *company*, which does come in for its share of criticism, and more.

2. Ivan Illich, *Tools for Conviviality* (New York: Harper and Row, 1973), 23.

3. Ibid., 24.

4. Ibid., 23.

5. Ibid., 69.

6. Jurgen Habermas, *Theory of Communicative Action*, trans. T. McCarthy (Cambridge: Polity Press, 1984), 2:184. See also *The Theory of Communicative Action*, trans. T. McCarthy (Boston: Beacon Press, 1984), vol. 1. A good secondary reference is S.K. White, ed., *The Cambridge Companion to Habermas* (Cambridge: Cambridge University Press, 1995).

7. For a highly accessible introduction to these issues in Habermas, see George Myerson, *Heidegger, Habermas and the Mobile Phone* (Cambridge, UK: Icon Books, 2001).

8. *The Age of Access, Information Technology and Social Revolution*, posthumous papers of Colin Cherry, compiled and edited by William Edmondson (Cambridge: Croom Helm, 1985), 64.

9. McLuhan, *Understanding Media*, 238.

10. Steven Lubar, *Infoculture* (New York: Houghton Mifflin, 1993), 132.

11. Casson, *The History of the Telephone*, 159.

12. Quoted in McLuhan, *Understanding Media*, 240.

13. Ann Moyal, "The Feminine Culture of the Telephone: People, Patterns and Policy," in *Information Technology and Society*, ed. Nick Heap, Ray Thomas, Geoff Einon, Robin Mason and Hughie Mackay (Cambridge: Sage Publications/Open University, 1995), 303.

14. Statistics are from the UN's International Telecommunications Union: www.itu.int/ITU-D/ict/statistics/

15. Derrick de Kerckhove, *Connected Intelligence: The Arrival of the Web Society* (London: Kogan Page, 1998).

16. Orange press release, July 13, 2000.

Chapter 10: The Invention of Radio

1. Sir William Crookes, *London Fortnightly Review* (1892).

2. It is a continuing challenge. Lawyers at Bell Laboratories were initially unwilling even to apply for a patent on the laser, on the grounds that it had no possible relevance to the telephone industry. At that time (1966) the best transatlantic phone cable carried 138 simultaneous conversations. The first fibre optic cable (1988) could carry 40,000. Fibre cable of the 1990s carried 1.5 million simultaneous telephone conversations— thanks to the laser.

3. December 2, 1932. Marconi was then exploring the VHF and microwave reaches of the radio spectrum.

4. Cable interests were to merge with Marconi's company in 1928.

5. Degna Marconi, *My Father, Marconi*, 2nd ed. (rev.) (Toronto: Balmuir Book Publishing, 1982), 95.

6. It operated at a wavelength of about 182 kHz.

7. In 1919, a third Cape Breton station, erected at the site of Fortress Louisbourg, was linked with Letterfrack, Ireland, for the first transatlantic wireless voice—wireless telephony—connection.

Chapter 11: Radio Goes International

1. Gleason L. Archer, *History of Radio to 1926* (New York: American Historical Society, 1938), 64.

2. It was at this conference that the word *radio* was formally adopted to describe communication through space without wires. The word took some time to catch on in North America, and the British continued to use the word *wireless* until only very recently. The conference also adopted SOS as the international distress signal; it had no literal meaning, but was easy to remember and send in Morse ($\cdot\cdot\cdot---\cdot\cdot\cdot$).

3. To some extent this fallacy of limited spectrum carried over into late-twentieth-century attempts to restrict competition among cable specialty channels. The argument (from owners of existing channels) was that bandwidth limits of coaxial cable were substantially used up. New digital technologies significantly reduced bandwidth needs, and that, in combination with competition from digital satellite television, eventually opened the floodgates to new layers of "diginets" or digital specialty channels.

Chapter 12: How Radio Works

1. The purpose of the plates was to provide capacitance in the circuit, a primitive means of tuning the frequency of the radio waves emitted.

2. Hermann Weyl, *Philosophy of Mathematics and Natural Science* (Princeton, NJ: Princeton University Press, 1949).

3. As usual, Marconi was making an inspired adaptation of someone else's discovery. The coherer was invented by the Frenchman Édouard Branly (1844–1940). Its potential for radio communication was realized by the English physicist Sir Oliver Lodge (1851–1940). It was Lodge who gave the first public demonstration of wireless transmission and reception, at the Royal Institution in London in June 1894. On his ninety-fifth birthday, in 1939, irked by wartime propaganda on the radio, Branly said, "It bothers me to think I had something to do with inventing it."

4. George Shiers, in Gene I. Rochlin, ed., *Scientific Technology and Social Change* (San Francisco: W.H. Freeman and Co., 1974), 141.

5. Quoted in Archer, *History of Radio to 1926*, 141.

6. John S. Belrose, "Fessenden and the Early History of Radio Science," *Radioscientist* 5, 3 (September 1994).

7. Quoted in A.F. Harlow, *Old Wires and New Waves* (Boston: Appleton, 1928).

8. Ibid.

9. Quoted in Asa Briggs and Peter Burke, *A Social History of the Media* (Cambridge: Polity Press, 2002), 159.

10. Carneal, *Life of De Forest*, quoted in Archer, *History of Radio*, 100.

Chapter 13: Commodifying the Airwaves

1. Owen D. Young, former undersecretary of the navy, a vice-president at General Electric, later to become founding chairman of RCA, quoted in Archer, *History of Radio*, 164.

2. Within less than five years the alternators, in their turn, would be made obsolete by new high-power vacuum tubes for transmitters—but that, of course, was not anticipated at the time.

3. Details of the government's role in the birth of RCA were made public during U.S. government antitrust hearings that were reported December 1, 1923.

4. Fessenden's lawsuit against his former partners and RCA, which took over his patents, was settled out of court in 1925 for $500,000, of which $200,000 went to his lawyers (Belrose, "Fessenden and the Early History of Radio Science").

5. They were, after all, no strangers to the notion of oligopoly. General Electric, formed initially in the merger of Edison's electric light interests with the Thomson–Houston electric company in 1892, had been created as a means of pooling the two companies' patents to place the new corporate entity in an unassailable market position vis-à-vis smaller competitors. And in 1896, General Electric and Westinghouse had in turn called a truce in their war for dominance in the electrical equipment market. With more than three hundred patent suits outstanding between them, they agreed to pool their resources, with GE assigned 62.5 percent of the business flowing from the shared patents. Not only did the deal allow the two companies to get on with the business of making money rather than spending it on lawyers, it served once again to limit competition, giving GE and Westinghouse a shared monopoly that was almost

impossible to penetrate. The public interest of course took a back seat to corporate comfort in these competition-limiting sweetheart deals, and government, prodded by public protest, was to become increasingly engaged in what was referred to as "trust-busting."

6. Amateur radio would be officially sanctioned in international law for the first time at the international radio conference of 1927, at which time amateurs were given exclusive use of several small slices of the high- and very-high-frequency spectrum.

7. Just prior to and following World War II, the high-frequency spectrum began to be populated by international shortwave stations, most of them operated by national governments, and most of them maintained primarily for propaganda purposes. Shortwave outlets of the major powers, Voice of America and Radio Moscow, broadcast in scores of languages, carrying their governments' message to the far corners of the world. Often, high-quality educational, musical and dramatic programming was served up as well. Other, less bellicose voices were heard from the countries of Western Europe, Canada, the Antipodes and the Spanish-speaking world, and from the standard-setter, the BBC World Service. Of course, this kind of cross-frontier communication was decidedly unwelcome with autocratic regimes, and a major feature of the shortwave bands, until the end of the Cold War brought blessed relief, was the idiot roar of the high-powered "jamming" station, whose signals blanketed unwanted shortwave broadcasts and anything else in their vicinity.

Chapter 14: The First Mass Medium

1. Despite their compact of 1896 to share the market in heavy electrical equipment, there was no love lost between General Electric and Westinghouse. In the 1880s, when Edison was introducing his electric lighting systems, George Westinghouse was perfecting a superior system based on a patent of the legendary electrical genius Nicola Tesla. It used alternating current (AC) as opposed to the direct current (DC) employed by Edison. The battle that ensued between the two systems was one of the most vicious in American corporate history, with Edison's side claiming that AC was a danger to public safety. As part of their campaign, the DC proponents went so far as to have a Westinghouse AC system adopted as the official means of public execution in New York State. Edison himself, in a series of gruesome late-night experiments at Menlo Park, had several animals of varying sizes killed with alternating-current shocks to demonstrate the hazard. Word of the "top secret" experiments was carefully leaked to the press. In the end, Westinghouse won the war because it was a superior technology, and the company was given the contract to

develop Niagara Falls for hydroelectric power. Edison's GE had to sue for peace.

2. The great radio trust would break down through internal bickering by 1924. Two years of secret negotiations among the players resulted in a series of deals that had historic implications. AT&T withdrew from broadcasting to stick to its knitting—long-distance telephony—selling radio station WEAF to RCA for $1 million. The telephone company retained exclusive patent rights to two-way telephone services by both wire and radio, while GE and Westinghouse received rights to all AT&T and RCA patents related to radio. Once again, the positions of these corporate giants had been consolidated and rationalized into an effective oligopoly, and it had become more difficult than ever for competing interests to enter their markets. Following the agreement, RCA, Westinghouse and General Electric together formed a new broadcasting venture that would network their respective stations and supply them with daily programming; it was to be called the National Broadcasting Company, or NBC. In 1932 the oligopoly was somewhat diluted as a result of a U.S. federal antitrust consent decree.

3. Donald G. Godfrey, "Canadian Marconi: CFCF, the Forgotten First," *Canadian Journal of Communications* 8, 4 (September 1982): 56–71. In The Hague, Holland, station PCGE began broadcasting in November 1919, the first station on the air in Europe.

4. Ibid.

5. Archer, *History of Radio*, 201–2.

6. Samuel Kinter, *Proceedings of the Institute of Radio Engineers*, December 1932.

7. KDKA may not have been, strictly speaking, the first U.S. radio broadcasting station. Other contenders for that distinction are WWJ in Detroit, KCBS (which was born as KQY) in San Francisco and WHA (9XN) in Madison, Wisconsin. But, as has often been observed, when KDKA started up, broadcasting started up.

8. Rogers, a pioneering amateur radio operator as a youngster, became an important innovator in radio technology in general, and in vacuum tube technology in particular. His son would eventually head the huge Canadian media conglomerate Rogers Communications.

9. George H. Clark, quoted in Archer, *History of Radio*, 174. Shades of the Macintosh versus IBM/DOS debate!

10. Quoted in several sources, including Tom Lewis, *Empire of the Air: The Men Who Made Radio* (New York: Harper Perennial, 1991), 115–17.

11. The designer Sarnoff went to for his prototype receiver was former Marconi and now RCA scientist Dr. Alfred Goldsmith. A man no less visionary than Sarnoff himself, Goldsmith had in 1918 written a book about radio in which he characterized the new technology as "the ultimate extension of personality in time and space." This predated Marshall McLuhan's publication of *Understanding Media: The Extensions of Man* by nearly half a century.

12. *Radio Broadcast*, May 1922.

13. Ibid.

Chapter 15: Broadcasting's Pot of Gold

1. Reproduced in Archer, *History of Radio*, 257–58.

2. AT&T salesman H. Clinton Smith, long deceased, owns the dubious distinction of having sold this, the first radio commercial. His descendants, if they are aware of this fact, no doubt take comfort in the anonymity afforded by their surname.

3. Gleason Archer, *Big Business and Radio* (New York: American Historical Company, 1939), 305.

4. Stewart Ewan, *Captains of Consciousness: Advertising and the Social Roots of Consumer Culture* (New York: McGraw-Hill, 1976), 62.

5. Frank P. Arnold (director of development for NBC), *Broadcast Advertising: The Fourth Dimension* (New York: John Wiley and Sons, 1931), 41–42.

6. There were exceptions in which high-minded sponsors practised non-interference in program decisions, but instances of this were rare in the extreme and generally short-lived. As well, certain performers have attracted such a wide audience that they have been able to, as it were, speak to their audience over the heads of their sponsors. Once again, however, the relationship between the sponsor and the performer in such cases is so unstable as to be short-lived.

7. G.E.C. Wedlake, *SOS: The Story of Radio Communication* (Newton Abbot: David and Charles, 1973), 189.

8. Broadcasting in New Zealand was initiated on the same day.

9. Briggs and Burke, *A Social History of the Media*, 221.

10. Ibid., 223.

11. Ibid., 220.

12. Licence fees were dropped in 1953 in favour of financing directly from the public purse.

13. Among those rules was one imposed in 1971 with a view to encouraging the Canadian music industry while keeping American cultural content at bay. It required radio stations to play Canadian content at least half the time. Derided on all sides at first, it is now universally acknowledged to have been responsible for an unprecedented flourishing of the Canadian music industry and its subsequent international success. An attempt in 1952 to impose Canadian content quotas on radio stations had failed in the face of intense lobbying.

Chapter 16: Television: 1

1. Some sources give joint credit for the discovery to another TCMC employee, Joseph (or Louis) May.

2. U.S. FCC annual report 1941, 7, 22, 31, 41.

3. Where facsimile transmission did have a large economic impact was in telegraphy. Transmitting a fax of a message was both faster and more accurate than translating it into Morse. Western Union began serious development of the fax in 1935.

4. Jim Percy, quoted in Briggs and Burke, *A Social History of the Media*, 178.

5. Current North American and European standards use 535 and 625 lines per second respectively. The results obtained are very similar from a viewer's point of view, with the European picture being of slightly better definition and greater subtlety of colour. "High-definition" television is an all-digital system to which these analog standards are no longer relevant.

6. Quoted in Lewis, *Empire of the Air*, 106–7.

7. Some see in Microsoft Corp. the current inheritor of these time-honoured tactics. Microsoft describes its approach to dealing with individual software developers as "embrace and extend." For some, it is an unwelcome embrace.

8. Neil Postman, "Philo Farnsworth," *Time*, March 29, 2000.

9. Only Dumont Laboratories, partly owned by movie giant Paramount, continued to broadcast throughout the war.

10. Briggs and Burke, *Social History of the Media*, 236.

Chapter 17: Television: 2

1. Quoted by Neil Postman in "Philo Farnsworth," *Time*, March 29, 2000.

2. Quoted in Derrick De Kerckhove, *The Skin of Culture* (Toronto: Somerville House, 1995), 14.

3. Postman, *Amusing Ourselves to Death*, 128.

4. A summary of the physiological impact of television viewing can be found in De Kerckhove, *The Skin of Culture*, 9ff.

5. Robert Kubey and Mihaly Csikszentmihalyi, "Television Addiction is No Mere Metaphor," *Scientific American*, Feb. 2002, 77–78.

6. Ibid., 76.

7. Ibid., 77.

8. Roger Parloff, "Is Fat the Next Tobacco? For Big Food the Supersizing of America is Becoming a Big Headache," *Fortune*, February 21, 2003. Available online at www.fortune.com/fortune/articles/0,15114,409670,00.html. A useful analysis of the most recent research into addictive qualities of foods, and links to papers by scientists prominent in the field, can be found at the British United Provident Association (BUPA) website: www.bupa.co.uk/health_information/html/health_news/190703addic. html.

9. F.B. Hu, T.Y. Li, G.A. Colditz, W.C. Willett and J.E. Manson, "Television watching and other sedentary behaviors in relation to risk of obesity and type 2 diabetes mellitus in women," *JAMA* 289 (2003): 1785–91; F.B. Hu, M.F. Leitzmann, M.J. Stampfer, G.A. Colditz, W.C. Willett and E.B. Rimm, "Physical activity and television watching in relation to risk for type 2 diabetes mellitus in men," *Arch Intern Med.* 161, 12 (June 25, 2001): 1542–48.

10. Reported in the *Proceedings of the National Academy of Sciences*, January 2001.

11. Quoted in the *Daily Telegraph* (London), January 8, 2001.

12. G.A. Comstock and H. Paik, "The effects of television violence on anti-social behavior: A meta-analysis," *Communication Research* 21 (1994): 516–46.

13. An increasing proportion of these "movies" never see the big screen, being released directly into the VCR market. As a rule, they are distinguished not by superior quality to television fare, as are many motion pictures, but by their willingness to traverse boundaries of taste in sex and violence in ways that would not be tolerated by on-air television regulators.

14. Not all "integration" is about a product, or even a brand. Two episodes of the Warner Brothers Network show *Dawson's Creek* integrated breast cancer into the plotline as part of a wider public service information project undertaken by sponsor Gillette, which included a print ad campaign in half a dozen magazines (*Entertainment Marketing Letter*, April 15, 2003).

15. "In a rare interview, Lauren Bacall appeared on the NBC 'Today' program in March [2002], telling Matt Lauer about a good friend who had gone blind from an eye disease and urging the audience to see their doctors to be tested for it.

   "'It's just—it's frightening because it—it can happen very suddenly,' she said. Ms. Bacall then mentioned a drug called Visudyne, a new treatment for the disease known as macular degeneration. She never revealed that she was being paid to tell the story, and neither did the network, NBC.

   "'We compensated her for her time,' said Dr. Yvonne Johnson, medical affairs director for the ophthalmics division of Novartis, the Swiss drug maker that sells Visudyne. Novartis chose Ms. Bacall for its marketing campaign, Dr. Johnson said, because she appeals to many people over fifty, the primary market for the drug.

   "'We realized people would accept what she was telling them,' said Dr. Johnson, who declined to say how much Ms. Bacall had been paid. 'Our whole intent is to let people know they don't have to go blind.'" (*New York Times*, August 11, 2002)

16. *Tyndall Report*, December 31, 1996.

17. Chuck Ross, "Ailes sets out to lead Fox into news business," *Advertising Age*, July 1, 1996, 71.

18. Michael Perelman, *Class Warfare in the Information Age* (New York: St. Martin's Press, 1998), 93.

19. I freely acknowledge that the BBC has had its share of censorship scandals and other programming outrages. I am speaking here in generalities, hoping to make a broader point. Public financing of television is certainly no guarantee against stupidity or cowardice in management, but then neither is commercial sponsorship, and it has a great many additional problems.

20. For more on the networks' convergence strategies, see chapters 28 and 29.

21. Roper-Starch Worldwide, December 1998.

22. The BBC, demonstrating that public institutions can be leaders in innovation, was by 2005 offering an array of Web/TV convergence features to its viewers. High-definition programming is available for viewing on demand for a week after initial airing, in formats ranging from standard television to mobile phones. News, sports, music reviews and other content is offered as RSS (Really Simple Syndication) feeds that allow the viewer to forward the programs. Other programs are being distributed in MP3 format for use on iPods. Portions of the corporation's enormous archives are being made available under a new Creative Archive Licence

to artists who want to rip, mix, and reuse music and video. (*Wired*, September 2005, 117)

Chapter 18: The Politics of Media

1. As reported by Peter Schwartz in *Wired*, November 1993, 64.

2. The new frequencies opened up were from 135.5 to 550 kHz, which is the bottom of today's AM broadcast band. Much more bandwidth was clearly available, but its use would have required building and marketing a new generation of receivers capable of tuning the higher frequency ranges.

3. It was a thoroughly modern radio design, built on an engineering foundation provided by Reginald Fessenden. Armstrong sold his patents for the "superhet" receiver to Westinghouse in 1920, but it was not until 1924 that the first home receivers were put on the market, and they were manufactured by RCA under the newly minted cross-licensing agreement with Westinghouse. Their more complex circuitry made them more expensive than the crystal sets and regenerative receivers then widely in use, but they would eventually take over the entire market because of their superior performance. Armstrong didn't stop there: he went on to invent and perfect FM radio.

4. R. Bierstedt, *Émile Durkheim (Life and Thought)* (London: Weidenfeld and Nicolson, 1969); Émile Durkheim, *The Division of Labour in Society* (London: Macmillan, 1933).

5. Hannah Arendt, *Between Past and Future: Eight Exercises in Political Thought* (New York: The Viking Press, 1968), 235.

6. Habermas, *Theory of Communicative Action*, 2:186.

7. Noam Chomsky and Edward S. Herman, *Manufacturing Consent* (New York: Pantheon Books, 1988), 1–2.

8. For more on the corporation and its impact on media, see my *Greed, Inc.* (Toronto: Thomas Allen & Son, 2005; New York: Arcade Publishers, 2006).

Part Two: The Digital Era

Chapter 19: "Reasoning Is But Reckoning"

1. Money is another digital system, as Karl Marx observed: "Since money does not disclose what has been transformed into it, everything, whether a commodity or not, is convertible into gold. Everything becomes saleable and purchasable. Circulation is the great social retort into which everything is thrown and out of which everything is recovered as crystallized

money . . . Just as all qualitative differences between commodities are effaced in money, so money, a radical leveller, effaces all distinctions." It is interesting to note the similarities between the conversion of economic value into money as Marx describes it and the conversion by digital technology of media content into an undifferentiated commodity called information, which can be stored, transferred and manipulated as symbols. Marx notes: "Money itself is a commodity, an external object, capable of becoming the private property of an individual." He goes further to observe: "Thus, social power becomes private power in the hands of a private person." The same could be said of information.

2. Thomas Hobbes, *Leviathan* (Cambridge: Cambridge University Press, 1991), 31.

3. René Descartes, *Meditations on First Philosophy*, in *Philosophical Works of Descartes*, ed. Elizabeth S. Haldane and G.R.T. Ross, vol. 1 (Cambridge: Cambridge University Press, 1967).

4. Letter to Henry Oldenburg, December 18, 1675, quoted in *The Correspondence of Isaac Newton*, ed. H.W. Turnbull, vol. 1 (Cambridge: Cambridge University Press, 1959), 401. I am indebted for this source and the two that follow to George B. Dyson's fascinating book *Darwin Among the Machines: The Evolution of Global Intelligence* (Cambridge, MA: Perseus Books, 1997).

5. Quoted in Henry Rosemont Jr. and Daniel J. Cook, trans. and ed., *Discourse on the Natural Theology of the Chinese*, monograph of the Society for Asian and Comparative Philosophy, no. 4 (Honolulu: University of Hawaii Press, 1977), 158.

6. "This [binary] calculus could be implemented by a machine (without wheels) in the following manner, easily to be sure and without effort. A container shall be provided with holes in such a way that they can be opened and closed, they are to be open at those places that correspond to a 1 and remain closed at those that correspond to a 0. Through the opened gates small cubes or marbles are to fall into tracks, through the others nothing. It [the container or gate array] is to be shifted from column to column as required." From a 1679 manuscript quoted in Dyson, *Darwin Among the Machines*, 37.

7. Quoted in D.E. Smith, ed., *A Source Book in Mathematics*, vol. 1 (New York: Dover, 1929), 180–81.

8. Boole's logic in fact obeyed all of the ordinary laws of algebra with just one exception, that being that in logic $x^2 = x$, whereas in algebra this is not the case. That is, in algebra it is not true that every x is equal to its square, whereas in Boolean logic it is true. In ordinary English the equation

$x^2 = x$ simply means that the class of all things common to a class x and to itself is simply the class x.

9. Noah Kennedy, *The Industrialization of Intelligence* (New York: Unwin Hyman, 1989), 75.

Chapter 20: The Amazingly Precocious Charles Babbage

1. He had an early and instrumental connection with Leibniz. As a young student at Cambridge University, Babbage was part of a movement to shake British mathematics out of a stultifying insularity and force it to recognize the stimulating work being done on the Continent and in particular in France. He and his fellow radicals were especially insistent on recognizing that the differential calculus notation of Leibniz, used in most of Europe, was much superior to that of Newton, stubbornly clung to in England for mainly patriotic reasons.

2. Johnson, *The Birth of the Modern*, 543.

3. Charles Babbage, *On the Economy of Machinery and Manufactures* (London: John Murray, 1846), 191–92.

4. The formula is a famous one, and speaks of Peel's erudition. It is a prolific generator of prime numbers (numbers that can be divided only by themselves), discovered by Leonhard Euler, eighteenth-century Swiss mathematician and pupil of Jakob Bernoulli.

5. The basic principle used by Babbage's Difference Engine is a simple one, adapted from an error-checking system conceived by Prony to validate results produced by his army of human calculators. The table below has been set up for the calculation of squares (a number multiplied by itself), but similar, more elaborate tables can be made for any computation that progresses by regular increments.

A number	B square	C difference	D 2nd difference
1	1		
		3	
2	4		2
		5	
3	9		2
		7	
4	16		2
		9	
5	25		

In Prony's case, if the "differences" followed their expected sequences, it was assumed the numbers that created them were also accurate. Babbage used the system in reverse. To get his Difference Engine to calculate and print a table of squares like the one represented by columns A and B above, he would set the wheel on the "number" shaft of his machine to 1, the wheel on the "first difference" shaft to 3 and the wheel on the "second difference" shaft to 2. The first turn of the crank would print a "1" (the square of 1). The next crank would add 3 to the 1, printing "4" (the square of 2), while at the same time adding 2 to 3 (the first and second differences) to produce a 5, which was stored in the middle shaft. The next crank would add 4 plus the stored 5 and print the result of "9" (the square of 3), while at the same time adding 2 to 5 (first and second differences) to produce and store the number 7. The next turn of the crank would add 7 to 9 for "16" (the square of 4) while adding and storing 2 plus 7—and so on. The numbers would be transferred from shaft to shaft by means of carefully calibrated gear teeth.

6. Doron D. Swade, "Redeeming Charles Babbage's Mechanical Computer," *Scientific American* 286, 2 (February 1993): 86. It is on view at the National Science Museum in South Kensington, London.

7. Charles Babbage, *Passages from the Life of a Philosopher* (New Brunswick, NJ: Rutgers University Press, 1994), 81.

8. Ada was only a few months old when her parents separated in one of the century's most famous scandals and Byron left England forever. The poet was angry and bitter to his death over losing his daughter. He opened the third canto of *Childe Harold's Pilgrimage* with the lines:

> Is thy face like thy mother's, my fair child!
> Ada! sole daughter of my house and heart?
> When last I saw thy young blue eyes they smiled,
> And then we parted—not as now we part,
> But with a hope.

As he lay dying in exile in Missolonghi, he said to his valet, "Oh my poor dear child!—my dear Ada! my God, could I but have seen her!" Ada specified in her will that she was to be interred in the family crypt beside her father.

9. Correspondence quoted in Maboth Moseley, *Irascible Genius: A Life of Charles Babbage, Inventor* (London: Hutchinson, 1964), 221.

10. Lady A.A. Lovelace, in "Sketch of the Analytical Engine Invented by Charles Babbage," *Notes upon the Memoir* by I.F. Manabrea (Geneva, 1842), reprinted in P. and E. Morrison, *Charles Babbage and His Calculating Engines*.

11. Ibid.

12. Babbage's son Henry completed parts of the Analytical Engine from his father's drawings in 1906 and used it to print multiples of pi to twenty-nine places as a test. It performed flawlessly.

13. Adrian Desmond and James Moore, *Darwin* (London: Michael Joseph, 1991), chapter 15.

14. Philip Mirowski, *Machine Dreams: Economics Becomes a Cyborg Science* (Cambridge: Cambridge University Press, 2002), 37ff.

Chapter 21: The Secrets of Automatic Formal Systems and the Enigmatic Alan Turing

1. The British decoding efforts were given a head start by Polish mathematicians Henryk Zygalski, Jerzy Rozyki and Marian Rejewski, who, assisted by French intelligence officers, were able to narrow the scope of the trial-and-error search. The work had begun as early as 1928, when Polish customs officials intercepted a German Enigma machine. For a concise and fascinating account of the technical aspects of the Enigma/Ultra saga, see Dyson, *Darwin Among the Machines*, 63–67.

2. Andrew Hodges, *Alan Turing, the Enigma of Intelligence* (London: Burnett Books, 1983), 496.

Chapter 22: The Computer Comes of Age

1. Vacuum tubes performed the same on-off function as electromechanical switches, but at electronic, rather than mechanical, speeds.

2. The world first learned of this in the 1970s when secret information was declassified under Britain's thirty-year secrecy rule. Colossus was designed by Thomas Flowers, S.W. Broadhurst and W.W. Chandler with assistance from Alan Turing and M.H.A. Newman.

3. The Macintosh PowerBook that this book was written on weighs five pounds, is about a million times faster than ENIAC and has about a million times as much storage. It cost less than a used car or a large kitchen appliance and can run for about two hours on a rechargeable battery that I can slip into a shirt pocket. A six-year-old child would have no difficulty handling most of its operations.

4. Herman Goldstine, *The Computer from Pascal to von Neumann* (Princeton, NJ: Princeton University Press, 1972), 86.

5. Details of Mauchly's security ordeal were first made public in Stan Augarten's *Bit by Bit* (New York: Ticknor and Fields, 1984), Appendix 1, 289.

6. *Life*, February 25, 1957.

7. A UNIVAC machine was used by the CBS television network as part of its coverage of the 1952 Stevenson–Eisenhower presidential election, the first time a computer had been used in journalistic coverage of a major event. With only 7 percent of the vote tallied, the UNIVAC predicted a landslide victory for Eisenhower. CBS producers, however, were reluctant to believe it and asked that it be reprogrammed. This time it predicted a result that was too close to call. In the event, of course, the initial prediction was proved to have been accurate.

8. Cherry, *The Age of Access*, 66.

9. Paul Edwards, "Close World: Systems Discourse, Military Policy and Post World War II Historical Consciousness," in *Cyborg Worlds: The Military Information Society*, ed. Les Levidow and Kevin Robins (London: Free Association, 1989), 149.

10. Simon Lavington, *Early British Computers* (Digital Press, 1980), 104.

Chapter 23: Information and Cybernetics

1. Norbert Wiener, *Cybernetics, or Control and Communication in the Animal and the Machine* (Cambridge, MA: MIT Press, 1961), 26.

2. Pulse code modulation was one of them. See chapter 8.

3. Information can thus be measured or quantified statistically by the number of yes/no questions that need to be answered to resolve uncertainty.

4. Norbert Wiener, *The Human Use of Human Beings*, 2nd ed. (New York: Doubleday, 1954), 33.

5. Mirowski, *Machine Dreams*, 63.

6. Norbert Wiener, *God and Golem* (Cambridge, MA: MIT Press, 1964), 92.

7. Ibid.

8. Claude Shannon and Warren Weaver, *Mathematical Theory of Communication* (Urbana: University of Illinois Press, 1949).

Chapter 24: The Prodigal Semiconductor

1. The reason for this is not difficult to explain in terms of holes and electrons and their properties. Connect the battery one way, with its negative terminal in contact with the *n* side of the silicon sandwich, and holes will be attracted from the *p* side toward the diode's depletion zone and through it. At the same time the battery's positive terminal, wired to the *p* side of the device, will attract electrons from the *n* side toward the depletion zone and across it, going the other way, and in this way a current

will flow in both directions. If the battery connection is reversed, its negative pole (now hooked up to the *p* side) will attract positively charged holes *away* from the depletion zone to one end of the diode, and its positive pole will attract negatively charged electrons *away* from the depletion zone to the other end of the device. The depletion zone has now become so wide a barrier that the diode is effectively neutralized and will act as an insulator (or very high resistance); no current will flow in this direction. It is as if the depletion zone in the transistor becomes a powerful suction device when the battery is hooked up one way, drawing current through itself in both directions, and behaves like an equally powerful blower when the battery terminals are reversed, preventing current from leaving the battery to enter the transistor.

2. It is relatively easy to understand the way a transistor amplifies if it is thought of as two diodes connected back to back, i.e., in series. The three zones of doped material that result are called the emitter (*p*), base (*n*) and collector (*p*). In a *pnp* transistor (*pn* + *np* diodes), a current of holes can be made to flow from the emitter to the base by the application of a small *positive* voltage or "bias," as in the case of the diode described above. If, as well, a small *negative* voltage is applied to the base-to-collector section of the transistor, the depletion zone in that region becomes an effective barrier to electron flow, but a powerful attractor of holes. Therefore holes from the base join holes from the emitter in flowing into the collector, as a tributary would join a river. In other words, a current beginning in the emitter is added to by the current arising in the base, and the two merge to flow out of the base to the collector: the original emitter current has been *amplified* by the time it reaches the collector. The extra energy has come from the batteries supplying the bias voltages. A weak radio or audio signal applied to the emitter can thus be stepped up several orders of magnitude by the time it leaves the transistor at the collector.

3. John von Neumann, "Defense in Atomic War," *Journal of the American Ordinance Association* (May–June 1956), 1090.

Chapter 25: Robert Noyce and the Integrated Circuit

1. Jack Kilby of Texas Instruments filed for a patent on an integrated circuit device of his invention several months earlier than Noyce. However, the U.S. Patent Office ruled that his description of the method for providing interconnections between components on the chip was not adequate, and gave the patent to Noyce. A ten-year lawsuit ensued, which Noyce won. The idea of an integrated circuit within a semiconductor chip was first proposed in public by the English engineer G.W.A. Drummer, in

1952, who worked on the idea on a contract from the Royal Radar Establishment.

2. It was a four-bit chip running at about sixty thousand operations per second. RAM, ROM and the input-output chip were external to the CPU chip.

3. Stan Augarten, *Bit by Bit—An Illustrated History of Computers* (New York: George Allen and Unwin, 1984), 265.

4. The first eight-bit chip, capable of processing data eight bits (binary digits) at a time. Intel also produced the first commercial sixteen-bit microchip, the 8086.

5. Tom Wolfe, "The Tinkerings of Robert Noyce," *Esquire*, December 1983, 346–74.

6. Stephen A. Campbell, *The Science and Engineering of Microelectronic Fabrication* (Oxford: Oxford University Press, 1996), 3.

7. Ibid., 491.

Chapter 26: The Personal Computer

1. Michael Shallis, *The Silicon Idol: The Micro Revolution and Its Social Implications* (Oxford: Oxford University Press, 1984), 95.

2. The dwarves being Sperry Rand, Control Data Corp., Honeywell, RCA, NCR, General Electric and Burroughs.

3. Steven Levy, *Hackers: Heroes of the Computer Revolution*, rev. ed. (New York: Penguin Books, 1994), 40–45.

4. Communism, we may note from the perspective of the century's end, appears to have done its worst and expired. Corporate capitalism has shown a sobering and unacceptable ruthlessness through a decade of downsizing and other forms of active disengagement from its responsibilities to the labour force and the broader community.

5. Quoted in Levy, *Hackers*, 431.

6. Roberts was assisted in the design by two former air force colleagues, engineers William Yates and Jim Bybee.

7. Rick Prelinger in a posting to Computer Memory forum.

8. Jean-Louis Gassé, *The Third Apple*, trans. Isabel L. Leonard (New York: Harcourt Brace Jovanovich, 1987), 25, 27.

9. The designers had the benefit of having seen leading-edge research into interface design being done at Xerox's Palo Alto Research Center (PARC).

10. Internet posting by Rod Perkins, Lisa interface designer, CPSR (Computer Programmers for Social Responsibility) Mail Digest 17. Perkins

also notes that in June 1979, Xerox PARC visits by Apple employees created enthusiasm for the mouse as an interface device.

11. Ibid.

Chapter 27: A Digital Mardi Gras

1. Bruce Sterling, in a speech to the National Academy of Sciences, Convocation on Technology and Education, Washington, D.C., May 10, 1993.

2. Howard Rheingold, "The Future of Democracy and the Four Fundamentals of Computer-Mediated Communication," paper delivered to *Ars Electronica*, Linz, Austria (1994).

3. RAND (Research and Development) was the successor to the U.S. Air Force's Project RAND, intended to create an environment for creative academics to contribute to national defence issues, especially intercontinental warfare.

4. A 1960 RAND report, "Cost of a Hardened, Nationwide Buried Cable Network," placed the cost of providing a system of two hundred linked communication hubs with 1,000 psi blast survivability at $3.4 billion in 1960 dollars. It was designed to provide "minimum essential communication" in the event of nuclear war, which meant being able to transmit the president's order to either "fire" or "stop." Baran's eventual solution to the problem would provide vastly more communication capability, more reliably, at a fraction of the cost.

5. Baran seems to have been among the earliest advocates of an "information highway." One of his recommendations in "On Distributed Communications" is for a national public utility to transport computer data, much in the same way as the telephone system handles voice data. "Is it time now to start thinking about a new . . . public utility," Baran asks, "a common user digital data communication plant designed specifically for the transmission of digital data among a large set of subscribers?" For a fascinating interview with Baran, see "Founding Father," *Wired*, March 2001. The interview is archived at http://www.wired.com/wired/archive/9.03/baran.html.

6. J. Abate, *Inventing the Internet* (Cambridge, MA: MIT Press, 1999).

7. Paul Baran, "Summary Overview" of *On Distributed Communications*, RAND Corporation Memorandum RM-3767-PR, Aug. 1964, 1.

8. Paul Baran, *Reliable Digital Communications Systems Utilizing Unreliable Network Repeater Nodes*, RAND Corporation Memorandum P-1995, 27, May, 1960, 1–2.

9. Baran, *On Distributed Communications*, vol. 9, v.

10. Dyson, *Darwin Among the Machines*, 152. Baran's system was never built, due largely to continued opposition from AT&T.

11. ARPANET Completion Report Draft, unpublished (September 1977), 111–24. Quoted in Michael Huber, "Behind the Net: The Untold Story of the ARPANET," WWW document (1995).

12. ARPANET Completion Report Draft, 111–21. The quotation is from Robert Taylor, Licklider's successor at ARPA.

13. Work was also being done independently in the U.K. at the National Physics Laboratory by Donald Davies and colleagues, and the world's first operational packet-switching network went on stream there in 1968. Davies coined the term "packet switching" as an abbreviation for Baran's "adaptive message clock switching." Another early packet-switching experiment was conducted by the Swiss firm Société Internationale de Télécommunications Aéronautiques in 1968–70.

14. The initial plan for the ARPANET was distributed at the October 1967 Association for Computing Machinery (ACM) Symposium on Operating Principles in Gatlingberg, Tennessee. The initial design called for networking four sites. The first ARPANET Information Message Processor (IMP), or gateway computer, was installed at UCLA on September 1, 1969.

15. J.C.R. Licklider and Albert Vezza, "Applications of Information Technology," *Proceedings of the IEEE* 66 (11) 1330 (1978).

16. Brian Reid, Usenet posting, 1993.

17. Ibid.

18. According to Paul Baran, there was at the time an almost universal agreement among defence researchers that as much information about American command and control capabilities as possible should be made public. It was widely recognized among scientists involved in the field, Baran has said, that it was in everyone's best interests that the Soviet Union have the best possible control over its nuclear arsenal. See "Founding Father," *Wired*, March 2001 (see note 279 for Web archive).

19. Steve Crocker, RFC 3 (1969).

20. Robert Braden, RFC 1336.

21. Vinton Cerf, Internet newsgroup posting (1995).

22. Ibid.

Chapter 28: How the Net Became a Mass Medium:
           Hypertext and Browsers

1. Chat areas of BBSs, like those provided today on AOL and other large Internet service providers, were typically open forums in which participants could meet and exchange messages in public before moving "off-line"

to private communication accessible only to themselves. They have been largely replaced by instant messaging software. As might be expected, the anonymity provided by the chat environment tends to make conversation in chat areas somewhat less inhibited than in real-life meetings between strangers. It might be compared to the masked balls of bygone days.

2. The first transatlantic telephone cable, installed in 1966, was capable of carrying 138 simultaneous telephone conversations. The fibre optic transatlantic cable opened in 1990 carries 1.5 million simultaneous conversations.

3. Interview with Gary Wolf in *Wired*, October 1994, 150.

4. Kevin Kelly, *New Rules for the New Economy: 10 Radical Strategies for a Connected World* (New York: Viking, 1998), 60.

5. A portal site is the default opening site selected by the user's browser whenever it is launched. Microsoft of course pre-set its Internet Explorer web browser to select the company's own portal (as did Netscape). This setting could be changed with a few keystrokes, but a majority of users didn't bother, or didn't wish to go to the trouble. Microsoft, Netscape, AOL, Yahoo! and a handful of search engines dominated this increasingly important market niche. In a wave of "portal mania" in early 1999, Disney and Infoseek (a search engine) combined to form SEEK; NBC and Cnet formed Snap; Netscape added Excite! (another search engine) to its Netcenter portal (and then merged with AOL); and Yahoo! purchased Geocities in a share deal worth $4.8 billion.

6. Clay Shirky, "The Semantic Web, Syllogism, and Worldview." First published November 7, 2003, on the "Networks, Economics, and Culture" mailing list. Available at http://www.shirky.com/writings/semantic_syllogism.html. For the "official" description of the Semantic Web see www.W3.org, the website of the World Wide Web Consortium, the Web's informal regulatory body.

Chapter 29: How the Net Became a Mass Medium:
Directories and Search Engines

1. Of course, there is always the risk that advertisers will attempt to integrate their messages directly into sites that are designed to appear purely informational, creating in the process the Internet equivalent of the television infomercial. (An example might be an allergy information site operated by an antihistamine maker.) It is a strategy that seems doomed to meagre successes, however, thanks once again to the Net's vast resources. Information, no matter how obscure or arcane, is almost always available from several different Net sources, at least some of which are certain to be non-commercial.

2. A novel, if distastefully Orwellian, strategy to surmount the "problem" of user sovereignty was adopted by a U.S. company called Free-PC, launched in 1999 with the support of USA Networks. Its aim was to give free computers and free Internet access to clients willing to supply personal information to advertisers and to put up with advertising on their screens whether they were using the Net browser or some other application.

3. Netscape saw in Yahoo! and other directories a means of sharpening competition with AOL and CompuServe, which, having switched from BBS to ISP/portal mode, were marketing themselves as making Web surfing a simpler, safer experience than using a browser. They were offering the package tour experience as opposed to the unguided, backpack adventure in cyberspace offered by Netscape. See May 1995 interview with David Yang: http://www.sun.com/950701/yahoo2.html.

4. "David and I and the rest of the Yahoos here really believe that the internet should remain as free as possible. At the same time we are a business and have fiscal responsibilities. If you look at the history of media, the 'free media' like radio and television have great programming and yet they are free. Our purpose/goal is the same, to keep the internet free to the users and make the business part work by finding sponsors and advertisers who want to reach our audience. I think it is one of the keys to keep improving the usefulness of the web and make sure that as many people as possible can use it and derive value from it." Jerry Yang in a July 1998 interview with *Time* Auditorium: http://www.time.com/time/community/transcripts/chattr072398.html.

5. Yahoo! press release, March 1, 2005.

6. http://www.google.com/corporate/tenthings.html.

7. Ibid.

Chapter 30: Anarchy and Public Space

1. David Johnson and David Post, "Law and Borders—The Rise of Law in Cyberspace," *Stanford Law Review* 48 (1996): 1367–1375.

2. Theodor Adorno, "The stars come down to earth: the *Los Angeles Times* astrology column," *Telos* 19 (Spring 1974): 88–89.

3. Theodor Adorno, "Culture industry reconsidered," *New German Critique* 6 (Fall 1975): 19.

4. Max Horkheimer and Theodor Adorno, *Dialectic of Enlightenment* (New York: Continuum, 1997), 144–45.

5. H.I. Schiller, *Mind Managers* (Boston: Beacon Press, 1973), 1.

6. Lawrence Lessig, *Code and Other Laws of Cyberspace* (New York: Basic Books, 1999). See also Andrew L. Shapiro, *The Control Revolution* (New York: Century Foundation, 1999) and James Slevin, *The Internet and Society* (Cambridge: Polity Press, 2000).

7. www.cauce.org

8. See www.spam.abuse.net for up-to-date information and links.

Chapter 31: The Information Economy

1. A useful and accessible treatment of information as a commodity is provided by Michael Perelman in *Class Warfare in the Information Age* (Toronto: Palgrave, 1998).

2. *Forbes ASAP*, 1995.

3. Don Tapscott, *The Digital Economy: Promise and Peril in the Age of Networked Intelligence* (New York: McGraw-Hill, 1996), xiv.

4. Stanford University Center for Economic Policy Research Report: "Computer and Dynamo: The Modern Productivity Paradox in a Not Too Distant Mirror" (1996).

Chapter 32: Network Society

1. See Manuel Castells's trilogy *The Information Age: Economy, Society and Culture*—Volume 1, *The Rise of the Network Society* (1996); Volume 2, *The Power of Identity* (1997); and Volume 3, *End of Millennium* (1997).

2. U. Beck, A. Giddens and S. Lash, *Reflexive Modernization: Politics, Tradition and Aesthetics in the Modern Social Order* (Cambridge: Polity Press, 1994), 95.

3. Manuel Castells, "An Introduction to the Information Age," in *City* 7 (1997), reprinted in Hugh Mackay and Tim O'Sullivan, eds., *The Media Reader: Continuity and Transformation* (London: Sage Publications, 1999).

4. Noah Kennedy, *The Industrialization of Intelligence* (London: Unwin Hyman, 1989), 156.

5. *Futures*, August–September 1995.

6. Kennedy, *The Industrialization of Intelligence*, 170.

7. Quoted in Simon Head, *The New Ruthless Economy: Work and Power in the Digital Age* (Oxford: Oxford University Press, 2000), 163.

8. Ibid., 163.

9. Ibid., 165.

10. Ibid., 166.

11. Ibid., 98.

12. Ibid., 109.

13. Heather Menzies, "Challenging Capitalism in Cyberspace: The Information Highway, the Postindustrial Economy, and People," in Robert W. McChesney et al., eds., *Capitalism and the Information Age: The Political Economy of the Global Communication Revolution* (New York: Monthly Review Press, 1997).

14. Castells, "An Introduction to the Information Age," 405–6.

15. Ibid., 407.

16. Manuel Castells, *The Information Age: Economy, Society and* Culture, vol. 1, *The Rise of Network Society* (Oxford: Blackwell, 1996), 428.

17. Thomas Homer-Dixon, op-ed, *New York Times*, August 13, 2005.

18. Lewis Mumford, *Technics and Civilization* (New York: Harcourt, Brace and Co., 1930), 269.

Index